LAWS HARSH AS TIGERS

The paper in this book meets the guidelines for permanence and durability of the Committee on Production Guidelines for Book Longevity of the Council on Library Resources.

"Poem by One Named Xu from Xiangshan Encouraging the Traveler" from *Island: Poetry and History of Chinese Immigrants on Angel Island, 1910– 1940*, edited by Him Mark Lai, Genny Lim, and Judy Yung, copyright 1980 by the HOC DOI project, reprinted by permission of the University of Washington Press.

Library of Congress Cataloging-in-Publication Data
Salyer, Lucy E.
Laws harsh as tigers : Chinese immigrants and the shaping of modern immigration law / by Lucy E. Salyer.
   p. cm. — (Studies in legal history)
Includes bibliographical references and index.
ISBN 0-8078-2218-3 (cloth : alk. paper). — ISBN 0-8078-4530-2 (pbk. : alk. paper)
1. Emigration and immigration law—United States—History. 2. Chinese—Legal status, laws, etc.—United States—History. 3. United States. Bureau of Immigration and Naturalization—History.
4. Administrative discretion—United States—History. I. Title. II. Series.
KF4845.S25   1995
342.73′082—dc20   94-48276
[347.30282]   CIP

99 98 97 96 95   5 4 3 2 1

FOR LEE AND NATE

CONTENTS

Acknowledgments *xi*

Introduction *xiii*

Chapter 1

From Counting to Sifting Immigrants *1*

PART I. JUDICIAL JUSTICE, 1891–1905 *33*

Chapter 2

Contesting Exclusion: The Chinese and the Administrators *37*

Chapter 3

Captives of Law: Judicial Enforcement of the Chinese Exclusion Laws *69*

Chapter 4

The Eclipse of Judicial Justice *94*

PART II. EXECUTIVE JUSTICE, 1905–1924 *117*

Chapter 5

Drawing the Sieve Tighter: The Rise of Nativism
and Administrative Power *121*

Chapter 6

Bureaucratic Tyranny: The Bureau of Immigration and Its Critics *139*

Chapter 7

A Fair though Summary Hearing: The Shaping of Administrative
Due Process *179*

Chapter 8

Its Own Keeper: Procedural Reform in the Bureau of Immigration *217*

Epilogue: Immigration Law in American Legal Culture *245*

Appendix: Methodology *253*

Notes *255*

Bibliography *309*

Index *325*

TABLES & ILLUSTRATIONS

TABLES

1. Chinese Admitted to the United States, 1894–1901 *67*
2. Non-Chinese Aliens Admitted to the United States, 1894–1901 *68*
3. Disposition of Chinese Habeas Corpus Cases in the District Court, 1891–1905 *80*
4. Disposition of Chinese Habeas Corpus Cases in the Circuit Court, 1891–1905 *82*
5. Disposition of Chinese Deportation Cases in the District Court, 1893–1900 *89*
6. Disposition of Chinese Deportation Cases before Commissioner Heacock, 1901–1905 *90*
7. Disposition of Deportation Cases by U.S. Commissioner, 1906–1924 *188*
8. Disposition of Chinese Habeas Corpus Cases, 1906–1924 *192*
9. Disposition of Non-Chinese Habeas Corpus Cases, 1906–1924 *193*

ILLUSTRATIONS

Interrogation at Angel Island, San Francisco *60*
A Section 6 certificate required of Chinese exempt from exclusion *61*
An advertisement from a prominent law firm specializing in Chinese exclusion cases *71*
William W. Morrow, U.S. District Court judge and Circuit judge *73*
Habeas corpus petition filed in the U.S. District Court at San Francisco *74*
Cartoon calling for restrictions on immigration from Europe *123*
"The Pens at Ellis Island" *146*
An immigrant appearing before the board of special inquiry at Ellis Island *148*
"Lady Liberty Is Ashamed" *160*

ACKNOWLEDGMENTS

My mother taught me that it is polite to send thank you notes for gifts. In this case, it is a pleasure rather than an obligation to express my gratitude to the many individuals who have given their time, resources, and support to bring this project to completion. The book has benefited from the thoughtful critiques of several scholars. I am particularly grateful for the detailed reading and comments provided by Charles McCurdy which helped me to reshape the manuscript in fundamental ways. Tom Green, the editor of the legal history series, willingly read multiple drafts and gently pushed me to tighten and refine the argument. Sucheng Chan and Dirk Hartog have read and commented on portions of the manuscript. Marianne Constable and Susan Sterett have not only been my closest friends but have read the entire manuscript several times, until they know it as well as I do. I am deeply grateful for their critical insights as well as their emotional support.

I have been very fortunate in my colleagues at the University of New Hampshire. My entire department has been extraordinarily supportive of the project. In particular, I thank Al Linden for his help with Chinese-language materials, Janet Polasky and Laurel Ulrich for their comments on grant proposals and chapters, and the chairs of the History Department, John Voll and Jeffry Diefendorf, for ushering me through administrative channels for research support. Beyond my department, I thank Mil Duncan and Lisa MacFarlane for their friendship and interest in the project, Deanna Wood for her help in locating legal sources, and the staff at the Faculty Resource Center for computer assistance.

Research can be relatively painless and even enjoyable when one has the help of knowledgeable experts. I wish to thank Waverly Lowell, archivist at the San Bruno branch of the National Archives, and her staff for their help in locating and using material, as well as Cynthia Fox of the National Archives in Washington, D.C. Michael Griffith, historian for the U.S. District Court in San Francisco, and Lynn Lundstrom, librarian for the court, have become good friends in part because of the amount of time we spent together as they aided me in my research. Rachel Bowman and Christine Fowler also provided valuable research assistance, and Elisabeth Nichols helped with the tedious task of proofreading. Thanks, too, to the editorial staff at the University of North Carolina Press for helping to bring the project to fruition.

Funding from a variety of sources allowed me the time and resources to complete the project. I appreciate the financial support of the National Endowment for the Humanities, the Committee for the Bicentennial of the Constitution of the Judicial Conference of the United States, and, at the University of New Hampshire, the College of Liberal Arts, the Graduate School, and the Center for the Humanities. I thank Dean Stuart Palmer for providing funds at critical times during the project. The Historical Society of the Northern District of California provided several photographs for the book.

I owe special thanks to Harry Scheiber for his mentoring over many years. I am grateful to Christine Fowler, Elizabeth Fowler, and Vicky Madden for their help on the home front in the last few years. Mary Odem has been a solid ally as we have commiserated together about the long, rocky road to publication. My debt to my parents is beyond measure, not only for teaching me the ways of the world but also for providing models of principled, caring people. My brothers and their families have provided unflagging encouragement as have my in-laws. But Lee and Nate, who have had to live with the ups and downs of the project on a daily basis, deserve special thanks for their love and patience. It is to them that I dedicate this work.

By 1905, policy makers had achieved their goal: the jurisdiction of the courts to hear Chinese and other immigration cases was sharply curtailed.[12]

The battle over the enforcement of the Chinese exclusion laws had particular importance for residents on the West Coast, but its outcome had much broader ramifications for the national development of immigration law and procedures. In particular, the Chinese resistance to exclusion provides a concrete explanation for the divergence of immigration law from other branches of administrative law. As Schuck suggests, the rise of nativism and the perceived connection between immigration and foreign policy concerns contributed to the willingness to vest greater discretion in the Bureau of Immigration. But to a significant extent, the more specific and immediate reason for the expansion of the agency's power lay in the difficulties in enforcing the Chinese exclusion laws. The successful litigation by Chinese provided the main impulse for taking away the jurisdiction of the federal courts in immigration matters and for placing immigration regulation, instead, under the firm control of the administrative agency. The Chinese litigation concerning administrative due process had "radiating effects" on other immigrants and other areas of administrative law.[13] Their early challenges set precedents that would influence later court decisions regarding administrative power. Thus the West and its immigrants, often treated by historians as peripheral to and separate from the immigration on the East Coast, had a powerful effect on the shape and enforcement of immigration laws throughout the nation.

With power over immigration firmly vested in the administrative agency after 1905, new questions arose. Congressional statutes and Supreme Court opinions clearly stated that immigrants were not entitled to a judicial hearing concerning their right to enter or remain in the United States. But were aliens to be denied all the procedural protections and guarantees associated with judicial hearings? Immigrants after 1905 focused on that question in their litigation challenging the Bureau of Immigration's summary administrative procedures as a denial of due process.

The attempt to forge a system of "executive justice" within the Bureau of Immigration after 1905 was not limited to Chinese on the West Coast. As other groups became subject to increasingly stringent laws, they and their American allies joined in the condemnation of administrative procedures that hindered their admission into the United States. Critics appealed to the long-standing American hostility toward bureaucracy and couched their challenges in well-worn phrases from American political discourse. Alleging that the Bureau of Immigration exercised arbitrary, dangerous power, unchecked by judicial control, aliens and their allies used a variety of tactics to subject the Bureau of Immigration to the rule of law rather than the rule of discretion. In their view, the rule of law meant, at best, judicial hearings with the attendant procedural rights and protections and, at least, the incorporation of judicial procedures into administrative hearings.

Such arguments, however, had lost some currency in the Progressive Era, when reformers hailed administrative agencies and the concomitant exercise of discretion by experts as the harbingers of a more enlightened, efficient age. The rule of law, Robert Gordon has suggested, became transformed by Progressives to require only the reasonable or fair exercise of discretion.[14] To impose more exacting procedural restraints upon government under a notion of rule of law would hamper social justice and effective policy making. Even Progressives who were sympathetic to immigrants' concerns failed to endorse the proceduralist definition of the rule of law, advocating instead better personnel and more elaborate administrative review to curb administrative abuses.

The federal courts, addressing the novel issue of what process was due persons appearing before administrative agencies, generally gave the Bureau of Immigration a wide berth, requiring only that aliens have a fair opportunity to be heard before being excluded or deported. Courts generally agreed that "judicial justice" was not always appropriate or necessary to administrative proceedings. Judges had felt obligated to follow the courts' institutional norms and practices when they decided the right of Chinese to enter the United States, but they did not believe administrative officials should be bound by the same rules. A strict insistence that agencies adopt formal judicial procedures could undermine the basic objectives of administrative government. The Bureau of Immigration had been given power, after all, to free administrators from the technical procedures that hampered courts and frustrated the enforcement of Chinese exclusion and other immigration laws. That the complainants were aliens, not yet members of the American polity, further affected the issue of procedural rights in immigration cases. Few judges were willing to concede to aliens the same rights and privileges citizens might enjoy in administrative hearings.[15]

The first chapter of this book explores the broad social, economic, and cultural factors that led the United States to enact increasingly restrictive immigration policies in the late nineteenth century. Although it addresses the substantive features of the new immigration legislation, it focuses on the particular institutional structure designed to implement the laws. The rest of the book falls into two parts. Part I, "Judicial Justice," explores the period between 1891 and 1905 in which Chinese successfully challenged the decisions of the administrative officials to exclude them under the Chinese exclusion laws through use of the federal courts in San Francisco. It analyzes the reasons for the victories of Chinese, focusing particularly on how institutional norms of the court made it a receptive forum for them. Chapter 2 analyzes the organization, perceptions, and goals of Chinese immigrants vis-à-vis those of the administrative officials responsible for enforcing Chinese exclusion. Chapter 3 focuses on the federal courts' treatment of Chinese cases and contrasts judicial and administrative approaches to immigration decisions. Chapter 4 describes the campaign to remove jurisdiction from the courts, which succeeded by 1905.

Part II, "Executive Justice," analyzes the rise of administrative discretion in immigration policy between 1905 and 1924 and its consequences for immigrants. Chapter 5 examines the proliferation of nativist legislation after 1905, which broadened its aim from Chinese to all "new" immigrants, culminating with the Immigration Act of 1924. As the nation embraced restriction as its dominant policy, the Bureau of Immigration's power grew and the summary procedures it had developed to exclude Chinese became the norm. Chapter 6 details the resistance of immigrants and their allies to these developments and their diverse strategies to challenge the bureau's practices, which, in their view, constituted "bureaucratic tyranny." Their unsuccessful efforts to impose limits on the bureau's power through litigation are explored in Chapter 7. Chapter 8 explores the effects of the courts' abdication of their role in immigration policy. Largely freed from judicial oversight, the bureau engaged in limited procedural reform but continued to tailor its practices to attain restrictionist objectives. The consequence, as the epilogue suggests, was the growth of an agency and a body of law that have never been fully assimilated into American jurisprudence.

LAWS HARSH AS TIGERS

CHAPTER 1

From Counting to Sifting Immigrants

The United States in the nineteenth century was a nation of immigrants.[1] Although American liberal ideology embraced this characteristic as a source of pride for most of the century, many Americans late in the century began to view the immigrant population as a threat. Instead of attracting honest, hardworking folk, America was becoming, in the words of one commentator, "an asylum for paupers, convicts, and cripples."[2] Nativists increasingly called for policies to "sift" the desirable from the undesirable immigrants.[3]

Congress in the 1880s began to make "selective" immigration the official United States policy. Scholars describing the restrictive nature of late nineteenth-century immigration legislation generally point to the growing number of categories of excludable immigrants.[4] Yet equally if not more important to restrictionists' goals was the administrative structure created by Congress in 1891. The Immigration Act of 1891 lodged the power to regulate immigration firmly in the hands of the federal government. Furthermore, the act delineated a novel relationship between the administrators of immigration law—the superintendent of immigration and the secretary of the treasury at that time—and the federal courts: the decisions of the federal administrative officers were to be final, suggesting that immigration cases would not be subject to judicial review.[5] The congressional decision to give federal administrators sole power to enforce immigration laws had significant ramifications for immigration policy, which are explored in later chapters.

Why Congress chose in 1891 to centralize immigration administration and to exclude federal courts from immigration decisions has not been adequately explained. Historians have not appreciated the importance of administrative structure to the implementation of immigration law. Immigration and administrative law scholars have been more sensitive to the effect of the clause forbidding judicial review, but they have looked only to doctrinal and theoretical explanations for the exclusion of courts from immigration policy.[6]

This chapter analyzes the social movement that gave rise to the restrictive legislation and to the particular administrative arrangement established by the act of 1891. The experience of Chinese immigrants in the United States is central to that story. The attention to Chinese may seem odd because Asians have long received different treatment than other immigrants, in law and in history. The Chinese exclusion laws regulated the entry of Chinese. The act of 1891 explicitly omitted Chinese from its reach, and until 1903 Chinese were not subject to the general immigration laws. Nevertheless, Chinese played an essential, though perhaps indirect, role in the development of immigration law. Beginning in 1882, Chinese began to use the federal courts, primarily in San Francisco, to challenge the administration of the Chinese exclusion laws. They were often successful, for the courts tended to interpret the laws more liberally than did the officer responsible for enforcing Chinese exclusion. I suggest that the difficulty administrators faced in implementing the Chinese exclusion laws affected the immigration administration created by Congress in 1891. Furthermore, Chinese litigation provided the precedent upon which much of later immigration law rested. Consequently, an understanding of the history and actions of Chinese immigrants is vital in reconstructing the history of early immigration administration and law.

THE CHANGING FEDERAL ROLE IN IMMIGRATION

For almost a century after its formation as a nation, the United States generally welcomed the arrival of new immigrants. Xenophobia had persisted in American communities since the colonial period, but both economics and ideology operated in favor of a benign immigration policy.[7] The country was rich in resources but deficient in the labor needed to exploit these resources. Filling this void, immigrants helped to settle the expanding American frontier and, as industrialization took hold after the Civil War, provided much of the labor in the new factories and mines.[8] A liberal ideology emphasizing equality and common humanity predisposed Americans to accept the new immigrants as well. The Declaration of Independence had set out the creed of inalienable human rights to life, liberty, and the pursuit of happiness. Such universal human rights, many Americans argued, mandated the free migration of people from country to country.[9] Because they themselves or their families had taken advantage of their right to better their lives by coming to the United States, most Americans upheld the right of others to pursue the same path.

Accompanying these beliefs was a faith in the process of assimilation. Americans, as historian John Higham describes it, had a certain cosmopolitan image of themselves. Throughout the history of the United States, the country had grown from the infusion of peoples from other lands. Many Americans saw the mixture of these different people as a strength, and they believed, as expressed by Ralph Waldo Emerson, that "the energy of Irish, Germans, Swedes, Poles, and Cossacks, and all the European tribes—and of the Africans, and of the Polynesians,—will construct a new race, a new religion, a new state, a new literature which will be as vigorous as the new Europe which came out of the smelting-pot of the Dark ages."[10] The conglomeration of many nationalities was seen as one of the country's unique characteristics.[11] Oliver Wendell Holmes summarized the sentiment aptly: " 'We are the Romans of the modern world, the great assimilating people.' "[12] Immigrants became Americans, according to the assimilationist outlook, by participating in the political, economic, and social life of the United States. American political institutions and processes transformed the foreigner into a self-governing republican.

There were, of course, notable exceptions to the spirit of acceptance. Nativist sentiment, aimed especially at people whose culture and religion seemed most different from the English tradition, arose periodically. Such sentiment gave birth in the 1840s to the anti-immigrant Know-Nothing party, organized in response to the arrival of large numbers of Germans and Irish Catholics.[13] Jews and Chinese were also continual targets of hostility.[14]

Anti-immigrant biases did not result, however, in any significant federal restrictive legislation during this period, and the major political parties distanced themselves from nativist movements. The dominant official stance toward immigrants remained one of open arms. The federal government demonstrated its positive attitude primarily by doing nothing to interfere with immigration. Aside from the Alien and Sedition Acts passed in 1798, Congress did not pass any restrictive legislation until 1875. It did, however, enact legislation in 1819 to protect immigrants and to provide basic information to the government on their arrival. The act of 1819 restricted the number of passengers allowed on a ship and required that immigrants be furnished with certain basic provisions on their voyage. The act also provided for the gathering of data on new immigrants, requiring the ship's captain to submit a list with the passengers' names and other pertinent information.[15] Thus the federal government assumed an accommodating and paternalistic role in the early history of immigration regulation, acting only to protect and to keep statistics on immigrants.[16]

The state governments, however, took a more active role in both promoting and restricting immigration. Many states, especially in the less populated West and South, encouraged immigration.[17] Other states, particularly in the Northeast, established inspection systems and passed legislation to protect the community from undesired immigrants, especially the impoverished and criminal, who, it was feared, might become public burdens. In response to a 1788 congressional resolution calling for such local legislation, several states adopted laws forbidding the entry of convicts into their states.[18] The poor were not welcome either, and states attempted through a variety of means to ensure that immigrants would not become public charges. New York and Massachusetts required masters of ships to post bonds guaranteeing that the state would not have to support immigrants who became indigent. States also collected a fee, known as a head tax, for each immigrant and placed it in a fund to help immigrants in need.

Masters and ship owners resented the states' impositions and successfully challenged the statutes in a series of cases before the United States Supreme Court. States defended their regulations as a legitimate exercise of their police power; they proclaimed their right to protect their people from the evil effects of disease, immorality, and pauperism that many associated with immigration. The Supreme Court in 1837 upheld state provisions requiring the master of a ship to submit a detailed report on the passengers, ruling that the states had a right to know who was coming within their boundaries.[19] The Court found other state laws unconstitutional, however, because they infringed on the federal government's power over interstate and foreign commerce. In a five-to-four decision in the *Passenger Cases*, the majority interpreted the transportation of passengers to be an act of commerce and viewed the states' head taxes as an attempt to regulate foreign commerce. Arguing that the Constitution gave Congress the exclusive power to regulate interstate and foreign commerce, the majority found the state head taxes to be an unconstitutional infringement on federal power.[20]

The decision did not deter the states from attempting to regulate immigration; it simply forced them to choose alternative methods. Justice John McLean in his opinion in the *Passenger Cases* had suggested that requiring ship masters or owners to post bonds for passengers likely to become public charges was a constitutional power of the states.[21] Apparently taking the cue from Justice McLean, New York quickly enacted a new law prescribing that masters or owners of ships post a $300 bond for each passenger, thus ensuring that the state would not have to care for the person if he or she became needy in any way. The requirement of a bond was not novel, but New York added a clause that departed from former policies. If the master did not wish to post the bond, New York's law permitted him to pay $1.50 for each passenger within twenty-four hours of his or her landing. In effect, New York was collecting a head tax under a thin guise of requiring a bond. The Supreme Court in 1876, noting the real thrust of the New York law, invalidated this and similar legislation in Louisiana as an improper interference with foreign commerce.[22]

The Court reserved its most scathing criticism for a California law that arose primarily in response to growing anti-Chinese sentiment. The law allowed the state commissioner of immigration to require a $500 bond or, in lieu of the bond, a sum of money which the commissioner thought adequate for any alien passenger who was likely to become a public charge because of physical or moral disabilities. (The main targets of the act, however, were Chinese women suspected of prostitution.) The state commissioner pocketed 20 percent of the fees collected, and the remainder went to the state treasury for the care of indigent citizens (not aliens). The Court denounced the law, saying, "in any view which we can take of this statute, it is in conflict with the Constitution."[23] Not only did the law infringe on congressional power over foreign commerce, but it also vested a state official with arbitrary power and went "far beyond" the police power of the state to protect itself from immorality and pauperism.[24]

With the 1876 cases, the Supreme Court effectively curtailed state involvement in immigration regulation. The federal government until this point still played a minimal role, primarily limited to protecting and keeping statistics on immigrants. But the shift to a more active stance was under way. Even before the Court delivered its opinions in 1876, Congress had passed its first restrictive law, the so-called Page Law of 1875.[25] The law represented a victory for anti-Chinese forces in California, who perceived that their state's attempt to regulate Chinese immigration would not survive the constitutional challenge brought by Chinese. They secured federal legislation forbidding the entry of Chinese, Japanese, and other "Oriental" laborers brought to the United States involuntarily, as well as that of women brought for the purpose of prostitution, a provision aimed particularly at Chinese women.[26]

The federal government faced additional pressure from eastern states to assume more control as the state regulatory system fell apart. Those states receiving the most newcomers remained anxious; without the immigrant fund fed by the head taxes, local governments would have to support sick and indigent aliens. The New York Board of Emigration Commissioners and New York Board of Charities, finally accepting the Supreme Court's rulings that only the federal government could legislate in the area, began to lobby Congress to enact head taxes and to exclude criminals and paupers.[27]

Though opposed by business interests who did not want to hamper immigration, New York succeeded in getting congressional action. With the Immigration Act of 1882, the federal government took a significant step toward a centralized and restrictive immigration policy. The act divided responsibilities between the federal and state governments: the secretary of the treasury assumed exclusive authority over immigration but awarded contracts to the states to administer the program on a day-to-day basis. The states thus retained a significant amount of control. They appointed the inspectors and commissioners of immigration, established rules for inspecting immigrants, and made the decisions whether to land applicants. The act also relieved the states' financial burden by authorizing a federal head tax of fifty cents for each immigrant. The secretary of the treasury distributed the money collected to the states, in proportion to the number of immigrants they received, to be used for distressed or needy immigrants.[28] Finally, the act denied admission to convicts, lunatics, idiots, and persons unable to care for themselves.[29]

In one sense, the Immigration Act of 1882 does not seem novel. The act followed the pattern of earlier colonial and state legislation in excluding paupers and convicts. Its main thrust aimed at protecting the states from the financial burden of indigent aliens. Yet the act of 1882 and, even more, that of 1875, represented significant departures for United States immigration policy. Whereas earlier nativist feelings had never penetrated official immigration policy, the movement to restrict immigration beginning in the 1880s was much more successful in molding federal legislation to its ends, as can be seen clearly in the campaign to exclude Chinese.

"LAWS HARSH AS TIGERS"

Poem by One Named Xu from Xiangshan
Encouraging the Traveler

Just talk about going to the land of the
   Flowery Flag and my countenance fills
     with happiness.
Not without hard work were 1,000 pieces of
   gold dug up and gathered together.
There were words of farewell to the parents,
   but the throat choked up first.
There were many feelings, many tears flowing
   face to face, when parting with the wife.

Waves big as mountains often astonished this
    traveller.
With laws harsh as tigers, I had a taste of all
    the barbarities.
Do not forget this day when you land ashore.
Push yourself ahead and do not be lazy or
    idle.

While the Immigration Act of 1882 foreshadowed the beginning of selective immigration, another piece of federal legislation passed in the same year moved more obviously toward an official policy of restriction. It was the Chinese Exclusion Act, a law that flew in the face of the traditional benign federal immigration policy. Abandoning the belief that it was the "inherent and inalienable right of man to change his home and allegiance,"[30] the United States embraced a less principled stand toward the Chinese. Congress, "in the opinion . . . [that] the coming of Chinese laborers to this country endangers the good order of certain localities," forbade the immigration of Chinese laborers for ten years.[31]

In restricting the admission of a particular race of people, Congress departed from the customary limits on immigration. The legislature did not act, as it did in the Immigration Act of 1882, out of concern that individual Chinese laborers would become financial burdens upon the community. On the contrary, Americans worried that Chinese succeeded *too* well. Congress barred Chinese laborers as a group, believing that as a race and an economic force, the Chinese as a whole were undesirable immigrants. In making a distinction based on race and nationality, the act augured a significant new era in federal legislation and American attitudes toward immigrants.

Chinese had been immigrating to the United States for over thirty years before the passage of the 1882 Exclusion Act. Like many immigrants to America, Chinese left their native homes to escape economic and social instability.[32] Drawn by the discovery of gold, many came to California beginning in 1849. Most initially worked in the mines, laboring as miners, cooks, or laundrymen. Chinese also undertook railroad construction when the Central Pacific Railroad Company needed labor to lay tracks through the rugged Sierra Nevada. When the railroad was completed and the mines were played out in the late 1860s, Chinese left the mountains for the central valleys and the cities. An increasing number entered new occupations in agriculture, fishing, trade, and manufacture.[33] Although the number of Chinese in the United States grew steadily, they remained a small proportion of the total immigrant and native population. In 1870, 63,199 Chinese were in the United States, growing to 105,465 by 1880.[34]

Despite their small numbers, Chinese immigrants encountered hostility from other settlers almost immediately after their arrival. A negative image of China and its people, propagated by traders, diplomats, and missionaries visiting that country, preceded the Chinese immigrants. American traders in their travel accounts laid the groundwork for later stereotypes in their descriptions of Chinese as "ridiculously clad, superstitious ridden, dishonest, crafty, cruel, and marginal members of the human race."[35] The establishment of the penny press in the 1830s gave many white Americans access to lurid accounts of bizarre Chinese customs, sexual aberrations, and cruelty to women and children.[36] These stories contributed to constructing what historian Alexander Saxton has described as a "psychological barrier" against Chinese in the minds of white Americans, who increasingly perceived the Chinese as being fundamentally different from themselves.[37]

Before 1870, anti-Chinese sentiment in California was clearly evident, if not particularly well-organized.[38] Some white laborers protested the presence of Chinese in the mines and in railroad construction, forming clubs and holding meetings to devise methods such as miners' taxes to keep Chinese out of these industries and out of California as well.[39] California's laws began to incorporate the idea that Chinese were fundamentally different. In *People* v. *Hall* in 1854, the California Supreme Court interpreted a California criminal statute excluding the testimony of blacks and Indians in cases involving a white person as also forbidding the testimony of Chinese. While the court went to great lengths to argue that the category of "Indian" incorporated Chinese,[40] the real reason for the court's decision appeared to be its belief that the Chinese were a "distinct people . . . a race of people whom nature has marked as inferior and who are incapable of progress or intellectual development beyond a certain point." The court professed astonishment that such a people should have "not only the right to swear away the life of a citizen, but the further privilege of participating with us in the administering of our Government."[41]

Hostility toward the Chinese coexisted during this time with pro-Chinese sentiment, especially from those who wanted their labor, their trade, and their souls. Industrialists saw in the Chinese a plentiful source of intelligent, inexpensive labor. Chinese labor was key to the completion of the transcontinental railroad, constituting 90 percent of the Central Pacific Railroad's workforce. This experience demonstrated to other employers the value of Chinese as workers.[42] The lure of a lucrative trade in the Orient persuaded other Americans that it made practical commercial sense to maintain good relations with China and her people.[43] Furthermore, though Protestant missionaries had been partially responsible for creating the negative stereotypes that fueled anti-Chinese agitation, several of them also defended the Chinese against criticism in the United States.[44] Finally, not all Americans agreed that Chinese were fundamentally different or that they should be treated as inferior if they were different. A bloody civil war had just been fought in part over the immorality of treating another race as inferior. The war and the ensuing civil rights acts served to reinforce, especially for old abolitionists and Radical Republicans, the principle of racial equality.[45] These strands of thought militated against anti-Chinese agitation.

Consequently, when China sent a goodwill mission to the United States under the leadership of the charismatic Chinese ambassador Anson Burlingame, many Americans, even in California, greeted the delegation with enthusiasm.[46] The visit resulted in the Burlingame Treaty of 1868. The main goal of the treaty, according to Secretary of State William H. Seward, was to increase commerce between China and the United States. "The essential element of that commerce and trade," argued Seward, "is . . . the free emigration of the Chinese to the American [continent]."[47] Chinese policy at the time posed the major obstacle to free Chinese emigration; for several centuries, Chinese law had defined emigration as a crime punishable by death.[48] China departed from this policy in the treaty, which allowed both Chinese and Americans to migrate to each other's countries, recognizing the "inherent and inalienable right of man to change his home and allegiance and also the mutual advantage of free migration and emigration of their citizens and subjects respectively from one country to the other for purposes of curiosity or trade or as permanent residents." The treaty further guaranteed Chinese citizens all of the "privileges, immunities and exemptions in respect to travel and residence" extended by the United States "to citizens . . . of the most favored nation."[49]

The pro-Chinese stance embodied in the Burlingame Treaty proved exceedingly short-lived. Almost as soon as the treaty was signed, forces began to lobby for amendments that would allow restrictions on Chinese immigration. A variety of circumstances beginning in 1870 contributed to the success of these groups.

A major factor was the unstable California economy. A severe depression between 1873 and 1878 resulted in reduced wages and widespread unemployment.[50] Labor groups increasingly blamed their problems on Chinese and their capitalist employers. Industrialists' enthusiastic welcome of Chinese laborers increased American labor's antipathy toward the Chinese. Workers were not soothed by employers' reassurance that Chinese, as "birds of passage," would soon return to China or, conversely, that the status and occupations of white workers would be elevated as Chinese entered the lower-scale occupations.[51]

Labor groups looked on with alarm as Chinese entered industry in large numbers during the period. By 1870, Chinese constituted 46 percent of the workers in the four main industries in San Francisco and 25 percent of the wage-earning force in California as a whole.[52] Henry George predicted that Chinese, willing to work for lower wages, would eventually push white workers out of one occupation after another.[53] Nor were these fears limited to California labor groups. In 1870, manufacturers in the Northeast began to experiment with Chinese labor; by 1875, there were enough Chinese to establish small communities within Boston, New York, and Philadelphia. Many easterners, particularly in labor organizations, were alarmed by the Chinese presence and formed clubs and held mass meetings in protest.[54]

The widespread belief that all Chinese laborers were part of the "coolie trade" exacerbated Americans' fear of Chinese immigration and attracted middle- as well as working-class Americans to the campaign for Chinese restriction. Under the coolie system, poor Chinese workers were taken, often by force or fraud, to labor under terrible conditions in foreign countries. Although such trade existed in some countries, Chinese laborers came to the United States voluntarily.[55] In much of the discussion in America, however, all Chinese were "coolies," no better than slaves.[56] The *San Francisco Chronicle* reported in 1879: "When the coolie arrives here he is as rigidly under the control of the contractor who brought him as ever an African slave was under his master in South Carolina or Louisiana."[57] The image of a "modern system of slavery" infiltrating the Pacific Coast alarmed "free-soil/free-labor" advocates and other Americans who had fought to eradicate black slavery.[58]

In part because of the identification of Chinese laborers with American slaves, nativists perceived Chinese as a racial and cultural as well as an economic threat. The most virulent racial attacks on Chinese came from the western states. California newspapers and literature focused on the perceived racial and cultural peculiarities of Chinese, at times explicitly comparing them to black Americans.[59]

But the West did not have a monopoly on racism; "scientific" theories of race developed in the East also affected Americans' perception of Chinese. The study of race differences became a major preoccupation of physical and social scientists in the nineteenth century.[60] Charles Darwin's theory of evolution and Herbert Spencer's application of the principle of natural selection to race spurred attempts to classify and rank races and to account for differences among them.[61] Scientists searching for the key to race differences busily measured and compared the size of human skulls, examined human brains, studied the structure of human hair, and scrutinized different social customs. Dr. Samuel George Morton found in his craniology studies in 1849 that Chinese skulls, along with those of blacks and Indians, were much smaller than those of white Americans or the English and concluded that the small size indicated an inferior intelligence.[62] A similar tendency to classify human development according to race flowered among historians and political theorists, who increasingly tied the capacity for representative, democratic government to a particular group of people, the ancient Germanic tribes and their Anglo-Saxon descendants. Believing Americans to be the descendants of the liberty-loving Anglo-Saxons, historians undertook studies of American colonial towns to demonstrate the natural democratic talent of Americans. The theorists further suggested that other races did *not* have the capacity for democratic rule. This argument gradually worked its way into anti-immigrant positions, in which people contended that peoples of different races should not be allowed to enter because they would never be able to understand the American governmental system and in fact might undermine it.[63]

All of the race theories shared the notion that races had certain fixed, immutable biological and cultural traits. This belief reinforced the drive for restrictionist immigration policies.[64] The idea that races were inherently different appealed to Americans who already felt that the Chinese were fundamentally unlike them. The influence of the new race theories was evident in the standard arguments that began to be formed against Chinese immigration in the 1870s. The faith in the American ability to assimilate newcomers began to fade, especially in the case of the Chinese. Opponents of Chinese immigration commonly argued, for example, that Chinese were *biologically* incapable of being assimilated into the American way of life and, consequently, they would pose a serious threat to American institutions.[65]

Anti-Chinese agitators often used rhetoric associating the Chinese with infectious diseases, both literally and metaphorically. They warned that Chinese culture could infect, contaminate, and eventually obliterate American culture. Americans also worried about the infiltration of biological diseases, which they increasingly associated with Chinese. The idea that diseases were transmitted through germs, and thus were contagious, developed in the 1870s and 1880s.[66] Scientists began to look for relationships between race and disease, and in America they began to link Chinese with dreaded illnesses. As early as 1862, Dr. Arthur Stout alerted Americans to the danger Chinese diseases posed to the nation's health in his book *Chinese Immigration and the Physiological Causes of the Decay of the Nation*. The American Medical Association singled out Chinese prostitutes as a special health concern and sponsored a study in 1875 of their effect on the "nation's bloodstream." Often the nature of the supposed diseases was left vague and undefined, further increasing Americans' fears. Just as Americans saw Chinese culture as impervious to the civilizing impulses of republican government, so, too, they considered "Chinese afflictions . . . to be the result of thousands of years of beastly vices, resistant to all the efforts of modern medicine."[67]

For all of these reasons—economic, racial, cultural—American opinion began to turn against the Chinese in the 1870s. The rising anti-Chinese sentiment became manifest in attacks on Chinese, particularly in California. Labor groups were in the vanguard of this agitation, in part because economic circumstances hit them the hardest and in part because the anti-Chinese stance served a useful unifying purpose. As the 1870s wore on, the depression became more severe for Californians, reaching crisis proportions by 1877. A long, devastating drought exacerbated an already difficult time for workers. Into this tense and discontented scene in California stepped Dennis Kearney and the Workingmen's party. In his famous "sand lot" meetings, Kearney spoke to, and for, thousands of frustrated, unemployed laborers, blaming their woes on greedy monopolists and the Chinese. Increasingly, Chinese became the scapegoat for the workers' problems, and the Workingmen's party adopted the slogan "The Chinese must go!" Even leaders who personally did not agree with the anti-Chinese stance found themselves mouthing the slogans before the crowds.[68] They did so, argues Alexander Saxton, because labor leaders had finally discovered a key issue—the expulsion of the Chinese—that could organize and unify laborers in California and consequently make labor a more formidable player in state politics. The appeal of the anti-Chinese position was so powerful that labor groups continued to find it a vital organizing tool well into the twentieth century.[69]

The Workingmen's party rode the crest of anti-Chinese hostility to win one-third of the seats in California's constitutional convention in 1878. The new constitution adopted in 1879, with its intense anti-Chinese tone and substance, clearly reflected the influence of the insurgent party. Among other things, the constitution denied Chinese the right to vote in state elections; forbade their employment by private corporations or on public works; authorized the legislature to make "all necessary regulations" to protect the state from dangerous or detrimental aliens, including removing aliens from the state who did not meet certain conditions; and empowered towns and cities to remove Chinese from their locale or to restrict Chinese to ghettos.[70] Immediately after the ratification of the constitution, the legislature began to exercise its newly granted powers in a series of discriminatory acts.[71]

The Chinese resisted the new wave of hostile legislation. Armed with their rights under the Burlingame Treaty and the Fourteenth Amendment, the Chinese community challenged California's laws in the federal courts. The courts invalidated most of the anti-Chinese laws and constitutional provisions, holding that in discriminating between Chinese and other aliens, the legislation violated the most-favored-nation clause of the Burlingame Treaty and the equal protection clause of the Fourteenth Amendment.[72]

In one crucial area of law, however, the Chinese did not succeed. In 1878, several Chinese petitioned the federal courts in San Francisco to become naturalized citizens. At issue was whether the naturalization statute encompassed Chinese aliens in its provision that "any alien, being a free white person" or "of African nativity or . . . African descent" could become a citizen of the United States. When the act had been amended in 1870 to include African Americans, Senator Charles Sumner proposed a bill to delete any reference to "white" in the naturalization laws, thus opening the possibility of citizenship to all immigrants. Many congressmen, especially those from the western states, had feared that such a law would result in the widespread naturalization and politicization of Chinese and, consequently, had defeated the bill.[73] Attorneys bringing the petitions of naturalization for the Chinese before the circuit court argued that the category of "white person" was ill-defined in law and could be interpreted as including Chinese. Circuit Court Judge Lorenzo Sawyer ruled, however, that a white person was someone of the Caucasian race and that Chinese were of the "Mongolian race"; consequently, Chinese were not white within the meaning of the naturalization statute and were barred from citizenship.[74]

At the time, the Chinese were the only immigrant group to be denied the privilege of naturalization. The legislative and judicial decisions denying them the opportunity to become citizens greatly aided the restrictionists' cause, both practically and symbolically. Without the right to vote and participate, Chinese had fewer avenues to combat the movement against them. Symbolically, the denial of naturalization reinforced the idea that Chinese were essentially different and racially inferior.[75]

Although the naturalization decision was a clear victory, anti-Chinese groups in California, as well as in other states, still faced two large obstacles to their goal of keeping Chinese out of the United States. One was the limit on state power regarding immigration. The other was the Burlingame Treaty, which secured the right of Chinese to migrate freely. To overcome these obstacles, they pressed for action on the federal level and for a new treaty with China.

Californians had reason to believe the federal government would be receptive to their anti-Chinese demands. Congress had passed the Page Law in 1875, aimed at so-called coolie labor and Chinese prostitutes.[76] A year later, Congress had appointed a special joint committee to investigate the nature and effects of Chinese immigration on the United States. The committee returned a report, written by California senator Aaron Augustus Sargent, warning of the economic and moral threat posed by Chinese immigrants and recommending that the United States modify its treaty with China so as to restrict Chinese immigration.[77] Unwilling to wait for the treaty modification and encouraged by the Democratic control in both houses of Congress, anti-Chinese forces proposed several bills in the late 1870s. After much debate over its legality, Congress passed in 1879 the Fifteen Passenger Bill, which allowed steamships to bring only fifteen Chinese passengers on each voyage to the United States. President Rutherford B. Hayes vetoed the act, however, on the grounds that it violated the Burlingame Treaty, but he soon appointed a commission to renegotiate the treaty with China.[78]

As the commission worked in China, the move for restriction became a key issue in the national election of 1880.[79] What had begun as primarily a regional issue had garnered more widespread attention, in part because many working- and middle-class Americans throughout the nation shared the concerns of Pacific Coast nativists that Chinese posed an economic as well as a cultural and racial threat. But as Elmer Sandmeyer argued in 1939, party politics also helped to move the Chinese immigration issue onto the national agenda. Neither major political party had a decisive majority in Congress in the late nineteenth century, and "control of both the presidency and the two houses of Congress shifted frequently" between the two parties.[80] Because of this situation, the Pacific Coast, regarded as the "swing vote" on several issues, gained more national power. Thus both the Democratic and the Republican party platforms in 1880 called for the amendment of the treaty and the restriction of Chinese immigration.[81] Though Democrats had been at the forefront of the national campaign to exclude Chinese, Republicans realized the necessity of endorsing similar policies if they were to maintain support on the West Coast.[82]

The commission returned from China with a new treaty that generally catered to the demands of Chinese exclusionists. Concern for trade and commerce and lingering liberal beliefs in an open immigration policy tempered certain sections of the treaty, however. The new treaty allowed the United States to limit the future immigration of Chinese laborers whenever the government thought that such immigration "affects or threatens to affect the interest of that country, or endangers the good order of the said country, or of any locality within the territory thereof." The United States could not, however, absolutely prohibit Chinese immigration.[83] Furthermore, the restriction applied only to Chinese laborers who had not yet immigrated to the United States; other "Chinese subjects, whether proceeding to the United States as teachers, students, merchants or from curiosity . . . and Chinese laborers who are now in the United States shall be allowed to go and come of their own free will and accord, and shall be accorded all the rights, privileges, immunities, and exemptions which are accorded to the citizens and subjects of the most favored nation."[84]

With the treaty in hand, anti-Chinese groups once again pressed Congress for federal legislation to restrict Chinese immigration, this time with more success. California representatives proposed one bill to suspend immigration of Chinese for twenty years; when this bill was vetoed by President Chester A. Arthur on the grounds that twenty years was an unreasonably long period of time, they proposed a very similar bill reducing the period to ten years. The second bill became the Chinese Exclusion Act of 1882.

The legislative debates over the various bills raised arguments that by then were familiar. The proponents of Chinese restriction warned of the economic threat Chinese immigrants posed to the well-being of American laborers. One of the leading proponents of the bill, Senator John F. Miller of California, for example, claimed that because of the overpopulation of China, Chinese laborers, engaged in a "dreary struggle for existence," had become, "by long training and . . . heredity . . . automatic engines of flesh and blood; they are patient, stolid, unemotional, and persistent, with such a marvelous frame and digestive apparatus that they can dispense with the comforts of shelter and subsist on the refuse of other men, and grow fat on less than half the food necessary to sustain life in the Anglo-Saxon." White laborers, Miller warned, could not compete with such "machines." If white laborers tried to work for the low wages Chinese workers accepted, their lives and those of their families would be reduced to "misery, want, self-denial, ignorance, and dumb slavery." The laborers' wives would be driven from their homes and children forced from the schoolhouse to the workplace to help eke out the family's subsistence. Only American manufacturers and capitalists would benefit from the admission of "servile labor" and the "debasement" of white labor.[85]

Intertwined with economic arguments were racial and cultural justifications to restrict Chinese immigration. The root of the racial argument was that Chinese could not or would not assimilate. Incorporating evolutionary thought to explain the inability of Chinese to become "American," Senator Miller contended that the American and the Asian civilizations were "of diverse elements and character, both the result of evolution under different conditions, radically antagonistic, and as impossible of amalgamation as are the two great races that produced them." Miller went on to stress the peculiarly static and insular nature of Chinese civilization. For "forty centuries or more," he declared, the Chinese "people . . . have endured without change," never seeking interaction with other peoples, never seeking "to teach nor . . . to be taught." This led to the inescapable conclusion, argued Miller and others, that Americans and Chinese, like "oil and water," would never mix.[86]

Restrictionists warned that if allowed to remain, Chinese with their distinctive character and traditions would endanger American civilization. They portrayed a Chinese character ill-suited to the American system of self-government and free labor. An imperial, despotic government had always ruled China, restrictionists argued, and as a consequence had created a people "utterly unfit for and incapable of free or self-government."[87] What would happen if two such disparate civilizations continued to live in the same country?

The Cassandras answered that a race struggle would inevitably ensue with the Chinese the victors because "the American people are far more impressible than the stoical Chinese." This pattern of Chinese conquest had occurred in "Manchooria, Thibet . . . Eastern Turkistan . . . the Philippine Islands . . . Siam and Formosa" and was already under way in California. The anti-Chinese congressmen pointed with alarm to the "immense" numbers of Chinese ready to pour into the United States. The law of self-preservation, inveighed the restrictionists, required the nation to protect itself against the incursion of Chinese civilization by forbidding further immigration.[88]

Opponents of restriction, led by Senator George Frisbie Hoar of Massachusetts, came primarily from the Northeast and represented commercial and religious groups.[89] They rejected the alarmist arguments of the anti-Chinese spokesmen. They reassured American workers that with time, Chinese laborers, as had other immigrants, would learn to demand higher wages and be good consumers. Further, with Chinese labor to fill the lower jobs, American workers would be elevated into the next grade of occupations. Opponents stressed the contributions Chinese immigrant workers had already made to the wealth and improvement of the United States.[90]

Others protested that the bill would hamper commercial relationships with China. China, argued Senator Joseph E. Brown of Georgia, is "a vast field opening to commerce" which ought to be "great . . . for white men's energy and thrift and gain." Predicting that soon trade with China would bring in "hundreds of millions a year," Brown questioned the wisdom of offending China with exclusion.[91]

Senator Hoar and others observed with disapprobation that the bill constituted a significant step away from the liberal immigration ideology of the past and, more important, from American ideals of equality. With this act aimed at the Chinese, Hoar exclaimed, the "self-evident truth" expressed in the Declaration of Independence—that all men are created equal—becomes a "self-evident lie." Hoar argued that legal distinctions based on race ran counter to the American Constitution as well as to the Declaration of Independence and, alluding to the Civil War, had in the past only served to discredit the nation.[92]

Opponents further rejected the restrictionists' emphasis on the unchangeable Chinese character. One senator angrily retorted that the Americans had never invited Chinese to assimilate and, in fact, had discouraged them from doing so. "Treat the subjects of any other government on earth as you have the Chinese in this country," said Senator Joseph E. Brown of Georgia, "and you will find they will not assimilate."[93]

Just as opponents downplayed the fears of economic competition, restrictionists dismissed the questions of principle. Such distinctions based on race, they argued, were allowed by the treaty with China and, furthermore, were required by the natural law of self-preservation and firmly rooted in American republican traditions.[94] "When [the signers of the Declaration of Independence] declared that all men were created equal, and were endowed with the inalienable right of life, liberty, and the pursuit of happiness," contended one restrictionist from Oregon, "they undoubtedly meant all men like themselves, and in like manner joined in the bonds of civil society."[95] Another senator pointed out, referring to the court decision denying Chinese the right of naturalization, that a legal distinction had already been made in regard to the Chinese.[96]

Evidently the restrictionists' arguments were persuasive; Congress passed the Chinese Exclusion Act of 1882 by a wide margin, and the United States, for the first time in its history, adopted a policy of excluding immigrants based on their race and nationality.[97] The act suspended the entry of Chinese laborers, both skilled and unskilled, for ten years. Chinese laborers who had been in the United States for ninety days before the act's passage were allowed to remain.[98] These laborers maintained the right to exit and return to the United States, though the act required them to obtain a certificate of identification from the collector of the port before departure.[99] The laborer had to present this certificate to the collector upon his return to the United States. Those Chinese exempt from the exclusion act by the 1880 treaty—merchants, teachers, students, and travelers—had to obtain from the Chinese government what came to be known as a "Section 6" or "Canton" certificate verifying that they were of the exempt class. This certificate constituted prima facie evidence of the Chinese applicant's right to enter the United States.[100] Finally, the act denied all Chinese the privilege of becoming naturalized United States citizens.[101]

It seemed to the anti-Chinese forces that their victory was finally at hand, even though the act was not as restrictive as they had hoped. The class of Chinese they found most objectionable would be forbidden to immigrate, at least for ten years. Yet the restrictionists soon found that the battle was not over. Just as they had challenged discriminatory state laws in the federal courts, Chinese turned once again to the federal courts to contest their exclusion from the United States.

Though the Chinese Exclusion Act placed the enforcement of the law in the hands of the collector of customs at each port, the federal courts in San Francisco—responding to suits filed by Chinese litigants—took a surprisingly active role in administering the law. The collector and his staff of inspectors issued the return certificates to departing laborers and investigated the right of returning laborers and exempt classes to enter the United States. If the collector denied them entry, Chinese often challenged his decision by filing petitions for writs of habeas corpus in the local federal courts.[102] The habeas corpus petition commonly alleged that the Chinese immigrant had a right to land and thus that the collector was detaining him or her unlawfully. The federal judges undertook a de novo review of the collector's decision, that is, they reinvestigated the Chinese petitioner's claim to enter the United States. As the judges frequently decided Chinese claims differently from the collector, it soon became clear that the federal courts were going to share in the enforcement of the Chinese exclusion law.

An antagonistic relationship quickly developed between the San Francisco federal courts and the local collector. The collector of San Francisco, under close public scrutiny, adopted a very strict reading of the act and a narrow view of the power of the courts in the cases. He seemed to invite the courts' interference. In several decisions, the federal courts rejected the collector's narrow interpretation of the law as unreasonable and lacking in good faith; and despite the collector's opinion that the courts had limited power over the cases, the federal judges continued to hear and grant numerous Chinese petitions.[103]

In a series of cases between 1882 and 1884, Chinese litigants obtained decisions from the district and circuit courts in San Francisco which mitigated the severity of the act in two important ways. The court expanded the "prior resident" class of Chinese who were exempt from the exclusion act. Many Chinese claimed to fill the residency requirement of having been in the United States before or within ninety days after Congress passed the act, but they left the United States before the collector began to issue the certificates of identification (or "return certificates" as they were commonly known). Consequently, they had no certificate to prove their prior residency as was required by the law. The secretary of the treasury instructed the collector to accept other types of proof in such cases, but the collector in San Francisco ignored the directive and refused to land Chinese in these situations. Judge Ogden Hoffman of the district court believed that the collector's interpretation of the law violated the spirit of the treaty of 1880 and ruled in 1883 that laborers who could establish their prior residency with other evidence must be allowed to land.[104]

The courts also relaxed the requirements for merchants trying to enter the United States. The act specified that merchants must present a certificate from the Chinese government affirming their status as one of the exempt classes. Some Chinese merchants who had been engaged in business in other foreign countries had arrived in the United States without a Section 6 certificate. Justice Stephen J. Field, sitting on the circuit court, held that it was unreasonable to force a merchant in such circumstances to return to China to obtain a certificate, and he allowed the merchant to present other evidence to prove his status.[105]

The courts also checked the collector's overzealous enforcement in other merchant cases. The collector was supposed to accept the Section 6 certificate as prima facie evidence of a merchant's right to land; however, the collector could refuse to accept the certificate if he had other evidence that the certificate bearer was not actually a merchant. Such proof was difficult to obtain, however, and the collector began to deny merchants the right to land simply on his belief that the certificates were fraudulent. When several merchants appealed to the court, Judge Hoffman, though also suspicious of the certificates' reliability, insisted that the collector treat them as valid unless he had concrete evidence of fraud.[106]

The courts' interpretations increased the number of Chinese allowed to enter. Within fourteen months of the act's passage, one historian estimates, the federal courts were directly or indirectly responsible for the entry of one-third of all Chinese landed during that period.[107] The influence of the courts did not go unnoticed. As criticism of the exclusion law's enforcement mounted, congressional representatives pressed for new legislation to counteract the courts' decisions.

Congress responded with an amendment to the restriction act in 1884. The amendment required *all* merchants and other exempt Chinese to present a Section 6 certificate from the Chinese government and endorsed by an American consul. The certificate was the only evidence allowed to prove exempt status. Furthermore, the new law mandated that all laborers had to have a certificate of identification issued by the collector to establish their right to land.[108]

In accordance with the new amendment, the San Francisco federal courts firmly applied a "no certificate–no entry" standard in cases that clearly required the certificates. Chinese laborers who failed to obtain certificates because of illness, mistake, or accident no longer received a sympathetic hearing from the judges.[109] But the federal courts continued to allow laborers residing in the United States before certificates began to be issued to enter by presenting other proof. Justice Field, sitting on the circuit court in California, ruled that such laborers must have certificates under the law. Judges Hoffman, Sawyer, and George M. Sabin, Field's colleagues on the circuit court, dissented based on their earlier decision in *In re Chin Ah On*. The Supreme Court agreed with the dissenters and held that laborers in this position did not need certificates.[110]

The courts expanded two other categories of Chinese who could enter. In a decision with far-reaching implications, the circuit court in 1884 ruled that even though Chinese could not be naturalized, children born in the United States of Chinese parents were United States citizens. These so-called native-born Chinese were not subject to the Chinese exclusion laws because "no citizen can be excluded from this country except in punishment for crime."[111] In a second set of cases, the district court in San Francisco differed from the collector by allowing the wives and children of Chinese merchants to enter the United States,[112] though the court did not allow the wives and children of Chinese laborers to enter, even if the laborer was exempt from the restriction act.[113]

Encouraged by these opinions, Chinese increasingly turned to the federal courts to challenge the collector's decisions. They enjoyed considerable success. A special agent for the Treasury Department estimated that by 1885 the courts were responsible for the landing of 2,695 Chinese, 20 percent of the total number landed since the passage of the Chinese Exclusion Act. By 1888, the agent calculated, 4,091 Chinese had petitioned the federal courts for a hearing and 85 percent received a favorable disposition.[114]

The Chinese litigants' success increased the antagonism between the federal judges and the collector and fueled public opinion against the courts. The collector, "a zealous opponent of Chinese immigration," accused the court of interfering with his job and argued that the cases "should [not] come before the judiciary at all."[115] Groups from the local community, incensed by the court decisions, called for the impeachment of the judges and established a committee to report on the court's actions in the Chinese cases.[116] An examiner for the Department of Justice, Leigh Chalmers, reported to the attorney general: "Two coorfinate [*sic*] branches of the Government are engaged in a hostile conflict, with the people and the press on the side against the courts, accusing them openly of all manner of bargain, intrigue and corruption, which threaten finally to do away with their usefulness, and bring the administration of justice into ridicule, contempt and utter disregard."[117]

Exclusion fervor again began to mount. Vigilante groups throughout the West carried out their own "exclusion campaign," peaking in 1885–86 with a series of violent riots in which many Chinese were murdered or forced to leave.[118] United States attorneys in California, Wyoming, and Washington sent urgent letters to the Department of Justice reporting the renewed efforts to expel Chinese from various communities and the impossibility of obtaining convictions of white rioters because of anti-Chinese juries.[119]

Once again, Congress received urgent demands for new, more restrictive legislation. Ironically, the federal judges of San Francisco, Ogden Hoffman and Lorenzo Sawyer, were among those who sent letters in support of sterner measures though the judges acted primarily out of their despair over their crushing caseload. In January 1888, Judge Hoffman explained their position to Representative Charles N. Felton of California. He urged that "it is of paramount and indispensable importance that something should be done to relieve the courts of the intolerable nuisance and obstruction to their regular business caused by the Chinese cases." Hoffman went on to describe the courts' attempts to deal with the cases: "Judge Sabin has been here on a summons of Judge Sawyer for one month, almost exclusively engaged in trying Chinese habeas corpus cases. There still remain on the calendars of the two courts in the neighborhood of two hundred and fifty cases undisposed of. The steamers arrive tri-monthly, and it may be anticipated that they will continue to bring their usual complement of Chinese passengers . . . unless something is done speedily." While pleading for relief, Hoffman cautioned that any legislation must conform to the treaties with China. In this respect, he clearly differed from the exclusionists. Hoffman recommended that Congress pass a law rescinding the right of Chinese laborers to enter the United States on the grounds of prior residence. Such an act would conform to United States treaty obligations and "would at once dispose of perhaps three-quarters or more of the cases presented to us."[120]

By this point, the Chinese government appeared willing to cooperate with the United States in forging a stricter exclusion policy. The Chinese government was appalled by the repeated violence against Chinese in the United States and frustrated with the apparent inability or unwillingness of the American government to protect Chinese immigrants. It volunteered to prohibit the emigration of Chinese laborers for twenty years in exchange for the United States government's guarantee of protection for Chinese residing in the United States and for monetary damages for those who had already suffered attacks by white mobs. China also requested that Chinese laborers who left the United States be allowed to return if they had property or debts owed them of at least $1,000 value or if they had a wife or parents who were lawful residents.[121]

Diplomats from China and the United States drew up a treaty incorporating these essential points. In anticipation of China's ratification of the treaty, Congress passed another exclusion law which exceeded the treaty provisions. It excluded Chinese laborers without any time limit (as opposed to the twenty-year limit in the treaty) and required Chinese laborers claiming to be exempt to undergo an elaborate investigation to establish their rights under the treaty.[122]

Soon after the bill was passed, however, rumors surfaced that the Chinese had rejected the treaty. Protests in Canton, the province from which the greatest numbers of immigrants to the United States came, had delayed ratification in China, but there was no concrete evidence that China intended to disapprove the treaty. Without waiting for confirmation of China's intentions, however, Congress rushed through another exclusion law, the Scott Act of 1888, which was quite severe.[123] Despite the 1880 treaty guarantee that Chinese laborers who resided in the United States at the time the treaty was signed could come and go at will, the new act prohibited the return of any Chinese laborers who had departed from the United States. The certificates of identity issued under the act of 1882 were declared null and void. Thus a Chinese laborer who left the United States could not return.[124] The proponents of the Scott Act anticipated that it would accelerate the depopulation of the Chinese communities in the United States.

Only seven days after the passage of the Scott Act, a Chinese laborer, Chae Chan Ping, arrived in San Francisco after a visit to China. He presented the return certificate he had obtained before his departure, but the collector denied him landing under the new law. Chae Chan Ping challenged the constitutionality of the law, protesting that it abrogated his rights under the treaty of 1880 and, further, that Congress had no constitutional power to exclude aliens, particularly those who had previously resided in the United States.[125] Judge Lorenzo Sawyer of the circuit court in San Francisco agreed that the act violated the terms of the treaty but still found it constitutional. The Constitution, said Sawyer, stipulated that both treaties and congressional acts were the supreme law of the land and did not specify which should take precedence if they conflicted. Sawyer concluded that the principle guiding courts in conflicts of law should apply, that is, the most recent law should stand as the latest expression of the sovereign's will.[126]

The Supreme Court affirmed the circuit court's decision but based its opinion primarily on the theory that Congress had the sovereign power to exclude aliens. Up to this point, courts had rooted congressional authority to regulate immigration in the constitutional provision empowering Congress to "regulate Commerce with foreign Nations."[127] Justice Field, writing for the Court, departed from this holding and did not ground federal immigration regulation on any of the powers expressly given to Congress in the Constitution. Field noted that the Constitution invested Congress with several powers—to declare war, regulate foreign commerce, and admit aliens to citizenship—which constituted a recognition of the sovereign status of Congress. Field reasoned that any independent nation must have "jurisdiction over its own territory," including the power to exclude aliens, if it were to be truly sovereign.[128]

The Court's decision was significant for Chinese and for other immigrants as well. Field's doctrine of inherent sovereign powers provided a more expansive notion of federal authority than had the foreign commerce clause. Whereas the earlier cases assumed that the Congress could exercise only those powers expressly delegated to it in the Constitution, the new theory made only a loose connection between the Constitution and federal power over immigration. Freed from constitutional moorings, the "inherent sovereign powers" doctrine expanded over the years to bolster the absolute power of the federal government to control immigration and to diminish the rights of aliens and the participation of courts in immigration decisions.[129]

More immediately, the decision supporting the Scott Act signified a defeat for Chinese immigrants. It has been estimated that more than twenty thousand return certificates were declared void;[130] but perhaps more important, the Court had upheld the legitimacy of exclusion. The Chinese minister to the United States regarded the act as "an affront to China."[131] By the end of the decade, Chinese had lost the major battle—exclusion was firmly in place. But they continued the war against "laws harsh as tigers" by fighting administrative officers over the enforcement of the laws.

TOWARD THE IMMIGRATION ACT OF 1891

By the time the Supreme Court endorsed the Chinese exclusion policy in 1888, the Chinese had the dubious distinction of being the only immigrant group to be specifically excluded from the United States and to be denied the privilege of naturalization. But they were no longer the only targets of restrictionist fervor. Antiforeigner sentiment began to spread in the late 1880s, particularly against those people Americans identified as the "new immigrants" from southern and eastern Europe.

The new nativism corresponded with concern over the economic and social effects of industrialization. Americans in the 1880s witnessed tremendous changes in their lives as their society became ever more industrial and urban. Immigrants were integral to the industrialization process. They provided both the labor and the market key to economic growth and expansion, but they also bore the brunt of many Americans' anxieties and dissatisfactions with the new economic order. While the United States expanded and increased its overall wealth during the late nineteenth century, the society also became increasingly polarized as the disparity between rich and poor grew and class lines sharpened. Unions such as the Knights of Labor formed to defend workers against employers. Rapid urbanization spurred by immigration and rural migration in the United States fostered other problems such as overcrowding, poor housing, and the lack of social services.

On the whole, immigrants tended to be poor workers living in cities. Consequently, Americans from all sides perceived them as a threat of one sort or another. Middle-class Americans associated the immigrants with the crowded, tense cities and with the growing, discontented working class. Pointing with alarm to the shrinking frontier, these Americans worried that immigrants clustered in cities would not assimilate properly and would endanger the American order.[132] Business leaders, too, became wary of immigrants. Although businessmen generally welcomed immigrants as cheap laborers, they suspected that the newcomers supplied the radical impulse to the burgeoning workers' movement. American laborers also expressed reservations about immigration because of its effect on their wages and working conditions. Immigration reached a high point in 1882; an industrial depression ensued between 1883 and 1886. Although these events were not necessarily causally related, many American workers blamed immigrants for their economic woes and began to press for restrictions.[133]

Organized labor succeeded in obtaining legislation to address some of the worst fears. American workers believed that imported labor was one reason for lower wages and for their difficulty in gaining bargaining power. Employers, they argued, contracted to bring in workers from other countries, thus driving American laborers out of work or at least forcing down wages.[134] Responding to their concerns, Congress in 1885 forbade such practices by enacting the Alien Contract Labor Law.[135]

Fears about immigration intensified in 1886, when a series of strikes and boycotts broke out. What really galvanized the anti-immigration movement, however, was the Haymarket Affair in May 1886 in which several policemen were killed by a bomb during a confrontation with striking laborers. Although it was unclear who actually threw the bomb, authorities charged seven German immigrants and one American with the crime, sentencing six of them to death. John Higham describes the strike as "the most important single incident in late nineteenth century nativism" because it inspired a wave of anti-immigrant sentiment throughout the nation.[136] Many Americans thought it was proof of the radical, violent nature of immigrants which threatened to destroy the fabric of American society.

The event sparked a widespread debate and calls for limits on immigration. In arguing for restriction, many commentators distinguished the newcomers arriving in the 1880s from previous immigrants. Whereas in earlier years, argued Richmond Mayo Smith, the immigrants were of a thrifty, industrious stock, they now were the "indolent, vagrant and vicious" castoffs of other countries.[137] Smith objected particularly to immigrants from southern Europe, quoting extensively from an 1885 report of the Connecticut commissioner of immigration on Italians: "The Italian's object in coming to this country is simple. He wishes to stay here until he can save two or three hundred dollars, and then go home again. . . . His expenses he is able to reduce to a minimum. In matters of personal crowding, he can bear an infinite amount of crowding, without apparently interfering with his enjoyment of life or sense of decency." Such observations bear a striking resemblance to those made earlier regarding Chinese laborers. Smith commented, in fact, that "it is the question of Chinese labor over again."[138] And he went on to draw similar conclusions, that is, that because of their low living standards, the new immigrants competed unfairly with American workers and drove down wages.[139]

As concern rose about the quality and quantity of immigrants, Americans turned their attention to the administration of the immigration laws and blamed the problems on lax enforcement. Several federal investigations of Castle Garden, the immigration station at New York, evoked charges of corruption and mismanagement by state officials. The reports of the investigations accused the state immigration commissioners of accepting many immigrants who should have been excluded, for example, as people unable to care for themselves under the 1882 immigration law.

In response to the charges of state incompetence, the secretary of the treasury in 1890 revoked the federal government's contract with New York and took over the administration of immigration at that port. In the same year, the House Select Committee on Immigration and Naturalization concluded its joint hearings with the Senate Committee on Immigration and recommended new laws to meet the goals of United States immigration policy. The intent of that policy, the committee suggested, was "not to restrict immigration, but to sift it, to separate the desirable from the undesirable immigrants, and to permit only those to land on our shores who have certain physical and moral qualities."[140] This policy of "sifting" required more efficient enforcement under the direction of a single federal authority and a finer distinction between desirable and undesirable immigrants.

Accepting the committee's recommendations, Congress passed a new immigration law in 1891.[141] The new act abrogated all contracts with state boards of immigration and created a federal superintendent of immigration who had sole control over the enforcement of immigration laws, subject to the review of the secretary of the treasury. For the first time, the federal government took full and exclusive control over immigration.

The law also extended the list of excludable classes. The 1882 immigration act had excluded convicts, lunatics, and "any person unable to take care of himself or herself." In 1891 Congress added to this list polygamists, people with contagious diseases, and people "likely to become a public charge." It further required immigrants whose fare was paid by someone else to prove that they were not contract laborers or likely to become public charges. The act also, for the first time, included a deportation provision, providing that aliens already in the United States could be deported within one year of their arrival if the government discovered they were excludable. To aid the superintendent of immigration in the enforcement of the new regulations, Congress mandated that steamship companies must, at their own expense, return aliens who were denied entry to their native countries. This, Congress hoped, would induce the steamship companies to winnow out undesirable immigrants before they reached the United States.

Two other features of the new law, less noticed by historians but central to this study, stand out. In section 8, the law stated: "All decisions made by the inspection officers or their assistants touching the right of any alien to land, when adverse to such right, shall be final unless appeal be taken to the superintendent of immigration, whose action shall be subject to review by the Secretary of the Treasury." The law also explicitly omitted Chinese from its reach in section 1, applying the provisions to all aliens "other than . . . Chinese laborers."

The first aspect—that "all decisions made by the inspection officers . . . shall be final"—turned out to be significant, for it came to be interpreted as severely limiting judicial review in immigration cases and provided the foundation for the unprecedented power of the Bureau of Immigration. Why Congress chose to make inspectors' decisions final is not immediately evident. The provision did not attract any attention or comment during legislative debates.[142] One possible answer is that Congress drew upon patterns already established in administrative law. Other statutes delegating power to administrative officers—such as the collector of customs and the commissioner of the General Land Office—sometimes contained similar finality clauses though they did not preclude judicial review.[143]

The finality provisions of such laws suggest only a partial explanation for the particular wording of the Immigration Act of 1891, for several statutes establishing administrative authority did *not* specify that administrative decisions were to be final. Nor did the federal courts appear to pose a particular threat to the administration of the general immigration laws. In the extensive testimony before the joint committee on immigration in 1890, only a few witnesses mentioned the courts.[144] Very few published opinions concerning non-Chinese immigration appear in federal case reporters before 1891.[145] The reporters are not the best indices of the volume of litigation, however, because lower federal courts often did not publish their opinions. The secretary of the treasury's annual report for 1892 suggests that some immigrants did challenge administrative decisions in court; the secretary observed that the 1891 act had "materially lessened the litigation at the landing ports."[146] Although this statement indicates that non-Chinese immigrants used the courts before 1891, it does not necessarily follow that their litigation provided the main impulse for prohibiting judicial review. If the litigation had been that problematic, one would have expected more mention of it in the extensive congressional hearings and debates.

Congress did know, however, of Chinese immigrants' use of the federal courts to contest admission cases, and it seems likely that it wished to avoid such litigation with non-Chinese immigrants. The damaging effects of Chinese litigation on the success of exclusion had been a central issue when Congress amended the Chinese Exclusion Act in 1888. In fact, Congress had inserted a similar finality clause in the Chinese Exclusion Act of September 13, 1888, which stated, "the collector shall . . . decide all questions in dispute with regard to the right of any Chinese passenger to enter the United States, and his decision shall be subject to review by the Secretary of the Treasury, and not otherwise."[147] Again, the debates in Congress did not explicitly address the finality clause, but the bill's main proponent, Senator Joseph N. Dolph of Oregon, clearly believed that the act would greatly reduce the litigation by Chinese immigrants.[148] Federal District Court Judge Olin Wellborn's explanation for the finality clause seems persuasive:

The books are full of cases in which the rights of Chinese persons to enter this country have been re-examined on habeas corpus, after denials of such rights by customs officials. . . . It was, doubtless, in view of this unbroken line of decisions, and for the purpose of changing the law . . . that congress enacted the twelfth section of the act of September 13, 1888. With this section in force, the action of the collector, in the absence of fraud, would be conclusive and final.[149]

The delay in ratifying the treaty of 1888 and the hasty enactment of the Scott Act threw the legality of the act of September 13, 1888, into doubt, however. The Circuit Court of Appeals for the Ninth Circuit and, later, the Supreme Court held that the finality provision in section 12 had never become law.[150]

Administrators in San Francisco did not have to read the appellate courts' opinions to know that the finality clause had not gone into effect, for Chinese immigrants continued to find a forum in the federal courts long after the September 1888 law had been enacted. The joint committee on immigration, which gathered testimony in preparation for the Immigration Act of 1891, sent a subcommittee to the West Coast to inquire into the enforcement of the Chinese exclusion laws. There, they heard ample testimony about Chinese use of the courts. An inspector for the customs service at San Francisco estimated that since the passage of the Chinese Exclusion Act of 1888, the local federal district court in San Francisco had reversed the collector of customs in 86 percent of the cases filed. Thus, the inspector concluded, the most serious hindrance to effective enforcement was the court's ability to review decisions of government officials.[151]

It seems likely, then, that the Chinese success in circumventing administrative processes provided the impulse for inserting the finality clause. Congress probably hoped to prevent other immigrants from resorting to the courts more than they already were. Similar attempts to preclude judicial review in Chinese cases came soon after the 1891 act.[152]

The Supreme Court had no difficulty in acquiescing to the exclusion of the federal courts from immigration decisions. Within months of the act's passage, the federal Circuit Court for the Northern District of California at San Francisco refused to review the decision of the federal immigration inspector denying a Japanese woman, Nishimura Ekiu, entry into the United States on the grounds that she was likely to become a public charge.[153] The circuit court held that under the act of 1891, it had no power to interfere with the inspector's decision and rejected the immigrant's argument that the act's finality clause, by precluding a judicial hearing of her right to land, denied her the constitutional right to due process. The United States Supreme Court in 1892 agreed with the circuit court. Its decision drew on the notion of inherent sovereign powers elaborated by Justice Field in *Chae Chan Ping*. The national government, the Court ruled, had as part of its inherent sovereign powers the "complete control" over aliens. Congress could choose whether or not to allow the federal courts a role in immigration matters. Because the act of 1891 clearly showed that Congress had decided to deny judicial review in these cases, Justice Horace Gray concluded, "It is not within the province of the judiciary to order that foreigners . . . shall be permitted to enter." Gray dismissed the due process arguments on the grounds that regarding "foreigners who have never been naturalized, nor acquired any domicil or residence within the United States, nor even been admitted into the country pursuant to law . . . the decisions of executive or administrative officers, acting within powers expressly conferred by Congress, *are* due process of law."[154]

Immigration law scholar Peter Schuck has suggested that the Court's deference to immigration officers in *Nishimura Ekiu*, as well as in *Chae Chan Ping*, established the basic relationship between judges and administrators which has long distinguished immigration law from other branches of administrative law. In that relationship, Schuck quips, "Judges should be seen—if absolutely necessary—but not heard."[155] Undeniably, the decisions set a lasting precedent for judicial restraint in immigration cases, though the courts continued to be active in cases involving Chinese immigrants. When compared to other decisions regarding administrative power at the time, however, the Court's deference in *Nishimura Ekiu* does not appear distinctive or unusual.

As the administrative tasks of government grew in the late nineteenth century, courts heard numerous challenges to the authority of state and federal officials. Courts generally extended to these cases the common law principle regarding public officers, holding that as long as administrative officials operated within their jurisdiction, their determinations of fact were to be treated as conclusive upon the courts, even in the absence of an explicit statutory provision for finality.[156] The rationale for judicial restraint lay in the theory of the separation of powers: each branch, when operating within its realm, was to be free from undue interference from the others. Judges presumed that public officials acted in good faith and within the proper scope of their duties.[157] Still, questions of *law* involved in administrative action fell within the proper scope of the judiciary and thus remained open to judicial review.[158] For example, the Supreme Court had generally refused to review the General Land Office's disposal of public lands, regarding such issues as whether applicants were qualified to file a claim for the land or whether they had made the necessary improvements on their claims to be questions of fact within the sole jurisdiction of the land officers. In one leading case, the Court explained, "When the law has confided to a special tribunal the authority to hear and determine certain matters arising in the course of its duties, the decision of that tribunal, within the scope of its authority, is conclusive upon all others."[159] Often, however, the Land Office's allocation of public lands depended on its interpretation of congressional statutes. Land officers had to decide, first, what the statute required claimants to do to secure the land before they determined whether claimants had complied with the law. In such cases, the Supreme Court had been willing to review the decision because a question of law (the province of the judiciary) was at stake.[160]

The same principle of review appeared to guide the Court in *Nishimura Ekiu*. The immigration inspector, in deciding that the Japanese woman was excludable as a person likely to become a public charge, investigated the reasons for her immigration to the United States, her moral character, and her financial resources and ability to support herself. Such questions were factual determinations which the Court left to the discretion of administrative officials. The Court did not address the conclusiveness of the officials' decisions on questions of law, but, based on past decisions in other areas, such questions would remain subject to judicial review.

The specific question of whether a statute making administrative decisions final constituted an unconstitutional denial of due process because it denied a judicial hearing of one's rights had not been directly addressed in many cases before *Nishimura Ekiu*. The issue had arisen primarily in tax cases. The Court had held that summary administrative proceedings satisfied the due process requirement in the Constitution and, consequently, that no judicial hearing was necessary.[161]

Although the Court's approach in *Nishimura Ekiu* fell within the established doctrines of the law of public officers, it must be emphasized that modern administrative law was in its formative stages and that the issue of administrative finality, according to one of the earliest administrative law scholars, John Dickinson, was "one of the largest and most confused [legal] topics" of the time.[162] Thus the Court's opinion cannot be fully understood as simply the elaboration of earlier precedent. The law/fact distinction may have worked in theory, for example, but it was notoriously difficult to maintain in practice. The difficulty in separating questions of law and fact prompted Dickinson to argue that it was purely a legal fiction used to mask true judicial intentions: "When the courts are unwilling to review, they are tempted to explain by the easy device of calling the question one of 'fact'; and when otherwise disposed, they say that it is a question of 'law.' "[163]

That Nishimura Ekiu was an alien who, as the Court pointed out, had established no ties in the United States, undoubtedly contributed to the Court's decision. It is difficult to imagine, for example, the Court allowing officials on the Interstate Commerce Commission the same degree of latitude as it did immigration inspectors, even if the 1887 statute establishing the commission had contained an administrative finality clause like that in the 1891 immigration law. Dickinson pointed out in 1924 that the type of administrative action involved and the interests at stake strongly affected the Court's willingness to review.[164] The Supreme Court, in fact, had exercised a much more zealous review of the Interstate Commerce Commission because of the potential danger it posed to the private property rights of citizens. Immigrants applying for admission, however, sought a privilege, not a right, in the Court's opinion, as did Americans who filed for land claims with the Land Office or who used the services of the Post Office. Because government privileges rather than common law rights were at stake, the Court deferred much more readily to the government as the bestower of the privileges. Similarly, courts allowed the government broad discretion in carrying out tasks essential to its maintenance such as collecting taxes and raising an army.[165]

The Supreme Court's opinion in *Nishimura Ekiu* had important ramifications for the development of immigration law because it strictly circumscribed the role that federal courts could play in immigration cases for decades to come. As a result of the Court's construction of the act of 1891's finality clause, the federal courts would not review the factual determinations made by immigration officials regarding the right of aliens to be admitted to the United States. The Court had also implied that aliens who had not yet entered the United States were not entitled to the procedural protections guaranteed by the Constitution. It is important to keep in mind, however, the issues the Court had *not* addressed in *Nishimura Ekiu* and which, ostensibly, remained amenable to judicial review. Questions of law involved in administrative decision making appeared to be open to judicial interpretation. Furthermore, the Court's opinion concerned only those aliens applying for admission to the United States; the Court said nothing about the rights of aliens who had already been admitted and had become residents of the United States.

Finally, the decision in *Nishimura Ekiu* did not address the right of Chinese to seek redress from the collector's exclusion decisions. In fact, for the Chinese, the federal district court in San Francisco continued to play an important role for several years after *Nishimura Ekiu*, intervening often and decisively in favor of the Chinese. Chinese were able to persevere in the courts in part because of the clause of the 1891 act which omitted Chinese from its reach: the immigration act reinforced the separation of Chinese from other immigrants by limiting the act to non-Chinese immigrants. As with the clause making immigration officials' decisions final, Congress gave no indication why it did not subject Chinese to the 1891 act. The legislature probably thought there was no need for debate or explanation; the idea that Chinese were fundamentally different from European immigrants was already implicit in the Chinese exclusion laws. Those laws adequately expressed U.S. policy on Chinese immigration and had established an administrative system for enforcement. The policy embodied in the act of 1891 responded to perceived problems with European immigrants, and thus Congress most likely saw no reason to include Chinese.

The act thus established a dual system of administration, one for the Chinese and one for all other immigrants. The collectors of customs at each port remained responsible for enforcing the laws regarding Chinese, while the newly created superintendent of immigration administered the laws governing non-Chinese immigrants. It was not until 1903 that the Chinese were placed under the aegis of the Bureau of Immigration and were made subject to the general immigration laws. The ironic consequence was that the prohibition of judicial review in the 1891 act did not apply to Chinese immigrants, and they could continue to challenge in the federal courts the administrative decisions denying them admission.

With the act of 1891 the United States had established the framework for a restrictive immigration policy. It entailed excluding aliens with specific undesirable characteristics and vesting great discretion in the administrative officers enforcing the law. Neither courts nor constitutional protections would hamper the immigration administration to any great extent.

The importance of administrative discretion to restrictive immigration policies is more clearly revealed in the next three chapters, which analyze the San Francisco federal court's role in the continuing contest over Chinese exclusion. By 1891, Chinese and anti-Chinese forces had developed strategies they would continue to rely on in the battle over the law and its enforcement. Chinese used litigation before the federal courts to gain entry into the United States, while exclusionists resorted both to intimidation and to stricter legal requirements. When administrators and exclusionists realized that the lower federal courts made strict enforcement of exclusion impossible, they waged a determined battle to remove jurisdiction from the court in Chinese cases. This effort, as well as the persistent Chinese litigation before the courts, is the focus of the next three chapters.

PART I

Judicial Justice, 1891–1905

By the time William W. Morrow took the bench as district court judge for the Northern District of California on September 18, 1891, the court had been barraged with Chinese immigration cases for almost a decade. In that time the Chinese filed more than seven thousand petitions for habeas corpus, and the court attracted the wrath of the public and the administrative officials by allowing the vast majority of these Chinese to enter freely.[1] An examiner for the Department of Justice warned the attorney general in 1887 that the court was in crisis: "The courts are already impaled upon the shafts of vituperation and ridicule by the Press of the State, and the danger is, that the people will lose all confidence in them, a result much to be feared, and than which there is nothing worse. Once tear away that 'divinity' which should 'hedge in' a court and let a people lose confidence in its integrity, and communism, anarchy and riot, follow as certainly as the morning follows night."[2]

When Morrow became judge, it seemed possible that the court's "divinity" might be restored. The deaths of Judge Ogden Hoffman of the district court and Judge Lorenzo Sawyer of the circuit court in 1891 brought to a close the first era of the Northern District Court's history. Californians had a new federal court staffed with judges—Morrow in the district court and Joseph McKenna in the circuit court—who had displayed their loyalty to anti-Chinese forces in Congress. As a California representative to Congress between 1885 and 1891, William Morrow had been at the forefront of the campaign to make the Chinese restriction acts more severe. McKenna, serving in the House of Representatives during the same period, joined his colleague as a vehement proponent of Chinese exclusion.

Furthermore, a new collector, Timothy Phelps, had been appointed to enforce the Chinese laws. Several observers realized that the tension between the courts and the local administration in the 1880s had resulted in part from the overly rigid interpretation of the laws adopted by the zealous collector John Hager.[3] With a new, more reasonable collector and the new judges, a more cooperative relationship in the enforcement of the Chinese laws seemed possible.

A new national consensus about the acceptability of exclusion had developed by 1891. The Supreme Court had upheld the constitutionality of the exclusion act in 1888.[4] When Congress considered amendments to the exclusion laws in 1892, no one questioned whether Chinese should continue to be excluded; only the particular form of the law was at issue. Senator William M. Stewart claimed: "There was a time when there was great diversity of opinion on the question of Chinese immigration to this country, but I think there is practically none now. The American people are now convinced that the Chinese can not be incorporated among our citizens, can not be amalgamated, can not be absorbed, but that they will remain a distinct element."[5]

U.S. commissioner for the federal courts Stephen Chase Houghton, commenting on the Chinese cases before the court, concluded that "the thing is really practically over." Because of the success of legislation restricting Chinese immigration, explained Houghton, the number of Chinese entering the United States had declined, and consequently, very few cases came before the court anymore.[6]

Yet the court's involvement was not over by any means. Between 1891 and 1905, the district and circuit courts heard more than 2,600 habeas corpus cases. And the courts, according to many observers, continued to frustrate the purposes of the Chinese exclusion laws.

Why did the district court continue to accept these Chinese immigration cases? And why did it decide so often in favor of the Chinese? An examination of the case files of the federal district and circuit courts for the Northern District of California between 1891 and 1905 reveals that their activity was due to a combination of factors.[7] Perhaps most important to the success of Chinese in court was the initiative and organization of the Chinese community in San Francisco. Many Chinese took advantage of the opportunity for judicial review, knowing from their collective experience that the federal courts, however reluctant, were often allies. The Chinese in California proved to be tenacious and sophisticated litigators, persistently bringing their claims before the court and fashioning persuasive legal arguments.

The litigants' determination and skill alone did not secure their victory, however. The federal court's adherence to certain institutional norms and practices made it an especially receptive forum, despite the personal opinions of the judges. The court felt bound to hear the cases because the requests for review came in the form of petitions for writs of habeas corpus. Once the Chinese got their claims before the court on habeas corpus, they were able to obtain favorable results because of the evidentiary practices of the court.

The next three chapters analyze the enforcement of the Chinese exclusion laws at San Francisco after 1891. Chapter 2 examines the perspectives and organization of the Chinese immigrants vis-à-vis those of the American officials responsible for enforcing the exclusion legislation. Chapter 3 focuses on the court's treatment of Chinese in admission and deportation cases. Chapter 4 describes the successful campaign to take jurisdiction away from the court.

Contesting Exclusion

THE CHINESE AND THE

ADMINISTRATORS

From the passage of the Chinese Exclusion Act in 1882 to its repeal in 1943, Chinese and federal administrative officials clashed over how the law should be interpreted and enforced. They were natural enemies with diametrically opposed goals: Chinese wanted to come to the United States as freely as possible while the federal officials attempted to restrict their entry. Frustration with the law on both sides fanned the dispute. Chinese resented the discriminatory law, described by one Chinese poet detained at Angel Island as a law "harsh as tigers."[1] The federal administrators, however, repeatedly complained that the law was "probably the most difficult piece of legislation to enforce ever placed upon the statute books."[2] If the law was a tiger, as the Chinese poet claimed, administrative officials thought its teeth dull and full of gaps.

Though apparently contradictory, both perspectives were grounded in reality; the law was both harsh and difficult to enforce. The law's severity stemmed in part from its discriminatory nature. By 1891 the Chinese were the only group of immigrants to be specifically excluded from the United States. American officials made it even more difficult for Chinese to enter through their stringent enforcement of the law. Yet officials did not find their task as America's gatekeepers simple or easy. Through protest, evasion, and, especially, persistent litigation, Chinese often thwarted the exclusion policy.

This chapter explores the contest between Chinese and administrative officials over the implementation of the exclusion laws. It analyzes the perspectives, goals, and organization of both groups, as well as the strategies they employed to pursue their objectives. One important Chinese strategy—litigation in the federal courts—is not examined here but is the focus of Chapter 3. This chapter concentrates instead on the administrative process established by the United States to implement exclusion legislation, analyzing both the government's rationale and the Chinese critique of the procedures.

ADMINISTRATIVE AND CHINESE ORGANIZATION

The Chinese immigrant and government inspector did not encounter each other as individuals. Rather, they were both part of larger social organizations that provided them with particular resources, pressures, and perspectives. An understanding of the structure of the Chinese immigrant community as well as that of the government bureaucracy is therefore crucial to the analysis of the exclusion laws and administrative policies.

When Chinese decided to come to the United States, they had to wind their way through the bureaucratic maze that had been established in piecemeal and incremental fashion by Congress over many years. The administration of the laws was fragmented and divided among several different federal offices under the control of the secretary of the treasury, the secretary of state, and the Department of Justice. The collector of customs at each port, supervised by the secretary of the treasury, assumed the primary duty of deciding whether to admit or exclude Chinese coming to the United States.[3] Other federal officials played supporting roles. United States consuls in China inspected the documents of Chinese claiming to be exempt from exclusion and attached their endorsement if all seemed in order.[4] When Congress enacted the Geary Act in 1892, requiring Chinese legally residing in the United States to register with the government, it gave the task of issuing registration certificates to the collector of internal revenue in each district.[5] Finally, the United States attorneys represented the government in all litigation involving Chinese exclusion.

Until 1903, when the enforcement of the Chinese exclusion laws became more consolidated under the control of the Bureau of Immigration, the collector of customs at each port served as the linchpin in their administration. The collector and his staff in the so-called Chinese Bureau of the Customs Service investigated all Chinese arriving in the United States and decided whether to admit or exclude the newcomers. The Chinese Bureau was just one of twenty-two divisions under the collector's control at San Francisco. In 1897, the San Francisco Chinese Bureau had a staff of seven: the inspector in charge, four inspectors, one interpreter, and one clerk.[6]

The collector of the port was intimately involved in local and national politics. In the age of patronage politics, the collector occupied one of the choicest and most powerful political positions available in the federal government. The advent of civil service reform in 1883 challenged the collector's role as dispenser of patronage, but he retained some discretion over promotions, transfers, and certain positions and actively used those resources to expand his political power.[7]

The collector's political ties made him subject to public and party pressure. His enforcement of the Chinese exclusion laws reflected on his party as a whole.[8] Upon John Wise's retirement as collector at San Francisco, the *San Francisco Call* described his administration as "characteristically Democratic" and predicted that the new collector's "administration will be characteristically Republican."[9] When problems arose, critics were quick to portray the trouble as indicative of the administration as a whole. The enforcement of exclusion became particularly charged during periods of volatile party politics, as in the 1890s.[10] If Californians were unhappy with the enforcement of laws regarding the Chinese, they voiced their dissatisfaction to congressional representatives and to the president, who, anxious to calm political waters, might pressure the collector to bring its local force into line. Newspapers in San Francisco kept a careful eye on the collector's Chinese Bureau, reporting on its routine business as well as "exposing" numerous scandals of the officials' corruption.[11] The watchfulness of the public encouraged the collector and his staff to take a restrictive, enforcement-minded approach to their work.[12]

Though vulnerable to public pressure, the collector and his staff did not act always or solely on political whim. The Chinese Bureau had to operate within the rules established by Congress and the secretary of the treasury. The Division of Special Agents in the Department of the Treasury monitored the collectors' practices, sending agents to each port to conduct routine as well as special investigations. In correspondence to their superiors, collectors and United States attorneys discussed how to interpret the laws, not only because they wanted to avoid departmental censure but also from a respect for rules.[13] Administrators with more legal training tended to be more concerned with following the letter of the rules, though other nonlegal officials shared their perspective.[14] John Sawyer, appointed Chinese inspector in 1904, expressed in his diaries an earnest desire to do his job fairly and efficiently. Sawyer praised his San Francisco superior in 1917 for having an "impersonal attitude" and "at the same time . . . maintain[ing] a very sympathetic attitude toward every subordinate and every Chinese coming before the office."[15]

Of course, consistency and a concern for rules did not necessarily imply leniency. Officials had discretion to develop local practices and interpret the exclusion laws. In deciding how to enforce the laws and regulations concerning exclusion, they proceeded on certain assumptions about Chinese as well as on the belief that their purpose was to enforce the laws as strictly as possible. Thus officials could operate within the law and still strive to satisfy exclusionists.

The implementation of the Chinese exclusion laws between 1891 and 1905 was thus a complex business. The division of responsibilities among several federal offices tended to lead to a diffused, uncoordinated administration of the laws, with each office exercising a significant degree of local control.[16] The secretary of the treasury curbed this decentralizing tendency to a certain extent because he reviewed the collector's actions in particular cases and through agents' reports on general procedures. Aside from departmental review, the collector and the Chinese Bureau proceeded within the constraints of public opinion, party politics, and legal requirements.

The Chinese had a simpler, more cohesive social organization with a more unified sense of purpose than did the government officials. The vast majority of Chinese arrived in San Francisco from Kwangtung Province in southeastern China and found a familiar network of family and service associations, led by the elite merchant class. All Chinese in California belonged to one of several surname or family associations based loosely on lineage.[17] Someone from the family association—an uncle or a distant cousin, for example—would meet the newcomer and help him or her with any immigration difficulties and would hire an attorney if necessary.[18] Once landed, the immigrant could rely on his family association to provide aid in getting settled.

In addition to the family organization, Chinese also belonged to one of several district associations or "huiguan," depending on the dialect they spoke and the region they came from in China. The huiguan performed many benevolent functions and also kept order within the Chinese-American communities. They promulgated rules to guide their members' behavior, required members to pay all debts and dues before leaving the United States, and resolved all "quarrels and troubles about claims in the mines."[19]

Each huiguan sent a representative to an organization that white Americans came to know as the Chinese Six Companies (officially named the Chinese Consolidated Benevolent Association). The original purpose of this board was to arbitrate disputes within the Chinese community. Eventually, however, the Chinese Six Companies took on a broader role, becoming the advocate for the Chinese community in the white world.[20] The organization kept an attorney on retainer to contest anti-Chinese legislation and practices.

Chinese immigrants might also belong to a third type of organization—

the secret or Triad societies, better known to white Americans as "tongs." In China, the Triad societies were associated with political rebellions and crime and thus had a subversive character. Similarly, Chinese joined the societies in the United States both to oppose the local merchant leadership and to profit from the organizations' business in gambling, opium, and prostitution.[21] The secret societies also provided many of the same benevolent services—lodging, medical care, and dispute settlement—as the family and district associations.[22]

Though tightly organized, the Chinese community was hardly harmonious. Conflicts among and between the various immigrant organizations flared up repeatedly as each group competed for economic, political, and social stature within the Chinese community. For example, two huiguan, the Sam Yup and the Sze Yup, fought for control over the Chinese Six Companies and the commercial life of San Francisco's Chinatown. Similarly, in much publicized "tong wars," Triad lodges vied for dominance over the vice business. Both the family associations and the Triads often challenged what they saw as the excessive power of the huiguan and its federation, the Chinese Six Companies, and, by extension, the rule of the merchant elite in Chinatowns. Political developments in China and traditional ethnic rivalries could further divide the Chinese community in the United States.[23]

Despite considerable infighting, the organizations of the Chinese community provided crucial assistance to individual immigrants and often cooperated in the face of American hostility.[24] Historian L. Eve Armentrout Ma argues that "the relative success of the various Chinatown social organizations depended on their ability to meet the challenge of American opposition."[25] For most of the nineteenth century, the Chinese Six Companies had been the most successful in this regard because it used its political and legal resources to check discrimination against Chinese. White Americans recognized the federation as the principal representative of the Chinese immigrant community, which enhanced its prestige and power among Chinese. When the exclusion laws made legal immigration impossible for the vast majority of Chinese, the Triad societies developed a flourishing business in illegal immigration, and their position within the Chinese community grew accordingly.[26]

The Chinese foreign ministry provided the final resource for immigrants and the Chinese-American community though the Chinese legation in Washington, D.C., and the Chinese consulate in San Francisco did not always act in accordance with immigrants' wishes. The offer by Chinese ministers in 1888, for example, to forbid further Chinese emigration to the United States for twenty years in exchange for better protection for Chinese already living in America engendered strenuous opposition and riots in the Kwangtung province, the region that depended most heavily upon free migration.[27] Despite such conflicts, the Chinese legation often negotiated with the United States for a more favorable and just immigration policy for Chinese. The Chinese ministers protested frequently, in passionate and eloquent tones, against the laws that discriminated against Chinese and against the violence perpetrated upon their countrymen. They appealed to the U.S. government to fulfill its treaty promises, holding out in exchange the allure of a profitable economic trade with China. Although the Chinese legation never succeeded in getting the exclusion policy reversed, it did influence the views of some policy makers and administrators and achieved some modifications in the law's enforcement.[28]

In addition to the aid of the social and diplomatic organizations, Chinese experience with bureaucracies in their homeland probably eased their interactions with administrative officials. The imperial government of China relied heavily on a hierarchy of magistrates and gentry officials to administer local government. The local gentry collected taxes, supervised public works and public schools, mediated legal disputes, and maintained a militia. Thus Chinese, at least those who were merchants, were probably accustomed to dealing with complex administration and to appealing to higher, more centralized authorities when necessary.[29]

Chinese newcomers could thus draw on their experiences with bureaucracies and the resources of several groups in their effort to land and settle in the United States. The importance of Chinese organization and experience with government was attested to by white Americans. American policy makers and administrators, bordering on paranoia, warned that "alert and quick-witted celestials" are familiar "with everything that takes place in our Federal Legislature and in our courts,"[30] and used that knowledge to evade the exclusion act. The commissioner general of immigration in 1906 further fastened on the "clannish" character of Chinese as one of the main obstacles in implementing the Chinese exclusion policy.[31]

The strength and sophistication of their community gave the Chinese the tools to combat exclusion. Chinese had been relegated to the periphery of American society through discriminatory immigration and naturalization laws. But many Chinese were not content to remain on the fringes or to be shoved out of the United States altogether.

The campaign in 1892 for more restrictive exclusion laws illustrates in more depth how the structure of the Chinese community and the American bureaucracy affected the struggle over exclusion. The passage and implementation of the new laws put both Chinese and administrators to the test, exposing the strengths and weaknesses of their relative positions.

By 1891, the United States had limited greatly the types of Chinese who could come to the country. Only those who were not laborers (including merchants, students, teachers, and travelers) or who were born in the United States and thus were American citizens were allowed to enter. Chinese laborers residing in California before 1880 were allowed to remain in the United States; once they left, however, they could not return.

The statutes did not address explicitly the admissibility of Chinese women and children. Their right to enter depended on judicial interpretation and administrative rules and hinged largely on the status of their husbands and fathers.[32] The courts ruled in 1884 that the wives of Chinese laborers were excluded under the law, even if their husbands were lawful residents of the United States.[33] But Chinese women and children would be allowed to enter if they were native-born American citizens or the family of citizens.[34] The lower federal courts disagreed, however, about whether the legislation permitted Chinese wives and children of exempt Chinese men to come to the United States and about the proof they needed to present to establish their right to land.[35] In 1900, the Supreme Court clarified the issue, holding, in essence, that the status of the wife and child followed that of the husband. Thus if the Chinese exclusion laws exempted the husband, the wife and child could also enter upon showing that they were the family of the exempt Chinese.[36]

Not surprisingly, Chinese expressed resentment toward the discriminatory exclusion laws. Secret Service agent Oscar Greenhalge reported meeting an unidentified Chinese woman, evidently involved in one of the secret societies: "She declared herself against the Chinese Exclosion [*sic*] Laws, sai[d] the Chinese had as much right to land in America as the Irish, who were always drunk and fighting."[37] "The most objectionable feature of the present exclusion laws," concluded Minister Wu Ting-Fang of the Chinese legation in 1901, "is that they single out the Chinese people alone for unjust exclusion." He advocated abolishing the Chinese exclusion laws and placing Chinese under the general immigration laws. "Why can not the test be made such as to exclude the undesirable elements of all countries from the American shores irrespective of race or nationality?" asked Wu Ting-Fang.[38]

By 1891, however, Congress was firmly committed to the exclusion policy and in 1892 took steps that made the laws even more harsh and offensive to Chinese. Sparked in part by the 1890 congressional report revealing the difficulties of enforcing the exclusion laws on the West Coast, legislators began to complain that "the coolie class . . . are filling up the country."[39]

One senator asserted (incorrectly) that, contrary to the aim of American policy, the number of Chinese in the United States had actually increased since the passage of the exclusion act in 1882.[40]

The problem, according to these legislators, was twofold. First, administrative and judicial officials failed to enforce the laws with much spirit or intelligence. Second, Chinese evaded exclusion and entered illegally through widespread fraud and smuggling rings. The contention that the vast majority of Chinese entered illegally merits closer attention because the actions of legislators, administrative officials, and federal judges largely rested on the core assumption that almost all Chinese lied to gain entry into the United States.

There is clear evidence that many Chinese did come to the United States illegally. When the United States enacted the Chinese exclusion laws, it forced the immigration of Chinese laborers underground and unwittingly created a flourishing business in illegal immigration.[41] The peasant families in the impoverished Kwangtung province in China relied heavily on the financial contributions of their kin working in the United States, as well as in other foreign countries.[42] Consequently, many families continued to send their sons to the United States after the passage of the exclusion acts, relying on false papers and their clan members already in America to help them land.[43]

Both Chinese and white Americans found the illegal immigration profitable. A Chinese merchant legally domiciled in the United States, for example, would claim the birth of a new son upon his return from each visit to China. He could then sell the "slot" to a young Chinese man who, by posing as the merchant's son, would be allowed into the United States.[44] At least eight thousand Chinese have admitted that they originally entered the United States as the "paper sons" of Chinese merchants or of Chinese born in the United States.[45] Clan members might also provide false testimony for Chinese trying to enter as United States citizens. Some white U.S. government officials aided the illegal immigration, providing documents from the Chinese Bureau to be altered and taking bribes to overlook problems with particular cases.[46]

The importation of Chinese prostitutes probably provided the most profit in illegal immigration. United States law severely circumscribed the entry of Chinese women. Only the wives and daughters of Chinese merchants or women born in the United States were allowed to land.[47] The resulting shortage of Chinese women in the United States created a lucrative business in Chinese prostitution run by the secret societies.[48] Although some Chinese women entered such prostitution voluntarily, it seems that most were sold into slavery by their families or kidnapped and brought into the United States.[49] The tongs would organize their landing, presenting the women as family members of merchants or as United States citizens. The tongs are estimated to have paid anywhere from $1,000 to $5,000 to purchase and land a Chinese prostitute.[50]

It is impossible to gauge the extent of illegal entry by Chinese in the period. The contemporary sources that express the belief that the vast majority, if not all, Chinese were in the United States illegally are suspect for their bias. Accounts of fraudulent entry by Chinese unfolded in an atmosphere heavy with suspicion and paranoia, in a society dominated by the images of deceptive Chinese and government boodlers. Americans looked for confirmations of their belief that Chinese were corrupt and thus exaggerated the extent of the fraud. So, too, it is unlikely that contemporaries gave an accurate portrayal of Chinese prostitution. Not only did racism distort their view of Chinese prostitution, but also the prevailing campaign against all types of prostitution may have influenced some observers' accounts.

Similarly, though scandals of government corruption periodically surfaced, investigation of the charges against administrators often revealed only minor indiscretions. Secret Service agent Oscar Greenhalge reported that, "with but one or two exceptions, there is nothing to indicate that the Officers, at this Port [San Francisco] are dishonest."[51] Furthermore, there is evidence that those making accusations sometimes falsely cried "corruption" as a way to get rid of officials who did not agree with their policies.[52]

Although allegations of fraud appear to have been exaggerated, the perception of Chinese as corrupt persisted and significantly influenced the move to tighten the exclusion laws and their enforcement. Legislators in 1892 relied heavily on the image of Chinese laborers sneaking into the United States in congressional debates on new exclusion legislation. The Exclusion Act of 1882 had prohibited the immigration of Chinese laborers for ten years. The end of the ten-year period in 1892 provided the nominal reason for placing Chinese exclusion on the legislative agenda. It was also a presidential election year, which, according to several critics, encouraged congressmen to demonstrate their parties' commitment to Chinese exclusion.[53] Legislators readily agreed that the exclusion policy should be renewed; the main debate centered on proposals to strengthen the enforcement of the laws by curbing Chinese fraud. The ability of Chinese to evade exclusion through legal and illegal means frustrated and humiliated anti-Chinese forces. "We have been mocked," said Senator Wilbur F. Sanders, "and that is why we are dissatisfied."[54]

Congress came up with the Geary Act, a law Senator Henry Teller of Colorado characterized as "exceedingly harsh in its provisions" but which was supported by "public sentiment."[55] The Geary Act required all Chinese laborers who were entitled to be in the United States to apply within one year to the collector of internal revenue for a certificate of residence. If they failed to register, these laborers could be arrested and brought before a United States judge or commissioner for deportation proceedings. The deportation hearings were intended to be summary proceedings in which the judges' actions were strictly circumscribed by the statute. The burden of proof was on the Chinese. If the laborer did not present a certificate, the judge had to order his deportation unless the laborer could prove that he had been unable to obtain one "by reason of accident, sickness or other unavoidable cause." At that point, the Chinese defendant still had to establish that he was lawfully in the United States, presenting the testimony of one white witness on his behalf. Chinese laborers who refused to register could be sentenced to one year in prison at hard labor before their deportation to China.[56]

The Chinese-American community fought vigorously against the new law, which once again singled out Chinese for discriminatory treatment. Yung Hen, a poultry dealer in San Francisco's Chinatown, complained, "For some reason you people persist in pestering the Chinese. . . . You now insist on labeling us."[57] The system of registration, charged the Chinese vice-consul in San Francisco, placed Chinese "on the level of your dogs."[58] The Chinese Six Companies lodged a strong protest with the collector of internal revenue at San Francisco, John Quinn, calling the Geary Act "an unwarranted and unnecessary insult to the subjects of a friendly nation . . . an insult that has not been inflicted upon the subjects of any other nation." Though the law applied only to laborers, the Six Companies predicted that it would be used to harass merchants as well: "The law, if enforced, will subject every Chinese merchant in the United States to blackmail of the worst type. A Chinese merchant who has resided in San Francisco for many years and who may desire to go to New York on business can be stopped at every little hamlet, village, and town on the line of the railroad and arrested on the charge of being a laborer who has failed to register."[59]

Chinese did not simply complain about the new law; they also refused to obey it. Collector of Internal Revenue John Quinn informed the Chinese Six Companies in September 1892, "I am now ready and willing to register all [Chinese] who may apply."[60] The Chinese Six Companies, however, had already posted circulars throughout San Francisco and the rest of the United States advising Chinese not to register. Describing the Geary Act as a "cruel" and "unjust" law, the Six Companies called upon Chinese to "stand together" and refuse to register. Resistance was justified, claimed the Six Companies, because the law violated both the U.S. Constitution and the treaty with China. Informing Chinese of their intent to fight the law in court, the organization requested that each member contribute $1 for legal fees. The Six Companies also petitioned the Chinese government to bring pressure to bear upon the American administration.[61]

The Six Companies' campaign for noncompliance was enormously successful, prompting consternation among exclusionists and government officials. With only one month remaining for registration, only 439 of an estimated 26,000 eligible Chinese had applied for certificates of residence in San Francisco. Furious with the Chinese resistance, Thomas Geary, the California Democrat who had authored the act, and other Californians tried, unsuccessfully, to get the U.S. attorney at San Francisco to indict the presidents of the Six Companies for interfering with implementation of registration, hoping for "the effect of frightening the members of that Association into a change of policy."[62] The Treasury Department adopted more conciliatory methods to persuade Chinese to register. Acting on its authority to prescribe regulations to govern the registration process, the department relaxed its rules by dropping the requirement for a photograph (for Chinese, one of the more offensive features of the law) and reducing the number of "credible" (i.e., white) witnesses from two to one. The attorney for the Chinese Six Companies, Thomas Riordan, was correct in his prediction that such changes would not "cut much figure in inducing the Chinese to register."[63]

As the deadline for registration neared, the atmosphere in San Francisco became more tense, probably fueled by the sensationalist stories in the *San Francisco Call*. The newspaper reported on March 28 that "for the past two weeks the gunstores of the city have been patronized pretty liberally by Chinese" and that the "Chinaman . . . usually purchases the most deadly and effective weapon he can find."[64] The Chinese vice-consul in San Francisco, King Owyang, angrily denied the rumors that Chinese would forcibly resist the enforcement of the Geary Act. Nevertheless, Collector of Internal Revenue John Quinn drew up a plan to place an armed guard of 180 federal marshals throughout Chinatown on the day registration ended.[65]

Far from armed conflict, the main weapon of choice for the Chinese in the struggle over the Geary Act was litigation. The Chinese Six Companies hired three of the most eminent appellate attorneys in Washington, D.C.— J. Hubley Ashton, counsel for the Southern Pacific Company, Joseph H. Choate, and Maxwell Evarts—to challenge the constitutionality of the Geary Act.[66] The attorneys set up a test case involving three Chinese laborers in New York. Fong Yue Ting and Wong Quan, residents of the United States for fourteen and sixteen years, respectively, had refused to register and, as a result, had been arrested and ordered deported. The third litigant, Lee Joe, had attempted to register but the collector of internal revenue in New York denied him a certificate on the grounds that Lee Joe's witnesses were not credible because they were Chinese. Lee Joe was later arrested for failure to have a certificate and brought before the district court for the required deportation hearing. Although the judge found that Lee Joe lacked a certificate for an unavoidable reason and proceeded to hear his case, the court ultimately decided that he had not proven to its satisfaction that he was a lawful resident of the United States and ordered his deportation.

The attorneys and the Chinese waited for the end of the registration period to press their case before the Supreme Court. At the request of Chinese minister Tsui Kwo Yin, Attorney General Richard Olney agreed to schedule the case in the Supreme Court for hearing soon after May 5, 1893, the deadline for registration.[67] By that date, only 13,242 Chinese in the United States had registered, leaving an estimated 85,000 subject to deportation.[68] The future of the unregistered Chinese laborers lay before the Supreme Court in the case of Fong Yue Ting.

The attorneys for the Chinese had prepared a lengthy brief for the Supreme Court's consideration. Although they argued that "if any aliens are to be registered, then *all* should be," the attorneys did not focus much attention on the legality of registration per se.[69] They concentrated instead on two main arguments: first, that Congress had no power to deport Chinese who did not register, and second, that the procedures established for the registration and deportation of Chinese violated the due process guarantees of the Constitution.

In establishing their first point, the attorneys for the Chinese had to confront the sweeping grant of power conceded to Congress by the Supreme Court in *Chae Chan Ping* v. *U.S.* and *Nishimura Ekiu* v. *U.S.* They vigorously asserted that the power to expel resident aliens was as far removed from the power to exclude "as the North Pole is from the South, and a decision against the appellants as to the *exclusion* of an alien is no authority as to the right to *remove* them."[70] Counsel emphasized that, unlike aliens applying for admission, the Chinese subject to deportation under the Geary Act were citizens in fact if not in law. They had lived in the United States for many years at its express invitation, extended in the Burlingame Treaty, and had accepted the obligations associated with that residence.

Such domiciled aliens, argued the attorneys for the Chinese, had rights under international law and the Constitution which Congress could not summarily extinguish. According to international law and English precedent, resident aliens could not be expelled except in punishment for a crime (after a full judicial trial) or in time of war. Neither did the Constitution provide Congress with the power to deport resident aliens. Congress could only pass laws based upon the express or implied power granted to it in the Constitution and could not base its action on the "sole ground" of an "inherent power of sovereignty." The counsel for the Chinese argued that "there is no such thing as an inherent power of sovereignty resting in Congress" because sovereignty lay with the people.[71] Congress *did* have the power to regulate foreign commerce, which allowed it to restrict admission of aliens into the United States. But once "immigrants have ceased to become immigrants, and have been transformed into our population," they become entitled under the Fifth Amendment to "the same constitutional rights to personal liberty as native-born citizens" and escape "beyond the reach of the commerce clause."[72] In regard to these aliens, attorney J. Hubley Ashton remonstrated, "It is not for Congress to devise any process by which they may be finally deprived of their liberty or property, and make it '*due* process of law' by its mere will."[73]

The contention that Chinese, though aliens, had the same constitutional rights as citizens was crucial to the attorneys' second major argument, that the Geary Act's procedures violated the due process guarantees of the Constitution. The attorneys examined in detail the registration and deportation system established by the Geary Act, concluding, "Every step of the procedure tramples upon a distinct constitutional right." The collector of internal revenue had the "absolute and arbitrary" power to determine whether an applicant was entitled to be in the United States before issuing a certificate of registration. The law did not specify the type of investigation or evidence the collector had to take, leaving such matters to the discretion of administrative officials. The law subjected a Chinese person to arrest without a warrant or probable cause and to a search for his certificate, both violations of the Fourth Amendment's protection against unreasonable searches and seizures. The government could proceed without a grand jury indictment as required by the Fifth Amendment for capital or infamous crimes.[74] During the administrative proceeding, the Chinese applicant or defendant had no power to summon witnesses on his behalf, to examine and rebut evidence considered by the government, or to consult with an attorney, all infringements on the Sixth Amendment. The attorneys finally argued that the punishment for failure to register—deportation—was "cruel and unusual" and thus a violation of the Eighth Amendment because it far exceeded the seriousness of the offense.[75]

But the fatal procedural flaw in the Geary Act, according to the attorneys, was the failure to allow unregistered Chinese a full judicial hearing of their right to remain in the United States. The act specified that a Chinese person charged with not having a certificate was to be brought before a United States judge, and the judge had to order deportation if the defendant did not produce the certificate or prove he could not obtain one for the reasons listed in the statute. Most cases would end here and the defendant would be remanded to officials for deportation. If the judge was satisfied that the defendant had been unable to obtain the certificate, he then proceeded to determine whether the Chinese was a lawful resident. But the act required the defendant to produce one credible white witness to prove his case before the judge.

In the attorneys' opinion, such a procedure did not constitute the judicial hearing contemplated by the Fifth and Sixth Amendments. The require-ment of white witnesses in the judicial hearing was "a reflection on the ability of the United States Judges [as] Congress has apparently taken it for granted that they are unable to determine for themselves whether a witness is to be believed or not." Furthermore, the requirement that there be a white witness was arbitrary and made it impossible for Chinese to have a full opportunity to establish their rights.[76]

But more important in the attorneys' minds, the act transformed the judge from an adjudicator into a ministerial officer. He "is commanded to get down from the bench, take off his robe, and see that the prisoner is exported out of the United States."[77] In his stead, the collector of internal revenue assumed the responsibility for adjudicating "the most sacred of all rights," liberty. Not only did this division of responsibility violate the sepa-ration of powers by usurping the judicial power granted in Article III of the Constitution, but it denied Chinese their right to due process. Such a summary hearing, Ashton intoned, "may be possible under a despotic government, but it cannot endure the atmosphere of a free country."[78] The Geary Act, concluded the attorneys, "is repugnant to the body and spirit, the very *soul* of the Constitution."[79]

The United States attorney dismissed the "sickly sentimentality" of the Chinese appellants' counsel. He reminded the Court of the practical prob-lem at hand: "We have here the willful violation of our law, upon the advice of counsel, by a large class of people owing allegiance to a foreign sovereign, by a people not suited to our institutions, remaining a separate and distinct race . . . not bound by any considerations of the sanctity of an oath, given to evasions of other laws of Congress."[80] Far from being cruel and unusual punishment, deportation was a just measure for aliens who have "deliber-ately defied the laws of the country" despite being "afforded every oppor-tunity to obtain the certificates required."[81]

Counsel for the United States set out his basic argument in support of the Geary Act in the first sentence of his brief: "These cases can not be distinguished from the *Chinese Exclusion Case*."[82] Just as Congress had the sovereign power to determine who could come into the United States, it retained the right, under international law, the common law, and the Constitution, to force resident aliens to leave. The U.S. attorney argued, contrary to the position of the appellants' attorneys, that the natural law of self-preservation, recognized by international law, allowed nations to expel aliens whenever necessary for the public welfare, not just in time of war. The nation's power to expel had an even firmer basis in the Constitution, which gave Congress "complete control" over foreign affairs. In conjunction with this delegated power, Congress, in the government's opinion, possessed a general police power that allowed it to regulate national and foreign affairs for the public's general welfare and protection. Such powers provided Congress with ample authority to deport "obnoxious subjects of China," concluded the U.S. attorney.[83]

In response to the due process claims raised by the attorneys for the Chinese, the U.S. attorney argued that aliens, unlike citizens, had no absolute rights under the Constitution. While "a citizen becomes such at birth, and inherits rights under the Constitution as his birthright without the will of the State . . . the alien acquires none without the consent of the State, and only such and for such time—short of citizenship—as the State continues such consent." Under international law, the nation owed aliens protection from other individuals, but aliens could not "appeal to the Federal Constitution for protection against the Federal Government itself." To allow aliens constitutional shelter against the government would be to deny the sovereignty of the United States against foreign nations.[84]

The Chinese defendants' length of residence in the United States was irrelevant in the opinion of the government counsel. They did not acquire "vested rights" in the Constitution by virtue of their residence nor did they become "de facto citizens," a conclusion the attorney drew from the Supreme Court's decision in *Chae Chan Ping*. Whereas the appellants' attorneys distinguished the earlier case as one concerning admission, not deportation, the U.S. attorney pointed out that Chae Chan Ping had been a resident of the United States for many years before he left for a visit to China and reapplied for admission. "If Chae Chan Ping had by his residence here acquired the rights of a citizen," reasoned the U.S. attorney, "he went abroad clothed with these privileges and immunities, and no legislation could have taken them away." Thus, he concluded, in denying his right to be readmitted, the Court recognized a difference between the rights of aliens and those of citizens.[85]

For aliens, then, according to the United States attorney, the guarantees of the Constitution were not rights, but rather mere privileges that could be revoked at the will of the government. The attorney conceded that if applied to citizens, the Geary Act would be an unconstitutional deprivation of due process.[86] But Congress had full authority over aliens and could establish any procedures it desired in providing for their deportation. Not only was a judicial trial unnecessary, but Congress could have chosen "to expel these alien residents without process, hearing, or evidence of any kind."[87]

Despite the U.S. attorney's impassioned brief, there was some reason to believe that the Supreme Court would agree with the Chinese that there was a fundamental difference between the power to exclude and the power to expel. When the Court in *Nishimura Ekiu* upheld a broad congressional power to dictate administrative procedures in admitting immigrants, it stated, "It is not within the province of the judiciary to order that foreigners who have never been naturalized, nor acquired any domicil or residence within the United States, nor even been admitted into the country pursuant to law, shall be permitted to enter."[88] Here, the Court appeared to recognize a difference between resident aliens and aliens applying for admission, and the possibility of judicial intervention on behalf of the former had not been foreclosed.

Yet when the Court announced its decision on May 15, 1893, it was clear that the more restrictive doctrines established in *Nishimura Ekiu* and *Chae Chan Ping* held sway over the majority. In a five-to-three decision, the Supreme Court upheld the constitutionality of the Geary Act.[89] Justice Gray, writing for the majority, found no difference between the power to exclude and the power to deport. They "rest upon one foundation, are derived from one source, are supported by the same reasons, and are in truth but parts of one and the same power."[90] That foundation was the nation's inherent sovereign power, elaborated in *Nishimura Ekiu* and *Chae Chan Ping*. Such power was "absolute and unqualified," and consequently, Congress could devise any procedures it saw fit to register and deport the resident Chinese aliens.[91]

The due process guarantees of the Constitution did not protect aliens from the plenary power of Congress. The majority agreed with the U.S. attorney that the Court in *Chae Chan Ping* had already distinguished between the rights of aliens and those of citizens. "In view of that decision," said Gray, "it appears impossible to hold that a Chinese laborer acquired, under any of the treaties or acts of Congress, any right, as a denizen or otherwise, to be and remain in this country, except by the license, permission and sufferance of Congress." While in the United States, aliens were entitled "to the safeguards of the Constitution, and to the protection of the laws, in regard to their rights of person and of property, and to their civil and criminal responsibility." But the Constitution could not shield them if Congress decided "their removal is necessary or expedient for the public interest."[92] The message was clear: aliens enjoyed constitutional rights only at the sufferance of Congress.

Gray further held that the constitutional provisions securing the right to a trial by jury and prohibiting unreasonable searches and seizures and cruel and unusual punishment did not apply in this case because the Geary Act procedures were "in no proper sense a trial," nor was "the order of deportation . . . a punishment for crime." Rather, deportation was merely "a method of enforcing the return [of an alien] to his own country." This process did not involve, according to Gray, a deprivation of life, liberty, or property nor did it constitute a criminal proceeding that might bring the protections in the Bill of Rights into play.[93]

Interestingly, Justice Stephen J. Field, the progenitor of the inherent sovereign powers doctrine in *Chae Chan Ping*, sharply dissented from the "extraordinary doctrines" expressed in the majority's opinion, as did Justice David J. Brewer and Chief Justice Melville W. Fuller.[94] Field stood by his earlier decision but asserted that there was a "wide and essential" difference between the power to admit and the power to deport.[95] All nations had the right to determine who should be allowed to enter their jurisdiction. Aliens not yet admitted to the United States remained outside of American political society and could not claim constitutional protection against administrative procedures. This had been the Supreme Court's holding in *Nishimura Ekiu*. Once the United States consented to admit the aliens, however, they became lawful residents, with all of the obligations and entitlements enjoyed by citizens, except the right to vote and hold public office. Congress could not deport aliens at will, just as it could not banish American citizens. Field expostulated, "Arbitrary and despotic power can no more be exercised over [aliens] with reference to their persons and property, than over the persons and property of native-born citizens."[96]

Justice Brewer further argued that even if Congress did possess an inherent sovereign power to expel aliens (which he seriously doubted), it could exercise that power "only in subordination to the limitations and restrictions imposed by the Constitution."[97] The Supreme Court had held, for example, that though "Congress has supreme control over the regulation of commerce . . . if, in exercising that supreme control, it deems it necessary to take private property, then it must proceed subject to the limitations imposed by this Fifth Amendment." Brewer reasoned that if the Fifth Amendment limited powers expressly given to Congress, "it must as certainly [limit congressional powers] that are only granted by implication."[98]

All three justices condemned the majority's holding that aliens possessed constitutional guarantees only at the sufferance of Congress. "Of what avail are such guarantees?" asked Justice Brewer.[99] The dissenters differed from the majority on this essential point: they believed that aliens could claim the same constitutional protections as citizens, by right, not by privilege. Thus, if Section 6 of the Geary Act constituted an illegal deprivation of due process if applied to citizens, then it must also fail constitutionally when applied to resident aliens.

Using that measure as their guide, the dissenters concluded that the Geary Act's procedures constituted a flagrant denial of due process. "If applied to a citizen," Justice Field argued, "none of the justices of this court would hesitate a moment to pronounce [the act] illegal."[100] The justices agreed with the Chinese appellants' attorneys that the act violated the Fourth and Sixth Amendments. In response to the majority's benign characterization of deportation, Chief Justice Fuller said, "No euphuism can disguise the character of the act."[101] Justice Brewer elaborated: "Deportation is a punishment. It involves first an arrest, a deprival of liberty; and second a removal from home, from family, from business, from property." Such punishment was "beyond all reason in its severity" and constituted cruel and unusual punishment, a violation of the Eighth Amendment. Furthermore, argued Justice Brewer, "no person who has once come within the protection of the Constitution can be punished without a trial. It may be summary, as for petty offenses and in cases of contempt, but still a trial, as known to the common law."[102] The judicial hearing provided for in the act did not constitute such a trial.

The dissenters warned that the "arbitrary and despotic" powers endorsed by the majority established a dangerous precedent. "It is true this statute is directed only against the obnoxious Chinese," said Justice Brewer. "But if the power exists, who shall say it will not be exercised to-morrow against other classes and other people?"[103]

Justice Brewer's words were prophetic, for the *Fong Yue Ting* decision had broad repercussions. It removed all aliens, not just Chinese, from the protective shelter of the Constitution and subjected them to the plenary power of Congress. The case established the basic principle that would distinguish immigration law from other branches of administrative law: aliens might have privileges, but, unlike citizens, they could not invoke the specific rights protected by the Bill of Rights against the government in administrative proceedings.[104]

More immediately, however, the decision subjected thousands of Chinese to deportation for failure to register. The prospect of imminent, massive deportation sparked mixed reactions. Most white Americans on the West Coast celebrated the Supreme Court's decision, but it had a "paralyzing effect" in San Francisco's Chinatown, according to the *San Francisco*

Morning Call, because "the confidence in the success of their fight had been so universal and supreme that the defeat stunned the leaders."[105] Their disappointment was shared by certain white Americans, including California fruit growers who feared their fruit would go unpicked and agricultural land "will certainly remain idle . . . should the Chinese be shipped away."[106] Others condemned the Geary Act and the *Fong Yue Ting* decision as unworthy of the United States and as a violation of American treaties with China.[107] The American Bar Association's Committee on International Law characterized the majority opinion as "very extreme," and John Russell Young, former U.S. minister to China, warned that American disregard of treaty rights would result in the atrophy of American trade and influence in China.[108] Another commentator argued that the Geary Act had been a purely political measure, passed "simply for the sake of votes." He hypothesized that many congressmen had voted for the act with the hope and expectation that the Supreme Court would invalidate it as unconstitutional.[109]

Despite such criticism, the legality of the Geary Act had been upheld and administrators were left with the thorny problem of enforcing the law. One of the Geary Act's critics was partially correct when he predicted that it would probably "remain a dead letter upon the statute book."[110] Before the Supreme Court's decision, the secretary of the treasury had instructed the collectors of customs and internal revenue not to enforce the law until further notice. Once the Supreme Court upheld the law, the secretary faced the impossible task—with a budget of only $25,000—of arresting and deporting tens of thousands of Chinese. The administration estimated that it would cost $7,310,000 to deport all of the Chinese who had not registered.[111] Confronted with massive noncompliance and a severe shortage of funds, the secretary chose to do nothing for the time being, hoping, no doubt, that Congress would repair the situation.[112] The secretary again instructed the individual collectors to refrain from enforcing the law, and the attorney general sent a similar order to his district attorneys.[113]

The restraint of the administration became intolerable to many Californians who clamored for the prompt deportation of unregistered Chinese. Criticism of President Grover Cleveland and his administration grew in California. "It is open war—Californians against the administration," declared one newspaper headline.[114] The Anti-Chinese Law and Labor League in San Francisco called for the impeachment of the "law-defying traitor known as Grover Cleveland."[115] Lampooning the president in cartoons and prose, the *San Francisco Call* cried, "The [Chinese] have invaded the White House and captured Grover the Great and Yang Yu [the Chinese minister] and his big retinue of Celestials are masters of the situation."

Attorney General Olney also came under censure when his order to refrain from enforcing the law became public.[116] Democratic senator Stephen M. White of California warned the attorney general that the "situation in California regarding the Chinese is critical" and could lead to the "destruction of the democratic party in that State."[117]

U.S. Attorney George Denis in Los Angeles reported to the attorney general: "Mass meetings have been held throughout this district calling upon me to enforce [the law]."[118] The economic stresses associated with the Panic of 1893 exacerbated Californians' frustrations. Denis described the tense situation:

> The wage-earners and farmers, instigated no doubt by the financial stringency of the times, have been doing everything in their power to remove the Chinese from the country, under the impression that their financial distress is due to the presence of this race. Hardship following hardship, these people have gone beyond the pale of public discussion and meeting, and have so menaced the business of the communities and of the district as to compel the sheriffs of the several counties to call upon the Governor of the State for troops with which to avert impending riots and threatened bloodshed. . . . Without such action, it is the confident belief of the people of this district that a number of Chinese lives would have been taken.[119]

While both Denis and Charles Garter, U.S. attorney at San Francisco, used tactics to delay enforcement, they impressed upon the attorney general the need to respond to public pressure.[120]

The attorney general reassured his staff attorneys that help was on the way because Congress was considering legislation to allow Chinese another opportunity to register. He instructed Denis to "preserve the existing status as far as possible until Congress has acted—inasmuch as to deport a few Chinamen for not registering while the like offences of all others equally guilty are condoned, would be manifestly and grossly unfair."[121]

True to the attorney general's word, Congress passed the McCreary Amendment in November 1893. Over the strenuous objections of several congressmen who did not think the Chinese deserved another chance, Representative James B. McCreary of Kentucky engineered the passage of the bill allowing Chinese laborers an additional six months to register. Western representatives to Congress did win important concessions in the McCreary Amendment, however. The law placed additional restrictions on resident merchants, a class usually favored under the Chinese exclusion laws. Californians had pressed earlier for the exclusion of merchants altogether, claiming, "There is no 'merchant class' in the sense we use the

word; they are traders among themselves and as a rule in a small way."
Further, Californians had argued, the exclusion of merchants, even legitimate ones, was necessary because it was too easy for Chinese laborers to
pretend to be merchants and to enter the United States based on this
fraud.[122]

Although Congress refused to prohibit merchants from coming to the
United States, it agreed to take steps to reduce the possibility of fraud. The
McCreary Amendment required resident merchants who were returning
to the United States after a temporary absence to prove their right to
reenter by following strict guidelines. The merchant had to "establish by
the testimony of two credible witnesses other than Chinese the fact that he
conducted such business . . . for at least one year before his departure from
the United States, and that during such year he was not engaged in the
performance of any manual labor, except such as was necessary in the.
conduct of his business as such merchant, and in default of such proof shall
be refused landing." Furthermore, the amendment defined a merchant as
"a person engaged in buying and selling merchandise, at a fixed place of
business, which business is conducted in his name."[123]

Hoping to modify some of the harsh elements of the Geary and McCreary acts, the Chinese minister, Yang Yu, entered into negotiations with the
United States for a new treaty. The United States denied most of his requests but extended one important right to Chinese laborers. Under the
Scott Act, Chinese laborers who left the United States could not return.
The treaty of 1894 made an exception for laborers who had a "lawful wife,
child or parent" living in the United States or property or debts owed them
of at least $1,000 in value.[124]

By 1894, the furor over the Geary Act had subsided. The registration and
deportation of Chinese laborers became an established feature of the administration of the Chinese exclusion laws. The fight over the Geary Act
reveals the complexities and difficulties in enforcing Chinese exclusion.
Though they lost in the end, Chinese put up a determined fight, and the
divided opinion in the Supreme Court shows how close they came to
winning. The strong ties in the Chinese-American community allowed the
Chinese to unite quickly against the law and to hamper its implementation.
Furthermore, Chinese leaders applied diplomatic pressure upon American
officials to delay action.

Administrators became caught in the crossfire between Californians, the
legislature, and the Chinese. While public opinion and political pressure
demanded that they enforce the law, the defiance of the Chinese, the shortage of funds, and the uncertain constitutionality of the law prevented them
from acting. The Democratic administration's position was made even

more awkward by the fact that the Democratic party had sponsored the Geary Act.

Though it is difficult to determine the lasting effect of the Geary Act fiasco on the Democratic party in California, it certainly left a stain on the Democratic record on Chinese exclusion. In 1900, the Republican party in California still used the Geary Act as a weapon against the Democrats. In contrast to the Democrats, who "nullified" the Geary Act with their lax methods, Republicans in California asserted that their administration was "enforcing the law to the very letter."[125] As this quote indicates, one important legacy of the Geary Act struggle was the tendency of later administrations to guard themselves against public criticism by emphasizing a more restrictive approach to Chinese exclusion.

Similarly, the Chinese defeat in *Fong Yue Ting* altered the balance of power within the Chinese community and provoked a decade of bitter infighting among the various associations. The major loser was the Chinese Six Companies, specifically the Sam Yup huiguan, which had dominated the federation up to that point and had led the fight against the Geary Act. After *Fong Yue Ting*, the more numerous Sze Yup challenged the leadership of the Six Companies and instigated a boycott of Sam Yup businesses with the aim of seizing economic as well as political power. The Triad lodges also gained power from the political upset.[126]

While Californians and Chinese coped with the political repercussions of the Geary Act fight, the legal ramifications of the *Fong Yue Ting* decision became quickly apparent. Chinese minister Wu Ting-Fang complained in 1901 that American administrative officials "treat the Chinese, not as subjects of a friendly power lawfully seeking the benefit of treaty privileges, but as suspected criminals."[127] In fact, as a result of *Fong Yue Ting*, suspected criminals in the United States received better treatment under the law than did Chinese facing deportation or seeking admission. The Supreme Court had confirmed the discretion of Congress and administrative officials to establish whatever procedures they deemed necessary in the admission and deportation of Chinese. Administrative officials wielded their discretion as a weapon to make Chinese entry more difficult.

ADMINISTRATIVE PROCEDURES

The procedures followed by the collector and his staff at the port of San Francisco varied according to the particular collector. Four different collectors served San Francisco between 1891 and 1905, and each had his own views on how to administer the exclusion policy. New laws pertaining to Chinese also resulted in changes in the investigation process. In general, however, Chinese arriving in the United States encountered more or less the same inspection between 1891 and 1903, when the commissioner of immigration assumed control over Chinese cases. And all of the procedures shared a common purpose: to restrict the number of Chinese entering the United States and to guard against any possibility of fraud.

The inspection began immediately upon a ship's arrival. According to one journalist, all Asians—Japanese and Koreans as well as Chinese—were immediately sent to the quarantine station on Angel Island to be fumigated while officials interviewed non-Asian immigrants and passengers.[128] The Chinese inspectors, through their interpreter, would then question each of the applicants, gather any documents (such as Section 6 certificates) supporting their claim to land, and compare them to those on file in the Chinese Bureau.[129]

Many Chinese did not have documents to prove their exemption from the exclusion laws. This was particularly true for those who claimed to be American citizens (by virtue of their birth in the United States), the child of a United States citizen, or the wife or child of a Chinese merchant. They relied instead on the testimony of witnesses to establish their identity and their right to enter.

The Chinese inspectors approached these cases with skepticism, expecting the testimony to be fraudulent. Officials believed that Chinese felt no obligation to tell the truth, even when they were under oath, and could easily obtain witnesses to substantiate their fraudulent stories. Secret Service agent Oscar Greenhalge warned the Department of the Treasury in 1899, "San Francisco is full of old men, that will, for $5 identify ANY Chinaman as his son."[130] In such cases, the applicant and his or her witnesses were carefully coached so that their stories would agree.

During his term as collector between 1889 and 1893, Timothy Phelps devised a system of investigation which attempted to expose fraudulent testimony.[131] The inspectors questioned the applicant and his witnesses separately and in great detail about their family and village in China. Inspectors would ask such questions as, How many steps were there out of the family's back door? How many houses were there in the village? Where did the applicant sit in the village schoolhouse? Did the mother have bound feet? If discrepancies existed in the testimony, the inspectors assumed that the parties did not know each other and that the applicant's claim was false.

Chinese immigrants dreaded the inspectors' investigations. Over the years, the inspectors' drilling became longer and more refined. In oral histories of Chinese who were detained at Angel Island, people remembered their confusion, fear, and anger at the questions that seemed arbitrary and designed only to trick them. "I couldn't understand why they

Interrogation at Angel Island, San Francisco. U.S. Public Health Service, File no. 90-G-124-479, National Archives, Still Pictures Branch.

asked such questions," said Mr. Poon of his interrogation in 1927. "They asked about everything and anything. . . . They even asked me where the rice bin was kept. Can you imagine?"[132] Mrs. Chin, arriving at Angel Island in 1913, remembered that "I was interrogated one day for several hours. They asked me so much, I broke out in a sweat. Sometimes they would try to trip you: 'Your husband said such-and-such and now you say this?' But the answer was out already and it was too late to take it back, so I couldn't say anything about it. If they said you were wrong, then it was up to them whether to land you or not."[133] Chinese remained apprehensive even when inspectors seemed fair. Mr. Low, coming to the United States in 1922,

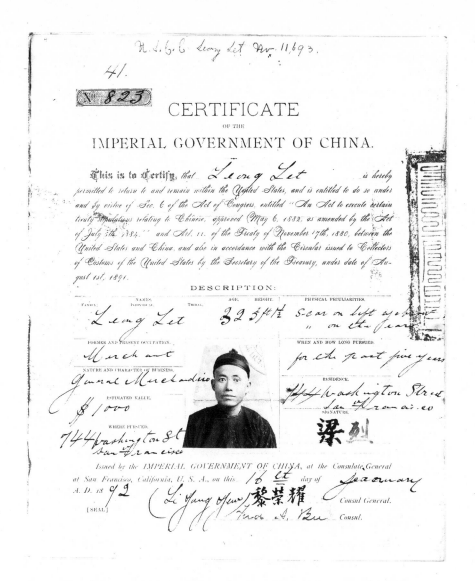

A *Section 6 certificate required of Chinese exempt from exclusion. Courtesy of National Archives, San Francisco Branch.*

thought "the inspector's attitude was non-threatening and pleasant, but I felt frightened and threatened anyway, having listened to people who returned to the village tell of interrogations."[134]

Ironically, in the opinion of one interpreter, the system of detailed questioning had the unintended result of easing the entry of illegal Chinese. "Paper sons . . . were so well coached that their testimonies jibed." But Chinese with the legitimate right to enter "hadn't gone to the trouble of making up coaching books and preparing for it. They were the ones who got the wrong answers, because they thought it was going to be cut and dry."[135]

Describing the collector's investigation as an "inquisition," Chinese minister Wu Ting-Fang sent a vehement letter of protest to the secretary of state in 1901: "The manner of these examinations is reprehensible. Men and women are examined alone, neither their friends nor a lawyer in their behalf being allowed to be present, and the interpreter is generally a foreigner. There are so many dialects of the Chinese language that one interpreter can not understand them all, hence misunderstandings often arise and injustice is inflicted."[136]

The Chinese minister was particularly perturbed that the collector even subjected Chinese with Section 6 certificates to a searching interrogation.[137] These so-called Section 6 certificates were supposed to be prima facie evidence of their bearers' right to land. Although the certificates created the presumption that the bearer was exempt, neither the law nor officials considered the certificates to be conclusive evidence, and inspectors could disregard them if they uncovered other unfavorable evidence or found the certificates to be faulty. They conceded "that the regulations are strict, but . . . they are necessarily so. . . . Strict as such regulations are, they yet fail to check extensive violations of law."[138] The collector and his staff believed it was necessary to keep applicants away from attorneys and friends who might "coach" them on the testimony.[139] According to departmental regulations, attorneys were not allowed to represent Chinese at the examinations or even to be present. Once the collector had decided to admit or deport the applicant, an attorney could then see the papers in his client's case and prepare a brief or additional testimony for the consideration of the secretary of the treasury upon appeal.[140]

Interpreters posed a special problem for the Chinese Bureau. Officials distrusted Chinese interpreters, suspecting them of colluding with the applicants. At one point in 1896, the Department of the Treasury instructed Collector Wise to discharge all his Chinese interpreters and to hire only white men in the future.[141] The department could not maintain this position for long, however, because few white Americans could speak Chinese fluently and even fewer were familiar with the many different dialects.[142]

Periodically, Chinese pressured the collector at San Francisco to allow them to have their attorneys and their own interpreters present at the examination. Some collectors, especially if they were new to the job, thought the request harmless and agreed until the Department of the Treasury brought them into line.[143] According to Agent Greenhalge, the real reason Chinese wanted their attorney and interpreter present "was on account of the applicant being so DUMB that the Cyndicate [*sic*] was in doubt as to his ability to remember his answers. . . . The Attorney heard the questions, he indicated (in English) to his companion [the interpreter], the answer the applicant should make to the question, the companion SIGNALED to the applican[t] . . . and the question was answered! . . . You will readily see the danger in having such persons present during an examination."[144]

Investigations often took days or even months to complete, during which time Chinese applicants were detained on the steamship. According to the Chinese exclusion laws, the steamship company bringing Chinese to the United States remained responsible for their keep until the collector decided whether they would be allowed to enter. If they were denied entry, the law required the company to return applicants to China at its own expense. The steamship companies often complained about the delay caused by this requirement because ships ready to leave on their next voyage had to wait until all of the passengers' cases were determined. The companies succeeded in obtaining the government's permission to house the detained Chinese in a shed on their dock, thus allowing the ships to come and go.

The detention shed located on the Pacific Mail Steamship dock was by all accounts an unpleasant place. The "accommodations" were cramped, dark, unsanitary, and, in the words of one government official, a "fire trap." Chinese frequently referred in their letters, poems, and recollections to the misery of detention. One anonymous author wrote, "Entering (the detention shed) one may look to the right and to the left and see only bunks and a few benches. 'You stay here, you stay here' is all they say. Here you are cramped and doomed never to stretch."[145] Because of the officials' fear that detainees would be coached, Chinese went outside only at noon, when the guards allowed them to stand on the stairway to get some fresh air.[146] The commissioner general of immigration visiting San Francisco from Washington, D.C., in 1903 was disturbed by the conditions in the shed and requested that the Pacific Mail Steamship Company make renovations, including adding a separate room for "Chinese of high caste" and making more windows. Even with these changes, complaints about the shed continued, in large part because of the indignity of the confinement. In a petition to the government, prominent merchants argued: "No matter how comfortable he [the Chinese passenger] is made in the shed, he is virtually a prisoner and more or less deprived of exercise and liberty of action."[147] Most Chinese stayed from a few days to a few weeks, but some remained confined in these quarters for as long as six months.[148]

The inspection and detention system helped to circumscribe Chinese entry, but it was not the only or the best method that officials used. The officials' power to interpret legislation and to impose additional evidentiary requirements upon Chinese applicants led to even more effective barriers to Chinese entry.

In the Chinese exclusion laws Congress had specified to some extent the evidence Chinese needed to present to prove their right to enter. The first of the Chinese exclusion acts in 1882 required, for example, that Chinese exempt from the act (nonlaborers) must obtain from their government a certificate that attested to their exempt status. The Section 6 certificate listed the applicant's name, age, height, physical description, and occupation; if the person was a merchant, the certificate included the nature and value of his business.[149] The McCreary Amendment imposed more strict evidentiary standards. The merchant had to present two "credible witnesses other than Chinese" who could testify that he had been a merchant for at least one year before he left the United States and, further, that he had not performed any manual labor during that time. The act also required that the merchant have a fixed place of business and that the business be conducted in his name.[150]

Even with such explicit congressional guidelines, there was much room for interpretation by the secretary of the treasury, the attorney general, and the Supreme Court. As the official ultimately responsible for the administration of the Chinese laws, the secretary of the treasury had the power to formulate more detailed rules and procedures to guide collectors and their staffs. Some of the secretary's regulations attempted to narrow the categories of admissible Chinese. The secretary decided, for example, that Chinese coming only to study English were not "students" within the meaning of the treaty of 1880 and thus not allowed to enter, even though the treaty did not specify what a "student" must study.[151] Another regulation instructed that laundrymen were laborers and thus excluded from entry even if they owned and ran the laundry and employed others.[152]

The secretary of the treasury also imposed additional evidentiary requirements upon Chinese. After initially allowing wives and children of merchants to enter the United States on the basis of testimony, the secretary later required the family of merchants to present Section 6 certificates.[153] In a different rule, the secretary authorized that merchants going on a visit to China should obtain before leaving a certificate of departure which documented their status. Although the secretary claimed that this new procedure was a convenience for the merchants, it is clear that the real intent was to narrow the possibility of fraud by imposing additional rules upon the merchants. Failure to obtain the certificate, threatened the secretary, "would be a fact exciting suspicion and discrediting to the application for readmission."[154]

Occasionally, the secretary of the treasury would ask the attorney general for his opinion on how to interpret the law as to who was allowed to come and upon what proof. Probably most significant was the attorney general's opinion in 1898 that defined which Chinese were exempt from the exclusion laws. The treaty of 1880 had allowed the United States to restrict the immigration of laborers but had specified that "other classes [were] not included in the limitations."[155] Exactly who constituted the "other classes" became an issue. The first interpretation, which seems truest to the language of the treaty, construed the "other classes" to mean anyone who was not a laborer.[156] The alternate meaning, which was embraced by the attorney general and became law in 1898, focused on Article III of the treaty, which explained the right of those exempt from restriction. The article began, "Chinese subjects, whether proceeding to the United States as teachers, students, merchants, or from curiosity. . ." Rather than interpret these groups as examples of those exempt from limitations, the attorney general construed the clause as a complete list of the exempt classes. "The true theory," he opined, "is not that all Chinese persons may enter this country who are not forbidden, but that only those are entitled to enter who are expressly allowed."[157] Thus *only* teachers, students, merchants, and travelers were allowed to enter. This reading of the treaty excluded many groups of Chinese who were not laborers but who did not strictly fall within the specified list. For example, "salesmen, clerks, buyers, bookkeepers, accountants, managers, storekeepers, apprentices, agents, cashiers, physicians, proprietors of restaurants" were not exempt.[158]

Though supervised by the central office, the collectors at each port retained a significant degree of discretion in administering the Chinese exclusion laws, especially in the early years. In general, the collectors at San Francisco used this power to impose greater restrictions upon Chinese trying to enter the United States and to guard against fraud.[159] Collector John Wise (1892–98) required evidence more stringent than that mandated by either Congress or the secretary of the treasury. He specified, for example, that Chinese alleging to be native-born citizens had to present the testimony of two white witnesses to establish their claim. Congress had not addressed the type of proof such Chinese needed, and the secretary had only cautioned the collectors to take "great pains" in citizenship cases.[160] In another instance, Wise disagreed with the secretary's ruling allowing wives and children of exempt Chinese to enter the United States. Though he agreed to abide by the regulation, he enforced it in a narrow and stringent fashion, requiring additional proof from the families. Wise required exempt men to present documents "from the proper authorities, Chinese or English in Hong Kong" establishing "that the woman he desires to bring is his wife according to our understanding of the marriage relations,—not the understanding that prevails in China—and that the children of tender age are his offspring born in legal wedlock."[161]

When collectors chose to enforce the laws more strictly than required, the secretary of the treasury generally did not interfere. When, however, Collector John P. Jackson in 1899 adopted more lenient standards than those established in department rules, the secretary quickly admonished him to engage in a "more faithful enforcement of the Chinese Exclusion laws."[162] Special agents for the treasury John Linck and C. J. Smith had reported several irregularities in Jackson's administration of the San Francisco port. According to the agents, Jackson accepted Chinese testimony in cases of alleged citizenship and did not require white witnesses; he allowed the applicant's attorney and interpreter to be present at the admission hearing; and he gave too much credence to Section 6 certificates.[163] Collector Jackson argued that statutes and court decisions concerning Chinese exclusion dictated that he follow such practices. He scoffed at the agents' suggestion that he should reject all citizenship cases and let the courts deal with the nuisance, saying, "I do not believe that I have any right to thus shirk the duty devolving upon me under the statute, and throw the entire burden of investigation upon another branch of the Government." Jackson summarized his views on the enforcement of the Chinese laws:

> If this Government does not want any Chinese admitted, then it can say so; if it wants Chinese admitted only on white testimony, then it can say so through legislation; but, if it intends to allow Chinese to be admitted to this country on Chinese testimony, as it has distinctly said by its legal enactments, then there is nothing left for the officers of the law, both executive and judicial, but to obey the will and mandate of the legislative power.[164]

The secretary of the treasury rejected Jackson's view and sent him a long letter of rebuke. According to the secretary, the collector paid too much attention to what courts had to say and too little to the rules and policy of the department. Furthermore, he misconstrued the statutes. The secretary stopped short of requiring white witnesses in citizenship cases, but he instructed Jackson to exercise "greater care" in such cases and to admit Chinese claiming American birth only if he was "fully satisfied" upon "reliable" evidence of the applicants' nativity. The collector should also investigate the Section 6 certificates more thoroughly because many of the documents were obtained "by fraud and collusion." And under no circumstances, the secretary continued, should attorneys be allowed at hearings.[165] Overall, the secretary's letter endorsed the recommendation of Special Agents Linck and Smith that "the Collector should be guided by the policy

TABLE 1 *Chinese Admitted to the United States, 1894–1901*

Year	Number of Chinese Arrived in U.S.	Number of Chinese Admitted	Percent Admitted	Percent Rejected
1894	6,840	5,559	82	18
1895	2,732	2,075	76	24
1896	3,925	3,510	89	11
1897	5,880	5,478	93	7
1898	5,553	5,273	95	5
1899	4,875	3,925	80.5	19.5
1900	4,867	3,802	78	22
1901	2,702	1,784	66	34

Source: Data gathered from the *Annual Report of the Secretary of the Treasury* for years 1894–1901. Figures for 1891–93 were unavailable.

of our law . . . that Chinese are an undesirable addition to our society—that their presence is a disturbing element that tends only to evil and corruption, and that every presumption, every technicality and every intendment should be held against their admission, and their testimony should have little or no weight when standing alone."[166]

Despite the stringent standards set down by the administrators, most Chinese, particularly those with the required documentation, succeeded in entering the United States. Unfortunately, statistics for the number of Chinese admitted at San Francisco are not available for all years. Table 1 indicates, however, the number of Chinese admitted at all ports of the United States. The percentage landed varied from a low of 66 percent in 1901 to a high of 95 percent in 1898. San Francisco figures are available for those years and indicate that the collector at that port landed fewer Chinese than the national average. In 1901, the collector admitted 59 percent of the Chinese applying for admission and in 1898 he landed 89.5 percent.[167] Although the number landed may appear high, given the stringent policy of the department, a comparison with the percentage of non-Chinese immigrants admitted and rejected during the same period provides a different perspective. As Table 2 shows, the Bureau of Immigration never rejected more than 1.3 percent of non-Chinese aliens applying for admission. Compared to other immigrants, Chinese were excluded in much greater proportions. Of course, the numbers do not reflect Chinese who, because of the exclusion policy, did not even attempt to enter the United States.

The ordeal of many Chinese ended with the collector's decision to land them, yet those without documentation—wives and children of exempt

TABLE 2 *Non-Chinese Aliens Admitted to the United States, 1894–1901*

Year	Number of Aliens Arrived in U.S.	Number of Aliens Admitted	Percent Admitted	Percent Rejected
1894	284,461	283,072	99.5	0.5
1895	257,997	255,578	99.1	0.9
1896	341,826	339,027	99.2	0.8
1897	227,469	225,852	99.3	0.7
1898	227,228	224,198	98.7	1.3
1899	310,055	306,257	98.8	1.2
1900	447,325	443,079	99.1	0.9
1901	485,459	481,943	99.3	0.7

Source: Compiled from Table 9, "Immigration to the United States, 1820–1910," and Table 42, "Aliens Debarred at All United States Ports during the Fiscal Years 1892 to 1910," in U.S. Immigration Commission, *Reports of the Immigration Commission. Statistical Review of Immigration, 1829–1910*, 61st Cong., 3d sess. (Washington, D.C.: GPO, 1911).

Chinese, Chinese born in the United States, and merchants returning to their businesses in California—who relied on the testimony of witnesses to prove their claims found the collector less willing to admit them.[168] If denied entry, the rejected Chinese had three choices. They could acquiesce to the collector's determination and return to China; they could appeal to the secretary of the treasury for a reconsideration of their case; or they could turn to the federal court in the hopes that it would reverse the collector's decision. As long as recourse to the court remained a possibility, most barred Chinese chose that option.

Access to the federal trial courts proved to be a vital resource for Chinese trying to come to the United States. Chinese resistance to the American exclusion policy had frustrated policy makers and administrators. But as long as the legislature and the agency remained the battleground for disputes over exclusion, the Chinese fought a losing battle. Once in the lower federal courts, however, Chinese had much more success in mitigating the severity of the exclusion laws, even though the federal judges supported the exclusion policy. That paradox is the focus of the next chapter.

CHAPTER 3

Captives of Law

JUDICIAL ENFORCEMENT

OF THE CHINESE EXCLUSION

LAWS

The Chinese, complained one legislator in 1893, "are always litigating."[1] If the collector denied them entry, Chinese did not necessarily accept his decision as their final fate. Chinese in the United States had quickly come to understand the value of what American political scientists today call "forum-shopping." They knew from their collective experience in fighting discriminatory state legislation that litigation in the federal courts provided a powerful weapon to combat the forces that opposed their entry. Consequently, they turned to the federal courts to challenge the exclusion laws and their enforcement by the collector.

The federal district court at San Francisco approached the Chinese cases with divided loyalties. On the one hand, the judges, sharing their contemporaries' negative, stereotypical view of the Chinese, openly supported the exclusion policy and thus allowed certain procedures that made it more difficult for Chinese to prove their claims. On the other hand, the judges were, in a sense, captured by law. When judges took the bench, they entered an institution that had particular procedural rules and practices rooted in Anglo-American common law tradition. Two practices of the court, respect for the doctrine of habeas corpus and the application of judicial evidentiary standards, were especially important to the success of the Chinese. Because of certain institutional norms—treating cases individually and applying general principles in decision making—the judges felt obligated to extend those practices to both Chinese and non-Chinese litigants. Thus in the

Chinese exclusion litigation the jurists' respect for institutional obligations trumped other personal and political loyalties.

MOBILIZING THE LAW

As of 1891, Chinese were the only immigrants who could obtain judicial review of administrative decisions denying them admission. The Immigration Act of 1891 made the decisions of immigration inspectors final except that it allowed appeals to the secretary of the treasury. Because the act specified that its provisions did not apply to Chinese, judicial review remained an option for this group.

The Chinese in northern California put the opportunity for judicial review to good use. By the time the Chinese exclusion laws were passed, Chinese had already proven themselves to be determined and skillful litigators in their challenges to other obnoxious, discriminatory laws before the federal courts.[2] Their success in the courts in these matters provided an example of how to use the legal system to challenge the decisions of the collector.

Several experienced white attorneys were willing to represent Chinese in the habeas corpus cases before the federal courts. Indeed, one of the complaints against the Chinese was that they hired the best legal talent.[3] The Chinese immigration cases became a new specialty; a small group of six to eight attorneys handled practically all of these cases before the district court, though other attorneys tried to compete for this profitable business. Attorneys could make between $75 and $100 per case, according to estimates sent to the attorney general.[4]

Chinese found attorneys in a variety of ways. White or Chinese "brokers" met Chinese when they arrived and offered to help them, for a fee, through the administrative maze. As part of their services, brokers arranged for an attorney if necessary.[5] Chinese friends and family already in the United States probably also referred lawyers whom they knew from experience or reputation. Thomas Riordan, well-known to the Chinese-American community as the attorney for the Chinese Six Companies, represented a large number of Chinese immigrants. Attorneys also advertised their services on business cards and in pamphlets written in Chinese.[6] Some attorneys had special expertise to offer. Drawn by the profitability of the work and the experience they had developed in the field, U.S. attorneys such as Marshall Woodworth who had defended the collector's decision to exclude the Chinese before the district court often worked on the side of the Chinese after their terms as district attorney ended. Former inspectors for the Chinese Bureau also became representatives for Chinese in the courts.[7]

An advertisement from a prominent law firm specializing in Chinese exclusion cases. The firm stressed its experience in handling all legal matters for Chinese and its contacts in Washington in case of an administrative or judicial appeal. From David Jones, The Surnames of the Chinese in America *(San Francisco: Chinese Name Spelling Company, 1904). Translation provided by Allen Linden.*

The Chinese litigants' success in obtaining talented legal representation was a key element in their victories in the federal courts.

BEFORE THE COURT

Once Chinese came before the federal court, there was every reason to expect that the judges would turn a deaf ear to their petitions. William W. Morrow—district court judge from 1891 to 1897 and circuit court judge from 1897 to 1924—had been one of the strongest proponents of Chinese exclusion in Congress in the 1880s. Morrow had championed several bills during his terms as representative, one of which proposed to make the decisions of the collector final and not subject to judicial review. Its purpose, he explained, was "to do away with the legal machinery now in use in determining the right of a Chinaman to land and come into the United States."[8] His speeches in Congress also suggested that as a judge, he would afford less protection to Chinese than had his predecessor, Ogden Hoffman. Whereas Judge Hoffman had tempered the effects of the Chinese restriction acts when they violated the treaty with China,[9] Morrow professed that the treaty should not stand in the way of congressional will. "The Congress of the United States is sovereign," he declared, "and if it is the desire of Congress to prohibit this immigration it may do so by legislating in any way, even though it be in contravention of the treaty."[10]

The congressional record of the other federal judges suggested that they too would be sympathetic to the exclusionists' goals. Joseph McKenna, circuit court judge from 1892 until 1897, when he was appointed to the United States Supreme Court, was Morrow's colleague in the House of Representatives and joined him in pushing for greater limits on Chinese immigration in the 1880s.[11] John De Haven, district court judge between 1897 and 1913, served in Congress for only one year before leaving to sit on the California Supreme Court. Though he was not involved with any Chinese legislation during that year (1889–90), an anti-immigrant stance is suggested by his advocacy of a bill to limit the sale of public lands to United States citizens.[12]

With such men composing the federal judiciary in northern California, one might very well doubt the chance for Chinese success in the courts. Yet in becoming federal court judges, these men were confined by certain institutional practices and doctrines that could not be easily ignored. The power of one such doctrine—habeas corpus—propelled Chinese cases into the court.

When a Chinese man or woman petitioned the court for a writ of habeas corpus, the court felt bound to issue the writ and to hear the case. The fact

William W. Morrow, U.S. District Court judge and Circuit judge, 1891–1929. Courtesy U.S. District Court, Northern District of California.

IN THE

District COURT OF THE UNITED STATES,

NORTHERN DISTRICT OF CALIFORNIA.

IN THE MATTER OF

Quan Wy Chung

ON HABEAS CORPUS.

To the Hon. *W. W. Morrow* Judge of the *District* Court of the
United States, Northern District of California:

The Petition of *Quan Foork* respectfully shows:

That *Quan Wy Chung* is unlawfully imprisoned, detained,
confined and restrained of his liberty by Captain *Frick*

Master of the Steamship *Peru*

in the City and County of San Francisco, State of California, Northern District of California.

That the said imprisonment, detention, confinement and restraint are illegal, and the illegality thereof consists in this, to wit:

That it is claimed by said Master that said passenger is a subject of the Emperor of China, and must not and cannot be allowed to land under the provisions of the Act of Congress of May 6th, 1882, entitled "An Act to execute certain treaty stipulations relating to Chinese," and the Acts amendatory thereof and supplemental thereto.

That said passenger does not come within the restrictions of said Acts, but, on the contrary, your petitioner alleges that said passenger was a resident of the United States, and departed therefrom on the Steamship *Gaelic* on the _____ day of _____ 18*79*
Quong Sui *5th* year, *1st* month, *29th* day.

That the said passenger is a *citizen of the United States and was born in the city and county of San Francisco State of California and is now about twenty-four years of age*

That *he* has applied to the Collector of the Port of San Francisco to be permitted to land, but said application was denied.

That your petitioner is the *father* of said passenger, and makes this petition on *his* behalf.

Wherefore, your petitioner prays that a writ of habeas corpus may be granted direct to the said Master, commanding him to have the body of said passenger before your Honor, at a time and place therein to be specified, to do and receive what shall then and there be considered by your Honor, concerning him, together with the time and cause of his detention, and said writ; and that *he* may be restored to his liberty.

Dated on the *13th* day of *April* 189*5*

Quan 陳福 *Foork*
Petitioner.

STATE OF CALIFORNIA,
CITY AND COUNTY OF SAN FRANCISCO, } ss.
Northern District of California,
United States of America.

Quan Foork being duly sworn, says that he is the Petitioner above
named, and that he has heard read the foregoing petition and knows the contents thereof, and that the same is true
of his own knowledge; that he is ~~a merchant~~ residing ~~and doing business in the firm of~~ *at the South*
East corner of Dupont & Jackson Streets

Sworn to before me this *13th* day }
of *April* 189*5*. } *Quan* 陳福 *Foork*

J. Macaulay

Commissioner of the Circuit Court of the United States
or the Northern District of California.

One of the thousands of habeas corpus petitions filed in the U.S. District Court at San
Francisco challenging exclusions by the collector. The use of standardized forms suggests how
common such petitions were. Courtesy National Archives, San Francisco Branch.

that the case came before the court on a writ of habeas corpus had special significance. Literally, habeas corpus means "you have the body."[13] A writ of habeas corpus requires the person detaining the petitioner to demonstrate to the court that the confinement is lawful. For the judges of the court, the writ of habeas corpus had an honored place in Anglo-American jurisprudence; it evoked the basic American principles of the rule of law and the liberty of the individual from arbitrary acts of government. The Constitution forbade Congress from suspending the privilege of habeas corpus except in "Cases of Rebellion or Invasion."[14] And the privilege was not limited to citizens.

Reconstruction legislation expanded the privilege of habeas corpus, giving the federal courts broad power to issue such writs in cases in which people (not just citizens) were held in violation of the United States Constitution, laws, or treaties.[15] When Inspector S. J. Ruddell suggested to a congressional subcommittee on immigration in 1890 that the problem of Chinese immigration could be solved by revoking the privilege of habeas corpus from the Chinese, Senator Watson C. Squire wryly queried: "That would be a little inimical to the spirit of the Constitution?"[16]

The district court under Judge Hoffman had upheld the right of the Chinese to habeas corpus in an 1888 case, *In re Jung Ah Lung*. The collector of San Francisco, furious with the intervention of the courts, had attempted to argue that the Chinese were not entitled to the writ of habeas corpus. Judge Hoffman had indignantly rejected the collector's arguments, declaring: "The petitioner is a free man, under our flag, and within the protection of our laws." Hoffman went on to celebrate the historic writ: "Such an abrogation of the writ of habeas corpus, which has always been considered among English-speaking peoples the most sacred monument of personal freedom, must be unmistakably declared by Congress before any court could venture to withhold its benefits from any human being, no matter what his race or color."[17]

Some spokesmen for the court emphasized that it had no choice but to issue the writs. Anxious to deflect the virulent public criticism of the court, United States commissioner for the court Stephen Houghton explained: "The courts are utterly powerless, under the law, to do different from what they have done. The Revised Statutes provide that, upon a proper application being made, all parties, except in certain excepted cases, and these cases don't come within the exception, are absolutely entitled to the writ of habeas corpus."[18]

Thus the judges of the district and circuit courts invariably issued writs of habeas corpus when petitions were filed, entitling the petitioner to a hearing in court as to whether he or she should be admitted into the United

States. Although the historic writ of liberty got Chinese into the court, the proceedings before the court fell short of the due process celebrated in Anglo-American jurisprudence. The proceedings in the habeas corpus cases were "novel and strange," as U.S. attorney John P. Carey put it. "There is no criminal that has ever been subjected by order of court to things the Chinese have been subjected to in the enforcement of these acts," said Carey.[19] Initially, Carey explained, the Chinese person would be brought immediately before the U.S. attorney for an examination, without his attorney present. Carey's staff would take down his statement and then release him on bail. The U.S. attorney could introduce and use the statement against the Chinese petitioner in court.

Judge Hoffman, who had authorized the procedure, had realized that such an extrajudicial proceeding would probably not stand if challenged. David Fisher, examiner for the Department of Justice, reported to the attorney general that

> Judge Hoffman endeavored to impress very deeply on my mind the fact that he believed this "Star Chamber" proceeding . . . to be absolutely necessary for the successful carrying out of the provisions of the Restriction Act. He does not attempt, nor seek to defend the proceeding as a legal one, but he thinks that, so long as the Chinamen do not raise the question of the legality of the thing, the Government ought not to, but, to the contrary, ought to give it its sanction and encouragement.[20]

Hoffman and the U.S. attorney felt the special procedure was a necessary abrogation of due process for the court to get at the truth of the cases. The usual court procedures did not work, thought government officials, for two reasons. One was that Chinese often lacked documentation to establish their exempt status. For example, petitioners claiming to be born in the United States and exempt from the Chinese exclusion laws had no birth certificates to prove their allegation of citizenship. Nor did laborers have proof of prior residence to establish their exemption from the exclusion acts of 1882 and 1884. They had only witnesses, usually Chinese, to verify their claims.

This lack of documentation led to the second issue that troubled officials involved in the legal proceedings. They shared the belief of most other white Americans that the Chinese and their witnesses lied to gain entry. "They are all liars and have no regard for an oath so that there is no reliance to be placed in anything they say," complained Carey to the attorney general in 1888.[21] Commissioner Stephen Houghton agreed: "The Chinamen are very adroit people; they are not scrupulous people at all in these matters; even the men who have good cases will swear to lies if they think the lies will help the cases on."[22] Thus the procedure adopted by the U.S. attorney was similar to that of the collector. The government's attorney would cross-examine the petitioner and his witnesses in great detail, trying to find discrepancies in their stories which would jeopardize their claims.

Though it appears the preliminary examination by the United States attorney was no longer used in the 1890s, the procedure employed by the court continued to be somewhat "novel and strange." The district and circuit courts in the 1880s had established a special system to handle the overwhelming number of Chinese cases coming before them. To free themselves to attend to the other business of the court, the judges referred the Chinese cases to a United States commissioner, who tried the cases de novo.[23] In other words, the commissioner reached his own decision about the right of the petitioner to land, independent of the collector's ruling. The referee took testimony, made a finding of facts, and recommended that the court either discharge the petitioner, that is, allow him or her to enter the United States, or remand the petitioner to the custody of the collector for deportation.

The decisions in the Chinese cases lay with one referee, Commissioner E. H. Heacock, for the period covered in this chapter. Unfortunately, very little information is available on Heacock. Like the judges, he was a Republican with a long history of public service. After his arrival in California in 1852, he, at different times, represented Sacramento and Santa Barbara counties in the state senate and later served as county judge for Santa Cruz and Santa Barbara counties.[24] Judge Morrow appointed Heacock as U.S. commissioner for the district court in 1892, which position he held until 1910.

The customary trial procedures and rules of evidence did not apply strictly in the hearings before Commissioner Heacock. Though both the petitioner and the government were allowed to introduce evidence and produce and cross-examine witnesses, the hearing was informal in many respects.[25] The commissioner often took an active role in the hearing, requesting, for example, that the attorney for the petitioner obtain further witnesses when the commissioner was not satisfied with the testimony. More striking, however, is the evidence Heacock allowed. The district attorney, appearing for the collector, relied on the same style of interrogation used by the Chinese inspectors in admission hearings.[26] That is, he used intensive, detailed cross-examination to disprove the petitioner's claim that he was exempt, for example, as either a merchant or a native-born citizen. In citizenship cases, the petitioner typically would claim that he had been born in San Francisco but left to live in China when young. To prove his claim, the petitioner would present witnesses who remembered his birth in the United States and who could identify him as the same person who was born here. The witnesses verifying his identity would claim that they had seen him in China with his family and thus could be sure he was the same person.

The district attorney, operating upon the assumption that the claim was fraudulent and that the witnesses and the petitioner did not actually know each other, would subject them to questioning, which was often incredibly detailed, about their visit in China. He would ask questions similar to those posed by agency officials: How many steps were there out the petitioner's back door? Where did the petitioner sit in the village schoolhouse? Did the petitioner's mother have bound feet? Who was present when the witness visited the petitioner's home? Did the petitioner accompany the witness to the door, or did he walk outside with him at the end of the visit? These questions were often about visits that had occurred several years earlier and, not surprisingly, were difficult to answer with great accuracy. Furthermore, unlike the procedure in a trial, there seemed to be no limit to the type or number of questions the district attorney could ask. Practically any subject was fair game.

In general, the petitioners' attorneys accepted this procedure, though attorneys new to the Chinese cases might object at first. When attorney Waldemar Tuska upset the usual routine of the hearings and objected to each of the district attorney's questions as immaterial and irrelevant, Commissioner Heacock overruled almost every objection and explained to the upstart that "in this class of cases the examination is intended to be very full, and the questions are sometimes asked that are immaterial."[27]

The court accepted this departure from normal procedure for the same reason that it had allowed the district attorney a preliminary examination of Chinese in the 1880s. That is, the judges and commissioners shared the belief that Chinese witnesses lied in the hearings. Judge Hoffman complained to California's congressional representative Charles N. Felton in 1888 that "if you could have attended court and listened to the hearing of any of these cases, you would have recognized how completely the court is at the mercy of Chinese testimony and how impossible it is to distinguish a genuine case from a fraudulent one."[28] U.S. Commissioner Houghton explained the need to take testimony that did not appear to be directly relevant: "It is difficult to get at the truth, particularly so for the reason that there have been so many of these cases running over a long period of time, and the Chinese have learned the routine thoroughly and they have drilled these men who come in here very thoroughly. . . . Now, in attacking the cases, the difficulty is this: If you cross-examine them on the lines they have testified about they are thoroughly fortified. You cannot catch them very well and therefore you must go into collateral matters."[29] When the system of intense, detailed examination was challenged, District Court Judge John De Haven strongly defended it as the only means to establish the credibility of Chinese testimony.[30]

Though the type of evidence allowed in the hearings worked to the Chinese petitioner's disadvantage, the commissioner often decided in his favor. This was largely because Heacock adhered to the general principles of evidence when he made his recommendations. Heacock's decisions hinged on the consistency of the testimony in these cases. If there were no discrepancies in the testimony, he followed the "general rule [that] positive testimony as to a particular fact, uncontradicted by any one, should control the decision of the court" and recommended that the petitioner be discharged.[31] Often he was convinced of the veracity of the petitioner's claim. Sometimes, however, he was dubious but felt bound by the evidence.

Heacock abided by this general rule even though the U.S. Supreme Court in 1890 suggested that a lesser standard could be adopted in the Chinese habeas corpus cases. In an appeal from the Circuit Court for the Northern District of California, the Supreme Court ruled in *Quock Ting* v. *United States* that the court could decide against the petitioner even though his testimony was uncontradicted. Justice Field reasoned that "there may be such an inherent improbability in the statements of a witness as to induce the court or jury to disregard his evidence even in the absence of any direct conflicting testimony," especially when the witness had a stake in the outcome of the case. In this case, the Court found the sixteen-year-old petitioner's testimony improbable because he was able to testify about the place of his birth (San Francisco) "with surprising particularity." The Court concluded that he could not have remembered these details on his own because he had not been in San Francisco since he was ten years old and thus his testimony must have been "coached" and fraudulent.[32]

The Circuit Court of Appeals for the Ninth Circuit addressed the issue again in 1901 in an appeal from the District Court for the Northern District of California. This case was unusual because the judge, rather than Commissioner Heacock, presided at the hearing. Though well-known Chinese merchants gave positive, uncontradicted testimony that the petitioner, a woman, was born in San Francisco, Judge De Haven impatiently refused to allow further testimony about the reputation and credibility of the merchant witnesses and decided against the petitioner, saying, "The court need not be satisfied beyond a reasonable doubt, but must be satisfied that it is not being made an instrument for the evasion of these exclusion laws. . . . I myself do not believe this testimony, and not believing it, I do not think the

TABLE 3 *Disposition of Chinese Habeas Corpus Cases in the District Court,*
1891–1905

Year	Discharge[a]	Remand[b]	Dismissal[c]	Unknown[d]	Total[e]
1891	73%	23%	3%	—	30
1892	88%	9%	3%	—	153
1893	66%	33%	1%	—	308
1894	80%	20%	—	—	207
1895	75%	25%	—	—	36
1896	89%	11%	—	—	35
1897	60%	40%	—	—	42
1898	49%	50%	0.4%	—	261
1899	46%	53%	0.5%	0.5%	182
1900	46%	52%	1%	0.5%	177
1901	52%	45%	2%	0.6%	162
1902	63%	36%	0.4%	—	242
1903	60%	40%	—	—	295
1904	60%	40%	—	—	127
1905	29%	68%	—	3%	31
Total					2,288

Source: U.S. District Court for the Northern District Court of California, *Admiralty Docket*, 1891–1905.

[a]*Discharge*: Court finds the petitioner should be allowed to enter the United States.

[b]*Remand*: Court upholds the collector's decision to exclude and remands the petitioner to the collector for deportation.

[c]*Dismissal*: Court dismisses the petition because, for example, the petitioner dies before the court hearing.

[d]*Unknown*: There is no record of the outcome.

[e]*Total*: Total number of petitions filed each year.

court should be required to found any judgment on it."[33] The circuit court of appeals upheld De Haven's decision. Though the court admitted that De Haven had not elaborated his reasons for not believing the testimony, and thus that the case "comes nearer the border line, beyond which courts must not go," the appellate court held it could not "assume that the court below acted arbitrarily in refusing to believe the testimony of any witness."[34]

Despite these decisions, however, Heacock continued to make his recommendations based on the general rule that positive, uncontradicted testimony required the release of the petitioner. If there *were* discrepancies, other factors, such as the seriousness of the discrepancies and the credibility of the witnesses, came into play. Heacock confronted the petitioner with the discrepancies and allowed him an opportunity to resolve them. If the explanation did not completely resolve the discrepancy, Heacock might still discharge the petitioner, citing most often the "manner of testimony" or the "appearance of the witnesses" as reasons. The testimony of respectable members of the "merchant class" or of white witnesses often helped the petitioner's case as well. If the contradictions in the testimony could not be resolved, Heacock generally remanded the petitioner to the collector for deportation.[35]

Heacock's recommendations carried great weight in the final disposition of the case because the judge routinely confirmed his decision. Either party could object to Heacock's findings and recommendation and the judge would review the transcripts of the commissioner's hearing. But the judge seldom reversed the commissioner except in the few cases where he differed with Heacock on a matter of law.[36] At times, the judge rereferred the case to Heacock to take further testimony and to make a recommendation on the new evidence. In general, however, the judge accepted the findings of the referee, operating on the principle governing judicial appeals. That is, the appellate body defers to the findings of the fact-finder, on the grounds that only he is in the position to evaluate things such as the credibility of witnesses which do not translate well into transcripts.[37]

Chinese generally fared well in Heacock's court. Until the late 1890s, the commissioner overturned the collector's decision to deny entry in more than 80 percent of the cases. The rate of reversal reached a low of 46 percent in 1899 but otherwise averaged well over 50 percent until 1905 (see Tables 3 and 4).

THE TENSION BETWEEN JUDICIAL AND ADMINISTRATIVE METHODS

In reviewing the collector's decisions, Commissioner Heacock's method of investigating cases was similar to that of the collector: both relied on detailed examinations to reveal discrepancies. Yet as the statistics in Tables 3 and 4 reveal, they frequently came to different conclusions. The court and the collector differed, claimed the latter, because Chinese had time to perfect their fraudulent stories by the time they came before the commissioner. Collectors told stories of intercepted "coaching letters" and of disreputable attorneys who used their right of counsel to visit their clients and instruct them how to testify.[38] Collector Wise prohibited the detained Chinese in San Francisco from speaking with their friends or attorneys but claimed he could not prevent coaching altogether, particularly when the

TABLE 4 *Disposition of Chinese Habeas Corpus Cases in the Circuit Court, 1891–1905*

Year	Discharge	Remand	Dismissal	Unknown	Total
1891	63%	27%	10%	—	206
1892	68%	29%	3%	—	71
1893	6%	94%	—	—	17
1894	—	—	—	—	0
1895	—	—	—	—	0
1896	—	—	—	—	0
1897	—	—	—	—	0
1898	50%	50%	—	—	2
1899	—	—	—	—	0
1900	—	—	—	—	0
1901	57%	43%	—	—	7
1902	69%	31%	—	—	16
1903	61%	39%	—	—	23
1904	77%	23%	—	—	26
1905	—	100%	—	—	1
Total					369

Source: U.S. Circuit Court for the Northern District of California, *Common Law and Equity Register, 1891–1905.*

U.S. marshal took the Chinese from his custody to attend their hearing before the court.[39]

Although there can be no doubt that many Chinese made fraudulent claims,[40] the disparity between the decisions of the collector and the commissioner was not simply the result of coaching. The high reversal rate reflected the different institutional orientation and practices of the court and the collector as well. Of particular importance was the evidentiary standard employed by each. Unlike the commissioner, the collector did not feel bound to land a Chinese person when there were no discrepancies in his story. If the collector felt the story was fraudulent or if he could find minor discrepancies, he would deny the Chinese entry. The court, hearing the same evidence, might admit the Chinese. The collector at Port Townsend, Washington, perceived the importance of judicial evidentiary rules to the success of Chinese in the courts: "The rules of evidence . . . which seem to have been adopted by the Courts, are not such as are used by the Collector, and as a result, most of the Chinamen are admitted."[41]

The collector also demanded additional proof, requiring, for example, the testimony of white witnesses to prove a Chinese applicant's claim of citizenship. The court, however, followed the dictates of the exclusion laws, which did not require white witnesses except in the cases of Chinese merchants returning to their businesses in the United States. Informing the secretary of the treasury of the court's stance, Collector Wise wrote, "[Heacock] does not rely entirely on Chinese testimony but he allows it, and if no adverse evidence is submitted he allows landing on that kind of testimony."[42] The court's acceptance of Chinese witnesses worked in the applicant's favor, particularly because few Chinese knew white Americans who could testify on their behalf.[43]

In addition to adhering to more favorable evidentiary standards, the court provided Chinese with certain basic protections which the collector did not, such as the right to representation and to subpoena witnesses. The right to counsel was crucial to the Chinese victories in court. Some Chinese may have been accustomed to dealing with a bureaucratized society, but it is unlikely that they had an intimate understanding of the American system of government. Chinese knew enough to hire advocates, however, who could decipher and manipulate the American laws.

The attorneys had both legal and practical knowledge that benefited their Chinese clients. Well-versed in American legal discourse, they understood how to frame their arguments and how to present testimony in the most favorable light. Through cross-examination and objections, attorneys for the Chinese could also expose weaknesses in the government's evidence. An extensive working knowledge of the collector's admission procedures, gained either through repeated litigation in the Chinese cases or through previous employment as inspectors or district attorneys for the government, supplemented the attorneys' legal expertise.

Chinese clearly profited from the representation of such experienced advocates in court. In contrast, the lack of counsel in the administrative hearings worked to their disadvantage. The secretary of the treasury explicitly forbade Chinese the right to counsel until after the collector had examined and decided to exclude an applicant. Without an attorney to steer the inexperienced applicant through the confusing and detailed questioning, the chances of damaging discrepancies creeping into the testimony greatly increased.

Ironically, even the government attorney's presence in the court could work to the Chinese petitioner's advantage. Although the U.S. attorney's job was to represent the collector and his decision to deny entry to Chinese, the U.S. attorneys often had more in common with the judges. The professional connection that drew the judges and attorneys together provided a natural alliance against the administrative orientation of the collector. As lawyers, the U.S. attorneys more readily understood and acceded to the procedures required in a court of law.

The U.S. attorneys' affinity to the judges' legal perspective often led to tensions between the U.S. attorney's office and the collector. Collector John Wise at San Francisco complained to the attorney general and the secretary of the treasury several times about lax prosecution by the U.S. attorney in his district and requested the appointment of government counsel "who, being in sympathy with the Administration and with this office, will act in harmony with me."[44] U.S. attorneys often took offense at such accusations and retorted that the collector and his inspectors, as well as the general public, had little understanding of or appreciation for legal requirements. When Collector Wise criticized Commissioner Heacock for accepting Chinese testimony, U.S. Attorney Charles Garter rushed to Heacock's defense, saying, "Any person of ordinary intelligence ought to know that evidence of Chinese persons cannot be excluded in this or any character of case merely on the grounds of the nationality of the witness, and no Court or Commissioner has any discretion but to 'allow' it, in any case where it is pertinent and offered."[45]

U.S. attorneys, in turn, criticized the Chinese inspectors' lack of attention to legal requirements in the habeas corpus cases. Collector Phelps admitted to the subcommittee on immigration in 1890 that because of a shortage of inspectors in his service, the U.S. attorneys often received very little help in preparing the government's cases.[46] Collector Phelps tried to remedy the situation by employing more inspectors and requiring his staff to make a written record of their investigation of Chinese applicants, but the U.S. attorney complained that his successor, Collector Wise, gave the government little assistance in developing its cases before the courts. Collector Wise did not require the inspectors to take written statements from the applicants, nor did he furnish names of witnesses. The government's representative entered the court without knowing the collector's reasons for denying the Chinese petitioner's landing and, consequently, was often ill-prepared.[47]

The U.S. attorney's complaints appear to have had some influence on the collector's methods. Or perhaps the collector became concerned about the possible reversal of his decisions by the district court or by the secretary of the treasury upon appeal. For whatever reason, Collector Wise for a time attempted to bring his procedures in line with those followed by attorneys and the court. Wise complained to the secretary of the treasury in 1895 that his staff's ignorance of legal procedures hampered enforcement of the Chinese laws and requested the appointment of a lawyer as a Chinese inspector who would be better equipped to "prepare in a legal manner the vast amount of evidence."[48] The collector also asked Commissioner Heacock to explain his "method of considering and judging the evidence" in Chinese habeas corpus cases. The collector hoped thereby, explained the special deputy collector, "to bring himself in accord with judicial methods as much as possible, so that in the case of an alleged merchant or other than a laborer, his action will hold water in case there should be an appeal from his decision."[49] Collector Jackson, successor to Wise, also evinced a concern to adjust his staff's practices to those of the court. Jackson explained in 1899, "I suppose the decisions of the Court to be the proper guides for my conduct."[50] For a short time, Jackson allowed Chinese testimony as sufficient proof of an applicant's birth in the United States and permitted attorneys to be present at the admission hearings.

The secretary of the treasury did not allow such legalistic tendencies to develop very far. Sharply critical of Collector Jackson's procedures, Treasury Department agents demanded that Jackson resume a more stringent approach, deny Chinese applicants entry promptly upon their arrival, and let Chinese appeal to the court if they were dissatisfied. Then, at least, "the Customs service would be relieved" of the problem.[51] Jackson responded that he felt he had no right to "shirk [his] duty . . . and throw the entire burden of investigation upon another branch of the Government." Jackson added, "I can not conceive that it makes any difference to the country whether Chinese are admitted by the Courts or by the Collectors of Customs."[52]

But it made a difference to his superior, the secretary of the treasury, whether the collector or the courts admitted Chinese. As discussed in Chapter 2, the administrators' susceptibility to public and political pressure encouraged them to take a more restrictive stance. Federal judges, sitting on the bench with life tenure, could more easily afford to allow Chinese traditional legal protections. The secretary was content to let the public blame the courts for admitting Chinese into the country.[53]

Thus, in deciding whether to admit Chinese, both the judges and the administrative officers, whatever their personal views, were caught between the often competing demands of policy and law. How they reconciled those demands depended in large part on their institutional mission. For administrators, the imperative to enforce the law strictly overwhelmed any inclination to adopt judicial methods. Conversely, the federal judges, though proponents of the exclusion policy, remained constrained by the court's norms and traditions. In a sense, the administrators were "captives of policy" just as the judges were "captives of law."

To this point, our discussion has centered on how Chinese used the courts to enter the United States. The courts played an equally important role in deciding whether to deport Chinese. The federal court judges' approach to deportation cases revealed a similar tension between policy goals and legal norms. In the struggle over the enforcement of the Geary Act in 1893, the federal judges in California displayed a strong sympathy for exclusionists and shared Californians' antipathy toward the cautious administrative officials.[54] Yet as the immediate crisis surrounding the Geary Act ebbed and the deportation cases became a routine part of the court's business, Chinese found the court more favorably disposed to their cases.

Under the terms of the Geary Act, the federal courts played a central role in deportation proceedings, though judicial discretion was limited by the specific requirements of the act. As will be recalled from Chapter 2, the Geary Act provided that all Chinese laborers in the United States must register with the government and obtain certificates of residence as proof of their lawful status. Chinese laborers without such certificates were liable to deportation. Only a federal judge or a U.S. commissioner had the power to hold a deportation hearing and to order a Chinese laborer deported.

The judicial officers presiding over the proceedings in San Francisco were resolute supporters of the deportation policy. As a congressional representative in 1890, Judge Morrow had introduced legislation very similar to the Geary Act. His bill required an enumeration of all Chinese in the United States and a system for their registration and deportation. His colleague in Congress, Judge McKenna, had strongly endorsed Morrow's bill.[55] Furthermore, as loyal Republicans, Morrow and McKenna probably delighted in the Democratic administration's dilemma over the Geary Act's enforcement.

Judicial support was especially valuable to exclusionists during the early fight over the Geary Act's implementation. When administrators, plagued by a lack of funding and by pressure from the Chinese, attempted to delay enforcement, private citizens in California decided to take the matter into their own hands. The exclusionists' strategy to expedite deportations was simple and bold. Rather than wait for U.S. attorneys to initiate deportation proceedings, private individuals (members of the San Francisco Labor Council) went directly to the federal district court in September 1893 and swore out complaints against suspected Chinese.[56]

Judges Morrow and McKenna evinced a readiness to bend or ignore certain procedural rules to facilitate the deportation process. Much to the chagrin of the administrators, the judges issued warrants for arrest upon the complaints of the private parties.[57] The legal basis for the judges' action was somewhat vague. The Geary Act did not specify who could swear out a complaint for the arrest of Chinese. The act simply provided for their arrest by a government official and a hearing before a judge. An earlier law—the act of September 13, 1888—had specified, however, that Chinese could be arrested for deportation upon a complaint "filed by *any party* on behalf of the United States."[58] The judges relied on this provision to justify their actions, though the validity of the law was disputed.[59]

Whether or not the judges theoretically had the power to issue the warrants, they clearly flouted customary legal practice. J. Hubley Ashton, an attorney for the Chinese, protested to the attorney general that the court's procedure was "irregular and unauthorized."[60] The U.S. attorney at San Francisco, Charles Garter, agreed. He called the court's actions a "remarkable departure from customary practice" and urged the court to issue warrants only upon the complaint of government officers. Otherwise, Garter warned, the court would "place itself at the mercy of irresponsible individuals who might be prompted by spite, revenge, personal ambitions and other motives of self interest." To bolster his point, Garter noted that in one case, "one of the affidavits was signed by a prominent representative of a labor union at Sacramento, California, while three others were signed by Dennis Kearney, the famous sand lot agitator."[61] Despite such criticism, the judges continued to hold that they had power to issue warrants on private complaints.

The judges' action placed local administrators in an awkward position, caught between the conflicting orders of the court on the one hand and those of the attorney general and the secretary of the treasury on the other. The U.S. attorneys did their best to appease both masters. In response to the attorney general's instructions, they tried to delay deportation proceedings as much as possible. The U.S. attorney in Los Angeles reported that "I have at present locked up in my safe nineteen warrants issued upon such complaints which I have refused and still refuse to put in the hands of the marshal for service."[62] Administrators also pleaded to the judges that they had no money to enforce the orders of the court. Judge Erskine Ross of the Southern District of California interpreted this argument simply as a ploy to hinder enforcement of the Geary law and refused to let the funding problem affect his rulings. Judge McKenna compromised and agreed to stop issuing warrants if and when the appropriated $25,000 had been expended.[63] To satisfy the demand for arrests, U.S. attorneys adopted a strategy of selective enforcement, directing "the arrest of Chinese gamblers, highbinders, and others of the criminal classes, so as not to interfere with the industrious and tax-paying portion of that population."[64] Judge Morrow clearly preferred such an approach, as he indicated in one deportation hearing: "'It would be much more to the interest of the country if the law was enforced against the gamblers, highbinders and opium smokers. . . . If any person will apply to me for warrants for [these Chinese] . . . I will issue the warrants.'"[65]

The passage of the McCreary Amendment in November 1893 brought an end to the standoff between the administration, the courts, and the public. At the end of the two-month deportation hysteria, one hundred Chinese awaited deportation in the San Francisco jail.[66] The amendment ordered the release of all Chinese arrested and ordered deported under the Geary Act and allowed them another opportunity to register.[67]

With the immediate crisis over, the court and the administrators began to develop more systematic deportation procedures. Only government officials—Chinese inspectors, internal revenue officers, or U.S. attorneys—could then swear out complaints for the arrest of Chinese. The U.S. marshal brought the Chinese defendant before the court or commissioner for a hearing. (Until 1901, the district court judges presided over the hearings in the Northern District of California. After that time, Commissioner Heacock heard and decided all of the deportation cases, though Chinese could appeal his decision to the district court.)

The deportation hearing in court was similar to the habeas corpus hearings regarding Chinese admissions. The defendants were entitled to an attorney, to subpoena witnesses on their behalf, and to release on bail.[68] But the Geary and McCreary acts strictly circumscribed the judicial officers' inquiry. The legislation mandated that the court must order deportation if the defendant had been convicted of a felony in the United States, had entered the United States illegally, or did not have a registration certificate.[69] If the Chinese defendant could prove that "by reason of accident, sickness or other unavoidable cause," he or she had been unable to obtain a certificate, or that the certificate had been lost or destroyed, the court proceeded to determine if the defendant was entitled to a certificate. In such cases, the act specified that the Chinese laborer had to present "at least one credible witness other than Chinese" to testify that he had been a resident of the United States at the time the Geary Act was passed.[70] If the defendant could meet these requirements to the satisfaction of the court, the judges would then issue a certificate of residence.

Initially, Chinese defendants did not receive favorable treatment by the court. In 1893 and 1894, the court ordered the deportation of 75 percent and 65 percent, respectively, of the Chinese coming before it. It seems clear that the high rate of deportations stemmed largely from the types of cases coming before the court. Practically all of the Chinese were convicted

TABLE 5 *Disposition of the Chinese Deportation Cases in the District Court,*
1893–1900

Year	Discharged	Deported	Dismissed	Total
1893	25%	75%	0	16
1894	12%	65%	23%	17
1895	42%	49%	9%	43
1896	41%	58%	2%	59
1897	51%	45%	4%	53
1898	54%	25%	21%	77
1899	35%	61%	4%	54
1900	44%	44%	11%	36
Total				355

Source: U.S. District Court for the Northern District of California, *Criminal Docket, 1893–1900*.

felons, a status which under the McCreary Amendment mandated immediate deportation. Felons could escape an order of deportation in only two ways. If the defendant could prove he was a native of the United States and thus a citizen, the court would discharge him.[71] Or if the defendant had obtained a valid registration certificate before being convicted of a felony, the court held that he was exempt from deportation.[72] Most Chinese felons could not meet those exceptions and instead found themselves the focus of early enforcement efforts.[73] (See Tables 5 and 6.)

Both white Americans and certain Chinese found the felons to be an ideal scapegoat. For many white Americans, Chinese involved in criminal activities—the gamblers, opium dealers, and the so-called highbinders who ruled the Chinese-American underworld—epitomized the sinister element of the Chinese character which, they believed, threatened American society. Stories of white girls being enticed to Chinatown and seduced in opium dens were common.[74] For those who wanted to maintain good relations with the "industrious" Chinese population, the arrest of felons assured exclusionists that the deportation program was under way but also caused less disruption in the Chinese-American community.

The Chinese Six Companies aided in the apprehension of Chinese felons, as well as of prostitutes. Their arrest not only deflected Californians' attention from other, more respectable Chinese, but it also gave the organization an edge in its power struggle with the secret societies, or tongs. After the Six Companies failed in its battle against the Geary Act, its prestige in

TABLE 6 *Disposition of Chinese Deportation Cases before Commissioner Heacock, 1901–1905*

Year	Discharged	Deported	Dismissed	Total
1901	35%	10%	55%	31
1902	46%	24%	29%	41
1903	58%	36%	6%	261
1904	60%	36%	4%	50
1905	23%	71%	6%	31
Total				416

Source: U.S. District Court for the Northern District of California, *Commissioner's Docket.*

San Francisco's Chinatown deteriorated somewhat and the tongs tried to reap the benefit of the leadership's declining popularity. The Six Companies retaliated with a movement to clean up Chinatown and to assist in the deportation of tong members. Thomas Riordan, the Six Companies' attorney, provided officials with a list of tong members.[75]

Eventually, the percentage of Chinese deported began to decrease, reaching a low of 10 percent in 1901. Again, this shift reflects the types of Chinese before the court. Not content to deport only felons, the Department of the Treasury began in 1896 to cast a wider net. The secretary instructed the collector of San Francisco to "make a canvass of all the Chinese in [San Francisco] and ascertain the names and addresses of all those who are not registered." He further directed the Chinese inspectors to arrest unregistered Chinese and institute deportation proceedings against them.[76]

Under the new crackdown, the court confronted a more diverse group of Chinese: laborers without certificates; alleged merchants, students, and U.S. citizens suspected of being laborers; merchants and students with deficient Section 6 certificates; alleged prostitutes; and Chinese smuggled into the country. As with the felon cases, many of the cases fell within the strict guidelines of the statutes, and the court had little discretion as to the outcome. Chinese caught being smuggled into the country had no chance of being released. A Chinese laborer without a certificate and without a sufficient excuse for not having one could expect to be deported. Conversely, Chinese laborers who established, for example, that they were working on ships during the entire registration period, or living in Alaska, which did not have a place to register, or were unable to reach the nearest registration point because of unseasonably bad weather, were allowed to remain after establishing their exemption from the Chinese exclusion laws.[77]

In other cases, the court had more latitude in its decision-making process which worked to the Chinese defendants' advantage. Commissioner Heacock, for example, generally allowed Chinese who had originally entered under Section 6 certificates to remain, even though they later became laborers.[78] In one such case, Chune Shea Wun had entered the United States as a merchant and had established a business in Vacaville which was subsequently destroyed by fire. Financially unable to reestablish his business, Chune Shea Wun became a laborer. Commissioner Heacock ruled he was entitled to remain because he was a legitimate merchant at the time of entry.[79]

As in admission cases, the court's evidentiary practices also led to more favorable outcomes. When a defendant claimed to be exempt from registration because he was a citizen, a merchant, or a student, or that his certificate had been lost or destroyed, the court based its decision on the testimony of the defendant and his witnesses. Although the court required white testimony to prove lawful residence, as specified by the Geary Act, it allowed Chinese alleging to be citizens to rely on Chinese testimony.[80] The customary evidentiary principles—the consistency of the testimony, the weight of the evidence, and so forth—applied in the deportation cases and made it easier for Chinese to establish their claims.

Most Chinese naturally sought to avoid the deportation process, but some actually tried to get arrested so that they could have their status determined in the more favorable judicial forum. In two cases, Chinese planning to leave the United States for a visit to China deliberately arranged for themselves to be arrested and brought before Commissioner Heacock for a deportation hearing, hoping to make their reentry into the United States easier. They obviously thought they had a better chance of proving to Heacock than they did to the administrators that they were U.S. citizens. Foreseeing the flood of arranged arrests that might follow, Heacock dismissed the cases, saying that "such procedure would tend to establish a dangerous precedent."[81]

CAPTIVES OF LAW

In both the admission and deportation cases, federal judges wavered between the competing demands of law and politics. The judges strongly supported exclusion and believed that the Chinese coming before them were making fraudulent claims to evade that policy. Thus the judges broke some procedural rules in order to expose Chinese who were lying, allowing, for example, the constitutionally questionable ex parte examination before the United States attorney, the "novel and strange" hearings before the commissioner, and the flouting of legal custom in issuing deportation warrants. But regarding other practices—the granting of habeas corpus petitions and the application of judicial evidentiary standards—the judges were less willing to deviate from legal tradition.

That leaves the perplexing question of why the judges chose to draw the line where they did.[82] The answer may be that the judges and the commissioner considered the doctrine of habeas corpus and the principles of evidence to be more closely tied to what it meant to be a court. Their conception of a court, although not explicitly stated, undoubtedly embraced a key principle in Anglo-American thought, that courts should be independent of personal or political influence. Certain legal procedures, such as the writ of habeas corpus and judicial evidentiary standards, were more important than others in maintaining judicial independence, or at least its semblance. As Judge Hoffman's vehement defense of the writ in *In re Jung Ah Lung* suggests, habeas corpus provided a powerful, historic symbol of the supremacy of law over the rulers. It promised that a government could not confine an individual without just cause and that the courts, as the parties responsible for issuing the writs, would guard against arbitrary government and preserve law from the influence of politics.

So, too, the evidentiary standards were central to the ideal of judicial independence because they committed judges to decide cases on the evidence presented, not on intuition or personal belief. The judges and the commissioner of the federal courts in San Francisco clearly felt torn between their personal beliefs and judicial evidentiary standards. They all believed that Chinese lied in the proceedings, but judicial norms did not allow them to take that belief into consideration unless there was proof of perjury. In one rare instance, Judge De Haven allowed his intuition to overcome evidentiary requirements. Although the circuit court of appeals upheld De Haven's decision in *Woey Ho v. United States*, the appellate court warned that the case "comes nearer the border line, beyond which the courts must not go." By basing his decision on his belief that the petitioner was lying rather than on the evidence presented, De Haven threatened to cross the line distinguishing judicial independence from arbitrary judicial power. The federal judges and commissioner in San Francisco were not often willing to transgress that line, perhaps because to do so would violate their notion of judicial duty and would undermine the conception of the court as an independent, neutral, and just institution.[83]

The court drew much attention and criticism for its decisions in the

Chinese cases from those who thought it was frustrating the purpose of the Chinese exclusion laws. The *San Francisco Call* protested, "Why should the Collector keep a force of men at work questioning and examining Chinese who come to this port if his work can be undone by the courts?"[84] Some charged that the federal courts, especially in New York and Vermont, deliberately released Chinese because they found the Chinese exclusion laws unjust.[85] Others, such as Ed Rosenberg, secretary of the San Francisco Labor Council, pointed to the political connections of the federal judges, "appointed and advanced through the influence of the trusts and corporations of the country. These trusts and corporations . . . want cheap and servile labor," argued Rosenberg, and it was natural, in his opinion, that the judges "wherever and whenever possible . . . will further the interests of those who befriend them."[86]

Most critics, however, hesitated to accuse the courts of being intentionally pro-Chinese. In a report to the commissioner general on San Francisco, an inspector said he found the legal officers "honest, conscientious, men." The "evil," he argued, "is in the system."[87] These observers tended to portray the court as the "dupe" of the Chinese. They laid the blame on the Chinese and their attorneys who "imposed" upon the dignity of the court by appealing to Anglo-American common law traditions to which, critics seemed to suggest, Chinese had no legitimate claim.[88] One U.S. senator complained, for example, that the Chinese person trying to enter the United States "unhesitatingly commits perjury, [and] is set free, by the 'sacred law of habeas corpus' writ (a process unknown in Asia)."[89] In a similar vein, the attorney general warned that "processes of the courts are being abused" by "disingenuous claims and fraudulent devices."[90] Thus, for the anti-Chinese forces and the policy makers, the court, as an institution, was a weak and ineffective enforcer of the Chinese exclusion laws. Hampered by legal niceties and traditions, the judiciary seemed unable to protect itself or American society from the intrusion of Chinese.

If "law," as represented by the courts, stood in the way of stringent enforcement of Chinese exclusion, the critics concurred that only one remedy could improve the situation: remove the court's jurisdiction to review the Chinese cases and expand the discretion of the administrative officials.

CHAPTER 4

The Eclipse of Judicial Justice

The exclusion laws of the 1880s significantly curtailed Chinese immigration, but they did not prevent many Chinese from entering. One senator, commenting on the weakness of the exclusion policy, lamented in 1892: "There are thousands of Chinese eager to circumvent this law and eager to come to the United States where the rewards of labor are so great."[1] Simply enacting restrictive laws did not guarantee exclusion of Chinese from the United States. Policy makers began to focus on effective enforcement as the key to ensuring that America's "gateways [would] be double locked and barred against the Mongolian."[2] A decision was made to remove the federal courts' jurisdiction to hear Chinese cases after increasingly stringent laws failed to keep them out.

Chinese success in the federal courts posed a primary, though not the only, obstacle to a stringent enforcement of the exclusion laws. Exclusionists and policy makers came to understand that the forum—a court or an administrative agency—affected enforcement of the laws. Experience taught them that courts, confined by certain legal practices and traditions, could not be strong gatekeepers. Administrative officials, however, had the distinct advantage of being free from traditional legal constraints and of being more accountable to public opinion. Thus policy makers and government officials embarked upon a campaign to remove jurisdiction from the courts and bolster the power of the administrators to enforce the Chinese exclusion policy.

Congress had made several attempts to limit judicial power in the habeas corpus cases since the passage of the first exclusion act in 1882. The acts of 1884 and 1888 imposed more specific evidentiary requirements on Chinese applicants in an attempt to close loopholes opened by federal court decisions. The act of September 13, 1888, made the decisions of the collector final, but as discussed in Chapter 1, that provision never took effect.[3] Finally, the Geary Act placed such strict limitations on the discretion of courts in deportation hearings that critics charged that the judges were left with "no judicial duties or functions to perform," making them "mere ministerial officers."[4]

None of those acts seriously checked the courts' involvement in the Chinese cases, however. The first major successful restriction on the federal district court's power to review the admission of Chinese came on the heels of the Geary Act of 1892 and the McCreary Amendment of 1893. Though the legislation placed onerous evidentiary requirements upon Chinese in admission and deportation proceedings, the San Francisco federal court mitigated the severity of the laws. The court's actions, according to critics, diluted and enfeebled the Chinese exclusion policy.

As described in Chapter 2, the McCreary Amendment of 1893 required resident merchants who were returning to the United States after a temporary absence to follow strict guidelines in proving their right to reenter. In passing the law, Congress aimed to curb what it perceived to be the fraudulent use of the merchant exemption. Chinese firms in the United States were usually composed of several individuals who often invested as little as $500 to $1,000 in the business. That investment made them merchants under the Chinese exclusion laws. Exclusionists believed that Chinese laborers purchased shares in businesses as a ploy to evade exclusion.

The McCreary Amendment sought to separate the impostors from the "real" merchants. The law specified that the merchant had to "establish by the testimony of two credible witnesses other than Chinese the fact that he conducted such business . . . for at least one year before his departure from the United States, and that during such year he was not engaged in the performance of any manual labor, except such as was necessary in the conduct of his business as such merchant, and in default of such proof shall be refused landing." Furthermore, the act defined a merchant as "a person engaged in buying and selling merchandise, at a fixed place of business, which business is conducted in his name."[5]

If enforced literally, these requirements would have had severe consequences. Several Chinese merchants, for example, had difficulty obtaining "two witnesses other than Chinese," which meant white witnesses. Segregated in Chinatown, Chinese merchants did not always know white residents, or at least not well enough to substantiate their claims as specified in the law. More serious was the requirement that the "business be conducted in his name." The attorney general interpreted this as meaning that the Chinese merchant's name must be part of the firm name. An attorney for the Chinese merchants explained to the secretary of the treasury the ramifications of such an opinion: "I am informed that there is not a Chinese mercantile establishment, in the country, whose firm name comprises or embraces the names of the individual partners." As a result, the attorney complained, the law would prevent the reentry of virtually all Chinese merchants.[6]

Initially, the district court in San Francisco adopted the attorney general's strict interpretation of the law, and it seemed that the exclusionists' goal was in sight. The controversy over the question of the firm name arose in the case of Quan Gin in 1894. Commissioner Heacock rejected a strict reading of the statute on the grounds that "such a construction of the law in my judgment, is narrow and unwarranted."[7] Judge Morrow, however, disagreed. Basing his decision on the attorney general's opinion, Morrow argued that dissatisfaction with the law should be addressed to Congress, not the courts. The judge went further to defend the policy of the act: "When it is considered how easy it is for a Chinese person seeking admission into the United States to claim a small interest in the business of buying and selling merchandise, it is evident that the statute has been wisely framed to prevent the admission of Chinese persons into the United States upon the fictitious and fraudulent claim that they are merchants."[8]

The commissioner and the judge differed again in the case of Loo Yue Soon. Heacock recommended the discharge of the petitioner, ruling that the McCreary Amendment did not apply because Loo Yue Soon had left China for the United States before the act was passed. Heacock felt his decision was on firm ground because the secretary of the treasury had come to the same conclusion. Judge Morrow, however, again put his foot down, saying, "I find nothing in the language of the statute to justify such an interpretation of its provisions," and dismissed Heacock's recommendation.[9]

In the end, however, the court's practices in handling the cases were much less severe than its opinions suggested. The interpretation by the attorney general and Judge Morrow on the firm name requirement aroused great consternation among the Chinese merchants, who pressured the government for a fairer standard. Noting the widespread tendency among merchants to choose "fanciful," lucky names for their businesses, the Chinese Merchants Exchange in San Francisco contended that "to hold that these merchants cannot now land will have the effect of depriving them of millions of dollars of property. [If Congress] intended to absolutely prohibit the further coming of Chinese merchants they should have said so in express terms."[10] The Circuit Court of Appeals for the Ninth Circuit also found the attorney general's interpretation too harsh and ruled that the law should be construed to mean that "the interest of the merchant must be real, and appear in the business and partnership articles in his own name, and not that his name must appear in the firm designation."[11]

Heacock's application of Morrow's decisions further weakened the exclusionary thrust of the court. Morrow sent several cases back to the commissioner for a rehearing, with instructions that the cases must meet the evidentiary requirements established in the statute (except the firm name requirement). That is, the petitioner had to establish upon the testimony of two witnesses, other than Chinese, that he had been a merchant for more than one year before leaving the United States and had done no manual labor. Heacock was willing to be somewhat generous in his findings. For example, if white witnesses could not swear that they knew the petitioner was actually a partner, Heacock would accept their testimony that it *appeared* from the petitioner's actions (helping customers, taking money, and so forth) that he was a partner. As long as he thought the commissioner was applying the rule of evidence specified in the statute, Judge Morrow was willing to accept Heacock's findings of fact and recommendations.

As a result, the court continued to order the discharge of Chinese in a very high percentage of cases, prompting calls for curbs on the courts.[12] Representatives in Congress, responding to public frustration, sought to remove the Chinese cases from the court's jurisdiction in a rider to the 1894 appropriations bill. The new law provided: "In every case where an alien is excluded from admission into the United States under any law or treaty now existing or hereafter made, the decision made by the appropriate immigration or custom officers, if adverse to the admission of such alien, shall be final, unless reversed on appeal to the Secretary of the Treasury."[13] In essence, the 1894 law extended to Chinese the same principle of review applied to non-Chinese immigration cases since the *Nishimura Ekiu* decision in 1891. That is, courts should treat the decisions of the administrative officials responsible for enforcing the Chinese laws as final and dismiss any habeas corpus petitions challenging administrative determinations, at least insofar as questions of fact were involved.

Judge Morrow was only too happy to apply the new law. He dismissed the habeas corpus petition of a Chinese merchant, Lem Moon Sing, returning to the United States after a brief visit to China, on the grounds that the court no longer had authority to review such cases. On appeal to the Supreme Court, Maxwell Evarts, attorney for Lem Moon Sing, focused his attack on the jurisdiction of the customs officials.

As discussed in Chapter 1, courts generally would not review the factual determinations of administrative officials as long as they were operating within their proper jurisdiction. Evarts noted that the act of 1894 gave the collector conclusive authority to deny admission to any alien " 'excluded from admission into the United States under any law or treaty now existing or hereafter made.' " It followed, argued Evarts, that the collector did not have final jurisdiction over aliens who were *not* excluded by statute or treaty.

Lem Moon Sing, as a resident merchant, was exempt from the exclusion laws and entitled by treaty to be in the United States; thus, Evarts concluded, his right to reenter the United States was not subject to the conclusive determination of the collector. Evarts urged that exempt Chinese, such as Lem Moon Sing, retained the right to challenge the collector's decisions in the federal courts.[14] Opposing counsel, J. M. Dickinson, conceded in his brief that Evarts's argument had force, especially if the language of the statute were taken at face value. But, he countered, Evarts's interpretation of the 1894 act, if "carried to its logical conclusion . . . makes the act practically almost ineffective" and was not consonant with the purpose of the law.[15]

The Supreme Court agreed with the assistant attorney general and affirmed Morrow's ruling in May 1895. Justice John Marshall Harlan, writing for the Court, held that the act of 1894 gave the collector "exclusive authority to determine whether a particular alien seeking admission into this country belongs to the *class* entitled by some law or treaty to come into the country, or to a *class* forbidden to enter the United States."[16] The interpretation insisted upon by Lem Moon Sing's attorney, Justice Harlan warned, "would bring into the courts every case of an alien who claimed the right to come into the United States under some law or treaty" and would defeat Congress's intention to take away "the authority of the courts to review the decision of the executive officers."[17]

The federal district court at San Francisco immediately felt the effect of the *Lem Moon Sing* decision. The number of petitions filed dropped dramatically from 207 in 1894 to 36 in 1895. The filings remained at this low level for the next two years.[18] But this inactivity did not last long. As attorney Thomas Riordan observed in 1895 while criticizing the decision in *Lem Moon Sing*, one class of cases was still open to the review of the court. "Of course," he said reassuringly, "no law of Congress could attempt to abridge the rights of a native-born Chinese to a writ of habeas corpus."[19] The *San Francisco Call* warned, "It will be a difficult task to exclude the 'native sons.' "[20]

The newspaper was correct: citizenship was to prove a particularly successful claim. The courts of the Northern District of California had long recognized the rights of American citizens of Chinese descent. The circuit court in 1884 had ruled that even though Chinese could not become naturalized, those born in the United States of Chinese parents were United States citizens and thus not subject to the Chinese exclusion laws because "no citizen can be excluded from this country except in punishment for crime."[21]

The district court signaled in 1894 that it would continue to accept jurisdiction in citizenship cases. Not long after his decision in *Lem Moon Sing,* Judge Morrow held that the 1894 "finality clause" did not apply to cases in which the Chinese person claimed to be a United States citizen. The judge ruled that the collector had jurisdiction only over aliens. To allow the collector to decide whether an applicant was a citizen would grant the collector power beyond the limits of his office.[22] The collector at San Francisco, John Wise, deplored Morrow's decision as frustrating the intent of the 1894 law. He predicted that there would now be "a great influx of youngsters from China" claiming to be born in the United States and "the old farce will be re-enacted of the Collector being merely the middle-man between the Chinese and the Courts, without power to enforce the laws of Congress."[23]

As more and more Chinese claimed to have been born in the United States (and thus to be beyond the reach of the exclusion law), exclusionists began to challenge the extension of birthright citizenship to Chinese. Concerned that birthright citizenship created a gaping loophole in the American exclusion policy, they pushed for an alternative conception of citizenship based on descent. Citizenship, exclusionists argued, should depend on the nationality of the parents. Although scholars attempted to make historical and principled justifications for following the descent rule, their underlying concern was clearly to prevent Chinese from becoming members of their community. The common law, according to lawyer George D. Collins, was "manifestly impolitic" because it allowed Chinese, "a people foreign to us in every respect," to become fellow citizens. Collins asserted that children of Chinese "born upon American soil are Chinese from their very birth in all respects, just as much so as though they had been born and reared in China." Such people, Collins continued, "are utterly unfit, wholly incompetent, to exercise the important privileges of an American citizen . . . and yet under the common-law rule they would be citizens."[24]

The Supreme Court rejected the descent argument in 1898 in *United States v. Wong Kim Ark* and upheld birthright citizenship for Chinese. The Court found the common law right too compelling a precedent to overcome and the language of the Fourteenth Amendment too plain to ignore merely for the sake of excluding Chinese. It warned that once established, a law based on descent would not affect only Chinese but would also deny citizenship to "thousands of persons of English, Scotch, Irish, German or other European parentage, who have always been considered and treated as citizens of the United States."[25]

Heartened by the Court's decision, Chinese in 1898 began to resort again to the court in large numbers (261 petitions were filed in that year), claiming that they were native-born citizens. Special Agent for the Treasury H. A. Moore and Collector John P. Jackson advised the secretary of the treasury of a great increase in the number of Chinese claiming to be "native sons." San Francisco officials pleaded for more staff to handle the increased arrivals and to stave off criticism by steamship companies and attorneys about delay in processing the cases. If he did not receive help, warned the collector, he would be forced summarily to reject incoming Chinese and "turn them over to the court without any investigation or examination by the Bureau or myself."[26]

Collector Jackson went on to describe what he perceived to be an alarming new litigation strategy adopted by attorneys for the applicants. The attorneys had decided to bypass the collector altogether when representing Chinese native-born citizens. It was "a matter of common report," Jackson said, that attorneys would take their cases directly before the federal courts after the ships arrived, on the grounds that the collector had no power to make any determination regarding the right of native-born Chinese to land. This procedure would have disastrous consequences for the enforcement of the exclusion laws, complained the collector, "for if their attorneys can get to communicate with them before the trial (as they will be enabled to do under the allowance of a writ of habeas corpus), their stories can be made to conform to any hypothesis which will secure their admission."[27]

The collector's letter highlights the major tensions that for the next several years dominated the relationship among the administration, the attorneys for the Chinese applicants, and the courts. The major complaint of the administrative officials was that the line between the function of the courts and the agency was blurred. The courts, they argued, usurped the role of the agency by trying the "native son" cases de novo. Attorneys for the Chinese contended that administrative officials had no jurisdiction to inspect Chinese-American citizens and further castigated the lack of due process in the administrative hearings in all of the cases involving Chinese applicants. The courts took a middle position, denying neither the authority of the collector to investigate the cases of Chinese-American citizens nor their own power to review the collector's decisions.

Over the next seven years (1898–1905), the administrative officials developed a variegated strategy that ultimately led to their victory over the attorneys and the courts. They tried, unsuccessfully, to convince the courts and commissioners to change their standards of evidence. They also consolidated administrative control over the Chinese cases in one agency, the Bureau of Immigration. Finally, and most important, they pushed for a sharper distinction between the court and the agency.

Evidence accepted by the courts in landing and deportation cases had been a source of constant annoyance to the collector and his superiors in

Washington, D.C. The collector subjected Chinese to stringent investigations and denied them access to attorneys and friends, justifying such procedures as the only way to get uncoached evidence. But, the collector argued, he was powerless to control the evidence or the outcome of the case once the federal court had issued a writ of habeas corpus. Upon serving the writ, the United States marshal removed the petitioner from the detention sheds on the wharf, which were under the collector's supervision, to the city jail to await his hearing. There, claimed the collector, the petitioner had access to his attorney and friends who helped him concoct a fraudulent story. As a result, the testimony and evidence presented by the petitioner at the court hearing could be quite different from that offered to the collector's inspectors and could result in the petitioner's discharge.

On the issue of detention, the administrative officials were able to obtain a concession from the court. Judge De Haven, who succeeded Judge Morrow to the district court bench in May 1897, agreed in 1904 to order that the petitioners remain in the detention sheds on the wharf, instead of in the city jail, pending their court hearing. Officials thought this rule would let them continue to control the access of attorneys and friends and the "purity" of the evidence.[28]

The collector and the U.S. attorney were less successful in changing the courts' evidentiary standards. Appeals to Congress by the secretary of the treasury for legislation requiring the testimony of non-Chinese witnesses in citizenship cases got no response.[29] The federal district court rejected arguments made by the U.S. attorney in San Francisco that the court should refuse to hear the cases de novo and should consider only the evidence taken by the Chinese inspectors. Commissioner Heacock was especially unwilling to concede this point because of the breaches of fundamental due process by the government. In his investigation before the Chinese Bureau, Heacock said disapprovingly, the party had not been allowed an attorney or the right to subpoena witnesses. By implication, Heacock was arguing that the court must allow more evidence to ensure a fair hearing of the petitioner's case because otherwise the petitioner was not allowed a chance to exercise his "personal rights" before the administrative officials.[30]

As the administrative officials tried to persuade the courts to adopt the agency's evidentiary standards, they worked simultaneously to obtain legislation that would clarify the jurisdictional boundaries between the federal courts and the agency. The first step toward success, officials thought, was to bring the administration of the Chinese exclusion laws under the centralized control of the Bureau of Immigration, headed by the commissioner general of immigration. This reform would "unify and simplify and thus render more effective a branch of the public service formerly conducted by various heads according to their varying interpretations of the laws."[31] Thus in 1900, Congress gave the commissioner general of immigration supervision over the Chinese exclusion laws, though the collector still administered the laws at the local level.[32] And in 1903, the local administration was removed from the collector's control altogether and transferred to the local commissioner of immigration.[33]

This consolidation undoubtedly led to more uniform rules, as the commissioner general of immigration had suggested, and made stricter enforcement more possible. More important, it seems, to the battle against judicial review in the Chinese habeas corpus cases, the administration of the Chinese laws was now under the Bureau of Immigration, an agency accustomed to operating free from court scrutiny. The "hands-off" doctrine in the 1891 *Nishimura Ekiu* case held firm in the courts' responses to petitions made by non-Chinese immigrants. For example, the district and circuit courts in the Southern District of New York with jurisdiction over Ellis Island very rarely intervened in immigration cases. The circuit court in New York received 165 habeas corpus petitions from immigrants between 1891 and 1906; it found in favor of the immigrant in only 16 cases. An order of discharge did not necessarily mean the courts allowed the immigrant to enter, however. Often the circuit court instead referred the case back to the commissioner of immigration at Ellis Island for reconsideration.[34] With this tradition of agency freedom behind the Bureau of Immigration, it seemed likely that the commissioner general would view judicial review in the Chinese cases as a serious problem.

Furthermore, the agency's leadership was firmly committed to the Chinese exclusion policy. When supervision over the Chinese cases was transferred to the commissioner general of immigration in 1900, the man holding that office was Terence Powderly, former head of the Knights of Labor. His successor in 1902, Frank P. Sargent, had also been a labor leader and was a friend of Samuel Gompers, president of the American Federation of Labor.[35] Their associations with labor unions encouraged the officials to approach the enforcement of the Chinese exclusion laws with zeal.[36]

A renewed legislative mandate gave added force to the commissioner general's campaign for stricter enforcement. Congress in 1902 had extended and broadened the exclusion policy, though not without significant opposition. The policy came up for reconsideration when the ten-year limitation imposed by the Geary Act expired in May 1902. Exclusionists along the West Coast organized a vigorous campaign to renew and strengthen the Chinese exclusion laws. In November 1901, a group of more than three thousand representatives met at an "exclusion convention" in San Francisco and drew up a petition for greater restrictions, which they sent to the president and

Congress.[37] The American Federation of Labor published a pamphlet advocating new exclusion laws, *Some Reasons for Exclusion, Meat vs. Rice, American Manhood against Asiatic Coolieism, Which Shall Survive?*[38] As those slogans suggest, the arguments for exclusion remained much the same as in earlier years: Chinese competed unfairly with white labor, driving down wages and preventing effective unionization; Chinese would not assimilate; they brought with them unsavory habits and morals; if not stopped, they would overrun white civilization.

The complaints were old ones, but new events in the United States prompted exclusionists to act with renewed zeal. The main change that concerned them was the imperialist expansion of the United States. In 1898, the United States annexed the Hawaiian Islands and, as a result of the American victory over Spain, acquired the territories of the Philippines, Puerto Rico, and Guam. The annexations sparked debate on several fronts, but what worried exclusionists was the presence of a large Chinese population in Hawaii and the Philippines. At least twenty thousand Chinese lived in Hawaii by 1898, many of whom were citizens or longtime residents, and an estimated hundred thousand lived in the Philippines.[39] Exclusionists protested that annexation would unlatch the door of the United States and result in a new invasion of Chinese immigrants. The *San Francisco Call* exclaimed that there were "hordes of coolies camped in Hawaii, waiting to come."[40]

Exclusionists were not able to prevent the annexation of Hawaii, but they did obtain a significant concession. Congress, by joint resolution in 1898, extended exclusion to Hawaii, prohibiting any further immigration of Chinese laborers to Hawaii and barring the entry of Chinese already there into the United States.[41] In 1900, Congress required the registration of all Chinese laborers residing in Hawaii, providing for the deportation of those who did not register.[42]

The status of Chinese living in the Philippines had still not been determined by 1902, however, and the issue of whether to extend exclusion to them was a major topic in the legislative debates over the renewal of the Chinese exclusion laws.[43] But it was not the only concern. The proposed bill—the result of collaboration among delegates from the exclusion convention in San Francisco, the American Federation of Labor, and western congressional representatives—was lengthy. It called for the exclusion of Chinese laborers without any time limit; the extension of exclusion to Chinese in the Philippines; the prohibition of Chinese immigration from the territories to the United States, even if the Chinese were citizens of the territories; and a ban on the hiring of Chinese sailors on American ships.[44]

The bill further proposed to incorporate the decisions of the attorney general and the regulations of the Treasury Department which restricted the definition of the exempt classes and imposed more stringent procedures for their admission. For example, the proposed law embodied the opinion of the attorney general, discussed in Chapter 2, that the treaty exempted *only* merchants, students, teachers, travelers, and officials, not just non-laborers. The bill also adopted the narrow definitions of the exempt classes developed by administrators, such as confining "teachers" to those Chinese who had taught for at least two years at institutions of higher education and were coming to the United States at the express invitation of a recognized educational institution.[45]

Such provisions clearly made the exclusion laws more restrictive and were aimed to overcome challenges to administrative regulations by courts and immigrants. Senator Henry Cabot Lodge complained, "We are now living under three statutes—innumerable Treasury regulations, decisions of the law officers of the departments, and of the courts of the United States." This led, he and others argued, to a "loose, contradictory administration of the law."[46] While proclaiming that the law simply straightened out confusions that had arisen, the bill clearly resolved any contradictions between administrative regulations and court decisions in favor of the more restrictive administrative decision.

Proponents enthusiastically proclaimed the bill to be "another grand step forward by this Republic in the majestic and progressive march of true Americanism," but several legislators disagreed, finding the proposed law "uncalled for, unnecessary, unwise, and un-American."[47] The opponents argued that the law would be a "slap in the face" of the Chinese government and would violate American treaties with China. Its definition of the exempt classes was too narrow, they argued, and the elimination of the time constraint on exclusion contravened the 1880 treaty provision that Chinese laborers could not be permanently barred from the United States.[48]

Opponents pointed out that the Chinese foreign minister, Wu Ting-Fang, had already filed a strong protest against the proposed bill because it was "so restrictive as to practically nullify the treaty."[49] Wu Ting-Fang warned that passage of the law "can not fail to seriously disturb the friendly relations" between China and the United States.[50] To ignore the Chinese minister's protests, argued opponents of the law, would be unethical as well as potentially unprofitable.

Of course, Congress had ignored such protests in the past, but by 1902 a growing, though still small, movement in the United States in favor of the Chinese encouraged some legislators to take such complaints more seriously. Increasingly, exclusionists had to compete with commercial interests who sought to expand American economic involvement in China as

America's "Open Door Policy," announced in 1899, promised to give American business a greater role in Chinese trade and economic development.[51] It was time, argued one commentator, for "the politicians to give way to the captains of industry."[52] American business interests organized the American Asiatic Association in 1898 to further good relations with China. The organization, fearing economic retaliation from China, took a strong stance against the renewal of the exclusion policy.[53]

Principle as well as economics motivated the new pro-Chinese groups. In addition to pursuing standard diplomatic remedies, Chinese envoys to the United States appealed directly to the conscience of Americans.[54] Minister Wu Ting-Fang was largely responsible for attracting the support of educated, upper-middle-class Americans to the Chinese cause.[55] Samuel Gompers complained that "there is never a social function in Washington at which [Wu Ting-Fang] is not an honored guest."[56] In speeches and letters, the minister questioned the justice of singling out the Chinese for exclusion and asked that they be subject to the same laws as all other immigrants.[57] He also pointedly argued that Americans could not expect an open door to China when they so firmly shut the doors on Chinese.[58]

Wu Ting-Fang's arguments evidently began to have an effect. In response to the American Federation of Labor's pamphlet *Meat vs. Rice*, a pro-Chinese group published another pamphlet under the title *Truth versus Fiction, Justice versus Prejudice, Meat for All, Not for a Few*. Stamped on its cover was the urgent message that the issue involved not only the "honor" of the country but also "an enormous foreign trade." The pamphlet urged that the Chinese exclusion laws not be reenacted, but instead Chinese should be subject to the same laws as all other immigrants.[59]

The recommendation that the Chinese exclusion laws be repealed had no support in Congress except for Senator Hoar, who had vigorously opposed Chinese exclusion from the beginning.[60] Some senators cautioned restraint, however, and proposed an amended bill that simply renewed the old exclusion legislation until 1904, when the treaty with China was due to expire. Then, they argued, the United States could perhaps negotiate for more restrictions, but in the meantime, the country would have abided by its treaty obligations.[61]

The House refused to agree to only a two-year renewal of the laws, and the final law reflected a compromise by providing for the exclusion of Chinese laborers "until otherwise provided by law," as long as it was "not inconsistent with treaty obligations."[62] The law thus catered to the exclusionists' demands for exclusion without time limit and to the opponents' insistence that treaty obligations be observed. The law further solved the question of the Chinese in the Philippines, extending the exclusion and registration of Chinese laborers to all American territories.[63] The law reiterated that the secretary of the treasury had power to make rules and regulations governing Chinese admission, though such rules must not be "inconsistent with the laws of the land." In a concession to American commercial interests, the act affirmed the privilege of Chinese to come to the United States to participate in fairs and expositions.[64]

Although administrative officials did not gain as restrictive a law as they would have liked, the act of 1902 reaffirmed the department's power and broadened the reach of the exclusion policy. With the support of this mandate, the commissioner general attempted to redefine the roles of the courts and the immigration agency so as to give the agency more control over Chinese cases.

Of immediate concern to the agency was the strategy adopted by attorneys for the Chinese of taking admission applications of Chinese alleging to be citizens directly to the courts, thus circumventing the investigation of the collector. The secretary of the treasury complained that the practice had grown to such an extent that it "practically destroy[ed] the power of . . . officers to enforce the law." The secretary urged the U.S. attorney at San Francisco to lay "the matter before the Judge of the court out of which the writs issue" to make him understand "that the effect of such issuance is to take the enforcement out of their [the officials'] hands."[65]

The U.S. attorney obtained the cooperation of the court with little difficulty. Commissioner Heacock was also frustrated with the number of cases coming before him without an investigation by the Chinese Bureau. Though Heacock heard the Chinese cases de novo, he usually referred to the collector's records "to test the accuracy of the testimony of the identifying witnesses." Heacock complained that the lack of investigation made it "exceedingly difficult" to have a full hearing of the case.[66] Thus, in response to a request by the U.S. attorney, Judge De Haven ordered that all petitions filed before the court had to indicate that the collector had made a decision in the case or that there had been an exceptional delay in the collector's investigation. If there was no indication that the bureau had made an investigation, the court would refuse to issue the writ of habeas corpus.[67]

Having obtained this victory, "one of the greatest reforms of recent years in the Chinese business at this Port," according to the inspector in charge of the Chinese Bureau, the Department of Justice went on to push for further limitations on the habeas corpus appeal.[68] Its next objective was to force those Chinese claiming citizenship to pursue all possible remedies within administrative channels before taking their cases before the court, a concept known as "exhaustion." Though the statutes provided that Chinese denied entry could take an appeal from the decision of the collector, and later of the commissioner of immigration, to the secretary of the treasury (later the secretary of commerce and labor) for review, the Chinese applicants preferred to take their appeals directly to the courts after the collector denied them entry.

Doctrinal developments regarding habeas corpus appeals in criminal law gave added force to the Justice Department's insistence that Chinese first exhaust their administrative remedies. The key development occurred in cases in which state prisoners petitioned federal courts for writs of habeas corpus, thereby challenging the legality of their confinement by the state. The power of the federal courts to issue habeas corpus writs in such cases had steadily increased in the mid-nineteenth century, especially following the passage of the Habeas Corpus Act of 1867. The lower federal courts had "viewed the 1867 statute as imperatively demanding federal discharge of state prisoners held for trial or after state trial-court conviction, notwithstanding the availability of still unexhausted state remedies." In 1886, however, the Supreme Court curbed the federal courts' liberal issuance of the writ and established the exhaustion doctrine in habeas corpus cases. In *Ex Parte Royall* and subsequent cases, the Court held that though federal courts had the power to issue habeas corpus to state prisoners before the state courts had full opportunity to determine their cases, the federal courts, in the interests of federalism, should refrain from interfering with state criminal processes until the prisoner had pursued his remedies at the state level.[69]

The Department of Justice sought to establish a similar principle in immigration cases. Special Assistant U.S. Attorney John Lott recommended to the attorney general in September 1903 that the government move to dismiss any writs in which the petitioner had not appealed to the secretary of commerce and labor. In this way, Lott hoped to impress upon the courts "the fact that the writ is being used as a means to perpetrate systematic frauds upon the Government" and that the courts "are, in large degree, usurping the functions of the officers."[70] The attorney general took Lott's recommendation and instructed the U.S. attorneys in various districts to file motions to dismiss in such cases.[71]

The attorney general decided to take the recommendation further, however, and instructed U.S. attorneys to challenge *all* habeas corpus petitions on the grounds that the decision of the Bureau of Immigration to allow or deny entry, under the review of the secretary of commerce and labor, was final and conclusive, whether or not the Chinese applicant purported to be a citizen.[72] This instruction aimed at the heart of the debate; if accepted, the courts would no longer review the findings of fact made by the administrative officials.

The issue soon came to a head in the Northern District of New York.

The ports of entry at Vermont and at Malone, New York, had become trouble spots for the officials because Chinese applicants, encouraged by favorable rulings by the court and commissioner there, came across the Canadian border in increasing numbers. A court decision limiting judicial review would greatly aid in checking the entry of Chinese at these ports, thought officials.[73]

The officials obtained the decisions they desired. Judge Hoyt Henry Wheeler of the district court in Vermont ruled in 1903 that the decision of the immigration officers on the question of whether a Chinese applicant was a citizen was final and not subject to judicial review.[74] The U.S. attorney from New York hailed this "exceedingly important decision. If it can be sustained it will, in my opinion, solve the problem which has made the Government so much trouble in this District and the District of Vermont."[75] A similar decision, *In re Sing Tuck*, by Circuit Court Judge George Washington Ray came soon thereafter from the Northern District of New York.[76]

The latter case, *Sing Tuck*, brought on behalf of thirty-two Chinese alleging to be citizens, was to make constitutional history. Though Judge Ray dismissed the case on the grounds that the court had no jurisdiction to review it, the Circuit Court of Appeals for the Second Circuit reversed his decision, holding that the petitioners were entitled to a judicial hearing because they claimed to be citizens.[77] The Ninth Circuit Court of Appeals had made a similar ruling in 1892, and on the strength of that case, District Court Judge De Haven in San Francisco upheld the right of alleged citizens to a judicial hearing shortly after Judge Ray's decision to the contrary in *Sing Tuck*.[78] To resolve the conflicting interpretations by the federal courts, hopefully in its favor, the government turned to the Supreme Court.

In his brief for the Court, the solicitor general tried to convey the government's frustration with the citizenship cases and its need to have complete control over all Chinese admissions. Since the Court's decision in *Wong Kim Ark*, the government complained, Chinese laborers had flocked to the United States and, with the help of "shrewd and unscrupulous agents" who advised them to claim American citizenship, had been wrongfully admitted to the United States by the courts. Although "the officers of the Immigration Bureau are diligent in endeavoring to carry out the provisions of the law . . . they have been greatly hindered by the rulings of the lower Federal courts, and find themselves in a maze of difficulties from which they can not hope to be finally released until this court settles the points in issue."[79]

The central issue to be decided was whether the act of 1894 had given administrative officers the conclusive power to determine whether an applicant was an American citizen and thus exempt from the exclusion laws.

The government argued that, by virtue of the act, immigration officials had the authority to determine conclusively *all* questions of fact, including allegations of citizenship. To hold otherwise would defeat the purpose of the exclusion acts and "would result in ousting the officers of jurisdiction in substantially every case, as there is ample reason for supposing that few Chinamen applying for admission would not find it convenient to claim birth within the United States."[80] The solicitor general urged that courts should issue a writ of habeas corpus only when the agency "acts contrary to law, or, possibly where a manifest wrong has been done, and only in such cases."[81]

The attorneys for the Chinese, upon the strength of earlier federal court cases, flatly denied that the agency had any power to detain or deny entry to Chinese claiming to be United States citizens because the act of 1894 applied only to aliens.[82] Citizenship was not simply a fact, like any other, to be determined by the officials. Rather, as Judge Morrow had explained in 1894, the determination of whether an applicant was a citizen or an alien "is the very fact upon which the jurisdiction of the collector depends." To allow the officials to decide the fact of citizenship would be to allow them to determine the boundaries of their own jurisdiction. Morrow had concluded, "It is difficult to see how [such a determination] can be deemed conclusive upon this court" because judicial review had always been possible in questions of jurisdiction.[83]

As citizens, the attorneys argued, Chinese Americans could not be deprived of their liberty or property without due process, which in this case meant a judicial trial.[84] And certainly, they continued, due process required more for citizens than the procedures outlined in the Bureau of Immigration's rules. These rules, promulgated in 1903, had been severely attacked by attorneys and a growing number of people who opposed the Chinese exclusion laws.[85] Even the U.S. attorney in the Northern District of New York doubted "whether the [bureau's] regulations provide for a proceeding which constitutes due process" and recommended that greater procedural protections be afforded alleged citizens.[86] Among other things, the rules denied the applicant the right of counsel at the investigation and provided that the hearings be "apart from the public." The attorney could review the evidence only after the officials made their decision and had just two days to file an appeal to the secretary of commerce and labor.[87] This lack of due process, the attorneys argued, made it even more imperative that Chinese alleging citizenship have the right to resort to the courts.[88]

The Supreme Court, with Justices David Brewer and Rufus W. Peckham dissenting, held for the government but on a narrower ground than either party asserted. Justice Holmes, writing for the majority, primarily limited the opinion to the issue of exhaustion. Sing Tuck and the other applicants had filed habeas corpus petitions directly after the immigration inspector denied them entry, forgoing their right to appeal the inspector's decision to the secretary of commerce and labor. Holmes insisted that "the first mode of attacking [the immigration inspector's] decision" is by appeal to the secretary of commerce and labor. The act of 1894 "points out a mode of procedure which must be followed before there can be a resort to the courts."[89] Holmes refused to decide whether administrative officers had jurisdiction to determine the fact of citizenship and argued that it did not pertain to his decision.

The majority was unmoved by the due process arguments, finding the department's rules to be reasonable, given the nature of the cases. "Whatever may be the ultimate rights of a person seeking to enter the country and alleging that he is a citizen," Holmes said, "it is within the power of Congress to provide at least a preliminary investigation by an inspector." Defending the specific procedures followed, Holmes concluded: "The whole scheme is intended to give as fair a chance to prove a right to enter the country as the necessarily summary character of the proceedings will permit."[90]

Justice Brewer rendered an ardent dissent. He argued that the act of 1894 explicitly limited the jurisdiction of the administrative officials to aliens. He assailed the majority opinion for allowing an inspector of immigration, "a mere ministerial officer," the power to decide whether a citizen could enter the country. Citizenship, Brewer reminded the Court, was an "inestimable heritage" and entitled one to "prompt access to the courts" and due process protections. And certainly, Brewer argued, citizens were entitled to more than the "Star Chamber proceeding" provided by the Bureau of Immigration. Continuing in the same vein, Brewer cut through the arguments of the majority to suggest that racial prejudice lay behind the willingness to subject Chinese-American citizens to such "harsh and arbitrary" proceedings:

> Must an American citizen, seeking to return to this his native land, be compelled to bring with him two witnesses to prove the place of his birth or else be denied his right to return and all opportunity of establishing his citizenship in the courts of his country? No such rule is enforced against an American citizen of Anglo-Saxon descent, and if this be, as claimed, a government of laws and not of men, I do not think it should be enforced against American citizens of Chinese descent.[91]

Brewer's angry dissent did not dampen administrative officials' pleasure with the decision. The U.S. attorney in New York said, "The decision . . . is very satisfactory and paves the way very fully accomplishing the purpose of the government in these cases."[92] The attorney general sent copies of the decision to all the U.S. attorneys involved in Chinese habeas corpus cases and ordered them to move for dismissals in similar cases.[93]

While the bureau pursued its strategy of litigation to limit the access of Chinese to the courts, the agency's advocates in Congress tried to bolster the bureau's power through new legislation. The opportunity for new legislation arose in 1904, when China, angered by the treatment of its subjects by American immigration inspectors, notified the Department of State that it would not renew its treaty with the United States.[94] After hearing of the Chinese government's intentions, anti-Chinese forces in Congress rushed to make the exclusion policy permanent, arguing that if the treaty ended, the laws would no longer be in effect.[95] The bill they proposed not only renewed exclusion indefinitely, but, like the 1902 act, tried to codify the restrictive administrative regulations. Furthermore, in a direct strike against the use of the courts by Chinese, the bill placed alleged native-born Chinese directly under the control of immigration officials, specifying that the agency had the power to decide their right to enter.[96]

The bill, introduced as part of the general appropriations act, did not receive much attention or debate, but pro-Chinese groups in Congress were able to ameliorate some of its more restrictive features.[97] The final law in 1904, passed only four days after the *Sing Tuck* decision, extended the exclusion laws already enacted without any time limit and reiterated that the exclusion policy would apply in the territories. Exclusion was firmly in place. It was the last time the exclusion of Chinese would be an issue until the repeal of the policy in 1943. But the attempt to close off the "habeas corpus route" to Chinese-American citizens through legislation failed.[98]

The *Sing Tuck* decision most likely took the sting out of that legislative defeat. Riding high on the success of his litigation strategy, the attorney general was eager to have the remaining question about judicial review settled as quickly as possible. Justice Holmes explicitly left open the crucial question of what action a court could take *after* the applicant had exhausted his remedies within the agency. "If the appeal [to the secretary of commerce and labor] fails," he said, "it then is time enough to consider whether upon a petition showing reasonable cause there ought to be a further trial upon habeas corpus."[99]

Assistant Attorney General J. M. McReynolds pressed Marshall Woodworth, the U.S. attorney in San Francisco, to set up a test case so the government could obtain a ruling on this issue. McReynolds and Woodworth settled on the case of Ju Toy, a cook from Oakland whom Commissioner Heacock had discharged as a citizen, saying that he found the evidence in his favor particularly compelling.[100] Complaining that "the orderly administration of the Chinese-exclusion law, where citizenship is claimed, remains impossible," the government successfully petitioned the Court to advance the case on the docket so that it could be decided as soon as possible. The *Sing Tuck* opinion, the government's attorney argued, had not fundamentally altered the intolerable situation facing the Bureau of Immigration except "that a formal appeal is now made to the Secretary of Commerce and Labor before the writs are sued out." Once the appeals had been denied, the Chinese carried on as before, suing "out writs of *habeas corpus* upon mere allegations of citizenship . . . and then demand[ing] entirely new trials upon that question before the court."[101]

As it had in *Sing Tuck*, the government argued that courts should treat all of its determinations, including allegations of citizenship, as conclusive, interfering only when fraud or a manifest wrong had been committed by the bureau. Assistant Attorney General McReynolds argued, on the government's behalf, that habeas corpus required only that courts inquire into the legality of the confinement. If the inspectors were carrying out their statutory duties in good faith, the confinement was lawful and the courts' inquiry should stop there. Under no circumstances should the court rehear the case or take new testimony or evidence into consideration, for "to allow an entirely new trial upon a wholly new record whenever citizenship is alleged would, in case of rejection, render the original investigation valueless—make it, indeed, an idle waste of time and energy."[102] Furthermore, it violated the manifest intent of Congress in the act of 1894 to make the decisions of inspectors final. Courts should intervene only if the habeas corpus petition provided evidence that the inspectors' decision was unlawful because of "mistake, fraud, injustice, or manifest wrong."[103] McReynolds concluded that a favorable outcome was crucial not only to the government's successful enforcement of the Chinese exclusion laws but to its administration of the general immigration laws.

The Chinese Six Companies hired experienced San Francisco attorney Henry C. Dibble to represent Ju Toy before the Supreme Court. Dibble reiterated the basic arguments presented by Sing Tuck's attorneys, that the Bureau of Immigration had no jurisdiction over alleged citizens and that, because of the "incalculable value" of the right at stake—citizenship—due process required a judicial hearing before an alleged citizen could be denied entry into his native country. Dibble rejected the government's attempt to limit the courts' review on habeas corpus, arguing that the nature of habeas corpus required that courts investigate the facts of the case to determine the legality of the confinement.[104]

The Supreme Court now confronted the issue it had sidestepped in *Sing Tuck* and in a six-to-three decision it found in favor of the government.

Justice Holmes, in what Felix Frankfurter allegedly described as one of Holmes's "cavalier opinions," disposed of the issue in a few pages.[105] Holmes presented the case as being firmly within the precedents established in *Nishimura Ekiu*, *Fong Yue Ting*, *Lem Moon Sing*, and *Sing Tuck*, stating that *Ju Toy* involved no new questions of law.[106] The precedents had construed congressional intent as giving broad authority to administrative officials over Chinese and other immigrants. To argue, as Ju Toy's attorneys did, that the act of 1894 limited officials' conclusive authority to aliens, not alleged citizens, would result in too "narrow an interpretation" of the statute and the cases. Holmes thus held that the act of 1894 intended to make the decision of the secretary of commerce and labor final and conclusive, even when the petitioner alleged citizenship.[107]

The precedents also settled the issue of due process in the government's favor, in Holmes's opinion. "If, for the purpose of argument, we assume that the Fifth Amendment applies to [an alleged citizen] and that to deny entrance to a citizen is to deprive him of liberty," Holmes said, "we nevertheless are of opinion that with regard to him due process of law does not require a judicial trial."[108] In addition to the immigration cases, Holmes cited as authority the landmark case *Murray's Lessee* v. *Hoboken Land & Improvement Co.*, in which the Court held that the Fifth Amendment did not require the government to institute judicial proceedings to recover property from a tax collector whose accounts were in arrears. Rather, in such cases the government could seize the property by summary administrative action.[109] The unelaborated analogy appears to be that if the Fifth Amendment allowed a citizen to be deprived of his property in tax collection cases without the benefit of judicial process, it also allowed alleged citizens applying for admission to the United States to be deprived of their liberty by administrative action.

Predictably, Justice Brewer, with Justice Peckham concurring, again dissented, protesting that "such a decision . . . is appalling."[110] Not only did the Court condone the Bureau of Immigration's "star chamber proceeding" but also, in allowing the bureau to deport Ju Toy, it sanctioned the banishment by ministerial officers of an American citizen, "who has been guilty of no crime." Such an action "strips him of all the rights which are given to a citizen." Brewer conceded the holding of *Murray's Lessee* that due process does not always require a judicial trial, but, he argued, it does when life and liberty are involved.[111] Brewer concluded: "I cannot believe that Congress intended to provide that a citizen, simply because he belongs to an obnoxious race, can be deprived of all the liberty and protection which the Constitution guarantees, and if it did so intend, I do not believe that it has the power to do so."[112]

Despite Holmes's insistence that the Court's opinion in *Ju Toy* could not be fundamentally distinguished from its earlier decisions in *Fong Yue Ting* and *Nishimura Ekiu*, the Court had carved out a decidedly new proposition in administrative and constitutional law. The former cases had made a sharp distinction between the constitutional rights of aliens and those of citizens, holding that aliens could not use the Constitution to shield them from administrative action. With the *Ju Toy* case, the Court appeared to blur the distinction between aliens and citizens and to subject both to the same bureaucratic discretion and authority.

Certainly, many within the scholarly and professional community considered the *Ju Toy* decision to be a serious departure from constitutional principles. There was no question in commentators' minds that the Supreme Court's opinion aimed to solve a particular enforcement problem rather than to elucidate grand jurisprudential questions. "No doubt," observed John Dickinson, "the determining motive behind the opinion of the majority was that an opposite holding would bring practically every Chinese exclusion case into the Federal district courts, since there would be nothing to prevent a claim of citizenship, however unfounded, from being set up."[113] While critics conceded that the Supreme Court was responding to "a notorious and difficult situation" and even that "the decision rendered . . . was probably necessary if the exclusion laws are to be effective," they argued that the damage to constitutional principles was too great a cost to pay.[114] Administrative law scholar Ernst Freund explained that "the reasoning in the *Ju Toy* case is unsatisfactory, if not obscure, and it may be doubted whether it is generally accepted as sound law. It seems to illustrate the saying that hard cases make bad law."[115] Critics particularly denounced Holmes's contention that due process did not require a judicial trial for citizens applying for admission. One legal commentator cried, "If the rights flowing from American citizenship when drawn in question are not of sufficient importance to entitle . . . one . . . to a judicial determination, it is difficult to imagine any right of sufficient magnitude to justify the exertion of judicial powers."[116]

Discomfort with the *Ju Toy* opinion would persist, but the Court's basic holding remained in force. Federal courts would no longer investigate the right of a petitioner to enter the United States. They accepted the Bureau of Immigration's investigation as final and refused to hear new evidence. When Chinese petitioned the court for habeas corpus after *Ju Toy*, the district court in San Francisco routinely dismissed the petitions unless there was evidence that the officials had taken unlawful or arbitrary action.

Although the *Ju Toy* decision curtailed the access of Chinese to courts concerning admission decisions, the Bureau of Immigration remained concerned about the courts' role in deportation cases. As discussed in Chapter 3, the Geary law authorizing the deportation of Chinese had given the courts the power to decide if Chinese were in the United States unlawfully and should be deported. What concerned immigration officials was the use by Chinese of the judicial deportation procedures to bypass the administrative admission hearing. Chinese sometimes chose to enter the country illegally, reasoning that even if they were arrested and brought before a U.S. commissioner or judge, they would have a better chance of proving their right to be in the United States than they would before immigration officials in the regular admission proceedings.[117]

The Bureau of Immigration complained repeatedly about the provision for judicial hearings in Chinese deportation cases. Chinese facing deportation often alleged that they were citizens, the bureau explained, and the procedures used in court and the "manufactured evidence" presented by Chinese often resulted in their claims being upheld. The agency warned that judicial deportation hearings worked to defeat the policy of exclusion, usually resulting in "conferring the boon of citizenship upon the Chinese, and not only 'legalizing' his unlawful residence but laying the foundation for the introduction of his foreign-born children and their descendants to the remotest generation."[118] The bureau further argued that the deportation policy unduly favored Chinese over other aliens who were entitled only to an administrative hearing before deportation. The commissioner general of immigration urged Congress to place Chinese under the full jurisdiction of the agency in deportation as well as admission cases.[119]

In 1917 Congress did remove the provision allowing Chinese a judicial hearing in deportation cases.[120] In the meantime, the Bureau of Immigration took steps to circumvent judicial deportation hearings. In 1901, the bureau succeeded in getting Congress to pass a bill allowing the U.S. attorney to choose which U.S. commissioner would hear the deportation case.[121] Previously, the cases were brought before the nearest commissioner. The law made it possible for the government's attorneys to bring cases before U.S. commissioners who might be more sympathetic to exclusion. The bureau developed a more important strategy in 1908, however. After much internal debate about the legality of the strategy, the bureau began to arrest Chinese for deportation under the general immigration laws whenever possible rather than under the Chinese exclusion laws.[122] Their policy was upheld by the Supreme Court in 1912, though the Court later held that if the deportable offense came only under the Chinese exclusion law, a judicial hearing was still required.[123] The bureau reported in 1913 that its new policy was "producing most valuable results" in discouraging illegal entries.[124]

In the end, then, Chinese became subject to the same administrative discretion as other immigrants. That they were able to challenge the discretion for so long and with such success was largely the result of the organization and persistence of Chinese and their attorneys. They continually brought their cases before the courts, and they fashioned their claims according to Anglo-American legal traditions that courts found difficult to refuse. Though the judges approached the Chinese habeas corpus cases with divided loyalties, the logic and norms of the court as an institution proved stronger than politics.

Exclusionists had good reason to hope that their policies would be more effectively enforced with the Bureau of Immigration more firmly in control. The Department of Justice and the Bureau of Immigration had succeeded in blocking the "habeas corpus route" which for over twenty years had allowed Chinese to temper the effects of exclusion. Chinese could no longer use courts in the same manner to review the administrative decisions denying them entry. They had lost an important, albeit a somewhat reluctant, ally in their resistance to exclusion.

PART II

Executive Justice, 1905–1924

The struggle involving Chinese, government officials, and exclusionists that culminated in *Ju Toy* clearly emerged from particular problems and dissatisfactions with the exclusion policy. But the battle over exclusion had a broader dimension with far-reaching effects. Because both sides sought principled arguments to gird their strategic positions, the debate over exclusion had exposed tensions among individual rights and policy, means and results, alienage and citizenship, and judicial and administrative methods. In short, the debate had focused attention on the rise of administrative power and its implications for traditional Anglo-American jurisprudence. In resisting exclusion, Chinese had challenged not only the justice of the discriminatory policy but also the boundaries of administrative power in a nation that professed to be guided by the rule of law. Only the possibility of substantive judicial review, they had argued, provided the regularity of proceedings and the protection from arbitrary government action so crucial to the notion of the rule of law. Conversely, the Bureau of Immigration had questioned the efficacy of a rights-based, court-centered jurisprudence in the modern world, which required more vigorous, flexible government action to achieve immigration policy objectives and to protect the nation's interests.

By 1905, the Supreme Court had endorsed the government's position, greatly restricting judicial review and expanding the authoritativeness and finality of immigration officials' decisions. Yet, if anything, the bureau's new authority over alleged citizens only served to heighten concern about its power and to draw more attention to its methods. One must conclude from the Court's decision, said one observer, that "either . . . an administrative tribunal will protect the liberties of the individual as scrupulously as a judicial court, or that the citizen has been deprived of one of his greatest historic rights."[1]

If aliens and alleged citizens could no longer obtain a judicial hearing on their right to be in the United States, critics argued, it became imperative to reform the bureau's procedures and curb its discretion. In their view, administrative power could be reconciled with the rule of law only by securing a system of executive justice that approximated that of courts. Attacks on administrative procedure thus formed the core of a new strategy embraced by immigrants and their allies between 1905 and 1924.

Although Chinese in the West had played the most important role in testing administrative power before 1905, the struggle after 1905 involved a broader, more diffuse group of people, particularly as immigration from southern and eastern Europe reached record numbers. These immigrants encountered an increasingly hostile reception and became subject to increasingly restrictive legislation. As the number of excludable classes grew, so too did the challenges to the Bureau of Immigration's interpretations of the law and its summary procedures.

In forging their attacks on immigration procedure, critics had only dim prospects for success. Nativist sentiment and the growing emphasis on administrative efficiency threatened to overwhelm concern about aliens' rights. The doctrines established primarily in Chinese litigation before 1905 —the extraconstitutional status of aliens, the characterization of deportation as a civil proceeding, the plenary congressional power over immigration policy, and judicial deference to administrative findings—provided a feeble basis for a rights-based strategy. Nevertheless, for immigrants and alleged citizens, the Bureau of Immigration's methods involved issues of great strategic and symbolic importance which were well worth a fight.

Reflecting the broader-based challenge to the Bureau of Immigration after 1905, the scope of Part II broadens to examine the national debate over immigration law and procedure and to include the port of New York, in addition to San Francisco, as a case study in the enforcement of the laws. Chapter 5 provides an overview of immigration policy between 1905 and 1924, demonstrating how nativist policies that originated against Chinese proliferated against other Asians and Europeans. So too the summary administrative procedures developed first in enforcing Chinese exclusion became the norm in general immigration administration. The rights-based critique of the Bureau of Immigration which developed in response to its summary procedures is detailed in Chapter 6. Immigrants and their allies asserted the importance of procedural guarantees in administrative hearings and limits on administrative discretion to the preservation of the rule of law. But as Chapter 7 reveals, the rights-based critique failed to penetrate the judicial barriers established in earlier Chinese cases. Federal judges maintained sharp distinctions between courts and administrative agencies and between aliens and citizens and refused to impose judicial standards of due process upon immigration proceedings. Chapter 8 examines the consequences of judicial reluctance to intervene in immigration policy. Left to regulate itself, the Bureau of Immigration pursued only the most superficial or self-serving steps toward procedural reform, continually emphasizing the objectives of restrictive immigration laws over the rights of aliens.

CHAPTER 5

Drawing the Sieve Tighter

THE RISE OF NATIVISM

AND ADMINISTRATIVE POWER

Nativism made its first inroads into federal immigration policy with the enactment of the Chinese exclusion policy in the 1880s and the Immigration Act of 1891, as detailed in Chapter 1. Between 1891 and 1924, the nativist movement gained momentum, though often in fits and starts. The movement cast an increasingly wider net to sweep out Asian and "new immigrants" from southern and eastern Europe who appeared to undermine the nation's economic and social stability. Nativists revealed a growing concern that the "aliens in our midst" did not fit—racially, culturally, or politically—into the American community.[1] They sought new policies that would eliminate the misfits from American society. Nativism reached its peak with the passage of the Quota Acts of 1921 and 1924, which successfully barred the entry of the "undesirable" immigrants.

As the struggle between Chinese and administrators that led to the *Ju Toy* decision had demonstrated, the passage of restrictive immigration policies was not sufficient to achieve nativists' objectives. They also needed to pay close attention to how those policies were enforced. Particularly important to the effective enforcement of restrictive laws, given the success that Chinese had achieved in the courts before *Ju Toy*, the bureau had to remain free from traditional legal constraints. Thus the move toward tighter restrictions was accompanied by the expansion of the Bureau of Immigration's unhampered discretion to administer the Chinese and immigration laws without the stultifying requirements of judicial notions of due process. Just as nativists finally in 1924 got the legislation they had long sought, they also had by that point an agency with broad powers to effect their restrictionist policies.

THE "ALIENS IN OUR MIDST":
THE GROWTH OF NATIVISM

The same factors that had contributed to the passage of the earlier federal legislation were at play in the nativist movement between 1891 and 1924. A troubled economy often fostered anti-immigrant sentiment.[2] John Higham, in his detailed account of American nativism, associates the periodic waves of antiforeigner feeling with economic recessions and depressions. The severe depression between 1893 and 1897, for example, sparked violent attacks on immigrants from all sectors of society. Even the American Federation of Labor joined the restrictionists' ranks during this period. Before 1893, the labor organization had been ambivalent about restriction because many of its members, including its president, Samuel Gompers, were foreign-born. As the depression worsened, however, unions began to fear the immigrants' effect on the economy and the strength of labor organizations as well.[3] Outbursts against immigrants also occurred during the depression of 1913–14 and in the post–World War I era, when the war-boom economy collapsed.[4]

The state of the economy was a constant factor in the rise of nativism, yet fears that immigrants were contributing to the social and political disintegration of the United States played an increasingly important role in the antiforeigner movement. America in the late nineteenth and early twentieth centuries was becoming, in historian Robert Wiebe's words, a "distended society." The sweeping changes brought by industrialization and urbanization strained communities and traditional social structures. Many Americans no longer felt that they were part of a cohesive community. Rather than a nation of small-town neighbors, they were becoming a nation of urban strangers. The society was becoming sharply divided and disrupted by class tensions, labor unrest, and city violence. As Wiebe summarizes the period, "America in the late 19th century was a society without a core. . . . Americans in a basic sense no longer knew who or where they were."[5]

Middle-class Americans thought immigrants were at the heart of the problem. Immigrants appeared to be implicated in the most threatening aspects of the social disorder—poverty, labor unrest, and city slum life. Aliens were associated with a whole litany of other social concerns as well. The underworld Black-Hand society of Italians, the importation of "white slaves" and Asian prostitutes, and the stealthy infiltration of anarchists and other foreign radicals were all produced as evidence of the dangerous and disruptive character of the new immigrants.[6]

The foreignness of the new immigrants exacerbated nativists' fears. The

By the turn of the century, non-Chinese immigrants also confronted growing nativist sentiment, as illustrated in this cartoon calling for restrictions on immigration from Europe. Courtesy William Williams Papers, Rare Books and Manuscripts Division, New York Public Library, Astor, Lenox and Tilden Foundations.

floods of immigrants coming from Russia, Italy, Austria-Hungary, Poland, Greece, Japan, and India had one thing in common in the minds of Americans—they were *different* from the old native stock. The new immigrants wore exotic clothes, spoke different languages, and had customs that seemed strange. Their religions were disparate as well. America until this point had been predominantly Protestant. In contrast, many of the new immigrants were Catholic and Jewish, even Buddhist and Sikh.[7]

Perhaps the most striking difference, however, was the variety of the immigrants' ethnic and racial backgrounds. The racial theories brought forth in the 1880s in support of Chinese exclusion became an increasingly important mainstay in the nativist movement. The obsession with racial differences and classification continued in the early twentieth century, under the advocacy of the Immigration Restriction League, a nativist group composed of eastern intellectuals. The fear of "race suicide" resulting from the introduction of "inferior" races became a widespread topic in popular journals and books after 1905.[8] It even prompted Theodore Roosevelt to exhort "old stock" American mothers to have more children to prevent the death of the Anglo-Saxon race.[9]

The Bureau of Immigration revealed an increasing pessimism about the impact of the new ethnic mix. In his 1907 annual report, the commissioner general of immigration, Frank P. Sargent, merely raised "the question that must arise in the mind of any person . . . as to whether or not our ability as a race to absorb foreign elements is not on the verge, at least, of being overtaxed."[10] Two years later, the new commissioner general, Daniel J. Keefe, broached the subject with much more alarm, calling attention to the "increase in the influx of peoples so different racially from the original settlers of the country. . . . There can be but little homogeneity between the people of southern and eastern Europe and the real American."[11]

The growth of the eugenics movement in the early twentieth century provoked further doubts about America's ability to assimilate different racial and ethnic groups.[12] The eugenicists claimed that all physical, mental, and even social differences were hereditary. Various racial groups were inferior, they believed, because they had poor gene pools. Reflecting the growing influence of the eugenicists, the commissioner general of immigration in 1910 encouraged Congress to require more rigorous physical examinations of immigrants. He asked, rhetorically, "Can we expect, if we continue to inject into the veins of our nation the blood of ill-formed, undersized persons, as are so many of the immigrants now coming, that the American of tomorrow will be the sturdy man that he is today?"[13]

"Racial nativism" had particularly strong appeal in the West and South, presumably because of those regions' history of racial conflict and greater diversity of racial groups. Although easterners felt threatened by the different ethnic groups coming from eastern and southern Europe, an even greater diversity of people lived in the West, including Asians, Indians, and Hispanics, as well as the "new" immigrants. Historian Patricia Nelson Limerick remarks that compared to "the diverse humanity of Western America . . . the 'melting pot' of the Eastern United States at the turn of the century begins to look more like a family reunion, a meeting of groups with an essential similarity—dominantly European, Judeo-Christian, accustomed to the existence of the modern state."[14] The mere presence of a variety of racial groups is not sufficient to explain the fierce hold of racism on white westerners, however. Limerick puts forth two further reasons for such strong attitudes toward race in the West: "First, Americans came West with high hopes for improved personal fortune, hopes that carried both the seeds of disappointment and frustration and, not far beyond, the need for someone to blame. Second, scapegoats were everywhere at this crossroads of the planet, meeting ground of Europe, Asia, and Latin America."[15]

As Limerick suggests, the West, in the American imagination, promised a new start, the "manifest destiny" of white Americans. Chester H. Rowell, a leading California Progressive, summed up in 1909 the importance of the West: "The Pacific Coast is the frontier of the white man's world, the culmination of the westward migration which is the white man's whole history."[16] The *San Francisco Examiner* asserted in a similar vein, "California stands for a white civilization—for homes filled with prosperous and happy families . . .—for industries that will support men in the American standard of comfort, and for a population that will maintain an American standard of civilization."[17]

As the experience of Chinese in America reveals, Californians, and westerners in general, perceived Asians to be a particular threat to the white society's West.[18] By 1909, Californians generally considered Chinese to be a "disappearing problem," though several nativists kept up an almost obligatory anti-Chinese patter in their speeches and articles.[19] Western nativists became more absorbed with what they perceived as the newest Asian invasion—the arrival of immigrants from Japan and India.

Japanese began to leave their homes and come to the United States in significant numbers after 1891. Like many other immigrants, these Japanese immigrants tended to be farmers facing economic dislocation in their native lands. Four prefectures in southwestern Japan provided the greatest proportion of emigrants. Drawn by recruiters' promises of employment on sugar plantations, many Japanese from those provinces went to Hawaii. Later, they moved to the Pacific Coast of the United States and settled primarily in the agricultural regions of California, though some owned small businesses or worked as domestics in San Francisco and other western cities. By 1900, 27,000 Japanese had immigrated to the United States. In the next eight years, their numbers reached 127,000.[20]

Immigrants from India arrived somewhat later and in smaller numbers but were driven by similar economic factors. Most Indian immigrants were Sikhs from the Punjab, a farming region that had been stricken by drought, famine, and epidemics in the late 1800s. Like the Chinese in Kwangtung province, the economic survival of Indian families became increasingly dependent on the migration of their sons to other parts of the world. Indians also left for political reasons when some became involved in the mounting opposition to British colonial rule. They sought asylum in other countries and a base from which to organize their resistance to Britain.[21]

In the early 1900s Indians often immigrated to Canada first and then came south to the Pacific Northwest to work in the lumber mills. Eventually many moved down to the Sacramento, San Joaquin, and Imperial valleys in California, where they became railroad and agricultural laborers.[22] The number of Asian Indians coming to the United States began to increase in 1904, reaching an annual high of 1,710 in 1908. Despite the paranoiac claims of nativists, the number of Indians immigrating to the United States remained small, amounting to only 8,234 between 1899 and 1924.[23]

The arrival of the Japanese in the 1890s initially provoked little comment, though some, such as the commissioner of immigration at San Francisco, Hart H. North, kept a cautious eye on their immigration.[24] In agricultural regions of California, farm owners welcomed Japanese laborers who were willing to perform tedious, backbreaking farmwork "which must be performed in a temperature of 100 to 110 degrees." Proponents of Japanese immigration claimed that the Japanese assimilated more easily than did eastern Europeans. Japanese, according to an admiring commentator, Colonel John P. Irish, "are very industrious, frugal, temperate, and orderly, with quick wit and intellectual alertness" and would soon become thoroughly Americanized.[25]

The vast majority of Californians did not share that confidence, however, and became increasingly hostile as the number of Japanese and later Indian immigrants increased. For exclusionists, the new Asian immigrants raised the specter of the Yellow Peril first encountered with the arrival of Chinese. Reminiscent of the economic arguments made against Chinese, nativists accused Japanese immigrants of "invading" one occupation after another and endangering the livelihood of white men.[26] But the Japanese posed a greater economic threat than did the Chinese, in the eyes of nativists, because they competed more directly with white men and appeared to be more upwardly mobile. Californians became particularly alarmed when Japanese began to purchase land and establish themselves as farmers.[27] U.S. senator James D. Phelan of California warned, "[Japanese] are rapidly acquiring the most productive lands. . . . They know no rest and respect no standards." For Phelan and others, Japanese ownership of land represented a severe blow to American stability, for "the soil is the foundation of everything. Race, family, citizenship, thrift, prosperity, patriotism, success in peace and security in war—all rest upon the soil. Dispossess the people and they are condemned to poverty and vagabondage."[28]

Racial concerns exacerbated the economic threat. One journalist in 1913 described the "white flight" resulting from Japanese settlement in California farm towns. The white farm families did not want Japanese for their neighbors, he reported. "The white farmer's wife does not run in and sit down to gossip with the Japanese farmer's wife and she does not want the Japanese farmer's wife running in to gossip with her. Their children cannot play together. Jenny Brown cannot go for a buggy ride with Harry Hirada. The whole idea of social intercourse between the races is unthinkable."[29] While Californians worried about the influence of the Japanese in their midst, they also feared a more overt invasion by Japan. The victory of Japan over Russia in 1905 led many Americans both to respect and fear Japanese military strength. Paranoia that Japan would invade America became widespread in California, particularly after Homer Lea published a book in 1909 detailing the probable Japanese occupation of the West Coast.[30]

Attacks against Asian Indians were even more virulent because nativists regarded them as the "most objectionable of all the Orientals" who had come to the United States.[31] Anti-Asian groups trotted out the standard economic arguments, that cheap Indian laborers were taking the jobs of "Anglo-Saxons, Celts, Teutons, Slavs and members of other races who are part of the real population of the country" and destroying the American standard of living.[32] But nativists dwelled much more on racial and cultural objections to Indians, arguing that the immigrants were unsanitary, evil, dirty, and infected not only with exotic diseases but with un-American ideas of caste. Indians, or "Hindus" as Americans incorrectly referred to them, made "delightfully interesting fiction from the fascinating pen of Kipling," but the "half-starved, superstitious, caste-bound Hindus" had little appeal to Californians in reality.[33]

Despairing that the rest of the nation failed to perceive the gravity of the "Asian invasion," Californians did not hesitate to begin their own anti-Asian campaign. The *San Francisco Examiner* exclaimed, "Californians must step to the front once more and battle to hold the Pacific Coast for the white race."[34] Physical attacks on Japanese and Indians were not uncommon, and people throughout the Pacific Coast forcibly expelled Indians from their communities. By 1905, the Asiatic Exclusion League had organized to bar the new Asian immigration. In San Francisco the league organized boycotts of Japanese businesses and sponsored a law that segregated Asian and white children in city schools. It later put intense pressure on the commissioner of immigration at San Francisco, Hart H. North, to deny admission to Asian Indians. The state's Alien Land Laws of 1913 and 1920 aimed to prevent Japanese from buying further land in California.[35]

These actions met with significant success. The segregation of the San Francisco schools sparked a diplomatic crisis between Japan and the United States which resulted in the Gentlemen's Agreement in 1907. Through this executive negotiation, Theodore Roosevelt obtained Japan's cooperation in voluntarily restricting the immigration of Japanese laborers. Japan agreed to issue passports only to nonlaborers and to laborers who already had parents, spouses, or children living in the United States.[36] The pressure placed upon the commissioner of immigration at San Francisco regarding Indian immigration also yielded results. The Bureau of Immigration capitulated to Californians' demands in 1910, forcing the resignation of Commissioner North and using its discretion to make the admission of Indians very difficult.[37]

Although California nativists had clearly obtained significant victories in their anti-Asian campaign, they remained dissatisfied. The Gentlemen's Agreement proved to be too lax, in their view, because it allowed the immigration of many Japanese women whose marriages to Japanese men living in the United States had been performed by proxy in Japan. The so-called picture brides came to the United States to join their new husbands, whom most of them had never met. Californians and the Bureau of Immigration objected that the arrival of picture brides violated the spirit of the Gentlemen's Agreement by introducing laborers who competed unfairly with American workers. And even more distressing to western nativists, the increasing number of Japanese women resulted in a greater number of native-born Japanese who were American citizens.[38]

For Californians and other westerners, exclusion was the only solution.[39] It seemed only natural to most commentators that if Chinese were to be excluded, so should all other Asians, especially inasmuch as "the Chinese are infinitely preferable" to other Asians, particularly "the Hindoos."[40] Walter Macarthur, editor of a prominent labor newspaper in San Francisco, advocated exclusion as "the only alternative [to] race degeneracy or race war." In demanding exclusion, Macarthur claimed he had the support of the master race theorist, Herbert Spencer. Macarthur quoted a letter allegedly written by Spencer, saying, "I have entirely approved of the regulations which have been established in America for restricting Chinese immigration. . . . If the Chinese are allowed to settle extensively . . . immense social mischief must arise and eventually social disorganization. The same thing would happen if there should be any considerable mixture of European races with the Japanese."[41]

Asians were the principal victims of nativism on the West Coast and in the mountain states, but southern and eastern Europeans also became targets of antiforeigner hostility, as did Mexicans. Labor groups in San Francisco had supported the restriction of Italian immigrants as early as 1890.[42] Such sentiments became more widespread after 1900, when the new immigrants began to migrate to the West in larger numbers. California became an increasingly popular destination for immigrants from Italy, Portugal, Armenia, and Russia.[43] Between 1900 and 1910, the number of southern and eastern Europeans living in the Far West more than tripled.[44] The *Santa Barbara Star* complained in 1910, "We are . . . getting more than enough indigestibles from the Balkan Peninsula and other parts of Southern Europe."[45] The popular novels of Californian Jack London portrayed southern and eastern Europeans as dire threats to the survival of the Anglo-Saxon race.[46] Chester Harvey Rowell, a leader in the anti-Japanese movement, considered southern Europeans on a par with the Japanese and argued that the campaign for Japanese exclusion should be made part of a general movement for immigration restriction. Nothing could be done about the Japanese, he argued, "until we can arouse the sentiment of the East, not on the Japanese question alone, but on the whole menace of unfit immigration."[47] Western nativists thus embraced a strict restrictionist approach toward immigration early on and consistently backed anti-immigrant legislation in Congress.[48]

Western nativists were somewhat less strident, at least until the 1920s, about the immigration from neighboring Mexico. Mexican immigrants began to cross the border in record numbers after 1900 to work in the booming commercial agricultural industry (principally in California), but their arrival did not provoke the same degree of antipathy as did Asian immigration. Historian Lawrence A. Cardoso argues that "Mexican immigration was perceived as distinct from that of other groups even in the eyes of the most rabid race determinists."[49] Mexicans were considered "safe" both because they were more familiar to western Anglos and because they were believed to pose less of a threat to the status quo. It was believed that Mexicans did not intend to become long-term residents but would return to Mexico after each farming season. There seemed little to fear from such immigrants and, in the view of agribusiness, much to be gained. Consequently, Mexican immigrants met little resistance when they came north until the 1920s, when the nativist movement reached its peak.[50]

Although nativism ran rampant in regions such as the Far West and among some sectors of the eastern intellectual community and the labor unions, the movement was not strong enough to secure stringent restrictionist legislation until World War I and its aftermath. Before World War I nativists encountered the determined opposition of immigrants and their industrial employers. As immigrants became naturalized citizens and voters, politicians found they had a new constituency to consider when restrictionist bills were proposed.[51] Furthermore, the liberal faith in an open immigration policy still lingered, and a sympathetic view of the new immigrants was encouraged by popular tales of their experiences.[52] Many people continued to believe that with guidance and support, the new immigrants could become good Americans. The settlement houses, for example, stressed the richness of the diverse immigrant cultures but tried to give immigrants skills to smooth their adaptation to their new home. These Progressives emphasized the influence of environment over biology, believing that all people could be "Americanized" once given the proper instruction and surroundings.[53]

Nativists thus were forced to restrict immigration in a piecemeal fashion. They continued the pattern established in the late nineteenth century of excluding immigrants with the most undesirable characteristics. The list of excludable classes eventually grew quite long. Economic considerations had been at the root of much of the early state and national immigration legislation, and such concerns continued to be important in the policies of the early twentieth century.[54] The exclusion of those "likely to become a public charge," a provision enacted in 1882, became the primary ground for barring aliens entry into the United States at the turn of the century. The law was used to protect American society from undue financial burdens but also, more broadly, to control American economic and social conditions.[55]

Closely tied to the economic provisions were the laws restricting the admission of aliens with physical and mental defects. The United States at various times excluded aliens who were mentally retarded, insane, feeble-minded, mentally defective, infected with a dangerous, contagious disease, epileptics, afflicted with a physical defect that affected their ability to earn a living, and chronic alcoholics.[56] A concern that mental and physical "defectives" would become public charges clearly motivated these policies in part, particularly the law that made the physical ability of an alien to make a living the test for admission. Other provisions, such as the exclusion of those with diseases, were framed as public health issues. But increasingly in the early 1900s, lawmakers and nativists justified the policy on biological grounds, accepting the eugenicists' argument that by excluding mental and physical defectives, they would prevent the deterioration of the American mind and body. The commissioner general of immigration in 1914 pushed for even greater restrictions, arguing, "Medical science has demonstrated that many, if not all, of these serious [mental] deficiencies are handed down from generation to generation, with steady increase in the strain; so that the importance of rejecting and expelling aliens of this class . . . can hardly be overstated."[57]

"Moral defectives" were the targets of another group of immigration laws. Prostitutes and convicted felons were the objects of the first restrictive immigration law in 1875, and later legislation further restricted their entry.[58] In 1891, Congress forbade the entry of aliens convicted of a crime involving "moral turpitude" and also denied admission to polygamists.[59] Alien prostitutes received increased attention, especially as reformers in the United States undertook campaigns to wipe out prostitution. Immigrant women coming to the United States were suspected of being "recruited by the human demons who seduce or buy the girls" in Europe and then brought them to the United States to be sold into prostitution.[60] In 1907, Congress broadened the immigration laws to exclude not only prostitutes but any woman coming to the United States for "immoral purposes" and those who brought the women into the country.[61]

Finally, the immigration laws penalized aliens for their political beliefs. The Immigration Act of 1903 excluded anarchists "or persons who believe in or advocate the overthrow by force or violence of the Government of the United States or, of all government, or of all forms of law, or the assassination of public officials."[62] An antiradical contingent of nativists had been arguing for such a provision for over a decade before it was adopted. A congressional committee had warned in 1889 that anarchists were being expelled from European countries and might be headed for the United States. Many Americans blamed the increased labor unrest on the infiltration of foreign radicals. The assassination of President William McKinley by an anarchist brought further wrath against foreign radicals and led to their exclusion in the 1903 law.[63]

Exclusion was not the nativists' only weapon. Deportation also became an ever more popular way to weed out and control undesirable immigrants. In 1891, the United States first embarked upon a policy of deportation when it allowed the expulsion of aliens who became public charges within one year of landing for causes existing before they landed. The time limit for deportation after landing gradually was extended from two to three and, finally, in 1917, to five years.[64] In 1910, the same year Congress passed the Mann Act aimed at "white slavery," the United States lifted the time limit for deporting alien prostitutes. They were subject to deportation at any time, regardless of the number of years they had spent in the United States and the lives they had built. The extended deportation time was an attempt to monitor the behavior of new immigrants and to shape the character of the American community. The Bureau of Immigration firmly supported a strong deportation policy, asking, "Why should any limitation be placed upon the Government's inherent right to remove them to the country of which they are citizens or subjects?"[65]

The move to lengthen and remove the deportation time limits reflects a change in the status of aliens in the United States and a growing tension regarding the constitution of the American community. Previous laws that set time limits on deportation seemingly operated on the theory that the longer aliens lived in the United States, the greater would be their economic, emotional, and political stake in America. The resident alien was more akin to a citizen than to the new immigrant in status.[66] Under this theory, deportation at any time would be an unfair hardship upon the resident alien. The move to extend the time limit weakened distinctions between newly arrived aliens and aliens who were longtime residents of the United States and created a sharper distinction between aliens and citizens. It signaled a growing intolerance of a foreign presence in the United States and reflected fears that aliens would remain alien to the American way of life. Such pessimism was particularly felt by Americans who believed that biology determined human characteristics. According to biological determinists, aliens were physically and mentally incapable of becoming American. Other Americans who believed in the positive force of environment in shaping people also worried about the foreignness of the aliens. They wanted aliens to shed their foreign ways as quickly as possible and to become good Americans.[67] One judge exclaimed, "The immigrant who won't get into our melting pot and melt—who does not Americanize in five years, is not desired."[68]

The extension of the deportation time limit responded to the concerns of both the determinists and the Americanizers by allowing the government to expel dangerous aliens before they "contaminated" the body politic. The policy further forced aliens either to become citizens with the incumbent responsibilities and privileges or to remain aliens subject to greater control.

Though harsh in many respects, the admission and deportation laws in force before World War I did not keep many immigrants out of the United States. In 1914, the year before the war began to affect immigration to the United States, the bureau denied admission to 2.3 percent of aliens, the highest proportion of non-Asian immigrants rejected up to that date.[69] It was also a banner year for deportation. The number of deportations rapidly increased beginning in 1908 after the time limit had been extended, and deportations reached an all-time high of 4,610 in 1914.[70] These events in the year before the war reflected the growing momentum of the nativist movement but did not significantly reduce or stem the flow of immigrants.

Significant restrictions on immigration occurred only with the antiforeigner frenzy whipped up during World War I. The "war for democracy" engendered an intense nationalism and a corresponding deep fear of disunity or disloyalty. The slogans from the war period demanded "Unqualified Loyalty" and "100 per cent Americanism." Such sentiments were directed particularly at the German Americans but also at all "hyphenates" who might be harboring ties to their native lands. Through repression and even violence, nativists pressured the foreign-born to become completely "Americanized" and to swear their loyalty to the United States. The war also brought antiradicalism to the fore of nativism. Hostility toward radicals had been growing since 1910, largely in response to the organizing activities of the Industrial Workers of the World (IWW). When war broke out in Europe, socialists and the IWW protested United States involvement and stressed class loyalty over nationalism. Their stance unleashed the fury of pro-war Americans who interpreted their actions as intensely disloyal and subversive.[71]

This context of suspicion and paranoia enabled nativists to obtain in the Immigration Act of 1917 some of the restrictionist policies they had long advocated. A literacy test for adult immigrants was one of their most important victories. The Immigration Restriction League had urged such a test since the 1890s, perceiving it as an indirect method of reducing immigration from southern and eastern Europe.[72] The 1917 law also bowed to the West Coast's demands for the exclusion of Asian Indians. Hesitant to exclude them directly on the grounds of race, Congress created a "barred zone," denying admission to aliens living within a certain geographical area. The "Asiatic Barred Zone" included India, Burma, Siam, the Malay States, Arabia, Afghanistan, part of Russia, and most of the Polynesian Islands.[73] Finally, the act of 1917 tightened restrictions on suspected radicals, excluding not only those who actually advocated violent revolution but also those who belonged to revolutionary or anarchistic organizations.[74]

The antiforeigner hysteria did not subside with the end of the war. If anything, antiradicalism, prompted by reverberations of the Russian Revolution and by domestic strife, reached new heights and gave way to the Red Scare of 1919.[75] Tensions between workers and employers—temporarily capped during the war—exploded after the war. Strikes and race riots erupted throughout the United States. Employer organizations and patriotic groups such as the newly formed American Legion blamed the disruptions once again on the foreign radicals who, they claimed, infected American workers with Bolshevik ideas.[76]

Nativists fastened on deportation as the key tool to rid the United States of the radicals' influence. Consequently, in the ensuing Red Scare between 1919 and 1920, the Bureau of Immigration and the Department of Justice came to play a prominent part in rooting out and expelling foreign radicals.

Commissioner General of Immigration Anthony Caminetti, a Californian, and Attorney General A. Mitchell Palmer led the assault on radicalism and arrested thousands of suspected alien radicals.[77] In one month alone, the acting secretary of labor issued more than three thousand warrants for the arrest of suspected alien radicals.[78] Between November 1919 and June 1920, the Bureau of Immigration ordered 802 accused anarchists and communists deported on the basis of its summary hearings. Many more would have been deported if not for the assistant secretary of labor, Louis F. Post, who disapproved of the "deportation delirium" and canceled many of the warrants for deportation.[79] Increasingly, too, prominent Americans and newspapers became disenchanted with the deportation craze and criticized the actions of administrative officials.[80]

The Red Scare soon subsided, but the desire for anti-immigrant legislation remained strong. By 1920, the war-boom economy had begun to collapse and immigration from Europe had revived.[81] Nativists found widespread support for restrictionist policies, though divisions remained as to how to restrain immigration. One proposal to suspend immigration failed in large part because of opposition from business interests. The Bureau of Immigration cautioned against suspension not only because of its "injurious effect" on American commercial interests but also because of the administrative difficulties involved. Though the proposed bill suspended immigration, it exempted certain people. Those exemptions, claimed the bureau, "would in fact produce . . . the same conditions and difficulties that are now encountered in the administration of the Chinese-exclusion law."[82]

A restrictive quota plan garnered more support than total suspension. The Quota Act of 1921, described by the commissioner general of immigration as "one of the most radical and far-reaching events in the annals of immigration legislation," was the first law successfully to restrict the volume of "new" immigrants from southern and eastern Europe.[83] The act limited European immigration to 3 percent of the number of foreign-born people of each nationality residing in the United States in 1910.[84] By 1923, the commissioner general of immigration proclaimed the Quota Act a success. Comparing the proportion of "old" and "new" immigrants admitted to the United States in 1914 and 1923, the commissioner general revealed that the percentage of southern and eastern European immigrants landed had decreased from 75.6 percent of the total immigration in 1914 to 31.1 percent in 1923. Conversely, the proportion of northern and western Europeans admitted had increased from 20.8 percent to 52.5 percent of the total immigrants landed.[85]

Such figures pleased nativists, but anti-immigrant groups still were not satisfied. They approved of the quota policy but wanted to reduce the number of immigrants even further. The Immigration Act of 1924 represented a compromise between the two houses of Congress. The act reduced the percentage admitted from 3 to 2 and made the base population the number of foreign-born of each nationality present in the United States in 1890 instead of 1910. This provision was clearly aimed at southern and eastern Europeans because relatively few immigrants from those regions had lived in the United States in 1890. The Senate, uncomfortable with such explicit discrimination, allowed the new 2 percent quota with the proviso that a new "national origins" test would be used beginning in 1927. The national origins provision appeared to be more fair but actually was just as restrictive, if not more so. It placed a cap on the total number of immigrants, limiting admissions to 150,000 each year. The law determined the number of immigrants allowed per nationality based on the 1920 census. But instead of using the number of foreign-born as its measure, the law divided the quotas based on the proportion of each "national stock," thus including both native and foreign-born people. This gave a definite edge to "old stock" Americans over the new immigrant population.[86]

The 1924 act also furthered the exclusion of Asians.[87] Though the law barred all aliens from entering the country who were "ineligible for citizenship" (i.e., those to whom naturalization was denied), Japanese immigrants were the real targets of the act because Chinese and Asian Indians had already been excluded. The Supreme Court in 1922 had decided that Japanese were not entitled to naturalization.[88] Congress probably chose to exclude Japanese through the phrase "ineligible for citizenship" for the same reason it excluded Indians via the "barred zone" provision in 1917: the devices seemed less blatantly offensive and more objective. The Japanese government was not fooled by the wording, however, and it lodged strong protests with the American government. But the western states were happy, having finally achieved the policy they had been seeking for over twenty years.[89]

The nativist campaign reached the pinnacle of its success with the act of 1924. Millions of immigrants had settled in the United States between 1880 and 1924, forever and drastically changing the nation's demography. Nativists could not alter that fact, but since the passage of the Chinese Exclusion Act in 1882, they had successfully used restriction and deportation laws to prune and mold American society. From a movement popular only in certain regions and social sectors, nativism had become an intense, nationwide phenomenon by the end of the war. Upon the strength of that movement, policy makers were able to put an effective end to the immigration considered to be the most racially, culturally, and politically threatening.

Just as the principles of exclusion and deportation had been established first with the Chinese and then expanded to other aliens considered undesirable, so too the summary administrative procedures sanctioned by the Supreme Court in the Chinese exclusion cases became the norm in the administration of the general immigration laws.[90] The Supreme Court's decisions in *Chae Chan Ping* and *Fong Yue Ting* were crucial to the proliferation of immigration procedures which Chinese and non-Chinese immigrants alike would refer to as "Star Chamber" proceedings. The "inherent sovereign power" doctrine enunciated in the former case became the foundation for the absolute power of Congress and, by delegation, the immigration officials, to exclude and deport aliens. The doctrine further justified, in the Court's opinion, the power of Congress and administrative officials to adopt procedures and regulations, however summary, to accomplish their tasks of exclusion and deportation. As the Court had made clear in *Fong Yue Ting* and *Nishimura Ekiu*, residence in the United States was a privilege extended to aliens and could be denied or revoked at any time, for any reason, and, it would seem, by almost any method that Congress specified.[91]

The Bureau of Immigration at times acknowledged that "the laws we are administering affect human rights and liberty" and took occasional steps to ensure immigrants a fair hearing; but its procedures aimed primarily to achieve the specific policy objectives embodied in restrictive legislation rather than to protect the individual rights of aliens.[92] The admission and deportation procedures followed by the Bureau of Immigration deviated significantly from the norms of due process elaborated in Anglo-American jurisprudence. As one critic succinctly noted, "The safeguards of a judicial trial are conspicuously lacking."[93]

Even in deportation hearings, which afforded the alien somewhat greater protection than admission proceedings, procedures appeared to be devised "with a maximum of powers in the administrative officers, a minimum of checks and safeguards against error and prejudice, and with certainty, care, and due deliberation sacrificed to the desire for speed."[94] Because the Supreme Court did not consider deportation a punishment for a crime but simply "a method of enforcing the return to his country of an alien," the Bureau of Immigration was not bound by the principles and prohibitions in the Bill of Rights which governed criminal proceedings.[95] Thus warrants were often issued without probable cause, bail was often excessive and detentions lengthy, and the evidence accepted was as loose and informal as that used in exclusion cases.[96] And the Bureau of Immigration's operations remained largely free of judicial review. One federal judge wryly remarked, "If the Commissioners [of immigration] wish to order an alien drawn, quartered, and chucked overboard they could do so without interference."[97]

As nativism gained momentum in the aftermath of World War I, the Bureau of Immigration revealed its willingness to use its discretion and summary proceedings to help rid the country of undesirable aliens. When the bureau joined forces with the Department of Justice to arrest and deport suspected radicals in 1919, the result, in the words of historian William Preston, was "a large-scale . . . violation of fundamental rights."[98] Such procedures provoked harsh criticism from several quarters, but as Preston notes, the bureau's actions in the "deportation delirium" were a natural outgrowth of the practices it had adopted and fine-tuned over many years.[99]

Such discretion had grown unchecked, in Preston's opinion, because the administration's procedures had been sanctioned by the Supreme Court and were "unrestrained by publicity or opposition." Preston argues that the aliens who came under the aegis of the bureau were largely outcasts— "prostitutes, procurers, lunatics, idiots, paupers . . . Chinese and Japanese. These were in the main friendless, despised, ignorant, defenseless people, and more important, *unorganized*." Thus, Preston concludes, they were unable to "make the protests that might have advertised the procedure and forced its reconsideration by the government" before the bureau unleashed its power on suspected radicals in 1919.[100]

For anyone familiar with the Chinese resistance to exclusion, Preston's account of the rise of the bureau's discretion strikes a wrong chord. For the Chinese, as we have seen, were anything but unorganized and defenseless. They had been extraordinarily resourceful in their battle against exclusion, relying on litigation, civil disobedience, and political negotiation. And they would continue to rely on these strategies in the years after *Ju Toy* in the attempt to force the Bureau of Immigration to afford them greater procedural protections. Other aliens, with the assistance of immigrant aid societies and public-spirited lawyers such as Max Kohler, also complained loudly and persistently about the bureau's methods and sought to change procedures through litigation and by lobbying Congress and the administration.[101] As the next chapter amply illustrates, there was no lack of protest on the part of aliens, though, undeniably, they were often outcasts in the eyes of the law.

Rather than the lack of organized protest on the part of aliens, the grip that nativism had on the country would appear to have played a greater role in the rise of the bureau's discretion. Anxiety over the "foreign" influence tended to overwhelm consideration of aliens' rights. What obligations did the United States have toward noncitizens, many of whom seemed to pose a threat to the nation just by the fact of their foreignness? The answer of nativists was "none." The earlier liberal belief in the international human right to migrate and to begin a new life had been trumped in the nativist era by the inherent national right of self-preservation and self-determination. In remarks aimed particularly at suspected alien radicals, Congressman Albert Johnson, chairman of the House Committee on Immigration and Naturalization, argued that constitutional rights were to be protected *from* aliens rather than be extended to them: "Free press is ours, not theirs; free speech is ours, not theirs, and they have gone just as far as we can let them go toward running over our most precious rights."[102] In such an atmosphere, most Americans were more concerned that the bureau be allowed to guard their gates effectively than that aliens be afforded greater procedural rights. Even after the well-publicized actions of the immigration officers in 1919, a fairly well-organized and well-positioned opposition group, in Preston's estimation, was unable to secure long-lasting reforms in the bureau's procedures.[103]

Thus in their challenges to the Bureau of Immigration's discretion, immigrants were fighting a battle they would ultimately lose. But the battle is worth examining, not only to recognize the efforts of immigrants and attorneys, which is important, but also because it is vital to understanding how the bureau came to exercise such unbridled discretion over its affairs and how judges and officials reconciled the summary administrative procedures employed by the bureau with traditional notions of due process and the rule of law.

CHAPTER 6

Bureaucratic Tyranny

THE BUREAU OF

IMMIGRATION AND

ITS CRITICS

Given the outcome in *Ju Toy*, it is not surprising that Commissioner General of Immigration Frank P. Sargent expressed great satisfaction in his annual report for 1905 with the agency's administration of Chinese exclusion. "In no [other] branch of its widespread activities," crowed Sargent, has the bureau "so thoroughly succeeded in carrying into effective operation the purpose of the laws." Yet he devoted the remainder of his report on Chinese exclusion to defending the bureau against severe criticisms mounted by "a large and somewhat vociferous element" who opposed the policy and denounced officials responsible for its enforcement.[1] Indeed, the bureau had only a few days to enjoy its victory in *Ju Toy* before Chinese launched a dramatic boycott of American goods, largely in protest against the Bureau of Immigration's treatment of them. Any hope that the bureau had that *Ju Toy* would end the struggle over Chinese exclusion was soon dashed by the boycott.

Ironically, the agency's success in the litigation leading up to *Ju Toy* provided the very impetus for new, broad-based challenges to its authority. The bureau had emerged in 1905 as an agency with unusual power over both aliens and alleged citizens. In the words of one critic, the Supreme Court had "emancipated" the Bureau of Immigration from the federal courts and, in its sanctioning of summary administrative methods, had loosened the hold of constitutional and judicial norms. Immediately preceding *Ju Toy*, well-publicized cases involving both Chinese and non-Chinese immigrants had generated concern about the possible abuses of administrative power; such fears only increased as the decision granted even greater authority to the agency's determinations and narrowed opportunities for judicial review.

As this chapter details, ethnic organizations and immigration lawyers in the aftermath of *Ju Toy* translated these fears into a well-articulated critique of the "bureaucratic tyranny" exercised by the agency. If judicial justice had been eclipsed, they argued, it was crucial to perfect a system of "administrative justice" which would hedge the Bureau of Immigration with the same procedural protections and judicial attitudes found in courts. Sargent's defensive posture in 1905 suggests the success of pro-immigrant groups in making their complaints heard. John Higham notes that despite a general rise in nativism, in the first decade of the twentieth century its hold on American policy ebbed and was challenged by "a fiercer, more militant immigrant opposition."[2] Moreover, this immigrant opposition proved adept at drawing the support of certain sectors of the American middle class. After describing the Bureau of Immigration's procedures in place by 1905 and their rationale, this chapter explores the immigrants' critique of the procedures and the strategies they used to mobilize public opinion against the agency's methods.

PROCEDURES IN THE BUREAU OF IMMIGRATION

In October 1903, John Turner, a labor organizer from England, arrived in the United States to deliver a series of lectures and to visit family. He planned to speak to a variety of organizations—the Brooklyn Philosophical Association, the Women's Henry George Club, and the Manhattan Liberal Club—with talks titled "Socialism and Politics," "The Essentials of Anarchism," and "The Legal Murder of 1887." Such topics were certain to be controversial, considering the antiradical furor unleashed after an anarchist assassinated President McKinley in 1901.[3] On the evening of October 23, Turner gave his first speech, "Trade Unionism and the General Strike," before a gathering at the Murray Hill Lyceum in New York City. Among the interested listeners were immigration inspectors Joseph Weldon and John J. McKee, who diligently took notes on Turner's impassioned speech. As Turner left the building, Weldon and McKee, armed with a warrant from the secretary of commerce and labor issued on October 19, arrested and searched him, confiscating various papers related to his lecture circuit. They brought Turner to Ellis Island for deportation proceedings, charging him with being an alien anarchist, a class Congress had excluded in the wake of McKinley's assassination.[4]

The next day, a board of special inquiry convened at noon to investigate whether Turner should be deported as an anarchist. The boards of special inquiry had been created by Congress in 1893 to hear deportation cases as well as cases in which aliens applying for admission were not "clearly and beyond a doubt entitled to land."[5] Each board consisted of three inspectors appointed by the local commissioner of immigration; members of the board were expected to be thoroughly acquainted with the immigration laws and regulations but were not required to be trained lawyers. Similarly, though the board had a "quasi-judicial nature," it did not follow judicial procedures.[6] The hearings were "separate and apart from the public," and the alien was not entitled by law or regulation to have an attorney or representative present or to subpoena witnesses or evidence on his behalf. Neither did the boards separate the functions of the inspectors as investigators and judges. In Turner's case, for example, one of the arresting officers giving testimony against him, Joseph Weldon, was also a member of the board of special inquiry deciding his case. Unlike in a court hearing, the roles of policeman, prosecutor, and judge were blended in the board of special inquiry.

Turner arrived at the hearing hours after his arrest without the benefit of an attorney's advice or representation to confront the evidence the inspectors had marshaled against him. Turner's own speech constituted the key evidence. Inspectors McKee and Weldon testified that in the course of his speech, Turner had said, "All over Europe they are preparing for a general strike . . . the employers are organizing, and to me, at any rate, *as an anarchist*, as one who feels that the people must emancipate themselves, I look forward to this struggle as an opportunity for the workers to assert the power that is really theirs."[7] The papers confiscated from Turner contained other damning material, thought the board members. The papers included an advertisement for one of Turner's lectures, "The Essentials of Anarchism," in a newspaper purporting to be "a periodical of anarchist thought, work and literature" and a quote from an announcement alleging that Turner had recently refused a candidacy to Parliament "because of his anarchistic principles."[8]

To the board, the case appeared to be an easy one. Both inspectors had heard Turner call himself an anarchist, and the papers taken from him suggested that he was associated with anarchism. Turner did not deny that association. When asked if, in his speech, he had called himself an anarchist, he replied that "it is a very probable statement—a statement that I would make."[9] Based on his testimony and the evidence submitted, the board voted unanimously to deport him as an alien anarchist. The hearing appears to have taken little time. The minutes consist of barely four pages of typescript. Two days later, the secretary of commerce and labor issued a warrant for his deportation. Turner would eventually be deported but only after his case had been appealed to the Supreme Court.

Turner was just one among hundreds of aliens ordered deported in 1903, yet, for a short time, he became a cause célèbre. The *New York Times* reported that on two separate occasions, protesters filled Cooper Union to object to Turner's fate at the hands of the immigration officials.[10] Such protest reflected the particular circumstances involved in Turner's case. American labor groups rallied around Turner, the chief organizer for the National Shop Assistants Union in England, because they saw in "the attempt to deport John Turner not merely a move against the undesirable element, but an attack on trade unionists and trades unionism."[11] Liberal intellectuals and free speech advocates joined in the condemnation of Turner's deportation because they saw the law of 1903 as imposing unconstitutional limits on political belief and advocacy. Because of the general principles at stake, the Free Speech League of New York hired attorneys Edgar Lee Masters and Clarence Darrow to fight Turner's deportation.[12]

Although the clamor against Turner's deportation was unique in several respects, the protesters articulated many criticisms of the bureau's methods which applied to all deportation cases and would persist over the years. "Nothing," said Turner's attorneys, Darrow and Masters, could be "more repugnant to the right of due process of law" than the deportation proceedings followed by the Bureau of Immigration. In their opinion, officials had violated almost all of the fundamental rights afforded persons in the Bill of Rights. After noting that the warrant to arrest Turner was issued before he had done anything for which he could be deported, thus violating the necessity that warrants be issued only on probable cause, Masters and Darrow went on to recapitulate the proceedings: "[Turner] was seized at the conclusion of a lecture by a federal inspector. He was searched. He was taken before a board of 'Special Inquiry' composed of his jailers, his prosecutors and the witnesses against him. He was tried in secret. He was subjected to an inquisition; and informed that the laws contemplated that he should give the immigration officers whatever information they desired." "If this is due process of law," concluded the attorneys, "any sort of an examination is due process of law."[13]

Critics also protested the discretion wielded by immigration officials in interpreting the law. The law of 1903 excluded "anarchists, or persons who believe in or advocate the overthrow by force or violence of the Government of the United States or of all government or of all forms of law, or the assassination of public officials."[14] Inspectors appeared to have little trouble applying the law, operating on the assumption that if Turner admitted to being an anarchist, he must be an anarchist under the law. Critics argued, however, that the law was aimed at those who believed in the violent and forceful overthrow of the government; not all anarchists embraced such beliefs. One person making such an argument was Louis F. Post, then an editor of a weekly publication, who would later, as the assistant secretary of labor, become more intimately involved in the affairs of the Bureau of Immigration and Naturalization. Post and others who knew Turner argued that he did not support the violent overthrow of any government but rather "expressed the most peaceable theories" and was an anarchist only insofar as he opposed the "direct government of man by man as the political ideal" and believed in "absolute individual liberty."[15]

As his case made its way through the federal judiciary, Turner grew "tired of the whole affair," saying he "would willingly leave the country as soon as he was free."[16] The Supreme Court soon obliged Turner, bringing the legal challenge to an end by upholding the bureau's order of deportation in May 1904. The Court easily dismissed the due process arguments, returning to the premises of the *Fong Yue Ting* decision that aliens were not entitled to the specific constitutional protections guaranteed in the Bill of Rights. The Court also found nothing amiss in the bureau's decision that Turner was an anarchist under the law of 1903, holding that Congress had made no distinction in the act between "philosophical" and other anarchists.[17]

The bureau's treatment of John Turner, though denounced by his indignant defenders, had not been unusual but rather standard operating procedure. The doctrines established in the early Chinese and other immigration cases had served to loosen immigration procedures from constitutional moorings. By 1905, the summary administrative hearing, devoid of most procedural protections, coupled with the agency's broad discretion to interpret and administer the law, characterized proceedings involving admission as well as deportation, Chinese as well as non-Chinese.

The Bureau of Immigration revealed little concern about its summary procedures, viewing them as necessary and appropriate to the agency's gatekeeping role. In officials' eyes, American immigration policy remained too lax and the procedures followed by the agency were unsatisfactory only because they failed to catch excludable aliens.[18] Commissioner General of Immigration Frank P. Sargent called in 1905 for "closer inspection and greater restriction of immigrants" and for more official discretion in enforcing the laws. His commissioner at Ellis Island, William Williams, shared his sentiments, arguing in 1903, "Aliens have no inherent right whatever to come here, and we may and should take means however radical or drastic, to keep out all below a certain physical and economic standard of fitness and all whose presence will tend to lower our standards of living and civilization."[19]

Agency officials believed their rapidly expanding workload also necessitated summary methods. The bureau exercised jurisdiction over Chinese as well as non-Chinese, over alleged citizens as well as aliens. In 1906, the bureau took on additional responsibilities to enforce federal naturalization legislation, hence the change in its title to the Bureau of Immigration and Naturalization. As the duties of the bureau expanded, so too did the workload and the size of the bureaucracy. In 1891, when the bureau was created, the central office consisted of the superintendent of immigration, a chief clerk, and two assistant clerks. By 1906, the Washington, D.C., office had 25 employees. Local immigration stations had much larger staffs, Ellis Island employing a force of 523 in 1911.[20] Local commissioners of immigration stressed the huge volume of work undertaken by their staff, in large part a result of the increasing number of immigrants coming through their ports. Fiorello H. La Guardia, hired as an interpreter at Ellis Island in 1906, remembered that for at least two years, employees at Ellis Island worked seven days a week.[21] The commissioner at Ellis Island, William Williams, tried to impress upon Commissioner General Sargent the great demands upon his large staff in 1904:

> The sending down to the Bay to board sometimes twelve vessels in one day, the inspection often of 5000 immigrants per diem, the hearing sometimes of 400 special inquiry cases a day, the daily board minutes of 160 to 190 close lined typewritten pages written out from stenographic notes, attending to 2000 people who may come here from New York in one day and fill the large outside waiting room to overflowing, the caring for and guarding of sometimes as many as 1800 people overnight, the placing on board of several ships in one day of over 150 people for deportation, the correct annual distribution of 30,000 telegrams relating to immigration,—these are a *few* of the larger items of work that present themselves frequently at the same time.[22]

San Francisco did not have nearly as many immigrants coming through its port, yet its commissioner of immigration also felt overwhelmed at times with the demands on his staff.[23] The procedures in Chinese admission and deportation cases were particularly labor-intensive, requiring much more paperwork and field investigations than did non-Chinese cases. In years in which Chinese applications for entry were particularly heavy, as in 1909, officials at San Francisco were hard-pressed to complete their investigations in a thorough and timely manner.[24] In a diary entry in 1917, Inspector John Sawyer expressed his frustration with the "way an inspector is sometimes driven in his work" in handling Chinese cases at San Francisco. Saying, "I think it is enough to sleep and eat with ears or eyes directed at an alarm clock without also doing all one's official work timed with a stop watch," Sawyer soon applied for a transfer to a less busy station.[25]

Confronted with such heavy demands on their workforce and the desire to maximize the restrictive thrust of the laws, immigration officials at each port devised procedures and rules designed to process aliens as quickly and efficiently as possible, sifting out the "desirable" from the "undesirable" and excludable classes. With as many as five thousand immigrants streaming through the station at Ellis Island in one day, immigration procedures, from the bureau's perspective, needed to be summary and systematic. Under such conditions, prolonged investigations recognizing full formal rights would not only be costly but inefficient because they would hinder immigration officials in performing their gatekeeping functions. Thus deportation proceedings, as in John Turner's case, provided for a hearing and an attorney on appeal but otherwise deviated significantly from judicial methods.

The admissions process existing in 1905 was even more summary and routinized, as is best illustrated in the procedures followed at Ellis Island.[26] The inspection began with preliminary investigations on board ship. Aliens from second-class cabin and steerage, wearing large tags bearing their names and ship manifest numbers, proceeded to the Ellis Island immigration station for further processing. There they climbed a huge staircase, unwittingly undergoing the first stage of their fitness examination. A medical inspector at the head of the stairs observed each alien to detect those who, "according to his trained eye," appeared to be particularly "inattentive" or "stupid-looking," traits that were considered to be signs of insanity or "mental deficiency." The officer marked suspected "mental defects" with an "X" in chalk on their clothing and detained them for further inspection. Other immigrants proceeded to the quick medical evaluation in which inspectors separated those with suspected diseases or physical deformities, again marking their clothing with a code for suspected problems.[27]

Healthy immigrants then entered long aisles to be investigated by the "line" inspectors who aimed to ferret out those who belonged to excludable classes. In 1905, those classes included persons with mental or physical defects, especially ones that would impair the ability to work; those with undesirable moral or political characteristics (i.e., polygamists, prostitutes and their procurers, anarchists, and persons convicted of a crime involving "moral turpitude"); paupers and persons "likely to become a public charge"; and contract laborers (those brought over by employers with an explicit promise of a job).[28]

Despite the immigration law's long list of undesirable immigrants, it did not specify how to determine such questions as whether a person was likely

Entitled "The Pens at Ellis Island" by the photographer, this picture shows immigrants waiting to be inspected in the Main Hall at Ellis Island. Courtesy William Williams Papers, Rare Books and Manuscripts Division, New York Public Library, Astor, Lenox and Tilden Foundations.

to become a public charge or whether a crime involved moral turpitude (beyond saying that convictions for "purely political" offenses were not crimes of moral turpitude). What the statute left silent, immigration officials, such as Commissioner of Immigration William Williams, filled in, often using their discretion to further the restrictive thrust of the immigration legislation. The effect of Williams's discretion was clearest in his interpretation of the phrase "likely to become a public charge." In its most literal sense, the clause seemed to exclude those who, at the time of admission, were likely to become dependent on charity and public funds for their survival. Rather than limit the clause to paupers, Williams stressed in his rules that "the really vital point for determination in each case is whether or not [an alien] will in fact be able to secure such employment and become self-supporting." To make that decision, inspectors were instructed to consider the immigrant's occupation, physical and mental capacity to engage in that occupation, employability given local labor market conditions, and number of dependents. Williams warned that "aliens with small amounts of money will be admitted only in exceptional cases, as where they are strong and intelligent persons with no one dependent upon them and it is reasonably certain that they will be able to secure profitable employment before their funds are exhausted."[29] By 1905, Williams had ordered that aliens must show $10 and a ticket to their destination to prove they did not fall within the "likely to become a public charge" class.[30]

Immigrants anxious to prove that they were employable and would not become public charges had to take care that they did not unwittingly arouse suspicions that they were contract laborers, another excluded class. Interpreter Fiorello La Guardia explained that if immigrants' "expectations [of a job] were too enthusiastic, they might be held as coming in violation of the contract labor provision. Yet, if they were too indefinite, if they knew nobody, had no idea where they were going to get jobs, they might be excluded as likely to become public charges."[31]

Women and minor children confronted the inspectors' assumption that they were dependent and likely to become public charges. Wives and children who would otherwise fall into that category could be admitted if the examining inspector was satisfied that "they are going to persons *able, willing and legally bound* to support them." Single women became automatic suspects not only of being likely to become public charges but also of entering for immoral purposes or being susceptible to the evil designs of white slavers and other corrupting influences. Thus unmarried pregnant women were always detained for further investigation.[32] Also as a matter of course, a young woman traveling alone was temporarily detained "till friends or relatives, of evident respectability, call for her—or she may be delivered to the agents of some national or religious society, or home, whose business it is to care for and protect such girls."[33]

Guided by the commissioner's rules on how to apply the immigration laws, the line inspector asked the immigrants about their destination in the United States, job prospects, financial security, and whether they had friends and relatives in the United States. Williams instructed the inspectors to evaluate not only the facts brought out in the questioning but also the immigrant's "appearance and general demeanor." According to the immigration law of 1903, only aliens who were "clearly and beyond a doubt entitled to land" should be admitted.[34]

If any doubt existed, the inspector turned the alien over to a board of special inquiry. As in deportation cases, hearings before the board were not public and aliens had no legal right to an attorney, though in practice, agents of immigrant aid societies often appeared to help aliens at their hearings.[35] The examinations were often brief because individual boards might hear up to one hundred cases in one day; as one board member at Ellis Island said, "To treat 100 cases, and treat them properly, does not leave

An immigrant appearing before the board of special inquiry at Ellis Island. Courtesy William Williams Papers, Rare Books and Manuscripts Division, New York Public Library, Astor, Lenox and Tilden Foundations.

much time for each immigrant." He reported that some cases were disposed of within a matter of minutes.[36]

Board members were granted even greater discretion than line inspectors over their proceedings. There were no specific guidelines in the statutes, regulations, or local rules specifying the type or weight of evidence to be considered by the boards, with one exception: the members' decisions were to be based on the evidence in front of them at the time of the hearing. The guidelines set by Commissioner Williams discouraged the boards from seeking additional evidence or deferring cases unless board members believed further evidence or time would substantially alter their decision. Williams also encouraged board members to take into account "the appearance or impression created by the aliens or witnesses."[37] Commissioner Williams justified the discretion given to the boards, saying that the point was to create "a body of experts," not "a body of automatons," who simply apply the rules of the superiors.[38]

An alien excluded or ordered deported by the board could appeal its decision, as could a dissenting member of the board, unless the exclusion was for mental or medical reasons.[39] The appeal went to the secretary of commerce and labor, whose decision was final.[40] The Department of Commerce and Labor's regulations limited the secretary in his review to the evidence that was before the board of special inquiry.[41] At the point of appeal, the alien could secure the services of an attorney or a representative who could review the record and submit a written brief.[42]

The procedure followed in Chinese cases in 1905 differed in significant ways from that adopted in general immigration admission and deportation cases. The most striking difference is that Chinese applicants for admission faced a much more extensive investigation than did non-Chinese immigrants. That was due, in part, to the more stringent nature of the exclusion laws, which created the presumption that most Chinese were not entitled to enter, to the determined resistance of Chinese to those laws, and to the particular strategies developed to test a Chinese applicant's right to enter.

But, though in some ways unique, the procedures in the Chinese cases, like those in general immigration cases, vested the officials with broad discretion and were administrative, not judicial, in character. The procedures did not provide for a board of special inquiry for Chinese unless their admission was questioned under the general immigration laws, but, like the boards, Chinese investigations were not public. A single inspector, with the aid of an interpreter and a stenographer, completed the investigation. The inspector determined which witnesses could testify; the Chinese applicant had no power to compel the presence of witnesses or the right to consult with an attorney.[43] Despite these liabilities, Chinese bore the burden of proof to establish their right to enter.[44] Attorneys for Chinese could examine the evidence on which the inspector based his decision to exclude and rebut it with written briefs and affidavits upon appeal. In preparing their appeals, however, they were often ignorant of the exact reason for the exclusion because they were denied access to the inspector's evaluation of the evidence. Instead, attorneys had to extrapolate the possible grounds for exclusion from the stenographer's record of the hearing.[45]

In a well-publicized case, two Chinese students arriving in the United States with a missionary, Luella Miner, on September 13, 1901, experienced the hardships such regulations sometimes engendered. Kung Hsiang Hsi and Fu Chi Hao came to the United States to further their studies at Oberlin College, but when they presented their passports to officials in San Francisco, they were denied entry because their papers were not in the correct form. They presented passports, rather than the Section 6 certificates provided for in the exclusion laws; the papers were issued by the viceroy, Li Hung Chang, rather than by his subordinate, the Chinese customs official authorized to issue such certificates under the law; finally, the passports were in Chinese rather than in English, as required by law. Even though the passports had been visaed by the American consul, who had assured Miner that the papers would be acceptable documentation for admission, officials at San Francisco considered their deficiencies serious enough to deny the students entry. Only after sixteen months' delay, considerable publicity, and the arrival of new papers did the students gain temporary admission.[46]

Officials' insistence that the papers of exempt Chinese be in the exact form prescribed by law stemmed from their general belief that Chinese sought to enter the United States unlawfully. Distrusting the oral testimony of Chinese, officials seized upon documents as a more reliable source of evidence of a right to land. The longer the exclusion laws were in existence, the longer the "paper trail" that was created. Administrative officials began to record the departures and arrivals of Chinese after the passage of the 1882 exclusion law and used such records to verify applicants' narratives. Similarly, the typescripts of earlier investigations were kept and checked when a Chinese man or woman returned from another visit to China or when their kin applied for admission. Eventually, administrators created a system for cross-referencing files making it possible to compare, for example, the testimony of a man, his brothers, and sons to see if there were any material discrepancies to suggest fraudulent relationships.[47]

Ironically, the documents created by officials to curb the possibility of fraud became valuable commodities and, in some ways, expanded the opportunities for those who wished to enter the United States illegally. "Paper" sons and daughters entered successfully because the immigration authorities had in their files documents in which fathers had earlier attested to their children's births in China. Illegal immigrants could purchase doctored certificates with their own photographs substituted. Thus inspectors scrutinized documents closely, looking for signs of forgery, tampering, or any other irregularities and used oral testimony to test the authenticity of the documents. Documents had to meet high standards; Section 6 certificates, for example, that did not provide all of the information required by law would not be considered sufficient evidence of a right to land.[48]

The Bureau of Immigration approached cases involving alleged Chinese-American citizens with even greater skepticism, seeing their attempts to enter as the greatest "menace" to the efficient enforcement of the exclusion laws. In admitting one Chinese-American citizen, the agency warned, it was also opening the door to his wife and children in China.[49] Consequently, the bureau felt it was crucial that the applicant's story could be verified through written documents on file in the immigration office, court records, or reliable testimony. They also relied on their impressions of the applicant and the witnesses, looking for signs of "Americanization" in the applicant and for statements that sounded rehearsed or too pat. In the end, admission of "native-borns" could hinge upon seemingly minor matters, as is illustrated in the case of Wong Gan.

Wong Gan had arrived in San Francisco on December 30, 1904, after a visit to China to get married. He claimed to have been born in San Francisco in 1885; his father now managed a "vegetable ranch" in Los Angeles, and his mother had died in San Francisco in 1898. Wong Gan made a favorable impression in his hearing before inspector John R. Dunn. Dunn noted at the end of his interrogation of Wong Gan, "Applicant speaks English fluently, reads and writes English, wears no queue and dresses in American clothes. His manner of testifying indicates that he is familiar with American customs, and it is quite apparent that he has resided in this country at least for quite a few years."[50] The inspector reported only one flaw in Wong Gan's case. Though Dunn had carefully searched mortuary records, he could find no "record whatsoever of the death of the reputed mother of the applicant."[51] This inability to verify the mother's death was sufficient, in the opinion of the Chinese inspector in charge, to deny Wong Gan entry.

In reviewing his decision, Commissioner of Immigration H. H. North noted that the applicant "is a very much Americanized Chinaman" and that there were no discrepancies in the record. He thus sent the case back for further investigation "as to the fate of [the applicant's] mother."[52] Wong Gan thought that his mother, Lee Shee, was buried in the Ning Yeong cemetery in San Francisco under a marker with the inscription " 'Wong Mon Lee Shee', meaning Lee Shee of the Wong family." Though he had only been to the cemetery once or twice, he thought he could show Inspector Dunn her grave. Dunn reported, however, that Wong Gan "was not able after arriving at the cemetery, to locate the grave of his mother with the ease anticipated at the Mail Dock. He finally settled on one slab, the marks on which had been almost totally obliterated by the elements, but on which could be easily discerned the characters 'Wong Mon', the rest of the name, if there were any more of it, being entirely washed away."[53] Wong Gan's attorney produced a certificate of death for his client's mother shortly thereafter. The name was the same, but the place and date of death differed from Wong Gan's testimony.[54] He had testified that his mother had died in February or March 1898 at 919 Dupont Street whereas the certificate stated that she had died on May 12, 1899, at 722 Jackson Street. On the strength of these discrepancies, North denied Wong Gan entry and ordered him deported. The Department of Commerce and Labor, however, reversed this decision on appeal on the grounds that "the fact that a woman answering the description of his mother did live and die in San Francisco is shown to at least a reasonable certainty. No discrepancies upon material points appear in the evidence."[55] Well over two months after his arrival in the United States, Wong Gan was released from detention on the Pacific Mail dock and allowed to go free. His residence in the United States remained precarious, however, because administrative authorities were not bound by their determinations, and if Wong Gan left the country again, they could later decide he was not a citizen and deny him reentry.

Chinese facing deportation under the exclusion law were entitled to judicial hearings, with some of the greater procedural protections such hearings implied. Yet all Chinese remained subject to the fear of periodic raids by immigration officials searching for illegal immigrants. Exempt Chinese felt particularly vulnerable because they were required by the bureau to leave their Section 6 certificates with officials at the port of entry, thus leaving them with no proof of their lawful residence in the event of a raid.[56] One such raid took place in Boston on October 11, 1903. According to Secretary of Commerce and Labor Victor Metcalf, the bureau conducted the raid at the request of the local police force, who reported a growing number of illegal Chinese residents in Boston involved in violent tong conflicts.[57] Officers swept Chinatown, arresting all Chinese who lacked the certificates of residence required by the Geary Act. In the words of former secretary of state John Foster, Chinese "were dragged from their hiding-places and stowed like cattle upon wagons."[58] Of the 234 Chinese arrested, 45 were deported.[59]

CRITIQUE OF THE BUREAU'S METHODS

Such incidents no doubt succored the hopes of exclusionists that the Bureau of Immigration was zealously guarding the nation's gates, but for a growing number of aliens and American citizens, they represented the epitome of "bureaucratic tyranny." Protesters filled Faneuil Hall in Boston to protest the "lawless acts of the officials," calling the raid a "brutal outrage."[60] For critics, John Turner, the alien applying for admission at Ellis Island, Wong Gan, and Chinese arrested in the Boston raid all had one thing in common: their right to enter and reside in the United States remained precarious, resting in the hands of powerful bureaucratic officials who exercised their considerable discretion with little restraint. Protesters believed officials elevated their gatekeeping function far above individual immigrants' rights and interests, leading to arbitrary decisions and inhumane treatment.

Procedures designed to sort people quickly often appeared impersonal and capricious to immigrants. The writer Louis Adamic, who emigrated from Austria in December 1913, recalled the inspection at Ellis Island, emphasizing the intimidating, confusing atmosphere: "The examiner sat bureaucratically—very much in the manner of officials in the Old Country —behind a great desk, which stood on a high platform. On the wall above him was a picture of George Washington. Beneath it was an American flag. The official spoke a bewildering mixture of many Slavic languages. He had a stern voice and a sour visage." The inspector almost denied Adamic entry. Adamic was coming to join the brother of a friend, Steve Radin. When questioned by the inspector, Radin said he was not related to Adamic but was only a friend. Though this statement corroborated Adamic's testimony, Adamic remembered that "the inspector pounced upon me, speaking the dreadful botch of Slavic languages. What did I mean by lying to him? He said a great many other things which I did not understand. I did comprehend, however, his threat to return me to the Old Country." It soon became apparent that the clerk had recorded, as Adamic's statement, that Radin was his uncle, not friend, and that this discrepancy had sparked the inspector's suspicions. When the error was discovered, the inspector did not apologize but, "waving his hand in a casual gesture, he ordered me released." Adamic left, embarrassed and "weak in the knees" and with the deeply ingrained impression of an arbitrary, uncaring officialdom.[61] Whether one was admitted, it appeared from Adamic's account, depended on small flukes and technical errors.

The Bitter Society, a novel published in China during the boycott of 1905, expressed a similar anger and bewilderment among Chinese merchants in San Francisco about their treatment at the hands of immigration officials. According to the anonymous author, Chinese in San Francisco lived in a state of constant anxiety, worried lest they lose their identification papers, be arrested during a raid, and confined in the "wooden cages" on the Pacific Mail Steamship dock. The immigration officials' decisions to deny Chinese entry seemed arbitrary and overly technical. When the two main characters in the novel board a ship to see a friend off who has been forced to return to China, they encounter many others who have been rejected for a variety of minor reasons: "See—that man is newly arrived from Shanghai, and the visa issued to him by the American consulate omitted an item. And over there, that man en route to Canada made a slip during interrogation. Yet another fellow's visa, which was issued by American customs in . . . [1882] has been declared invalid. . . . Isn't this nonsense detestable?"[62]

In the opinion of immigrants and their allies, such arbitrary treatment flourished because of the unhampered discretion of immigration officials and the lack of procedural protections afforded during inspections. The critics saw the discretion wielded by immigration officials at practically every step of the inspection and in the local and departmental rules issued to guide the application of the laws. Commissioner Williams's interpretation of the "likely to become a public charge" clause became particularly controversial, especially when Williams proudly announced in 1903 that exclusions had doubled in the first year of his administration at Ellis Island.[63] Under Williams's rules, inspectors based admission decisions on their predictions about the employability and future financial security of immigrants, considering, among other things, the amount of money the immigrant had upon landing, local labor market conditions, and the number of dependents. Williams's interpretation, according to a wide variety of ethnic associations, exceeded the plain meaning of the statute and resulted in unjust exclusions. Immigration officials were allowed too much leeway to guess what might happen to the immigrant and to allow guesswork to substitute for decisions based on solid evidence.[64]

The discretion wielded by men like Williams to interpret the law turned immigration officials from "law-enforcers" into "self-constituted, law-maker[s]," in attorney Max Kohler's opinion. Under Williams's administration in 1911, Kohler argued, 15 to 25 percent of the Jewish immigrants denied entry had been excluded unjustly, and the percentage of such unwarranted exclusions was "daily increasing." Kohler warned that all immigrants, not just Jews, were "apt to become victims of unjust administration of the law." But it was difficult to predict just who "will next become a victim of a blundering administration of the law" because men, not law, governed the process.[65]

Chinese similarly challenged the Bureau of Immigration's authority to interpret the law and establish its own rules and practices. Such discretion, charged one Chinese-American critic, led to "exclusion by regulation" rather than by law. He accused the bureau of examining Chinese "with the aim in mind of seeing how he may be excluded, rather than of finding out whether he is legally entitled to land."[66] The author of *Bitter Society* charged that the bureau's intentions, "which can't be stated openly, are but to chase every single one of us out of here! They'll resort to tighter and tighter regulations and make it so difficult that we'll be forced to leave."[67]

Among other things, Chinese persistently sought a broader definition of the exempt classes than that construed by the attorney general in 1898 and followed by the bureau.[68] The attorney general had decided that only those classes that were explicitly exempted from the law—merchants, teachers, students, teachers, diplomats—could be admitted. Chinese argued that Congress intended only to exclude laborers; the attorney general's opinion, in their view, unjustly forbade the entry of many professional Chinese who were not laborers but who also did not fall within the classes specifically exempted.[69]

Chinese similarly protested when, again by departmental fiat, the attorney general subjected them in 1903 to the general immigration as well as the exclusion laws. Representatives of the Chinese had often argued that they should be treated just the same as other immigrants under the general immigration laws, but they assumed that in such an event the exclusion laws would be repealed. Now Chinese faced two restrictive laws and those exempt from exclusion had to prove they were also admissible under the general immigration laws.[70] Chinese complained, too, when the bureau developed its plan to bypass the federal courts in Chinese deportation cases and submit Chinese to the same procedures used in deporting non-Chinese aliens.[71]

Official discretion appeared to go unchecked, in the immigrants' opinion, in part because of the lack of significant judicial review. When the *Ju Toy* decision removed the federal courts ever further from immigration administration, critics sought to recreate a more active role for the courts. The Chinese Six Companies asked President William Howard Taft in 1909 to recommend new legislation, "eliminating from our jurisprudence the pernicious doctrines laid down by the Supreme Court" in the *Ju Toy* decision.[72] Similarly, Kohler urged the Immigration Commission in 1910 to recommend the repeal of the finality clause in the Immigration Act of 1891 and allow judicial review of exclusion and deportation decisions, arguing that "no other class of cases is beyond judicial review."[73]

If courts were not to review the actions of officials, then at least, critics argued, immigrants should be entitled to certain procedural protections to ensure the fairness of the bureau's investigations. The inspection system established by the Bureau of Immigration was faulty in many respects, according to critics. While non-Chinese immigrants objected to the summary, superficial hearings that did not allow them sufficient time to develop their case, Chinese complained of the detailed examinations that bordered on the "third degree," especially for exempt classes who had Section 6 certificates, which, they argued, should be sufficient evidence of their right to enter.[74] Chinese further protested against the bureau's decision-making process, which "disregards the weight of evidence and the circumstances surrounding the individual case and resolves the slightest doubt against the applicant."[75]

The decisions to admit or deport—decisions involving precious rights to liberty which had a profound impact on aliens' lives—were too often in the hands of men who had little judicial training or temperament, critics continued. This argument was particularly directed at the men who sat on the board of special inquiry. The inadequacies of the board members were revealed, argued critics, by the fact that the Department of Commerce and Labor reversed their decisions in nearly 50 percent of the cases on appeal.[76] Immigrant groups suspected that rather than acting after a full consideration of the evidence, line inspectors and the boards of special inquiry sought "to reach the results which their superior requires . . . under penalty of removal"; the desired result was "to exclude with great frequency."[77] Thus, while inspectors performed judicial functions in deciding personal rights and weighing evidence, they did not operate with the independent, neutral stance expected of judges. The fact that inspectors often wore more than one hat, figuratively speaking, performing prosecutorial and judicial roles simultaneously, also compromised their objectivity.

Advocates for both Chinese and non-Chinese immigrants persistently demanded what they considered to be basic procedural rights: admission and deportation hearings before immigration officials should be public; aliens should be allowed to consult attorneys and friends; they should have a reasonable opportunity to hear and rebut all of the evidence against them and to submit briefs upon appeal; arrests for deportation should be made only upon warrants and those warrants should be issued only upon probable cause. Such were the rights granted "even to murderers," argued the German-language newspaper, the *Volksblatt*, and "to deny [them] to immigrants is barbarous."[78] Articulating a critique of the Bureau of Immigration which drew on familiar precepts of Anglo-American jurisprudence was only half of the battle, however; substantive changes in immigration procedure would come only if immigrants and their allies could develop successful strategies to bring pressure to bear upon the bureau.

STRATEGIES FOR CHANGE

The political and legal climate in the early twentieth century did not appear to favor the campaign for greater rights for immigrants. As Commissioner Williams noted in 1913, the layperson who labeled the immigration laws defective usually meant that they did not keep enough immigrants out.[79] In the years immediately preceding the *Ju Toy* decision, Congress reflected the growing anti-immigrant sentiment among Americans by expanding the list of excludable immigrants in 1903 and making Chinese exclusion permanent in 1904. The Bureau of Immigration operated under the leadership of officials with strong allegiance to labor organizations and nativist sympathies.[80] The Supreme Court appeared to acquiesce to the efforts of political and administrative officials to bar entry to "undesirable" immigrants.

Though political and legal institutions appeared to be aligned against them, immigrants often had powerful incentives as well as valuable allies with resources to challenge the restrictionist status quo. Ethnic organizations and immigrant aid societies, rather than individual immigrants, generally led and organized the campaign against the Bureau of Immigration. They often found support for their actions in the growing number of foreign-born voters, the foreign-language press, and certain sectors among the American-born middle class. No single strategy dominated in their campaign; rather, pro-immigrant groups used whatever devices were available to them, whether they be political and diplomatic pressure, economic sanctions, personal influence, publicity, or litigation, to perfect a system of "executive justice" within the Bureau of Immigration.

The importance of ethnic organizations in providing a base for political action has already been demonstrated in the analysis of Chinese resistance to exclusion. Although the Chinese-American community often experienced intense infighting, it frequently united to defend itself against discriminatory treatment. Chinese were not unique in their reliance upon ethnic associations; a plethora of immigrant aid associations and ethnic organizations flourished in the early twentieth century with a variety of objectives and proved to be a significant counterweight to the nativist movement.[81] Although the goals of the organizations frequently conflicted with the immediate interests of newcomers, their distinct interests did not prevent them from being effective, passionate advocates of immigrants in devising strategies to curb the Bureau of Immigration's discretion.[82]

The watchdog role played by various organizations began as soon as the immigrants arrived at the immigration station. Representatives of various religious and immigrant aid societies had desks at Ellis Island to greet immigrants as they entered the station. Though the immigration laws did not specifically allow immigrants to have representation at special inquiry hearings, members of the societies sometimes testified on behalf of such aliens and, in addition, offered to guarantee that an alien would not become a burden on the community.[83] The intervention of the agents, who obviously had greater experience with immigration procedures than did the newcomers, could make a significant difference in the outcome of a case. One society reported that in 1907 it had appealed 1,906 cases, of which 1,252 were successful.[84]

The most active and vocal defenders of non-Chinese immigrants came from the Jewish immigrant aid and philanthropic organizations. At the core of these organizations was a group of well-established, often wealthy, men, several of whom had emigrated from German-speaking countries in the 1840s. Simon Wolf, an immigrant from Germany in 1848, was a lawyer and a leader in several of the major Jewish organizations—B'nai B'rith, the Union of American Hebrew Congregations, and the Hebrew Sheltering and Immigrant Aid Society.[85] Jacob Schiff, the prominent banker and financier, originally from Germany, and Louis Marshall, corporate attorney and well-known community leader, were instrumental in establishing the American Jewish Committee in 1906, which, among other things, sought to provide refuge for Jews escaping persecution by easing their immigration to the United States.[86] Working closely with these men was one of the most vociferous critics of immigration policies and their administration, attorney Max J. Kohler. Kohler had been an assistant U.S. attorney from 1894 to 1898 and in that capacity had gained considerable experience with, and a distaste for, the Chinese exclusion laws. After his term expired, he represented aliens frequently in court, wrote several articles on immigration policy for newspapers and journals, and served as chair for the Committee on Immigration Aid and Education for the Baron de Hirsh Fund and the Committee on Immigration of the American Jewish Committee.[87]

These men championed individual immigrants' cases while pushing for broad reforms in immigration policy and procedure. They did not hesitate to use their social positions to intercede on behalf of individual immigrants threatened with exclusion or deportation.[88] Simon Wolf, in his official position in the United Hebrew Congregations, maintained a close lobbying relationship with immigration officials and the secretary of commerce and labor in Washington, D.C. Secretary Charles Nagel commented in 1911 that Wolf "keeps a pretty close eye on us. If we ever miss him, we think the world is going to stop. I frequently inquire about eleven o'clock, 'Has Wolf been here?' That is the situation there."[89] The Hebrew Sheltering and Immigrant Aid Society credited Wolf with "preventing the deportation of no fewer than 103,000 Jewish immigrants" in his many years of service.[90] Representatives from the group never missed an opportunity to testify before various congressional committees investigating immigration procedures or changes in the immigration laws. Louis Marshall, for example, was largely responsible for preventing for a long time the introduction of a literacy requirement into the immigration laws. Jewish leaders also protested to local commissioners, U.S. attorneys, Washington officials, and even the president against particular interpretations and rules adopted at immigration stations.[91]

These men were especially concerned with what they perceived to be the disparate impact of immigration policies on Jewish immigrants, but they also opposed laws that appeared to discriminate on the basis of race or ethnicity. Kohler, for example, vigorously assailed the Chinese exclusion laws and represented Chinese-American groups in New York City, and Marshall represented Japanese before the Supreme Court in their challenge to California's Alien Land Laws and served as a director for the National Association for the Advancement of Colored People.[92] Thus Jewish activists, in critiquing immigration laws and procedure, took a broad view of their advocacy role.

While such organizations often worked quietly, through official channels, the foreign-language press took a different approach. The success of the foreign-language press depended largely on the volume of immigration. As immigration swelled in the late nineteenth and early twentieth centuries, so, too, did the number of foreign newspapers and their circulation.[93] Their stories were directed at their particular audiences. It is thus not surprising that the foreign-language press often turned its attention to an issue with which almost all could identify: the experience of immigrants as they entered the United States. It used publicity and the power of the pen to expose perceived abuses in the enforcement of immigration laws and to lobby for reform.[94] Periodic investigations of Ellis Island were often instigated by the foreign-language press.[95]

Other exposés addressed a different audience—the American-born middle class. Edward Steiner, an immigrant from Hungary and professor of applied Christianity at Grinnell College, provided a complete account of the immigrants' journey from their homeland to their landing in the United States in *On the Trail of the Immigrant*, with the partial aim "to humanize the process of admission to this country."[96] Though Steiner praised immigration officials' efforts to enforce the laws impartially and accurately, he repeatedly used metaphors that stressed the administration's mechanistic, impersonal qualities—qualities that made the law impartial, in Steiner's opinion, yet also cold and unyielding to the immigrant. The very structure of the immigration station, Steiner suggested, imparted an imposing, official impression to the arriving immigrants. That impression was soon reinforced by the "sifting process" of the immigration investigation. "Let no one believe that landing on the shores of 'The land of the free, and the home of the brave' is a pleasant experience," cautioned Steiner. Rather, "it is a hard, harsh fact, surrounded by the grinding machinery of the law, which sifts, picks, and chooses; admitting the fit and excluding the weak and helpless."[97]

Steiner juxtaposed the impersonal, mechanical administration of the laws with the very personal and human reactions of immigrants as inspec-

"*Lady Liberty Is Ashamed.*" *Cartoons such as this one from the German-language newspaper* Staats-Zeitung *sought to arouse opposition to the "Czar of Ellis Island," Commissioner William Williams, and his harsh procedures. Courtesy William Williams Papers, Rare Books and Manuscripts Division, New York Public Library, Astor, Lenox and Tilden Foundations.*

tors began the "sifting process," sometimes separating families. "A Polish woman by my side has suddenly become aware that she has one child less clinging to her skirts, and she implores me with agonizing cries, to bring it back to her. . . . 'Gdeye moya shena' (where is my wife?) an old Slovak cries as he looks wildly about for her, whose physique was suspected of being below the normal and who was passed on for further examination."[98] Those detained for special inquiry appeared especially tragic and heart-rending as their journey to America threatened to come to an abrupt halt. Two boys have arrived to join their mother in the United States. After anticipating the moment for several years, their reunion is marred by the medical officer's suspicion that they have a contagious disease and will not be allowed to land.[99]

Accounts such as Steiner's clearly aimed to turn the faceless, menacing throngs pouring into the country into individuals, with their own particular histories, families, hopes, and fears, little different from those of any human being.[100] He also confronted the reader with the human costs and consequences of restrictive legislation and impersonal procedures. Immigration laws separated families and returned unfortunates to uncertain and even dangerous futures in their homelands. Procedures that appeared harsh and confusing to immigrants made an indelible impact as well, forming the immigrants' first and most striking impression of the United States. It was vital, therefore, that the first impression be a good one. "The more humanely the immigrant is treated [at Ellis Island]," said Steiner, "the better citizen he is likely to become . . . and the more humanely he will deal with us when he becomes the master of our national destiny."[101]

Personal appeals could be quite successful in mobilizing public opinion. Immigration laws "may be endorsed in the abstract," observed one official, "but the public will always be found against their enforcement in concrete cases."[102] Thus, despite the growing strength of nativism, there also grew a vocal corps of Americans who opposed restrictive legislation and who pushed for more humane and less rigid enforcement of the laws. Such sentiments might be embraced only periodically by some Americans, provoked by reports of a particularly heartrending exclusion or harsh treatment of immigrants. But the organization of the National Liberal Immigration League in 1906, which brought together foreign-born and American-born supporters of immigrants, attested to the more systematic efforts of some Americans to oppose nativism.[103] They responded to the appeals to the immigrant heritage of the United States as well as to the idea that it was at the nation's gates that "this vast throng of 'Americans in the rough'" first learned "American principles of justice and fair play."[104]

Other Americans joined in the condemnation of the Bureau of Immigration, not out of sympathy for immigrants but from a general hostility to the expansion of administrative power. Justice Brewer, for example, evinced little concern for the "obnoxious Chinese" in his passionate dissents, aiming his wrath instead at the unprecedented power given to a "mere ministerial officer" to determine crucial questions of liberty in a "star chamber proceeding of the most stringent sort."[105] Characterizing the American Revolution as a struggle to protect civil liberty from the encroachment of executive power, Brewer and others looked with alarm upon the new expansion of administrative power at the turn of the century which threatened to undermine the "fundamental principles of our Government." The *Ju Toy* decision, extending the bureau's authority over alleged citizens, only heightened concern over the "great power that may be granted to the administration."[106]

Some political officeholders, particularly those representing large foreign-born constituencies, responded to the pressure from bureau's critics. Even those who supported restrictive immigration legislation occasionally found it politically expedient to intercede on the behalf of individual immigrants as the Democratic and Republican parties increasingly vied for the votes of ethnic communities.[107] Immigration officials frequently blamed such political maneuvering for their inability to enforce the laws. One official associated with the service at Ellis Island for many years blamed the inability of even so popular and skilled a leader as Commissioner General Sargent fully to enforce the laws upon President Theodore Roosevelt, who "found it was good politics to have stringent immigration laws to point to [but] it was poor politics to enforce them impartially."[108]

THE CHINESE BOYCOTT OF 1905

Thus immigrants were far from defenseless as they sought to curb the Bureau of Immigration's power through procedural reform in the post–*Ju Toy* years. Of all the tactics employed, the Chinese boycott of 1905 provides the most striking illustration of how immigrant groups developed concrete and potentially powerful strategies to challenge the Bureau of Immigration. Chinese in the United States had already resorted to civil disobedience, political and diplomatic pressure, and litigation to resist the discriminatory exclusion laws and their administration. In 1905, within days of the Supreme Court's decision in *Ju Toy*, Chinese merchants once again took the offensive, this time turning to economic sanctions to protest American immigration policy. They helped to engineer a boycott of American goods in China, which for a time seemed to suggest that appeals to American pocketbooks held greater sway than appeals to American consciences.

Chinese leaders of the boycott made clear that the movement was not a sudden or isolated act against the United States; rather, as the leader of the Chinese Reform party, K'ang Yu-wei, stressed to President Roosevelt, "two decades' rigid enforcement [of the exclusion policy] has brought about the ill-will of four hundred million people."[109] Though the boycott resulted from years of resentment, it was more immediately a response to particular events in 1904 and 1905 as well as to a growing nationalism within China. Well-publicized stories in such books as *The Bitter Society* telling of rough and insulting treatment of the Chinese exempt classes had fueled Chinese resentment in the years immediately before the boycott. One Chinese official warned Americans in 1904: "Every Chinese ill-treated in America or sent back from it spreads the story of his wrongs amongst his friends and their acquaintances."[110]

The expiration in 1904 of the Gresham-Yang Treaty provided an opportunity, in the view of the Chinese Foreign Office, to ameliorate some of the more offensive practices involved in the administration of the exclusion policy and to afford Chinese residing in the United States greater protection from harassment. The Chinese foreign minister denounced the Gresham-Yang Treaty in January 1904 and informed the United States that it wished to create a new treaty to remedy what it perceived to be overly zealous enforcement by the Bureau of Immigration. When news of China's denunciation of the treaty was made public, exclusionists in Congress took advantage of the lapse of the treaty to pass a law extending exclusion without time limit and independent of any treaty. For the Chinese, passage of the 1904 law made a more liberal treaty all the more vital.

In particular, the Chinese foreign minister sought to broaden the attorney general's restrictive interpretation of what Chinese were exempt under the exclusion laws as well as to provide Chinese laborers with greater protections, including the right to counsel, bail, and appeal in administrative proceedings.[111] Primarily because of opposition from the Bureau of Immigration, the United States rejected the Chinese proposal and offered another treaty, which, if anything, was even more restrictive than the 1894 treaty. Negotiations over the new treaty stalled, and it appeared that for the first time since exclusion had been adopted, the policy would be implemented without the consent of the Chinese government. On the heels of these developments came the *Ju Toy* decision, the culmination of the bureau's campaign to curb Chinese access to the federal courts in exclusion cases.

Anger and frustration with these developments dovetailed with a growing nationalism in China to spawn the boycott.[112] The Shanghai Chamber of Commerce officially initiated the call for the boycott of American goods on May 10, 1905.[113] Through the organization's efforts, the boycott soon spread to major cities throughout China and attracted wide popular support. The Chinese-American community actively promoted the boycott, forming a Resist Treaty Committee in San Francisco and raising money to send to boycott leaders in China.[114]

Some supporters of the boycott demanded an end to exclusion, but most sought only to temper the policy, particularly removal of the restrictive interpretations and practices imposed by immigration officials.[115] They remained primarily concerned with the treatment of the exempt classes. They demanded more respectful treatment by officials, a broader interpretation of the exempt class, preembarkation investigations, bail in lengthy investigations, and the elimination of requirements for photographs and body measurements.[116]

The boycott brought the United States's attention to bear upon the Bureau of Immigration's methods. American merchants, worried that the boycott might "ultimately destroy American trade" in the Chinese empire, joined in the demand that the agency treat exempt Chinese with greater respect and that it refrain from an overzealous enforcement of the laws. Other Americans became embarrassed by stories detailing the harsh methods of the immigration service. The *New York Times* asserted on May 16, 1905, "Americans of liberal and intelligent minds hold substantially one opinion about the Chinese Exclusion act now in force. It is a barbarous measure, brutally enforced." The *Times* clarified that it did not want to allow the immigration of Chinese coolies; "the flood of highly undesirable immigrants that is now coming to us from Europe is about all we can stand." What bothered the *Times* and other Americans was the "indecent ... exclusion [of] educated and highly intelligent Chinese gentlemen."[117]

President Theodore Roosevelt took steps to avert the escalation of the boycott. Even before the boycott, Roosevelt had expressed reservations about the way the exclusion laws were enforced. The government should ease rather than hamper the entry of exempt classes, said Roosevelt in 1904, because "we wish to enlarge our trade with China. We wish to make ever firmer our intellectual hold upon China."[118] After meeting with various Chinese leaders, Roosevelt instructed Secretary of Commerce and Labor Victor Metcalf on June 16, 1905, to "issue specific and rigid instructions to the officials of the Immigration Bureau that we will [not] tolerate discourtesy or harsh treatment in connection with the Chinese merchant, traveler, or student."[119] Roosevelt publicly endorsed the Chinese demand that the exclusion laws be framed so as to exclude only Chinese laborers and proposed in his annual message to Congress in December 1905 that the laws be amended to that effect.[120] He also exhorted American consuls to investigate exempt Chinese more thoroughly in China before visaing Section 6 certificates so that the bureau would give them more credence.[121]

The Bureau of Immigration proved less yielding than the president to the pressure applied by Chinese boycotters.[122] In June 1905, the bureau stressed the difficulty of enforcing the Chinese exclusion laws and defended its examinations of exempt Chinese as necessary to prevent fraud. It further warned of the danger of giving in to the Chinese. If China had an "influence sufficiently potent, by using the boycott against a great nation, to secure the relaxation of regulations which have been enforced for years," the country would grow more confident and "be emboldened to demand all its wants—the emasculation, if not repeal, of the exclusion policy."[123]

The tone of the next year's report indicated that the Bureau of Immigration felt under siege. With the combined forces of the Chinese, the press, and the "educated, enlightened [American] populace" joining in the condemnation of the bureau's practices, the commissioner general commented, "the only wonder is that the force of Chinese inspectors was not demoralized." The bureau, in a more placative mood, reassured its critics that "every possible effort has been exerted to extend to Chinese of the classes entitled by treaty provisions to enter the United States exactly the same treatment as is accorded Europeans." The bureau reported that through better communication established with the consulate in China since the beginning of the boycott, it could give more weight to the Section 6 certificates presented at American ports.[124]

Under intense pressure from the administration, Secretary of Commerce and Labor Metcalf reluctantly instituted in 1906 further changes in the bureau's regulations as a conciliatory gesture to Chinese. Most of the changes concerned the treatment of exempt Chinese. The bureau dropped some rules which exempt Chinese had found particularly offensive, no longer requiring, for example, photographs of exempt Chinese who were in transit through the United States and eliminating the Bertillon system of identification. The bureau also allowed exempt Chinese to retain their Section 6 certificates after landing in the United States, though it warned of the danger of stimulating a market in fraudulent certificates. And, most likely in response to complaints that exempt Chinese were excluded on technical grounds, the bureau dropped the rule which stated that any omissions on a Section 6 certificate would "be fatal to its sufficiency." The bureau liberalized some of its procedures in hearings as well. It specifically guaranteed the right of Chinese to present witnesses on their behalf, allowed counsel of Chinese to make copies of the testimony, and informed the

Chinese consul at the port of entry of all exclusions and provided him the opportunity to review the records in those cases. The time for appeal was expanded from two to five days as well.[125]

A more accommodating administrative attitude became evident when Oscar S. Straus was appointed as secretary of commerce and labor in 1907. Like Roosevelt, Straus expressed sympathy for Chinese demands, agreeing that "it is not surprising . . . that both the Chinese government and the Chinese people should feel aggrieved." He urged that admission should be the rule in Chinese cases and "exclusion the exception."[126] Under his supervision, the bureau broadened its definition of the exempt student class. Whereas earlier rules had admitted only those students coming for a secondary or professional education, excluding those who came only to "study English" and strictly forbidding students from working while in the United States, the new rules allowed students to pursue elementary studies as well and to work at the same time as long as they did not become "laborers" within the meaning of the exclusion laws.[127] Also in 1907, the bureau conceded to Chinese the right to have an attorney and interpreter present during admission hearings, though they were forbidden to participate in the proceeding.[128]

These were not insignificant victories for the Chinese boycotters, who, under pressure from the Chinese government, had ended the boycott by March 1906.[129] But their main objectives were not realized in the new regulations. The bureau refused to budge in its restrictive interpretation of the exempt classes. It insisted that the plain meaning of the exclusion laws limited entry only to those explicitly exempted—merchants, teachers, students, travelers, and officials. And the agency refused to provide further procedural protections beyond the right to an attorney in admission hearings. The Bureau of Immigration pointed out that the procedures in Chinese cases "are much more extended and much less summary" than those followed in general immigration cases, and it was unwilling to concede that anything, except more fraudulent entries, would be gained by making the hearings more formal.[130]

Although the boycotters had not achieved their main objectives, they had succeeded in capturing the nation's attention and in mobilizing public opinion against the administration of the laws. Compared to the Chinese campaign of civil disobedience in response to the Geary Act of 1892, the boycott of American goods had been a much more effective strategy in mitigating the severity of the exclusion laws, at least in the short run. The boycott, for one thing, drew broader support. The movement against the Geary Act had been primarily carried out by Chinese within the United States, whereas the boycott had marshaled the support of influential groups within China as well as the overseas Chinese. Chinese in 1892, seeking allies among Anglo-Americans, could rely on the aid of certain economic groups, particularly the railroads and agriculturalists, but their main appeal was to legal and moral principles embodied in the Constitution and international law. In contrast, boycotters applied economic sanctions, just at a time when American business was looking with hungry and expectant eyes at the opportunity for markets and development within China. This economic pressure, coupled with the potential political threat of growing Chinese nationalism and anti-Americanism, proved a more successful tool for change.

Chinese in the United States learned valuable lessons from the boycott which they drew on in their continued fight to liberalize the exclusion policy. The boycott had reinforced their reliance on their own organizations to build resistance, through newspapers, handbills posted in Chinatown, and associational ties.[131] But perhaps even more important, they had learned how to press their allies into action. Since at least 1900, Chinese merchants in California had formed their own chambers of commerce and made connections with organizations of white businessmen, who frequently supported their fight against exclusion.[132] After the boycott of 1905, American business organizations wrote letters on behalf of Chinese experiencing immigration difficulties and even conducted investigations of the Angel Island immigration station in San Francisco to appease Chinese and improve economic relations with China. Trade between China and the United States after the boycott did not automatically resume at preboycott levels. Secretary of Commerce and Labor Oscar Straus pointed out that American exports to China had more than quadrupled between 1897 and 1905, amounting to $57 million in the latter year, but exports had fallen dramatically to $26 million in 1907.[133] Thus when threats of new boycotts periodically surfaced, American businessmen took them seriously.[134] In 1910, for example, the San Francisco Chamber of Commerce urged the secretary of commerce and labor to allay Chinese irritations over "unreasonable examinations" and thus fend off a potential boycott. The organization wrote, "We are aware that our Government claims there will be no boycott. This was said before the last one. It came without warning and effectually paralyzed the trade between the two countries."[135]

Chinese also continued to find support among a certain middle-class sector of Americans. Ng Poon Chew, editor of the Chinese-language newspaper in San Francisco, *Chung Sai Yat Po*, became a polished public speaker on the Chautauqua lecturing circuit and did much to educate Americans throughout the United States on Chinese culture and society.[136] The publication of the book *Chinese Immigration* by sociologist Mary Roberts Coolidge in 1909 further bolstered the Chinese cause. Coolidge's sympathies clearly rested with the Chinese as she analyzed the growth of the anti-Chinese movement in the United States. While Coolidge lashed out against California labor unions and politicians, she saved her most damning criticism for the Bureau of Immigration. Its officers, she argued, were mainly to blame for the "odium attached to the administration of the [exclusion] law." In Coolidge's assessment, the inspectors and interpreters were over-zealous, corrupt, prejudiced, and unqualified. Reflecting her own class bias, Coolidge noted the low pay of the inspectors and remarked, "It could scarcely be expected that their manners would be equal to the social requirements of one of the politest nations of the world. . . . In various ways the officials have shown a lack of tact and judgment in the rather delicate task of cross-questioning their social superiors."[137]

Coolidge's "startling tale" quickly became controversial and quite popular.[138] At one point, even the commissioner general of immigration was unable to obtain a copy from the Library of Congress because the book was in "constant demand."[139] While San Francisco newspapers denounced the book as "a gross libel on the entire community," Chinese and their American allies seized upon it as a potent weapon in their battle against the bureau because it "set forth the whole long story of political chicanery, abuse, fraud, misrepresentation, coercion, illegality, and indecency in which the record of the treatment of the Chinese in this country is enshrined."[140]

In a short story sure to tug at the heartstrings of its middle-class audience, another author, Sui Sin Far, viewed the harsh nature of the exclusion laws and their enforcement from the eyes of a Chinese mother, Lae Choo.[141] "In the Land of the Free" opens as Lae Choo and her two-year-old son, born in China, return to her merchant husband in San Francisco after a prolonged visit to China. When the ship docks, however, customs officials refuse to admit her son because there is no mention of him in his parents' papers. " 'There was no child when the papers were made out,' " explains the father. The officers are sympathetic but unyielding in their insistence that the son must have proper documentation. They take the boy away and place him in a mission to be cared for by white women while the case is appealed to Washington, D.C. Her husband, Hom Hing, reassures Lae Choo that "there cannot be any law that would keep a child from its mother!"[142]

Months go by. Lae Choo and her husband spend all of their money trying to retrieve their son. Lae Choo becomes "listless, wan and hollow-eyed"; her husband fears that "before another moon, she will pass into the land of spirits." Their opportunistic lawyer offers, as a last resort, to travel to Washington to present their case personally. "Of course," the lawyer adds, "it will cost a little money." They have none left so Lae Choo gives all of her jewels to the lawyer. Finally, after ten months, they are allowed to reclaim their son.

Yet when Lae Choo goes to the mission to get her son, it becomes apparent that although the law has officially restored him, it has just as surely, by virtue of the length of their separation and the "Americanizing" influence of the mission, taken him from her. She arrives to find her son, dressed in blue cotton overalls and renamed "Kim" by the mission women:

> "Little One, ah, my Little One!" cried Lae Choo.
> She fell on her knees and stretched her hungry arms toward her son.
> But the Little One shrunk from her and tried to hide himself in the folds of the white woman's skirt.
> "Go 'way, go 'way!" he bade his mother.[143]

Here the story ends. The once prosperous and happy family coming to the "land of the free" ends up destitute and virtually childless. As in *The Bitter Society*, the exclusion laws appear unjust, at odds with basic standards of human decency ("There cannot be any law that would keep a child from its mother!"), and with American principles of liberty, as the play on the title of the story makes clear. The laws are made even more harsh by their technical and rigid enforcement by officials, which makes Chinese vulnerable to the overtures of unscrupulous attorneys, anxious to make money from their misfortunes. The editors of the *Independent*, in which the story appeared, assured its readers that "truth is stranger than fiction." Such tales were bound to reinforce the impression given by Coolidge and others of an arbitrary, heartless law; articles in liberal journals of the era such as the *Independent* and *Outlook* attest to growing middle-class distaste for the treatment of Chinese, a turn in public opinion that gave Chinese another weapon in their resistance to exclusion.

A NEW LITIGATION STRATEGY

While Chinese and other immigrant groups resorted to a variety of tactics—economic sanctions, publicity, lobbying—to exert pressure on the Bureau of Immigration, their lawyers simultaneously turned to the courts in the effort to "regulate the regulators." The Supreme Court had narrowly circumscribed the scope of judicial review since 1891, dealing a crushing blow to Chinese litigation strategies in the *Ju Toy* decision. Other tactics such as the boycott appeared to attract more national attention and more pressure for change than had litigation. Not surprisingly, the number of habeas corpus petitions filed by Chinese in the Northern District of California plummeted after the *Ju Toy* decision, from a total of 153 cases filed in 1904, to 32 in 1905, to a low of 9 in 1906.[144] But immigrants needed as many weapons as possible in their arsenal. Litigation would at the very least delay an alien's exclusion or deportation, allowing more time to pursue other channels of appeal and perhaps even result in the alien's release. At best, litigation could serve as a more general check on official discretion and provide a means to set higher standards for administrative procedures.

The task was to resurrect a litigation strategy from the limited avenues of judicial review left open by the Supreme Court by 1905. Because the Court had foreclosed the substantive review of the decisions made by the Bureau of Immigration, attorneys turned their attention to the procedures followed by the agency, hoping to make them less summary and administrative and more judicial in character. The attorneys' attack on its procedures, as outlined in its regulations, came as no surprise to the Bureau of Immigration. If attorneys could modify or eliminate regulations they found objectionable, the commissioner general of immigration predicted in 1905 that "they will care nothing for the Ju Toy decision and will suddenly become earnest advocates" of the bureau's administrative hearings.[145] Indeed, Henry Dibble, Ju Toy's attorney, had suggested that if the bureau afforded aliens and alleged citizens all of the protections they would receive in judicial hearings, there would be no cause for complaint.[146] The greater success Chinese had experienced in establishing their right to land before the federal courts gave immigrants cogent reasons for preferring judicial methods.[147] Just as obviously, the bureau had ample grounds for resisting such procedures, fearing that if adopted, they would result in unwarranted entries as well as delay.

Immigrants' attorneys probably brought their procedural challenges to the Bureau of Immigration before the federal courts with some trepidation because the Supreme Court had not displayed much sympathy for immigrants' demands for greater procedural protections. It had repeatedly held that due process did not require a judicial trial for aliens applying for admission or facing deportation and had further allowed the bureau broad discretion to establish its own procedures. In administrative agencies other than the Bureau of Immigration, the Constitution might be invoked as a check on officials' methods. But aliens appearing before the Bureau of Immigration could not lay claim to the specific constitutional guarantees embraced in the Bill of Rights; they enjoyed such protections only as privileges and only at the sufferance of Congress. Having acknowledged Congress's plenary power to regulate immigration, courts had conceded, as an incident of that power, the congressional authority to establish any procedures it thought necessary or appropriate. If Congress decided to authorize summary administrative procedures to establish an alien's right to be in the country, as it had in the act of 1891, then those procedures constituted due process of law regarding aliens.[148] Even when threatened with deportation, aliens appeared to have no greater procedural rights, primarily because the Court had characterized deportation in *Fong Yue Ting* as a civil, administrative proceeding to remove aliens from the United States for various policy reasons, not as a criminal proceeding. Because the "order of deportation," in the Court's words, "is not punishment for crime . . . the provisions of the Constitution securing the right of trial by jury and prohibiting unreasonable searches and seizures, and cruel and unusual punishments, have no application."[149]

The Court's decision in *Wong Wing* v. *United States* (1896) clarified its distinction between deportation and criminal proceedings. The Court invalidated section 4 of the Geary Act of 1892, which provided that Chinese found, after a summary hearing by a judge or commissioner, to be unlawfully in the United States "shall be imprisoned at hard labor for a period not exceeding one year" before deportation.[150] Unlike deportation, this provision, according to the Court, prescribed a genuine punishment, one that could be imposed only after a finding of guilt by "a judicial trial," not the summary hearings established by the Geary Act.[151] Although *Wong Wing* invalidated one of the harshest provisions of the Geary Act, the decision also served to reinforce the Court's benign characterization of deportation as an administrative proceeding free from judicial norms of due process. When John Turner's case reached the Supreme Court in 1904, the Court quickly dismissed his attorneys' arguments that immigration officials had violated the First, Fifth, and Sixth Amendments to the Constitution, holding as well settled that aliens in deportation proceedings "cannot assert the rights in general obtaining in a land to which they do not belong as citizens or otherwise."[152]

As the quote above suggests, the Court's opinions from *Nishimura Ekiu* to *Turner* had rested on a fundamental distinction between the rights of aliens and those of citizens. No matter how long their residence in the United States, aliens stood on the outskirts of the political community, enjoying constitutional guarantees only at the sufferance of Congress. The *Ju Toy* decision, however, blurred the earlier distinction between aliens and citizens, as Holmes held that even alleged citizens applying for admission to their own country were subject to the discretion of the Bureau of Immigration. Immigration officials had the power, in the Court's opinion, to determine whether an applicant was in fact a citizen entitled to land; due process, in such cases, "does not require a judicial trial" but could be satisfied by summary administrative proceedings.[153]

This line of reasoning did not appear to lay a particularly promising foundation for a legal campaign to force the Bureau of Immigration to afford aliens and alleged citizens greater procedural protections. Attorneys for immigrants fastened their hopes for change on the Supreme Court's holding in the *Japanese Immigrant Case* of 1903 and qualifications made in the *Ju Toy* opinion. In the *Japanese Immigrant Case*, a sixteen-year-old Japanese woman, Kaoru Yamataya, had landed in Seattle, Washington, on July 11, 1901, without authorization, according to the Bureau of Immigration. Several days later, immigration officials arrested her and ordered her deported as a person likely to become a public charge. On arguing her case before the Supreme Court, her attorney, Harold Preston, did not contend that she was entitled to a "judicial trial before a *court*" but did insist that even in administrative proceedings, Yamataya must have notice of the investigation against her as well as an opportunity to be heard before officials could deport her.[154] The failure of the Immigration Act of 1891 to provide the basic right of notice and a hearing made it unconstitutional, in Preston's opinion. He cited a wide range of nonimmigration cases involving due process challenges to administrative action as support for his claim that notice and a hearing were fundamental to a notion of due process. Preston admitted that the cases cited "involve property rights, but can it be said that the right to property is, in the eyes of the law, more sacred than the right to liberty?"[155] Yamataya, according to her attorney, spoke no English and had little understanding of the charges against her, realizing that she was to be deported only a few hours before her ship was due to sail. Under such conditions, he concluded, she had not had a genuine opportunity to be heard.

The government's attorney scornfully dismissed the appellant's arguments as "roving, experimental and general allegations"; officials had conducted the investigation honestly and fairly and had operated under the broad authority conferred upon them by Congress and affirmed by the Court in several cases.[156] The appellant's references to other cases involving administrative power were irrelevant, in the government's opinion, because "we are dealing with a special subject. . . . Judicial statements as to property and liberty under entirely different circumstances do not remotely affect the present case." The enforcement of immigration laws, in other words, was unique in that the traditional restraints of due process, even in their limited application to administrative processes, did not operate.[157] Paraphrasing the Court's opinion in *Fong Yue Ting*, the government's attorney argued that "deportation merely enforces the withholding of the privilege of coming here or remaining here" and, thus, "liberty is no more involved than property or life."[158]

The attorney for Yamataya scored an important legal victory but lost his particular case. The Supreme Court once again reaffirmed the broad discretion of the Bureau of Immigration and the constitutionality of summary administrative proceedings, comparing them, as it would in the *Ju Toy* case, to the summary procedures traditionally allowed in tax collection cases. But the Court's deference to the discretion of immigration officials did not mean that it would condone all of their actions. Justice John Marshall Harlan wrote, "This court has never held, nor must we now be understood as holding, that administrative officers, when executing the provisions of a statute involving the liberty of persons, may disregard the fundamental principles that inhere in 'due process of law' as understood at the time of the adoption of the Constitution." One of those fundamental principles was that "no person shall be deprived of his liberty without opportunity, at some time, to be heard." This basic procedural right did not necessarily require "an opportunity upon a regular, set occasion and according to the forms of judicial procedure, but one that will secure the prompt, vigorous action contemplated by Congress, and at the same time be appropriate to the nature of the case upon which such officers are required to act."[159]

Turning to the question of whether the act of 1891 was unconstitutional because it did not explicitly require notice and a hearing before deportation, Harlan held that congressional statutes must be construed, whenever possible, to be in harmony with the Constitution. Nothing in the language of the statute gave absolute, arbitrary power to immigration officials, and consequently, Harlan implied, the statutes should be interpreted as incorporating fundamental principles of due process such as notice and a hearing.

The opinion departed in significant ways from the Court's earlier immigration decisions. In *Nishimura Ekiu* and *Fong Yue Ting*, the Court had held that the congressional statutes provided the gauge to determine whether due process had been afforded. Presumably, if the immigration officials departed from the procedure established by Congress or the bureau's regulations, that constituted a violation of due process. In the *Japanese Immigrant Case*, however, the Court had grounded the right to be heard, not in the immigration statutes but in the "fundamental principles that inhere in 'due process of law.' "[160] A "fundamental principles" approach provided a much more promising basis from which to raise the standards in immigration procedure because it suggested that there existed a "higher law" to which congressional statutes and bureau regulations must conform.

Although the Court appeared to broaden the procedural rights available to aliens, the outcome in the *Japanese Immigrant Case* cast doubt on its potential to lead to far-ranging change. And the Court's rare interjection in immigration procedure probably came as cold comfort to Yamataya as it found that she had been afforded the required notice and opportunity to be heard. "If the appellant's want of knowledge of the English language put her at some disadvantage in the investigation," said Harlan, "that was her misfortune and constitutes no reason . . . for the intervention of the courts."[161] The proper person to redress such potential injustices, Harlan noted, was the officer designated by the statute to oversee the administration of the laws, the secretary of the treasury, not the courts. Thus the Court maintained a stance of deference, and it was not clear how significant the requirement of notice and a hearing would be in practice.

The Supreme Court's decision in *Ju Toy* left a similarly ambiguous legacy, broadening the bureau's discretion to determine the right of alleged citizens to enter the country while, at the same time, suggesting possible avenues for judicial review. In preparing the questions to be certified by the Circuit Court of Appeals in the *Ju Toy* case, Assistant Attorney General McReynolds had acknowledged to U.S. Attorney Marshall Woodworth that the government left open the possibility that courts might issue writs of habeas corpus if it appeared that administrative officials had "failed to grant a proper hearing, abused their discretion or acted in any unlawful or improper way upon the case presented to them for determination."[162] Indeed, Justice Holmes's opinion in *Ju Toy* began with the assumption that "no abuse of authority is alleged," nor was there any complaint of "evidence not laid before the Secretary [of commerce and labor]" in the petition challenging Ju Toy's exclusion.[163]

Within months of the *Ju Toy* decision, habeas corpus petitions filed in the Federal District Court for the Northern District in San Francisco revealed that attorneys were attempting to parlay the qualifications made in the *Ju Toy* case into a new litigation strategy. In planning that new strategy, Chinese probably could not have found a more experienced attorney than Marshall Woodworth, the U.S. attorney who had represented the government in *Ju Toy* and to whom Assistant Attorney General McReynolds had confided the limits of the government's case. Woodworth had an intimate knowledge of the federal courts in San Francisco, having served as a clerk to Judges Ogden Hoffman and William W. Morrow before being appointed as assistant U.S. attorney in 1898.[164] Woodworth now worked for the Chinese and joined forces with Oliver P. Stidger, an attorney who appears to have worked briefly for the Chinese Bureau in the collector's office but who now represented a variety of Chinese organizations (including the Chinese Six Companies), to construct new challenges to the Bureau of Immigration's decisions.[165] They limited their initial petitions to cases involving alleged Chinese-American citizens, complaining in each case that the commissioner of immigration had abused his discretion and acted arbitrarily in rejecting the testimony of the applicant and his or her witnesses. Furthermore, the petitions alleged, the commissioner had failed to provide Chinese-American citizens with such basic procedural protections as the right to an attorney, to present evidence on their behalf, to view evidence used against them, and to a public hearing before exclusion. Without such protections, the attorneys implied, the hearing before immigration officials was not proper.[166]

The district court in San Francisco routinely dismissed such petitions, but one of the cases involving a Chinese-American man, Chin Yow, made it to the Supreme Court and resulted in a potentially significant check on the Bureau of Immigration's methods. Chin Yow claimed to have been born in San Francisco and to have left for a visit to China in 1904.[167] He returned a year later but was denied entry by the immigration officials, who believed his case to be fraudulent because he spoke little English and his witnesses' testimony sounded coached.

Maxwell Evarts, the attorney representing Chin Yow on appeal to the Supreme Court, did not try to reargue the *Ju Toy* case, but he did highlight, somewhat sarcastically, some of the decision's wide-reaching and troubling implications:

> It is somewhat disconcerting to think that a citizen of the United States of French or German descent, might be ordered deported because he had ophthalmia, and the immigration inspector at the port of landing believed him to be a Frenchman or German (inasmuch as he looked like one and talked like one), and to be making the claim of citizenship solely for the purpose of enabling him to land in spite of the contagious trouble with his eyes. If the immigration officer is honest in his belief, and gives a full hearing to this citizen of the United States, then the latter can have no relief from any court, but must be banished from his country.[168]

Evarts elaborated the implications of the *Ju Toy* opinion to bolster his main argument that given the high stakes involved—the possible banishment of a citizen from his country—the courts had to ensure that immigration officials acted in good faith and after due deliberation. Citizens might be disbarred even after a full hearing by officials, but the chance of an unjust exclusion was even greater if officials did not follow proper procedures. In the case on appeal, Evarts pointed out, Chin Yow had not been allowed to present all of the available witnesses who could have proven overwhelmingly the fact of his American birth, nor were his attorneys (Woodworth and Stidger) allowed to consult with him or to view the evidence and proceedings against him.

Significantly, Evarts did not argue that Chin Yow was entitled to consult an attorney by virtue of the Sixth Amendment—an argument that would have gained him little ground given the Court's persistent refusal to extend the Bill of Rights to immigration cases; rather, Evarts implicitly tied the right to an attorney to the right of Chin Yow to present all of the relevant evidence on his behalf. In other words, the right to consult with an attorney was essential to an opportunity to be heard.[169] If officials deprived an alleged citizen of a full opportunity to present his or her case, they were guilty of arbitrary action and an abuse of discretion, charged Evarts.[170]

The government perceived the *Chin Yow* case as a deliberate "attempt to avoid the ruling of the Supreme Court in the Ju Toy case" by curbing the discretion of immigration officials to determine the fact of citizenship.[171] Assistant Attorney General Alford W. Cooley acknowledged that the Court in *Ju Toy* had implied that judicial review might still be possible if officials abused their authority. But in this case, the government argued, no such abuse was evident. The only rule that inspectors had potentially violated was the regulation giving attorneys the right to examine the evidence after the investigation; but if inspectors had infringed upon that right, Cooley urged that the Court follow its lead in the *Japanese Immigrant Case* and assign the power to redress irregularities in the administrative proceedings to the secretary of commerce and labor.[172]

The Supreme Court, perhaps responding to the outcry against the *Ju Toy* decision and the growing public criticism of the Bureau of Immigration's methods in Chinese cases, found for Chin Yow. Justice Holmes again wrote the opinion for the Court, clarifying that while "the decision of the Department is final . . . that is on the presupposition that the decision was after a hearing in good faith, however summary in form." If it appeared from a habeas corpus petition that "the petitioner had been allowed nothing but the semblance of a hearing," without a "fair opportunity to produce the evidence that he had desired . . . in the mode provided by the [Chinese exclusion] statutes," then courts should issue the writ of habeas corpus to determine whether, in fact, officials had provided a fair hearing.[173] If the court found that an applicant did not have a fair hearing, Holmes suggested that the court could then proceed to rehear the case on its merits, that is, it could determine whether the petitioner was an American citizen as alleged. Holmes cautioned, however, that courts could not take jurisdiction if the applicant simply proved "that the commissioner and the Department of Commerce and Labor did not accept sworn statements as true, even though no contrary or impeaching testimony was adduced," or that the decision was wrong. Furthermore, Holmes reiterated, the hearing could be summary in form.[174]

By the time the Supreme Court had decided in his favor, Chin Yow, discouraged and ill after more than two years of confinement in the Pacific

Mail detention shed in San Francisco, had allowed himself to be deported to China. When informed of the opportunity to return to the United States, he reportedly said that "he would rather die than take chances of again being confined."[175] Though the decision apparently came too late for Chin Yow, the Court's opinion must have pleased his attorneys. Constitutional law scholar Thomas Reed Powell noted at the time that the Supreme Court had significantly limited its decision in *Ju Toy* with the caveat that immigration officials' decisions were final only if they followed proper methods. Holmes's suggestion that federal courts might hear cases de novo on the question of citizenship if officials failed to provide a fair hearing was an even more dramatic qualification of *Ju Toy*.[176] Furthermore, Holmes's caution that judges should not review the bureau's decisions simply upon allegations that they were wrong would be difficult for judges to heed, predicted Powell, for "the evidence produced to show the hearing was unfair may convince [the judge] the decision of Commissioner was erroneous." In such a case, Powell thought a judge who believed a citizen was being wrongfully excluded from her country would find it difficult "to eliminate this and other considerations from his mind in judging the fairness of the hearing."[177] Thus the judicial review of the bureau's procedures might lead to the review of its factual determinations as well and might potentially unravel the bureau's determined campaign, believed to have been cinched with the *Ju Toy* decision, to have its determinations treated as final.

The *Chin Yow* requirement that hearings before immigration officials must be "fair" also offered a promising avenue for both Chinese and non-Chinese immigrants to attack the procedures in agency regulations and congressional statutes. In its most expansive interpretation, *Chin Yow*, in conjunction with the "fundamental rights" approach to defining due process in the *Japanese Immigrant Case*, could provide the basis for overcoming some of the legal liabilities imposed upon aliens in *Nishimura Ekiu* and *Fong Yue Ting*. Although the Supreme Court in those decisions had held that aliens could not avail themselves of the specific guarantees in the Bill of Rights in hearings before the Bureau of Immigration, the *Chin Yow* decision opened the possibility that attorneys might be able to elaborate a definition of "fair hearing" which incorporated several of those procedural rights as fundamental to securing a fair opportunity to be heard.

Thus immigrants' challenges to the bureau's methods took place in a variety of forums, from the Supreme Court to the local newspapers, and made use of diverse appeals to the American immigrant heritage and notions of fair play, hostility to administrative power, and American economic and international interests. It is clear that immigrants' complaints were heard. Upon leaving as commissioner general of immigration in 1913,

Daniel Keefe stated to Congress that "the present immigration law has but little effect in reducing or checking the great influx of aliens," in part because of the actions of immigrant aid societies intervening on behalf of aliens and of "those who constantly criticize the Immigration Service on every conceivable ground."[178] Commissioner Williams at Ellis Island appeared to spend much of his time, when not engaged with his daily administrative tasks, defending his staff's enforcement of the law against attacks by pro-immigrant groups.[179] Immigrants' complaints were not only being heard, but sometimes, as the bureau's grudging reforms in response to the Chinese boycott and the Supreme Court's decision in *Chin Yow* reveal, acted on. It remained to be seen, however, whether the pressure applied by pro-immigrant groups or the new appeals made to the federal courts were sufficient to obtain the significant substantive and procedural changes sought by aliens.

CHAPTER 7

A Fair though Summary Hearing

THE SHAPING OF

ADMINISTRATIVE

DUE PROCESS

The *Chin Yow* "fair hearing" requirement gave attorneys for immigrants a toehold in their new campaign to bind the Bureau of Immigration to higher standards of due process. Though it was an important victory, the decision's long-term significance remained uncertain. The new litigation launched attorneys into largely uncharted legal territory, exploring the vague parameters of procedural due process and its application in the nascent administrative state. The highly controversial debates surrounding due process of law at the turn of the century, as well as the gathering momentum of the nativist movement by the 1910s, provided the broader context for attorneys' efforts to shape a new administrative due process.

Due process, always a vague concept, became particularly contested in late nineteenth-century struggles over expanding government regulation. Critics, seeing "governmental interference" as a dangerous encroachment into the private sphere, turned to the due process clauses of the Fifth and Fourteenth Amendments to challenge regulatory efforts. They condemned the administrative proceedings of new agencies such as the Interstate Commerce Commission (ICC) as a violation of due process and also "transformed the Fourteenth Amendment . . . into a charter identifying fundamental [substantive] rights and immunizing them from all legislative regulation."[1] Not surprisingly, reformers perceived an appeal to due process as merely a "convenient technicality" used by their opponents to demolish their cherished reforms in the courts.[2] So-called Progressives sought a more interventionist, flexible government, placing their hopes in the administrative agency staffed by objective experts who exercised discretion to achieve the social good. Due process, with its emphasis on uniformity, precedents, and individual entitlements, stood at odds with the administrative values of discretion, flexibility, and the public interest. In reformers' eyes, due process had become an antiquated concept ill-suited to the demands of modern society.[3]

Although attorneys and federal judges made few references to developments outside of immigration law, their efforts to delineate appropriate procedures within the Bureau of Immigration were undoubtedly informed by this rich discourse on the meaning of due process in the administrative age. In elaborating the definition of a fair hearing, for example, immigrants' attorneys drew on a "fundamental principles" approach as elaborated in the *Japanese Immigrant Case* to argue that certain procedures were inherent in the notion of due process and to be followed, regardless of the forum (judicial or administrative) or the status of the individual (alien or citizen).[4] In deciding attorneys' challenges to immigration procedure, some judges rallied with great passion around the fundamental principles approach, but on the whole, the courts overwhelmingly endorsed a more flexible definition of due process. The courts frequently referred to the distinct nature of administrative agencies as well as to the hold of earlier immigration precedents in upholding the bureau's summary methods. But as their equivocal holdings regarding alleged citizens reveal, membership in the American polity and the objectives of American immigration policy remained, as in *Fong Yue Ting*, the key determinants in shaping the courts' approach to due process in immigration proceedings. When nativism peaked by the 1920s, so too did judicial willingness to abide by precedents emphasizing deference to the broad discretion of immigration officials.

THE AMBIGUITIES OF *CHIN YOW*

Despite Thomas Reed Powell's speculation that *Chin Yow* could lead to significant restraints on the Bureau of Immigration, the decision appeared to have little immediate effect. In San Francisco, Chinese petitions for habeas corpus jumped from only one case filed in 1907 to twenty-seven cases filed in 1908. Few of the 1908 cases, however, rested on the claim of an unfair hearing. In 1909, the number of Chinese applying for admission to the United States rose 38 percent from the previous year, yet only six petitions were filed in the federal court at San Francisco, none of which was successful. The situation was much the same in other judicial districts. Commissioner General of Immigration Daniel J. Keefe reported in 1909, with evident satisfaction, that "attorneys who have endeavored to have Chinese cases reviewed by the courts should be discouraged by the fact that in 15 instances in the past year [of a national total of 16 habeas corpus cases] their efforts failed." Based on such numbers, Keefe predicted that despite the *Chin Yow* decision, "it seems altogether improbable that any Chinese refused admission will ever hereafter be able to resort to the courts and overturn the decision of the immigration officers."[5]

Keefe's prediction was not fully borne out, but he was correct that attorneys moved cautiously in their initial forays into the new legal territory opened by the *Chin Yow* decision. The doctrine expounded in the case had great potential, as discussed in Chapter 6, for it appeared to offer an avenue for securing basic procedural protections denied aliens since *Nishimura Ekiu* and *Fong Yue Ting*. But the *Chin Yow* opinion left unresolved several legal issues that made it difficult to predict the decision's long-term significance. This uncertainty probably accounts, in part, for attorneys' tentativeness in the immediate aftermath of the case.

The most perplexing issue arising from *Chin Yow* centered on how to determine what was a fair hearing for aliens and alleged citizens involved in proceedings which Congress had explicitly designated as summary. A fair hearing involved the notion that the Bureau of Immigration had to follow regular procedures, but it was unclear what legal authority—the statutes, the common law, or fundamental principles—provided the standard to which immigration proceedings should be held. A notion of fairness incorporating fundamental principles of due process clearly represented the best definition for aliens' attorneys. But *Chin Yow* might mean only that the Bureau of Immigration had to follow the procedures established in congressional statutes. The Supreme Court had held in *Nishimura Ekiu* that the procedures created by Congress or its delegated authority, the Bureau of Immigration, constituted due process for aliens. Similarly, Justice Holmes in *Chin Yow* used the immigration statutes as his baseline for determining fairness, holding that "if one alleging himself to be a citizen is not allowed a chance to establish his right *in the mode provided by those statutes* . . . the statutes cannot be taken to require him to be turned back without more."[6]

Furthermore, a fundamental rights approach, though a more promising foundation than the statutes for defining fairness, would not necessarily lead to more formal legal procedures in the Bureau of Immigration for the Supreme Court had identified few "fundamental principles" inherent in procedural due process.[7] Even rights considered to be at the core of due process might not be guaranteed in all proceedings. Much depended, as the Supreme Court had said in the *Japanese Immigrant Case*, upon what process "is appropriate to the nature of the case."[8]

In assessing the nature of immigration proceedings, the distinct characteristics and purposes of administrative tribunals as compared to courts were important factors. Legislatures created administrative bodies in increasing numbers in the early twentieth century, often precisely to avoid the cumbersome and procedure-bound courts. The new administrative tribunals, noted one commentator in 1906, "aimed at expedition and economy," in short, "the accomplishment of things," goals that could easily be hampered if they followed more elaborate judicial procedures.[9]

Certainly, the campaign to vest final jurisdiction in the Bureau of Immigration, described in Part I, developed out of a concern that courts, because of their judicial standards and procedures, frustrated the enforcement of restrictive policies. But though the judges had felt compelled to extend certain procedural rights and practices to Chinese in court hearings, they had thus far refused to hold the Bureau of Immigration to the same standards. The summary character of the proceedings, according to Justice Holmes in *Sing Tuck* v. *United States*, provided the basis from which to determine what process was due. Upholding the legality of the bureau's Chinese regulations, Holmes explained, "The whole scheme is intended to give as fair a chance to prove a right to enter the country as the necessarily summary character of the proceedings will permit."[10]

The Court did not defer to all administrative agencies so readily, however. Administrative law pioneer Frank J. Goodnow had cautioned in 1905 that courts should not "impair governmental efficiency," but neither should they tolerate "serious violation of private rights."[11] The federal courts perceived certain private rights and interests as in need of greater protection than others. For example, the Supreme Court had exercised a particularly vigilant review over state utility commissions and the Interstate Commerce Commission because the common carriers they regulated often had large property interests and common law rights at stake. Other administrative activities concerning taxation, the dispersal of public lands, customs duties, and the postal service were seen either as essential to the government's support or defense or as an extension of a privilege, rather than regulation of a right, by the government; in such cases, the Court had perceived the government's policy goals to be paramount and the rights of individuals involved to be weak.[12]

Significantly, the Supreme Court, in upholding the broad authority of the Bureau of Immigration, had relied most frequently on precedents involving administrative power over taxation, customs, the dispersal of public lands, and the postal service. The Supreme Court had early treated aliens' claims to enter and remain in the United States as a privilege, not a right, which could be suspended at any time by Congress under its inherent power to police and defend the nation's borders. The Court further had refused to see deportation as a deprivation of liberty. In the Court's view, aliens apparently had few compelling interests at stake, and the requirements of a fair hearing might not be very elaborate.

The challenge for aliens' attorneys would be to persuade the federal courts that aliens had greater interests at stake than, for example, an importer contesting the amount of duties to be paid on his goods and that, consequently, they deserved a higher standard of due process. Attorneys would stress, as Evarts did in *Chin Yow*, the serious deprivation of liberty resulting from the Bureau of Immigration's decision to exclude or deport aliens and alleged citizens. Less frequently, they would also propose new analogies to the Court, likening the Bureau of Immigration to other administrative agencies, such as the Interstate Commerce Commission, which received greater judicial scrutiny and followed more elaborate procedures.

Thus the definition of a fair hearing would be drawn from a variety of elements—the nature of the admission and deportation proceedings, the statutes and agency regulations, and the "fundamental principles" of due process—but the exact weight that should be given to each was a matter of debate. Immigrants' attorneys in the major ports of New York and San Francisco had to navigate their way through the uncertain implications of *Chin Yow*, but the decision provided them with a foundation from which to build a new litigation strategy. They worked from the premise that for a person to have a fair opportunity to be heard, certain rights—the right to an attorney, to confront evidence, to cross-examine witnesses, to a public hearing, and to a finding based on substantial evidence—were essential. Attorneys also took advantage of other available routes to judicial review, charging that immigration officials acted arbitrarily by disregarding the weight of the evidence or that they misinterpreted the law. But their success in exploiting the potential of *Chin Yow* and the exceptions made in *Ju Toy* depended, of course, on the federal courts' reception of their arguments.

THE CAMPAIGN FOR PROCEDURAL RIGHTS

Attorneys focused their efforts first on obtaining greater procedural protections in immigration hearings as fundamental to due process. In attacking administrative procedure, they challenged one of the prime characteristics distinguishing courts from administrative agencies. In the view of its supporters, the agency's "freedom from the bonds of purely traditional . . . and technical rules" allowed it the discretion to respond flexibly and efficiently to changing social conditions and to accomplish policy objectives.[13] Attorneys' procedural claims also contested, though more subtly, congressional and administrative power to determine in statutes and regulations the rights of aliens and alleged citizens in immigration hearings.

Federal judges' responses to the procedural complaints were shaped by two concerns: the function of due process in administrative proceedings and the hold of Supreme Court precedent, which deferred broadly to Congress and its delegated authority to enforce immigration policy in whatever manner they saw fit. Most federal judges shared the opinion of District Court Judge Emile Henry Lacombe of the Southern District of New York, who repeatedly supported the Bureau of Immigration and expressed little concern or compunction about its discretionary power or the lack of procedural protections. He stressed the differences between courts and administrative bodies, declaring that examinations by immigration inspectors were not "trials at law" and should be restrained only by the explicit instructions of Congress or the Bureau of Immigration.[14] Too great an emphasis on procedural form would hinder the bureau from effectively fulfilling its administrative objectives and depart from Supreme Court rulings recognizing the necessarily summary character of immigration proceedings.

A vocal minority saw the disjuncture between administrative and judicial proceedings as reason to exercise more, not less, vigilance over immigration officials. Those judges had less faith that officials, operating without procedural constraints, would conduct hearings fairly. Officials' "zeal to elicit adverse testimony [was] inconsistent with that degree of fairmindedness required of a trier in passing" on questions in which the stakes for aliens and alleged citizens were so high.[15] The point of immigration hearings, stressed Judge Maurice T. Dooling, appointed to the district court at San Francisco in 1913, was "the ascertainment of the truth."[16] As opposed to the majority of federal judges, who believed the "truth" could best be reached if the agency were freed from technical procedural rules, the minority asserted that procedural rights would lead to better, more accurate substantive outcomes. They deplored the bureau's deportation proceedings, in particular, saying "it is obvious" that they disregard "almost every fundamental principle established in England and this country for the protection of persons charged with an offense."[17]

These judges, sympathetic to immigrants and their demands for fundamental procedural rights, spoke more often and passionately about the requisites of a fair hearing. Yet even they failed to transform the *Chin Yow* decision into a vehicle for patrolling the Bureau of Immigration's methods in any significant way. If earlier judges, such as Judge Morrow, had been "captives of law" in admitting Chinese despite their support of exclusionary legislation, a minority of federal judges who now wished to offer greater protections to immigrants similarly professed to be constrained by law—the Supreme Court precedents that had checked the federal courts' power to intervene in immigration proceedings.

The first major Supreme Court decision concerning procedural rights after *Chin Yow* revealed just how thick was the barrier of precedent. The case arose after the bureau and the San Francisco police instituted a series of raids between 1910 and 1913 on houses suspected of being brothels. Officials ordered the deportation of many women, particularly Chinese, for practicing prostitution. In the litigation challenging their deportation, both sides agreed that immigration officials had proceeded according to agency regulations. This, argued government attorneys, was all that the fairness mandate of *Chin Yow*, understood within the context of earlier immigration decisions, required.

Attorneys for the women sought to circumvent, without directly challenging, the limits placed on procedural due process in *Nishimura Ekiu* and *Fong Yue Ting*. They argued that simply following administrative regulations did not make a hearing fair. Rather, the test was whether agency rules comported with fundamental norms of due process. In these cases, the bureau failed the test because the procedure it followed was "destructive of liberty and fair play, is contrary to law, and does not protect the person proceeded against from fraud and loss." In particular, attorneys complained of the rules promulgated by the Bureau of Immigration in 1911, which, while providing the right to counsel for aliens in deportation proceedings, gave officials the discretion to decide at what stage of the investigation to afford that right. For example, immigration officers detained one woman, who was eight months pregnant, for four days and conducted extensive preliminary examinations before advising her of the right to an attorney. Such an "impaired right of counsel" left naive aliens vulnerable to manipulation and intimidation by immigration officials, in the opinion of the immigrants' attorneys. Furthermore, immigration officials, though acting within bureau regulations, did not compel the testimony of witnesses on the aliens' behalf, forced the women to testify against themselves, and accepted the hearsay evidence of informants without allowing the women an opportunity to confront their accusers. The warrants for the arrest and deportation of the women were also vague and general, charged the attorneys, and did not meet the requirements for warrants in criminal proceedings.

Attorneys rejected the government's contention that the administrative and summary character of the proceedings required abbreviated procedures. They stressed instead the potential serious deprivation of liberty suffered by the alien women who might be unjustly deported and the harm done to their American families as well. In the case that eventually came before the Supreme Court, attorneys argued that the common law right of the Chinese-American citizen husband to the company of his wife was as much at stake as the liberty of the Chinese woman accused of prostitution. Attorneys emphasized the weak qualifications of immigration inspectors who acted in a "quasi-judicial capacity" without the "learning or experience of the judiciary." The stakes involved, attorneys argued, required that such men be bound by the "fundamental legal principles" that guided courts.[18]

The federal district court at San Francisco, however, sided with the government, emphasizing the need to free administrative tribunals from judicial procedures. Judges acknowledged that the deportation proceedings did not conform to the "strict rules of legal procedure" and that "it is somewhat difficult for the mind, accustomed to . . . investigations conducted strictly in accordance with the time-honored rules of judicial procedure, to adjust itself to the informal and sometimes ex parte methods of administrative officers."[19] Yet, judges stressed, such an adjustment must be made because the Bureau of Immigration, by necessity and design, was not required to follow the same procedural guidelines as courts. They held that the procedures established by the bureau did not deny the alien women a fair hearing and dismissed the attorneys' challenges.

The Supreme Court affirmed the district court's position in *Low Wah Suey* v. *Backus* in 1912 and narrowed the implications of *Chin Yow*. Stressing the summary character of the hearing and the agency's good faith effort to provide aliens with notice and the opportunity to present evidence, the Court proceeded to evaluate the bureau's standards against the language of the immigration statutes. Because the statutes did not explicitly require counsel throughout the whole hearing nor provide officials with the power to compel the attendance of witnesses for the alien, the Court found the agency's regulations and practices lawful. The Court emphasized that immigration proceedings must be "manifestly unfair" or reveal a "manifest abuse of discretion" before it would intervene.[20]

The *Low Wah Suey* opinion was not an encouraging sequel to *Chin Yow*. Not only did it raise the threshold for judicial review by requiring a showing of "manifest unfairness," it rejected a fundamental principles approach in favor of a statutory definition of due process. The statutory definition of due process rested firmly upon earlier precedent, which held that aliens in immigration proceedings had only those rights explicitly granted them by Congress. Because Congress had plenary authority over immigration policy, the Court deemed it also had the power to establish whatever methods for enforcement legislators and administrators thought prudent. "Fairness" meant only that Congress and the Bureau of Immigration had to follow the administrative rules they created.

Despite the discouraging outcome in *Low Wah Suey*, the Court had not foreclosed further litigation over procedural issues, and attorneys had some hope for success in the lower federal courts. Judges agreed that certain rights, particularly the opportunity both to present and confront the evidence, must be guaranteed. Inspectors could not withhold any material evidence from the immigrant or the secretary of commerce and labor upon appeal.[21] For example, though the bureau generally allowed the alien's attorney to view and copy evidence collected by the government, it usually did not share the bureau's correspondence regarding the case or the commissioner of immigration's recommendation to the secretary of labor upon appeal.[22] Attorneys suspected, often with good reason, that the bureau's correspondence contained damning information or interpretations of the evidence which the alien was never allowed an opportunity to confront. Judges sometimes found the withholding of information in the communication from the alien to be unfair, especially if it contained evidence critical to the decision to exclude or deport.[23] They also found the failure to forward all of the evidence to the Department of Commerce and Labor upon appeal to be unfair. Such decisions lay clearly within the ambit of the *Chin Yow* decision in which Justice Holmes had explicitly linked the "fair opportunity to produce . . . evidence" to the right to a fair hearing.[24]

Judges also uniformly conceded that the statutory test, as outlined in *Low Wah Suey*, required the bureau to follow its own rules.[25] Yet the statutory test of due process did not always yield easy answers, nor did federal judges always agree on what statutes or agency rules required. Sometimes, for example, statutes appeared to authorize conflicting procedures, as became particularly evident in the struggles over the deportation of Chinese. The Chinese exclusion laws provided for a judicial hearing before deportation, but subsequent general immigration laws required only an administrative hearing. The Bureau of Immigration attempted to circumvent the courts by arresting Chinese whenever possible for violation of the general immigration laws rather than the Chinese exclusion laws, freeing inspectors to pass on the case in an administrative hearing (see Table 7 for the varying disposition of deportation cases). When Chinese challenged that action as a violation of the due process established in the exclusion statutes, the Supreme Court first sanctioned the bureau's policy but later held that Chinese arrested specifically for violating the Chinese exclusion law, rather than the general immigration laws, retained the statutory right to a judicial hearing with its "safeguards of impartiality and providence."[26]

Even when the statutes did not conflict, they established few explicit

TABLE 7 *Disposition of Deportation Cases by U.S. Commissioner, 1906–1924 (Federal District Court for Northern District of California)*

Year	Discharged N (%)	Deported N (%)	Dismissal N (%)	Unknown N (%)	Total N
1906	6 (50)	6 (50)	0 (0)	0 (0)	12
1907	23 (32)	47 (65)	1 (1)	1 (1)	72
1908	5 (21)	18 (75)	1 (4)	0 (0)	24
1909	16 (53)	14 (47)	0 (0)	0 (0)	30
1910	12 (48)	13 (52)	0 (0)	0 (0)	25
1911	5 (38)	6 (46)	2 (15)	0 (0)	13
1912	12 (36)	19 (57)	1 (3)	1 (3)	33
1913	13 (42)	12 (39)	5 (16)	1 (3)	31
1914	3 (25)	6 (50)	0 (0)	3 (25)	12
1915	6 (50)	5 (42)	1 (8)	0 (0)	12
1916	0 (0)	1 (100)	0 (0)	0 (0)	1[a]
1917	3 (60)	1 (20)	0 (0)	1 (20)	5
1918	0 (0)	4 (100)	0 (0)	0 (0)	4
1919	0 (0)	0 (0)	0 (0)	0 (0)	0
1920	0 (0)	1 (100)	0 (0)	0 (0)	1
1921	0 (0)	0 (0)	0 (0)	0 (0)	0
1922	0 (0)	0 (0)	0 (0)	0 (0)	0
1923	4 (28)	9 (64)	1 (7)	0 (0)	14[b]
1924	3 (100)	0 (0)	0 (0)	0 (0)	3
Total					292

Source: Compiled from U.S. Commissioner's Dockets, Federal District Court for Northern District of California, 1906–24.

[a]The drop in the number of deportation cases probably reflects the Bureau of Immigration's campaign to arrest Chinese under the general immigration laws which required only an administrative hearing, a strategy that had been approved by the Supreme Court in *United States* v. *Wong You*, 223 U.S. 67 (1912).

[b]The rise in the number of deportation cases probably reflects the Supreme Court's holding in *Ng Fung Ho* v. *White*, 259 U.S. 276 (1922), that alleged Chinese-American citizens were still entitled to a judicial hearing as to their citizenship before they could be deported.

procedural guidelines, leaving the details to the discretion of administrative officials. Attorneys mined the ambiguities of the statutes and provoked an often spirited debate among federal judges over such questions as the alien's right to an attorney, the extent of the attorney's participation, and the evidentiary rules to be followed by the bureau. Yet even judges defending aliens' rights remained constrained by precedent that urged deference to the unique administrative objectives of the Bureau of Immigration.

Consider, for example, judicial responses to immigration attorneys' efforts to expand the participation of counsel in immigration hearings. The immigration laws did not explicitly allow an alien an attorney in hearings before the board of special inquiry; but after the boycott, Chinese in 1907 won the right to have an attorney present at admission hearings.[27] Other immigrants did not have access to attorneys during admission hearings, but the bureau did provide in 1911 that aliens facing deportation be allowed representation by an attorney at some point during the investigation.

Even when conceding the right to counsel, the Bureau of Immigration sought to limit attorneys' participation, allowing inspectors discretion to decide when, and to what extent, they would be allowed to participate. The commissioner general of immigration advised the San Francisco bureau that the attorney should be brought in near the end of the proceedings, saying, "Ordinarily the government's case can be practically completed before counsel is allowed to intervene for any purpose." The commissioner general cautioned the inspector to keep a tight rein on the attorney's participation: "When intervention is allowed, it is not for the purpose of cross-questioning and grilling the Government's agents, but to enable counsel to acquaint himself with the nature of the evidence already of record, and to offer any further evidence that he may be able to produce bearing upon the questions actually in issue."[28] Cross-examination, the bureau emphasized, was not necessary to secure a fair hearing.[29]

Concerned that hearings had become "unduly prolong[ed]," the commissioner general of immigration initiated reforms that curbed cross-examination even further. He instructed local commissioners to dispense, whenever possible, with the practice of having the government's witnesses testify in person at the hearings and instead to use ex parte affidavits, that is, the written statements of witnesses.[30]

Immigration attorneys, not surprisingly, vigorously challenged the bureau's attempt to limit their effective participation. In their view, the right to counsel was meaningful only if aliens had representation from the very beginning of the proceeding to ensure that aliens knew the charges against them and to protect them from making damaging statements in the preliminary examinations. Attorneys further argued that once selected to represent an alien, they should be able to participate fully in immigration hearings, with full access to all of the evidence and the ability to subpoena and cross-examine witnesses. Attorneys complained bitterly about the new "hearings by affidavits," which were designed "to obviate all examinations" by immigrants' counsel.[31] Such statements would never be allowed in a "court of justice," the attorneys argued. The affidavits were taken "secretly" and "in private," allowing no opportunity for the attorney to cross-examine or clarify points in the testimony.[32] Such restraints upon lawyers made it impossible for aliens and alleged citizens to have a full opportunity to submit and rebut evidence, the essence of the "fair hearing" requirement of *Chin Yow*.

Challenges to the bureau's regulations regarding attorneys' participation prompted different judicial responses, though all professed to be bound by the statutes. In the face of the statute's silence regarding the right to counsel, federal judges proved unwilling to impose such a requirement as fundamental to a fair hearing.[33] Access to attorneys in deportation cases was only a privilege granted by the bureau, not a fundamental right; thus judges generally allowed the bureau considerable latitude to regulate attorneys' participation even though they might disagree with the regulations.[34]

District Court Judge Frank Dietrich, for example, had serious misgivings about the use of affidavits in the case of Pedro Garcia, ordered deported in part on evidence given in ex parte affidavits. Garcia's attorney, Marshall Woodworth, argued that it was impossible to defend his client adequately and rebut opposing evidence without the ability to cross-examine witnesses. Dietrich stressed that "the petitioner has been domiciled in this country for more than a decade, and may have acquired large property interests and formed close social ties. . . . Where . . . deportation is fraught with such dire consequences," Dietrich continued, "to subject his right to remain here to a trial by ex parte affidavits is . . . far out of harmony with the procedure which I think ought to prevail."[35] Despite his appreciation of the high stakes involved, the judge concluded after a review of Supreme Court authority and the general immigration laws and regulations that a hearing based on affidavits was not a denial of due process in the administrative realm. While, according to the bureau's rules, "evidence may be offered to rebut evidence produced by the government . . . there is no suggestion of a right to cross-examination," concluded Dietrich.[36]

Other judges who disapproved of the bureau's methods construed the statutes and regulations more liberally in favor of aliens to achieve what they thought was a fair hearing. Judge George Chandler Holt of the Southern District of New York did not believe he could substantially alter the procedure established by statute and agency regulations, but he held that aliens "are at least entitled to the rights which such a system accords them." He found that the right of Arthur and Lambertine Bosny to an attorney had been denied in the deportation proceedings even though it appeared from official records that the Bosnys had declined the assistance of counsel when offered. Upon appeal, the Bosnys claimed that they had acted on the advice of an immigration inspector who told them several times that "the Department generally would take umbrage at their employing a lawyer, but would be inclined to be lenient with them if they did not employ a lawyer," a charge that immigration officials adamantly denied. Judge Holt concluded that the inspector had "by a course of constant persuasion and intimidation prevented these aliens from engaging counsel to represent them in the proceeding" and thus the hearing was unfair.[37]

Judge Dooling at San Francisco, who generally demonstrated greater than usual sympathy for immigrants and a higher regard for proceduralism, ventured even closer to the fundamental principles approach.[38] He held, for example, that though the statute did not provide aliens with the right to subpoena witnesses, "ordinary fairness" required that an alien be allowed to cross-examine the government's witnesses already present at the deportation hearing. In response to the agency's argument that it would be a "'nuisance' to permit cross-examination," Dooling said, "Perhaps it would, but to the petitioner the whole proceeding is probably a nuisance. The rights of the petitioner may not be wholly measured by the convenience or inconvenience to the immigration officers in affording her a fair hearing."[39]

Dooling also held that a hearing could not be fair if the immigrant did not understand the charges or have an opportunity to refute them. For example, Wong Quen Luck was denied admission to the United States in 1915 because of conflicts between his and his father's testimony. Wong protested that the bureau's interpreter spoke a different dialect and that any discrepancies arose from misunderstandings in the translation. Dooling held that the hearing could not be fair if the immigrant did not understand the interpreter.[40] Dooling also disapproved of warrants for deportation which did not specify the reason for deportation. The warrant for the arrest of Lew Lin Shew simply alleged that he was in the country in violation of the Chinese exclusion laws. Dooling conceded that the administrative warrants did not have to be as detailed or specific as those used in court proceedings, but he argued, "This does not mean that an omnibus charge of being in this country in violation of law, which does not in any degree whatever advise the alien as to just what he is called upon to meet, will satisfy the requirements of the law, or of good faith, or of fair dealing."[41]

Such decisions encouraged immigrants and their attorneys, and, not surprisingly, the number of habeas corpus petitions filed by immigrants in the San Francisco federal district court again began to climb after Dooling's appointment.[42] The chief law officer of the Bureau of Immigration complained in 1919 that "it looks as though Dooling is seeking to run our business" in San Francisco.[43] Yet, though Dooling's decisions caused a stir

TABLE 8 *Disposition of Chinese Habeas Corpus Cases, 1906–1924*
(Federal District Court for Northern District of California)

Year	Discharge N (%)	Remand N (%)	Dismissal N (%)	Unknown N (%)	Total N
1906	1 (11)	8 (89)	0 (0)	0 (0)	9
1907	0 (0)	1 (100)	0 (0)	0 (0)	1
1908	0 (0)	12 (44)	15 (56)	0 (0)	27
1909	0 (0)	4 (67)	1 (17)	1 (17)	6
1910	0 (0)	8 (57)	5 (36)	1 (7)	14
1911	2 (15)	9 (69)	2 (15)	0 (0)	13
1912	0 (0)	7 (58)	5 (42)	0 (0)	12
1913	3 (19)	13 (81)	0 (0)	0 (0)	16
1914	11 (32)	22 (65)	1 (3)	0 (0)	34
1915	12 (29)	27 (66)	2 (5)	0 (0)	41
1916	7 (14)	38 (77)	4 (8)	0 (0)	49
1917	7 (21)	25 (76)	1 (3)	0 (0)	33
1918	6 (19)	24 (75)	1 (3)	1 (3)	32
1919	7 (32)	10 (45)	5 (23)	0 (0)	22
1920	4 (10)	34 (85)	2 (5)	0 (0)	40
1921	2 (3)	53 (77)	13 (19)	1 (1)	69
1922	8 (14)	36 (63)	12 (21)	1 (2)	57
1923	15 (15)	61 (63)	17 (17)	4 (4)	97
1924	24 (18)	80 (61)	15 (11)	12 (9)	131
Total					703

Source: Compiled from U.S. District Court for the Northern District Court of California, Admiralty Docket, 1906–24.

Note: Percentages rounded to the nearest decimal point.

among bureau officials in Washington accustomed to deferential judges, they had a relatively minor impact on the campaign for greater procedural rights in immigration hearings in the long run. Most of the complaints of the immigrants—their limited access to attorneys, the hearings by affidavits, their inability to subpoena witnesses on their behalf, and, more generally, the discretionary power wielded by immigration officials—were not remedied by the federal courts (see Tables 8 and 9 for the disposition of habeas corpus cases).[44] Judges rejected challenges to the composition of the boards of special inquiry, holding, for example, that the arresting officer in a deportation case could also be a member of the board without compromis-

TABLE 9 *Disposition of Non-Chinese Habeas Corpus Cases, 1906–1924 (Federal District Court for the Northern District of California)*

Year	Discharge N (%)	Remand N (%)	Dismissal N (%)	Unknown N (%)	Total N
1906	0 (0)	1 (100)	0 (0)	0 (0)	1
1907	0 (0)	0 (0)	0 (0)	0 (0)	0
1908	0 (0)	1 (100)	0 (0)	0 (0)	1
1909	0 (0)	1 (100)	0 (0)	0 (0)	1
1910	0 (0)	3 (100)	0 (0)	0 (0)	3
1911	1 (33)	2 (66)	0 (0)	0 (0)	3
1912	0 (0)	22 (92)	1 (4)	1 (4)	24
1913	7 (41)	8 (47)	2 (12)	0 (0)	17
1914	8 (44)	5 (28)	5 (28)	0 (0)	18
1915	2 (10)	11 (58)	5 (26)	1 (5)	19
1916	2 (17)	6 (50)	4 (33)	0 (0)	12
1917	2 (100)	0 (0)	0 (0)	0 (0)	2
1918	1 (12)	4 (50)	2 (25)	1 (12)	8
1919	1 (10)	6 (60)	3 (30)	0 (0)	10
1920	23 (82)[a]	2 (7)	3 (11)	0 (0)	28
1921	3 (43)	3 (43)	1 (14)	0 (0)	7
1922	1 (5)	20 (95)	0 (0)	0 (0)	21
1923	1 (5)	16 (76)	4 (19)	0 (0)	21
1924	0 (0)	7 (87)	1 (12)	0 (0)	8
Total					204

Source: Compiled from U.S. District Court for the Northern District Court of California, Admiralty Docket, 1906–24.

Note: Percentages rounded to the nearest decimal point.

[a]These cases involved Japanese immigrants whose cases were apparently decided upon the same principle, but neither the case files nor published court opinions reveal the reason for their discharge by the district court.

ing the fairness of the deportation hearing.[45] Unlike a court, the Bureau of Immigration was not bound by its previous determinations.[46] Nor did an acquittal on criminal charges in a court prevent the bureau from arresting and deporting an alien on the same charges. For, as the Supreme Court emphasized, acquittal did not necessarily imply innocence and immigration authorities were not bound by the same high standard of proof imposed in criminal proceedings.[47]

Judges freely acknowledged that the liberal rules governing immigration proceedings would never be acceptable in a court, but as Judge Lacombe succinctly stated, "Inspectors are not 'courts of justice,' nor are the examinations by them of incoming aliens touching their qualifications 'trials at law.' "[48] Even the rights the courts did protect were often tempered by administrative needs. When Dooling, for example, required the bureau to allow aliens to cross-examine witnesses present at the deportation hearing, he conceded that the bureau retained discretion to decide how extensive the examinations should be. Furthermore, the courts generally refused to uphold "technical" formal rules or to correct "mere error[s] of procedure" which might be irrelevant to the issue of whether someone should be landed or deported.[49] Few judges, for example, agreed with Dooling that the warrant for arrest in deportation cases had to specify the exact charge, holding instead that the important consideration was whether the alien, at the time of the hearing, understood the essential grounds for deportation.[50] Administrative action, thought most federal judges, should not be unduly hampered by legal niceties, especially when it involved aliens whom the Supreme Court had found to have few rights at stake.[51]

THE WEIGHT OF THE EVIDENCE

The attempt to secure a broad range of procedural rights through the fair hearing requirement generally failed, but that effort did not exhaust the grounds for attorneys' challenges to the Bureau of Immigration. Almost every petition filed in the federal court at San Francisco also alleged that officials' decisions to exclude or deport aliens rested on insufficient evidence and thus were arbitrary and unfair. From *Nishimura Ekiu* to *Ju Toy*, courts had readily deferred to the administrative evaluation of evidence as questions of fact within the sole jurisdiction of the agency. But attorneys persisted in their claims because they thought the bureau's discretion to gather and weigh evidence led to unjust and unlawful exclusions.

Immigrants' attorneys surely would have agreed with administrative law scholar John Dickinson's admonition that a refusal by federal courts to examine the sufficiency of evidence for immigration decisions "would obviously open a dangerous door for executive oppression."[52] A hearing could hardly be fair, attorneys argued, if official determinations were not grounded on an objective evaluation of pertinent evidence. The Supreme Court had recognized the potential for abuse in opinions concerning other administrative agencies, holding, for example, that decisions of the Interstate Commerce Commission had to be based on "substantial evidence"; a "mere scintilla of proof" would not be sufficient.[53] Without a judicial check on their consideration of evidence, officials could easily abuse their discretion and allow their beliefs or prejudices to determine their decisions. Even more significant, the Bureau of Immigration, operating from behind the protective cloak of administrative discretion, could (and did) further nativist goals through restrictionist interpretations of the immigration laws. When attorneys alleged that there was insufficient or no evidence for a decision, they often appeared to be challenging indirectly the bureau's constructions of the statute and its assumptions of policy-making power.

The federal courts found challenges to the bureau's evaluation of evidence unpersuasive, and they routinely dismissed petitions alleging insufficient evidence. As one judge noted, the claim of "insufficient evidence" usually meant "that the immigration officers found contrary to petitioner's concept of the evidence. In other words, decided wrong."[54] Justice Holmes in the *Chin Yow* case had explicitly said that the immigrant could not prove an unfair hearing by showing that the decision was wrong.[55] Thus, though the federal courts had used the preponderance of evidence standard when they had jurisdiction over Chinese cases, they now held that the bureau could decide against the weight of the evidence and the hearing would still be fair.[56] "As long as there is some evidence to support the finding of the immigration officials," said Judge Henry Wade Rogers of the Second Circuit, "we cannot say that the order of deportation was invalid, even though we might regard the testimony as not sufficiently convincing."[57]

Judges upheld even bureau decisions that worked particular hardship on aliens. Judge Holt called the deportation of Vincenzo Canfora, a sixty-year-old engraver and bookbinder from Italy who had lived in the United States with his wife and six children for sixteen years, "an act of cruel injustice." Canfora traveled to Italy to visit his mother in 1910, but upon his return to the United States, officials ordered his deportation as an alien "likely to become a public charge," even though he had over $200 in his bank account and the potential support of his adult children. Holt thought there was little reason to suspect that Canfora would become a public charge, but he felt compelled to uphold the deportation order as a matter within the exclusive jurisdiction of the bureau. Holt's only recourse was to appeal to the officials' sense of compassion, and he expressed "the hope that the immigration authorities would reconsider the case" before deporting Canfora "to die in a distant land, far from his wife and children, and from the home in this country in which he has lived a blameless life for so many years."[58]

The judges' unwillingness to act on claims of insufficient evidence reflected in part the traditional deference given to fact-finders as the ones who, having observed the witnesses and heard their testimony, were best situated to evaluate the evidence. This traditional deference was reinforced by the long line of Supreme Court cases acknowledging the power of Congress to decide that the Bureau of Immigration, not the courts, had authority to determine the facts in such cases.[59] "It is not within our province to weigh the evidence," said one appellate judge.[60] Courts were not willing to second-guess the agency, holding that "the authorities' mental processes can not be guided or controlled by the courts."[61] Federal judges also believed that administrative agencies such as the Bureau of Immigration should not be required to follow judicial rules of evidence just for the sake of form.

Although virtually all federal judges dismissed petitions that simply alleged insufficient evidence, they lacked the same unanimity regarding claims that there was *no* evidence to support the bureau's decisions to exclude or deport. Judge Learned Hand of the Southern District of New York refused to consider whether there was any evidence for immigration officials' decision to exclude Georgios Glavas. In his opinion, courts could intervene only if the alien had been denied a statutory right or when a question of law was involved.[62] His colleague, Judge Lacombe, agreed, pointing out that in *Nishimura Ekiu* the Supreme Court had recognized "in unambiguous language" the final and exclusive jurisdiction of the Bureau of Immigration over factual determinations, though, he lamented, that holding "seems to be frequently overlooked."[63] As Lacombe's comment suggests, not all judges shared his view. Circuit judges Alfred Coxe and Henry Ward, sitting on the Court of Appeals for the Second Circuit, affirmed Lacombe's dismissal of a habeas corpus petition challenging a deportation order, but in so doing, they clarified that while "the findings of [immigration] officials are practically conclusive upon questions of fact . . . some evidence must be presented to justify a judgment of deportation and . . . conclusions of law must have some facts upon which to rest."[64]

Judges proved to be even more troubled by immigrants' protests that the stated ground for their exclusion or deportation was simply a subterfuge to exclude them for reasons not encompassed by the immigration laws. Provisions mandating the exclusion of aliens "likely to become a public charge" or "who have been convicted of or admit having committed . . . a crime . . . involving moral turpitude" were notoriously vague.[65] Not surprisingly, the clauses became perfect vehicles for bureau officials to banish aliens thought to be undesirable for various policy reasons but who technically might be admissible under the statute. For example, the Bureau of Immigration excluded Regina Kornmehl, the mother of a child afflicted with a contagious disease. Kornmehl had met the requirements for entry, but officials rejected her as "likely to become a public charge," basing their decision on a departmental regulation that authorized the exclusion of a parent if a minor child had been denied entry.

Judges hesitated to endorse the bureau's ready use of the public charge and moral turpitude clauses, for in expanding the definitions of those clauses, the bureau ventured beyond its undisputed jurisdiction over questions of fact into the judicial territory of questions of law. In such cases, federal judges would occasionally depart from their customary restraint in immigration matters to curb administrative exuberance. Questions of fact could seldom be neatly separated from questions of law, however, and courts differed as to when the bureau had exceeded its authority.

Yet even Judge Lacombe, the staunch defender of administrative discretion, held in 1898 that the bureau had erred in excluding Regina Kornmehl. The bureau could make regulations "to carry out the statutes and facilitate the exclusion and return of persons belonging to the classes whose immigration congress has forbidden," Lacombe conceded. But, he thundered, "no mere rule of the department can operate to exclude persons not belonging to one or other of the classes named in the statutes. . . . The alien is entitled to the honest decision of the inspecting officers, wholly untrammeled by any instructions not authorized by the statutes." Congress had not provided for the exclusion of parents in such cases so Judge Lacombe found the action of the bureau unwarranted.[66]

Lacombe's colleagues in the Southern District of New York also found fault with the bureau's interpretation of the moral turpitude clause of the immigration statute in two prominent cases decided within five days of each other. One involved Edward F. Mylius, an English native and publisher who had been convicted of criminal libel in England after he printed a story alleging that the king was a bigamist. Mylius's exclusion in 1913 sparked a debate not only over the loose standards of journalism and freedom of the press but also over the bureau's interpretation of crimes involving moral turpitude.[67] Judges hearing the case in the district court and in the Second Circuit Court of Appeals were troubled by immigration officials' tendency to retry offenses, to "go behind judgments of conviction and determine . . . the questions of purpose, motive and knowledge which are often determinative of the moral character of the acts."[68] Immigration officials, the judges argued, should not be guided by the moral character of the particular perpetrator or victim but must decide whether, in general, the type of crime committed—here, defamatory libel—was of such a nature as necessarily to involve "moral turpitude," which the district court defined as "an act of baseness, vileness, or depravity." Holding that defamatory libel was not a crime involving moral turpitude, the Second Circuit Court of Appeals affirmed the lower court's order to admit Mylius into the United States.

The second case involved an even more notorious alien, General Cipriano Castro, the former president (and virtual dictator) of Venezuela, who had left his country in 1908 and remained in exile.[69] When he applied for entry into the United States in 1912, he was under indictment in Venezuela for the murder of one of his opponents, General Antonio Paredes.[70] Upon the urging of the United States State Department, the Bureau of Immigration instructed officials at Ellis Island that in examining Castro, "everything that can be developed by the Board [of special inquiry] should be brought out, and whether or not any specific reason is ascertained for his exclusion under the immigration law, Castro should be detained until the case can be referred to the Department for consideration and decision."[71] The board members took the bureau's instructions to heart and doggedly attempted to discover grounds to exclude Castro. When Castro imperiously declined to participate in the hearing and went to his bedroom at the Ellis Island station, the board "followed him to the door of his bedroom" and continued to question him.[72] Castro's refusal to answer immigration officials' questions convinced the bureau "that there exist damaging facts which he desires to conceal." Construing his "silence and behavior [as] an admission of guilt" and relying on evidence gathered by the State Department, immigration officials excluded Castro on the grounds that he had committed a crime—the murder of General Paredes—which involved moral turpitude.[73]

Castro's behavior in Venezuela and at Ellis Island had clearly not endeared him to the American government or the American public. But the federal district court held that the bureau had excluded Castro unlawfully and ordered his admission into the United States. Judge Ward rejected the bureau's presumption of Castro's guilt, holding that the law intended to deprive immigration officials "of the right to try the question of guilt at all." Under the law of 1907, aliens could be excluded for crimes involving moral turpitude only if they had been convicted of the crime or if they had made "an explicit and voluntary" confession; mere indictment for murder was not grounds for exclusion.[74]

The back-to-back decisions against the Bureau of Immigration's decisions in the *Mylius* and *Castro* cases provoked even the usually moderate journal, the *Outlook*, to denounce judicial intervention in immigration matters. "This country is an asylum, not an insane asylum; a school, but not a reform school," the editor cried. "The determination of what particular cases come under the general provisions that exclude undesirable aliens is an administrative function . . . not . . . a judicial function." The "legal technicalities that safeguard the rights of citizens" should not burden immigration officials faced with the task of passing upon the "eligibility of a million immigrants a year." Aliens, in the journal's opinion, must prove affirmatively their right to enter; they were presumed unfit until they established the contrary.[75]

The outraged public response to the judicial opinions in *Mylius* and *Castro* suggests that just as particularly heartrending cases could mobilize public opinion against the bureau, as described in the last chapter, the court-ordered admission of especially "undesirable" immigrants could provoke defenses of the agency's methods. The *New York Tribune*, supporting the bureau's exclusion of Castro, recognized the bureau's "exceptional extent of authority" over immigration matters and "the possibility of abuse of that power by an unscrupulous or unreasonable official." When balancing the evil of an abuse of administrative power against the evil of undesirable aliens entering the United States unchecked, the *Tribune* argued that "a prudent regard for our own welfare suggests that of the two evils excessive strictness in excluding dubious applicants is preferable to too great leniency in admitting them."[76]

Such sentiments were not limited to the *Castro* and *Mylius* cases. Nativists were relatively weak in the first decade of the 1900s but had gathered momentum by the second decade as the nation experienced an economic downturn in 1913 and became embroiled in worldwide conflict.[77] They exerted greater pressure on the Bureau of Immigration to use its discretion even more broadly to limit immigration. The agency readily complied, relying increasingly on the "likely to become a public charge" clause of the immigration law to further restrictionist goals. By expanding the definition of the clause, the agency was making immigration policy as well as enforcing it and thereby straining the limits of its jurisdiction and exposing the consequences of unrestrained administrative discretion. Not surprisingly, immigration attorneys mounted their most impassioned attacks on the bureau's methods in such cases, culminating with *Gegiow* v. *Uhl* in 1915, and used them to illustrate the dangers of administrative discretion unfettered by judicial procedural norms.

The bureau's bold use of immigration provisions to broaden the exclusion of immigrants flourished first on the West Coast. The Asiatic Exclusion League, founded in 1907, persistently lobbied the bureau at San Francisco to exclude higher numbers of new Asian immigrants.[78] For example, exclusionists railed against the number of Japanese families, which grew despite the Gentlemen's Agreement limiting the immigration of Japanese laborers. The agreement did not forbid the immigration of Japanese women coming to join their husbands who were already residing in the United States. Often, Japanese women married Japanese-American men through proxy marriages arranged by their families. Responding to nativists' complaints, the bureau reported that it could not prevent the immigration of the Japanese women because the marriages were legal.[79] But the bureau could use its discretion in creative ways. For example, it excluded as likely to become a public charge a Japanese woman who, while single, had allegedly lived with a man in Japan. The bureau reasoned, rather tenuously, that because she had a "loose sense of morality . . . she should not be admitted to proceed to a community where there would be every incentive to ply an immoral calling, such as would render her extremely likely sooner or later to fall a charge on the public," presumably because she would be arrested as a prostitute.[80]

The bureau's use of the "likely to become a public charge" ground to reject Asian Indian immigrants provides an even more dramatic example of its policy-making power. The commissioner of immigration at San Francisco turned to the clause in 1910 in response to constant pressure from Californians who viewed the arrival of Asian Indians as the latest "invasion" of Asians.[81] Organized opposition to Indian immigration had begun in 1908 when the Asiatic Exclusion League in San Francisco mounted an attack on the allegedly lax enforcement policies of Commissioner of Immigration Hart North. The league insisted that the commissioner find some way to bar all Indians, but North maintained that unless Congress enacted legislation to exclude Indians, he could not lawfully deny them entry.[82]

In 1910, the issue exploded; California groups petitioned Commissioner General Daniel Keefe, President Taft, and Congress for the dismissal of North and the exclusion of Indians.[83] Some inspectors on North's staff filed official complaints about him with the Bureau of Immigration.[84] Taft suspended North, and the assistant secretary of commerce and labor publicized a new approach to Indian immigrants. Regretting that the law did not allow a total exclusion of Indians, the assistant secretary said reassuringly, "All the restrictions at our command will be applied strictly. We will resort to a broader construction of the law."[85]

Indians arriving in San Francisco thereafter were subject to "higher scrutiny." Inspectors investigated all Indians thoroughly, searching for any reason to exclude them. The *San Diego Tribune* reported approvingly, "All along the coast the Hindu is being shut out on one pretext or another."[86] The medical officer at Angel Island gave exclusionists hope when he discovered that many Indians were afflicted with hookworm and could be rejected because they had a "dangerous, contagious disease."[87] But the Bureau of Immigration discovered an even better means of prohibiting

Indians from landing. San Francisco immigration officials began in 1910 to deny entry to Indians on the grounds that because they were Indian, they were likely to become public charges. The bureau reasoned that because of strong anti-Indian prejudice in California, no Indian would be able to get a job, despite his or her physical capabilities, and thus would eventually become a public charge.

Indians challenged the bureau's interpretation in the district court, objecting to its use of the public charge provision to exclude a whole group of people.[88] The immigration law, attorneys argued, provided for an investigation of each individual and could deny entry only if he or she personally had certain undesirable characteristics. There was no evidence in these cases that individual applicants would become public charges or that Indians already in the United States had become public charges. Indians had plenty of opportunities for employment, they argued. "If the Hindu is to be excluded," the attorneys concluded, "let Congress exclude him. Let us be governed by law, not by departmental fiat."[89]

The government responded with thousands of newspaper articles, affidavits, and letters to prove its contention that widespread prejudice would prevent Indians from getting jobs. It also pushed for a broader construction of the category "public charge." Whereas public charge narrowly referred to a person who depended financially on charity or public support, the United States attorney argued that under a more general definition, "the term might mean a person who would be a nuisance to a community . . . who would be a detriment to a community, who would hinder its progress rather than aid its upbuilding."[90] The Indians' attorneys rejected the government's documentation, saying that it "is not evidence, but is purely the expression of biased individuals and organizations bitterly opposed to all forms of Oriental Labor."[91]

Judge Dooling in the district court was troubled by the case but upheld the bureau's exclusion of Indians. Dooling felt constrained by the limited role of the courts in immigration matters: "If it were a new question," he said, "I would not hesitate for a moment" to find the bureau's policy unlawful. "But," he continued, "the Supreme Court has gone so far in holding that the findings of the department cannot be reviewed, if there be any testimony at all to support them that I am not prepared to deny to it the power" to implement such a policy. The government had some evidence for its decision, Dooling found, albeit evidence resting on prejudicial conditions in the United States rather than on the particular qualities of the individuals. Furthermore, the immigration inspectors provided an opportunity for the Indians to be heard and to present and rebut evidence, and thus, the judge concluded, the petitioners had a fair hearing.[92]

The Indians appealed to the United States Supreme Court, but the Court decided the issue in a case arising out of New York at the same time. In *Gegiow* v. *Uhl*, immigration inspectors at Ellis Island denied entry to several young Russian men who planned to join their countrymen already settled in Portland, Oregon. The board of special inquiry decided, based on news reports of the poor labor market in Portland, that the immigrants would not be able to obtain jobs and further that they had insufficient money (about $25 each) to tide them over. And though they all had friends or relatives in the vicinity, there was no one who would be legally obligated to support them should the men become unable to support themselves. Finally, Commissioner of Immigration Byron Uhl pointed out that only one of the men—Ali Gegiow—was literate; the rest were illiterate and spoke a dialect not understood by an interpreter at Ellis Island. Illiteracy would not become grounds for exclusion for several years, but Uhl concluded that "their ignorance has a tendency to cause them to form a gang or clique, which constitutes a detriment to any community of which they might become members, and also renders them a much more easy prey to exploitation by unscrupulous persons."[93] The bureau consequently barred the men as aliens likely to become public charges.

Attorneys Ralph Barnett and Morris Jablow challenged the exclusion in the Southern District of New York. Judge Lacombe dismissed their petition, pointing out that although "opinions may differ as to whether or not [the immigrants] were . . . liable to become a charge upon the public," the only opinion that mattered under the law was that of the Bureau of Immigration.[94] In a split decision, the Second Circuit affirmed Lacombe's decision, though in contrast to Lacombe's unwillingness to review the evidence at all, the appellate court held that there must be some evidence to support the bureau's decisions. The evidence need not be "established with the same formality and certainty which is required in courts," said Judge Coxe. "No immigration act could be enforced" if such requirements were imposed. Deferring broadly to the fact-finding responsibilities of the bureau, the court upheld its decision as founded on some evidence.[95]

The Bureau of Immigration's broad interpretation of the public charge clause, condoned by the federal courts, alarmed attorneys active in Jewish immigrant aid and civil rights organizations, such as Max Kohler and Abram Elkus who represented Ali Gegiow and Sabas Zarikoew on appeal to the Supreme Court.[96] Kohler had condemned the bureau's construction of the public charge provision in 1911, arguing that many of the exclusions under that clause were unwarranted as they rested upon the "narrow and erroneous opinion and beliefs of what is best for the country" instead of on the actual law.[97] This case was typical, in Kohler's eyes, of the bureau's tendency to search for grounds to exclude eastern and southern Europeans, generally seen by officials as "undesirable" aliens. None of the grounds upon which the bureau's decision rested—labor market conditions, literacy, the amount of money possessed by the men, and the existence of family legally obligated to support the men—were specified in the statute nor did they, in the opinion of Kohler and Elkus, predict the likelihood of the men becoming public charges. If the bureau's exclusion were allowed to stand, they argued, "there are no limits to administrative authority to exclude aliens."[98]

The Bureau of Immigration similarly recognized the important issues at stake in the case and sought to defend its discretion. The bureau argued that Congress intended to give it the flexibility to respond to changing conditions in the United States and to give the broadest possible protection to the American people. "If the administrative officers are not vested with a sufficient discretion to exclude aliens because . . . the economic situation in the United States is such as to make it reasonably certain that they will be charges upon the public if landed," said the commissioner general, "the law is not as comprehensive as it should be and is much less potent to protect the people of this country than the bureau has always supposed it to be."[99]

Gegiow v. *Uhl* thus brought to a climax the battle over the bureau's growing discretion since *Chin Yow*, and the briefs filed by Kohler and Elkus and by the U.S. attorney led to an elaborate debate over the Bureau of Immigration's power to elaborate policy, the definition of due process in immigration and other administrative agencies, and the role of the courts in shaping administrative due process. Kohler and Elkus tried to use the *Gegiow* case as an opportunity to submit the Bureau of Immigration's discretion to more exacting standards and to expand the meaning of a "fair hearing" to include evidentiary as well as procedural practices. Kohler and Elkus focused their attack on the bureau's failure to introduce evidence regarding labor market conditions in Portland, arguing that inspectors merely assumed, based on unidentified newspaper accounts, that the immigrants would be unable to find work. The inspectors' reliance on opinion and hearsay rather than on solid evidence constituted a denial of due process, asserted Kohler and Elkus, because due process required not only a hearing according to regular procedures but also a decision based on competent evidence. The inspectors' failure to produce evidence on labor market conditions, even in the form of affidavits, also violated due process because the immigrants never had clear notice of the grounds for exclusion or the opportunity to rebut the assumptions through evidence and cross-examination.

To support their arguments, Kohler and Elkus made the relatively unusual move of looking to judicial decisions regarding other administrative action. The attorney in the *Japanese Immigrant Case* had employed the same tactic to underscore the widespread judicial acceptance of a fundamental right to be heard. But government attorneys had usually succeeded in isolating immigration law as unique and not subject to the same constraints circumscribing other administrative action. Kohler and Elkus hoped to bring the Bureau of Immigration back into the mainstream of Anglo-American jurisprudence by making its work analogous to that of such agencies as the Interstate Commerce Commission.

The attorneys pinned their hopes on a 1913 Supreme Court decision, *Interstate Commerce Commission v. Louisville and Nashville Railroad Company*. In that case, the Court confronted the government's assertion that the Hepburn Act of 1906 gave the ICC the final jurisdiction to decide whether carriers' rates were reasonable, a decision that could not be set aside by the courts "even if the finding was wholly without substantial evidence to support it." The courts should presume, argued the government, that the ICC had acted in good faith upon information "even though not formally proved at the hearing."[100] Justice Joseph Rucker Lamar treated the government's argument as heresy, saying "a finding without evidence is arbitrary and baseless. And if the Government's contention is correct . . . it would mean that where rights depended upon facts, the Commissioner could disregard all rules of evidence, and capriciously make findings of administrative fiat."[101] Though conceding that administrative bodies were not limited by strict rules of evidence, Lamar insisted that the liberal practices followed by administrative tribunals made it "imperative . . . to preserve the essential rules of evidence by which rights are asserted or defended." Officials could not "act upon their own information" but must apprise parties of "the evidence submitted or to be considered" and allow them "opportunity to cross-examine witnesses, to inspect documents and to offer evidence in explanation or rebuttal."[102]

The ICC case was especially useful for immigrants' attorneys because Lamar turned to immigration cases to elaborate a definition of procedural requirements in administrative hearings. In doing so, the Court implicitly suggested that immigration and ICC cases were analogous; this meant, in turn, that immigrants' attorneys could draw upon ICC cases, which generally placed greater limits on administrative discretion, in their attempt to raise the standards of due process in immigration hearings. The Eighth Circuit in 1915 relied heavily on *ICC v. Louis. Nash. R.R. Co.* to strike down a deportation order based on hearsay evidence.[103] Kohler and Elkus hoped for a similar result and quoted from Lamar's opinion at length to attack not only the bureau's lax evidentiary practices but the lower federal courts' reluctance, based on *Nishimura Ekiu*, to review the bureau's decisions even when there was no direct evidence for its findings.

Kohler and Elkus argued that statutory and judicial developments since *Nishimura Ekiu* had modified the finality of the bureau's decisions. Statutes passed after that case creating the boards of special inquiry and requiring records of their proceedings revealed Congress's intent to make the Bureau of Immigration more accountable and judicious in its decision making; judicial opinions such as those in the *Japanese Immigrant Case* and *Chin Yow* had suggested the limits to the bureau's discretion when procedural questions came into play. Simultaneously, the Bureau of Immigration's jurisdiction had broadened over the years to reach "difficult questions of law and fact . . . even rights to citizenship." These complicated questions, touching upon "the rights of a million persons a year," were being decided, Kohler and Elkus warned, by "$1,800 a year Inspectors . . . who are notoriously lacking in education, and weak, in general." To treat their decisions in such cases as conclusive "would be a great public calamity." Given the greater responsibilities of the bureau and the weaknesses of the inspectors, Kohler and Elkus argued it was imperative that administrative proceedings be in "closer conformity to judicial procedure."[104]

In opposition to the immigrants' claims, the solicitor general, John W. Davis, sought to secure the victory achieved in *Ju Toy* and to remove all questions concerning the bureau's reliance on evidence from the federal courts' review. He returned to the basic premise of *Nishimura Ekiu* and *Ju Toy* that Congress had complete power over immigration matters and had vested final authority in the Bureau of Immigration to determine an alien's right to enter under the law. It followed, Davis reasoned, that "any inquiry [by the courts] into the evidence" relied upon by the bureau "is improper" even if judges believed the officials' decision to be wrong or misguided.[105] Citing *Chin Yow*, Davis argued that administrative officials "may be woefully mistaken but they need not be in consequence dishonest or unfair." And there was no reason to believe, as Gegiow's attorneys implied, that judges would make better, more just determinations if they assumed power over admission decisions. It was far better, argued Davis, to leave the matter as Congress intended in the expert hands of immigration officials "constantly engaged in this work and handling hundreds of such cases day by day."[106]

Davis dismissed the due process arguments made by Kohler and Elkus. The requirements of due process, he insisted, depend on the nature of the case. Here, the case involved an immigrant with no constitutional rights at entry, who "simply stands at the gate and knocks" and an administrative agency with the overwhelming job of deciding on thousands of applications for entry every day.[107] Given the status of immigrants and the pressing nature of the government's business, Davis argued that the summary proceedings provided by Congress were sufficient.[108] Whereas Kohler and Elkus had relied on *ICC* v. *Louis. & Nash. R.R.* to delineate the requisites of administrative due process, Davis turned to customs and land cases to uphold the summary and absolute power of government over essential government business. The Interstate Commerce Commission and the Bureau of Immigration were not comparable, Davis argued. Not only did the statutes governing the ICC provide for more elaborate procedures, but its orders affected the property rights of citizens, protected under the Constitution. Consequently, "the appropriate form of hearing . . . is far different from the summary proceedings made necessary by the conditions under which one million aliens come to this country each year."[109]

In his opinion for the Supreme Court, Justice Holmes bypassed the debate concerning the procedural and evidentiary practices of the Bureau of Immigration as well as the authority of courts to review the sufficiency of evidence for the agency's decisions. Instead, Holmes framed the issue as a question of law, clearly within the Court's jurisdiction to review. The only question to be decided, Holmes asserted, was whether the immigration statutes authorized the exclusion of an alien as likely to become a public charge "on the ground that the labor market in the city of his immediate destination is overstocked." Holmes noted that the act included "persons likely to become a public charge" among a list of other excludable aliens such as professional beggars, paupers, convicted felons, prostitutes, and idiots. By implication, the act excluded persons "on the ground of permanent personal objections accompanying them irrespective of local conditions," and the Bureau of Immigration could not assume the "amazing claim of power" to adjust admissions based on current labor market conditions that had no relation to an individual alien's personal qualifications.[110]

The Bureau of Immigration expressed dismay and surprise at the Supreme Court's decision, perceiving it as an important victory for immigrants. Holmes implied that the bureau could not use the public charge provision as a pretext to implement policies not embodied in the law. On the strength of this decision, the Indians in San Francisco were allowed to enter, and the lower federal courts in New York and San Francisco began to scrutinize the bureau's decisions on public charges more closely.[111]

Yet the narrow grounds of the *Gegiow* decision limited the impact of the case. Holmes said nothing about the authority of the courts to review the sufficiency of evidence in immigration decisions nor did he venture to discuss the requirements of due process in immigration or administrative proceedings more generally. Consequently, Kohler and Elkus' effort to alter judicial perceptions of the interests at stake in immigration cases and to raise the requirements of due process in immigration hearings by analogizing the rights of immigrants with those of common carriers before the Interstate Commerce Commission went unnoticed in Holmes's opinion. Citing only immigration cases, Holmes reiterated and strengthened the proposition already established by the Supreme Court in earlier cases that the courts retained jurisdiction to check the bureau's interpretations of law. In most cases, however, questions of law and fact were intertwined, and the courts remained reluctant to intervene if there were "some evidence" for the agency's decision.[112] Only the boldest forays of the bureau in expanding the reach of the immigration statutes provoked the courts to step in.

THE CLAIMS OF CITIZENS

Thus, neither purely procedural nor evidentiary challenges on the behalf of aliens fared well in the courts. But when similar complaints were made by persons claiming to be citizens, the judges proved to be more ambivalent about the agency's practices. Despite the *Ju Toy* decision submitting alleged citizens as well as aliens to the discretion of immigration officials, judges continued to perceive a difference between the rights of aliens and the rights of citizens. At times, the courts treated alleged citizens and aliens the same, subjecting both to the discretion of the agency. In other cases, they made distinctions between citizens and aliens and called for a higher standard of due process in administrative hearings involving citizens.

The courts' inconsistencies regarding citizens revealed a tension within legal and social constructions of citizenship at the time, constructions which simultaneously endorsed an expansive liberal and a more narrow ethnocultural definition of membership.[113] The conflicting notions of membership had been manifest in the law regarding citizenship since the nation's birth. As the American Revolution sparked an elaboration of a distinct American political ideology drawn from liberal and republican roots, so, too, Americans grappled with the requirements for membership in the new republic. Lockean liberalism, which stressed universal natural rights and membership through voluntary allegiance, resulted in the affirmation of universal birthright citizenship and a generous naturalization policy based on swearing political allegiance to the United States. Republican emphasis on the need for a homogeneous, virtuous citizenry capable of self-rule tempered the broad liberal definition of citizenship, however. In response to republican concerns, the federal naturalization policy adopted in 1790 not only imposed a residency requirement (allowing a probationary period for the "training" of future citizens in the the virtues and responsibilities of republican self-government) but also limited naturalization to free white persons.[114] Thus, from the nation's beginning, the law embraced potentially contradictory notions, at once a broad, universal definition based on birth and voluntary political allegiance and a more exclusionary policy that made racial distinctions.

These different conceptions would remain in tension throughout the nineteenth century. Justice Roger Taney in his *Dred Scott* opinion elevated the ethnocultural definition to new heights, using the racial qualification in the 1790 law to argue that birthright citizenship was also limited to the white race. After the Civil War, Republican congressmen sought to reassert the liberal definition of citizenship with the Fourteenth Amendment's encompassing provision that "all persons born . . . in the United States . . . are citizens of the United States and of the State wherein they reside" and by amending the naturalization law in 1870 to allow those of "african nativity or descent" as well as "free white persons" the privilege of becoming United States citizens.[115]

With the rise of immigration and the declining faith in assimilation at the turn of the twentieth century, racial distinctions in laws regarding citizenship again came to the forefront, especially in debates as to whether Asians and those of Asian descent could be American citizens under existing law. The Supreme Court had held that the common law rule adopted in the United States and reinforced in the Fourteenth Amendment guaranteed citizenship to anyone, including Chinese, born in the United States.[116] While the Court upheld a liberal definition of membership in recognizing the citizenship of native-born Chinese Americans, it simultaneously upheld restrictive naturalization policies based on race. The circuit court in San Francisco had denied naturalization to Chinese in 1878 on the grounds that United States naturalization laws limited that privilege to "free white persons" and persons of "African descent." Chinese, the court decided, were not "white" and thus could not become citizens.[117] The prohibition on Chinese naturalization was incorporated into the 1880 treaty and the Chinese exclusion laws. The Supreme Court later denied Japanese and Asian Indians the privilege of naturalization on the same racial grounds.[118]

The Court's decisions left Asians in a strange situation regarding citizenship. They could gain citizenship by birth but not by naturalization. As exclusionists never tired of pointing out, there was an inconsistency in the Court's approach which revealed fundamental conflicts in Americans' notions of membership. Confronted with the Court's unequivocal holding regarding birthright citizenship, Bureau of Immigration officials and exclusionists urged that though native-born Asian Americans might be "technical" citizens, they would never become "real" citizens sharing the same values and characteristics of Anglo-Americans and should not be treated in the law as genuine Americans. Consequently, the bureau frequently subjected alleged Chinese Americans to more rigorous examinations than it did other alleged citizens.

The perceived distinction between "technical" and "real" citizens posed a problem for federal judges when deciding procedural challenges to the Bureau of Immigration. Should native-born Chinese Americans, "accidental" citizens in the words of immigration officials, be treated more like citizens or aliens? The federal courts never explicitly framed the issue in that way, but the difficulty courts had in citizenship cases may have been owing to a feeling that Chinese Americans were not really citizens, either because they made fraudulent claims or because they remained "alien in heart." In handling citizens' challenges to immigration procedures, the court vacillated between treating them just like other aliens and granting them greater protections because of their citizenship.

The *Ju Toy* decision placed alleged citizens on the same level as aliens in admission proceedings before the Bureau of Immigration. The act of 1894, in the Supreme Court's opinion, made the bureau's decision final, "whatever the ground on which the right to enter the country is claimed."[119] The Ninth Circuit Court of Appeals extended the rule in *Ju Toy* in 1910 to allow the bureau complete control over the deportation of alleged citizens as well. Haw Moy had originally been admitted into the United States as a returning native-born citizen but was later arrested and ordered deported under the general immigration laws as an alien prostitute. Upholding the procedure, Judge Morrow indicated little concern at the possibility that the Bureau of Immigration might be deporting an American citizen, probably because he did not believe Haw Moy's claim of citizenship. It was not the court's business to interfere, he argued. "If Congress had intended that the courts should have jurisdiction" in such cases, Morrow explained, it "would have indicated such intention" in the immigration laws.[120]

In other cases, the court extended greater protections to Chinese alleging to be citizens, in part because the Bureau of Immigration clearly placed greater burdens of proof upon Chinese than it did on other citizens. The bureau asserted, "Citizenship of this country should rest upon substantial elements, not upon mere technicalities." Its policies aimed to make it more difficult for "technical" citizens to enter.[121] Before 1906, the bureau tried to stem the tide of Chinese applying for entry as native-born citizens. It boldly denied admission to adult Chinese who claimed to have been born in the United States but to have grown up in China. The bureau justified its policy on the grounds that one who "remained in China until after his majority had, in effect, expatriated himself or been expatriated by his parents, and was not, therefore, entitled to be regarded as an American citizen."[122] The naturalization law of 1906 brought the bureau's policy to a halt, however, by providing that a citizen could expatriate himself only by swearing allegiance to another country.[123]

The bureau also sought to bar Chinese claiming to be the foreign-born children of American citizens. It was not unusual for Chinese or Americans of Chinese descent to visit China, marry and have children, and return to the United States. Under United States law, children born in China of Chinese-American fathers were citizens of the United States, regardless of their age when applying for admission.[124] The Bureau of Immigration, suspecting all Chinese of fraud, approached all such cases with extreme skepticism, and inspectors at San Francisco routinely denied entry to adult children of citizens of Chinese descent. The agency's rules virtually limited entry to the dependent members of a Chinese American's household.[125]

Though the court usually did not interfere with the bureau's consideration of the evidence, Judge Dooling observed that the real reason for the inspectors' decisions was not that the children lacked evidence of their citizenship. The bureau in some cases conceded that they had a "technical right" to enter as citizens. But this technical right was insufficient to gain them entry; the bureau determined that Chinese children and their citizen fathers must pass a "test of allegiance." In the case of Leong Wah Jam, for example, there were only slight discrepancies in the applicant's testimony. Officials denied him entry because "the evidence of Chinese allegiance is so pronounced, the applicant being 24 years old and having a family of his own in China, and neither he nor his father indicat[e] any tendency to Americanism."[126] Dooling found the hearings unfair because the bureau refused to acknowledge the statutory right of children born of citizens to be admitted into the United States. "When one's right as a citizen is examined in that spirit, the hearing given him appears to me to be anything but fair," the judge ruled. He admonished the agency that "it . . . [is] the duty of executive as well as judicial officers fairly and freely to administer the laws of Congress as they find them, whether they agree with the policy . . . or not."[127]

The Supreme Court also applied a higher standard of due process to the immigration bureau when citizens were involved. In 1920, the Court found the hearing of Kwock Jan Fat to be unfair because the examining inspector did not submit crucial evidence supporting his claim of citizenship to the commissioner of immigration at San Francisco or to the secretary of labor on appeal. Kwock Jan Fat's claim that he had been born and raised in Monterey had strong support, both because of his command of English and the manner of his testimony and because of the corroborating statements of three well-known white men from Monterey. The testimony of the white men had been noted by the inspector, but he failed to mention in the record that they had positively recognized and identified Kwock Jan Fat during the hearing. Despite the strength of his case, Kwock Jan Fat had been denied entry because of damaging anonymous testimony against him. The Court held that the omission of the white witnesses' identification of Kwock from the record made the hearing unfair because that evidence was so important that it could have led to his admission.

The Supreme Court's intervention appears to have been prompted by a concern that the bureau was unduly trampling on the rights of citizens, a concern provoked by administrative abuses during the Red Raids of 1919, discussed in the next chapter. The Court admonished the bureau to administer its power, "not arbitrarily and secretly, but fairly and openly, under the restraints of the tradition and principles of free government applicable where the fundamental rights of men are involved, regardless of their origin or race." The Court's parting shot revealed that the fundamental rights of citizens were its main interest. It declared, "It is better that many Chinese immigrants should be improperly admitted than that one natural born citizen of the United States should be permanently excluded from his country."[128]

Such a strong declaration represented a significant turnaround in the Court's attitude toward Chinese-American citizens, unmistakably placing them on the same level as other citizens. *Kwock Jan Fat* also seemed to reveal a greater concern with the procedural rights of citizens in immigration cases than had earlier decisions. In *Ng Fung Ho*, decided two years later, the Court took its concern for the procedural protection of citizens a step further.

The *Ng Fung Ho* opinion limited the Bureau of Immigration's power in deportation proceedings. Two petitioners, Gin Sang Get and Gin Sang Mo, claimed the agency had no power to order their deportation because they were American citizens. Both had been admitted, after extensive investigation, to the United States as the foreign-born sons of an American citizen. In a surprising move, the Supreme Court upheld their challenge, ruling that an alleged citizen deserved to have a judicial hearing before he or she could be deported. The Bureau of Immigration had the power only to deport aliens; when a petitioner alleged to be a citizen, the case involved a jurisdictional issue which the courts had to determine. If the court decided the person was a citizen, the bureau clearly could not proceed against him.[129]

The Court clarified that its decision applied only to deportation cases. The *Ju Toy* opinion still ruled admission cases. For those outside the "borders of the United States, seeking entry, the mere fact that they claimed to be citizens would not have entitled them to a judicial hearing." The Court's distinction between *Ju Toy* and *Ng Fung Ho* seems a bit strained, however, and was not elaborated. For a citizen, to be denied entry into his or her country or to be expelled from it would seem to be equally oppressive. Both result in a "loss of liberty; a loss . . . of all that makes life worth living."[130] The Court may have extended greater protection in deportation cases because the Chinese men had substantial proof that they were citizens. The Court pointed out that the petitioners had evidence of their citizenship because the bureau had thoroughly investigated their claim and admitted them as citizens. Chinese who had gone through the investigation and were residing in the United States were more likely, in the Court's opinion, to be genuine citizens.[131]

Though the Court granted Chinese Americans greater protections, it still did not treat them in the same way as other citizens. In 1925, the Court interpreted the 1924 Quota Act, which forbade the entry of anyone "ineligible for citizenship," as denying Chinese-American men the right to bring their Chinese wives to the United States.[132] Chinese-American women suffered even greater inequities. Women of Chinese descent who were born in the United States were citizens. But as of 1907, United States law provided that any American woman who married an alien lost her citizenship.[133] The law proved very unsatisfactory to American women, and after they gained the vote, Congress passed the Cable Act in 1922 which made a woman's citizenship independent of that of her husband.[134] Yet women who married men "ineligible for citizenship" (i.e., Asians) still forfeited their American citizenship.[135] The Cable Act and Supreme Court opinions combined to place severe limits on the freedom of Asian-American women and men to marry and have families, a result that no doubt satisfied exclusionists.[136]

In summary, claims of citizenship were much more successful than other procedural claims in getting the court's attention. The federal judges tended to believe that greater procedural protections were owed to alleged citizens before the immigration bureau, and the fact that the claimants were Chinese Americans, so-called "technical" citizens, generally did not preclude them from the benefits and rights of citizenship. Yet judges were not consistently protective of alleged citizens except in deportation cases. Courts might admonish immigration officials to take more care in admission hearings, but they never seriously challenged the bureau's power over alleged citizens in admission cases and continued to allow it considerable discretion over its procedures.

PROCEDURE FOLLOWING UNFAIR HEARINGS

The dominant posture of judicial deference was evident even when the courts *did* find the bureau's proceedings to be unfair. Judges then had to address another question left open by *Chin Yow*, that is, whether the merits of the alien's case then should be determined by the federal courts or be remanded to administrative authorities for a rehearing. It was an important question for it involved the issue of administrative finality over factual determinations, so vigorously sought by the Bureau of Immigration in the litigation leading to *Ju Toy*. The *Chin Yow* decision offered hope to aliens that they could still have their cases determined in the more favorable judicial forum (once they had achieved the difficult task of persuading judges that their hearing before immigration authorities had been unfair). But here as well, the potential of *Chin Yow* was not realized.

In the immediate aftermath of *Chin Yow*, federal judges appeared to interpret Justice Holmes's opinion as requiring them to hear the case on its merits after finding the administrative hearing unfair, whether the petitioner was an alien or an alleged citizen. Judge Learned Hand ruled in 1909: "Under *Chin Yow v. United States*, it seems to me that, once I have taken jurisdiction, I must dispose of the question as to the alien's freedom."[137] Judge Dooling also regularly heard the cases de novo in such instances rather than remanding them to the Bureau of Immigration. But as Thomas Powell had noted soon after *Chin Yow*, Holmes's opinion appeared to suggest, rather than mandate, that judicial rehearings should be the logical procedure. The alternative—remanding the case to the agency—corresponded better with the pattern of judicial deference which dominated the federal courts' handling of immigration cases. It is not surprising, then, that the federal courts increasingly opted for that alternative.

The Ninth Circuit, for example, agreed in 1915 with Judge Dooling that failure to provide an interpreter who understood the alien's dialect denied "an essential requirement of a fair hearing," but it held that Dooling erred in ordering the unconditional release of the applicant. "The order of discharge should not have been final," the court held, "but conditional, to be effective only in case the Immigration authorities should fail to give the applicant a fair hearing required by law within a reasonable period, say 30 days hereafter."[138] Subsequently, Dooling usually, though not always, allowed the Bureau of Immigration thirty to forty-five days to correct the procedural error before ordering the release of the petitioner.[139] Thus, even when aliens could successfully show that they had been denied a fair hearing, increasingly their remedy lay with administrative authorities and they could not be very confident of a favorable outcome.

By 1924, the Supreme Court had endorsed the procedure of remanding cases for administrative reconsideration and had further suggested that the fair hearing requirement established in *Chin Yow* had different significance for citizens than for aliens. In *Tod v. Waldman*, the government challenged the Second Circuit's discharge of a woman and her three children after finding that the Department of Labor had unfairly denied her the right to administrative appeal. The Supreme Court held that instead of releasing the petitioners the court should have returned the case to the Department of Labor to allow it to correct its error. In support of its decision, the Court emphasized the administrative expertise of immigration officials "who have constant practice and are better advised" in determining the admissibility of immigrants. "The court," concluded Justice William Howard Taft, "is not as well qualified in such cases to consider and decide the issues." The Court suggested, however, that it had greater expertise when the cases involved the question of alleged citizenship, "a question of frequent judicial inquiry," and consequently implied a greater willingness to allow judicial rehearings in such cases.[140]

With the *Tod* v. *Waldman* case, according to administrative law scholar Walter Gellhorn, "the Chin Yow case was distinguished away practically to the vanishing point."[141] Indeed, by 1924 the promise of the *Chin Yow* case and the litigation strategy developed by aliens' attorneys had gone largely unfulfilled. In litigation between 1908 and 1924, federal judges, on the whole, proved reluctant to venture outside the basic requirements established in the *Chin Yow* and *Japanese Immigrant* cases, and they persistently refused to impart a strict judicial notion to the concept of a fair hearing in immigration matters. "Judicial justice" was not seen as particularly essential or relevant in the administrative realm. Implicit in the courts' decisions was the belief that the Bureau of Immigration could best do its job if it were not constrained by technical judicial procedures. Congressional statutes and bureau regulations, rather than fundamental principles, provided the yardstick for determining whether due process had been afforded aliens; only occasionally did federal courts reach beyond the statutory definition of due process to ensure aliens an opportunity to be heard.[142] Even when certain procedural rights such as the right to cross-examine were recognized by courts, they were never granted to their full extent. Judges acknowledged the agency's discretion to control the format of the hearing and the extent of the cross-examination.

The courts might intervene when aliens' attorneys could show to their satisfaction that the Bureau of Immigration had gone beyond its undisputed authority over questions of fact into the judicial realm of questions of law. But here, too, the courts moved cautiously, arguing that they were constrained by the established doctrine of judicial deference, even when they doubted the wisdom or correctness of the bureau's actions. Referring to Judge Dooling, among others, the bureau's chief law officer observed, "A good many of the courts have sustained us really because they had to sustain us, not because they believed in us."[143] Dooling, unlike the other federal judges in the Northern District of California, did not appear to endorse the summary immigration procedures. He never made the sort of disparaging remarks regarding the character of the immigrants that Judges Morrow and De Haven frequently uttered. Yet he, too, generally conceded power to the Bureau of Immigration because he felt bound by the tradition of judicial deference. In his opinions, Dooling repeatedly suggested that if the question of the extent of review had not already been settled, he would have decided the issue differently.[144]

Courts also deferred to the Bureau of Immigration because of the tenuous social and legal status of Chinese and other aliens. That the claims of citizens received greater attention highlights the importance the court attached to membership in determining what process was due. Only in those cases were judges persuaded that the stakes involved (the potential banishment of a citizen) mandated a higher degree of vigilance. For the most part, judges did not budge from the premises laid down in *Nishimura Ekiu* and *Fong Yue Ting* that aliens, standing outside the political community, had few rights which the government was bound to respect in exercising its sovereign right to police its borders.

The growing hostility toward aliens undoubtedly influenced the judges' assessment of the stakes involved in immigration cases. In balancing the danger of administrative abuse against the evil of undesirable immigration, the *New York Tribune*, commenting on the *Castro* case, had opted in favor of excessive administrative power. Most judges, with the notable exception of men such as Maurice Dooling and George Holt, came to similar conclusions and were fairly sympathetic to the policies embodied in the Chinese exclusion and general immigration laws and to the bureau's problems with enforcement. When immigrants barred under the Quota Act turned to the district court in San Francisco, for example, the newly appointed Judge John S. Partridge aligned with the nativists. In one case involving Russian immigrants fleeing persecution, Partridge observed: "It is a daily experience of this Court . . . that the Melting Pot does not always melt; that there are many who come to this country of such a character that it is impossible to fuse them into our national life. They have brought here their prejudices and their radical tendencies, which they maintained in their own country and they have found it, in many instances, impossible to realize the fact that there was no place and no occasion for such ideas in a free America."[145]

By 1924, then, the federal courts had helped to create a new administrative due process in immigration which incorporated, in abbreviated form, a few judicial procedures, but which remained defined primarily by the agency itself. Congress, of course, could alter the procedures and, thus, the definition of due process in immigration cases, but in practice, statutes tended to be vague or silent on such issues, leaving primary authority over practices to the Bureau of Immigration and its supervisory officials at the Department of Labor. Because judges, for the most part, tended only to insist that the bureau follow its own rules, procedural reform, if it came at all, would have to come through the Bureau of Immigration or Congress.

CHAPTER 8

Its Own Keeper

PROCEDURAL

REFORM IN THE

BUREAU OF

IMMIGRATION

In August 1915, commissioners of immigration from all over the nation came to San Francisco for an "Immigration Consultation," a conference in which they shared their experiences and views in an effort to forge more uniform practices. A. Warner Parker, chief law officer for the Bureau of Immigration, launched the consultation on the first day with an admonition he felt was of utmost importance. The immigration service had to become more uniform in its procedures, but, even more important, it had to place a high standard on fairness. Parker cautioned, "We have a great responsibility, a great deal of power placed in our hands. There never has been in the history of this country so much power vested outside of the courts as is put in the hands of the Immigration officers and we have to watch ourselves very carefully, and we have to watch every man serving under us to see that that power is not abused."[1]

Parker's words seem to suggest that, despite growing nativism, the immigrants' critique of the bureau was not without effect. To some extent, the agency by the eve of World War I had adopted more formal legal procedures of the sort advocated by pro-immigrant groups. Some officials supported the move out of a spirit of fairness and a solicitude for aliens' rights. Awed by their own power, several commissioners at the immigration conference agreed that inspectors owed *both* "the alien and the Government a square deal."[2] But even more important, a more legalistic approach also provided a solution to internal demands for rationalizing the agency's decision-making process while alleviating the growing criticism of the agency by immigrants and their defenders. The primacy of the latter objectives undercut the significance of the reforms for aliens. Although the Bureau of Immigration operated with a greater regard for uniformity and procedural regularity, the intent and result of legalization was largely to strengthen the bureau's decisions against external attacks.

Parker's message suggests additional limits to the effectiveness of the immigrants' critique. The federal courts' deference to immigration officials left an agency, in Parker's vision, of unprecedented power. While encouraging fairness, Parker implied that it was up to the bureau to determine the boundaries of its own discretion and the requirements of "fairness." Given those assumptions, the success of immigrant groups pressing the bureau to alter its procedures depended upon the amenability of particular administrations to their pleas as well as the general political atmosphere. Consequently, "fairness" to immigrants, manifested in greater procedural rights, proved to be an easily expendable principle when nativism reached a fevered pitch during World War I and the subsequent Red Scare.

In 1915, Louis F. Post, at a meeting of the American Political Science Association, denounced the power of the Bureau of Immigration and the "extremely administrative" procedures followed in deportation cases. "Culprits of whatever race or nationality have judicial trials and appeals, and in special cases of hardship there is for them at the last a fountain of mercy in the Chief Executive," Post observed. "But for the hapless person, whether citizen or alien," Post cried, "who is arrested as an alien and found to be an alien—all by administrative decision—there is neither judicial trial nor fountain of mercy, though his case call for it never so loudly, if the secretary of labor becomes satisfied that he is in this country contrary to law." Post had harsh words for the bureau's power over the admission of alleged citizens as well. By administrative process, he argued, "citizenship is awarded or denied much as a new public building may be contracted for or an old one ordered to be torn down."[3]

Such criticisms had been heard before. These comments are striking, however, because the man who voiced them was the assistant secretary of labor from 1913 to 1921, responsible for overseeing the enforcement of immigration laws. Before accepting that position, Post had practiced law briefly but was best known as a leading advocate of Henry George's single tax and as the editor of the *Public*.[4] He had been associated with a variety of liberal causes, including opposition to the deportation of alleged anarchist John Turner in 1903.[5] The Bureau of Immigration was only one among twelve offices operating under the auspices of the Department of Labor, and it appeared to be one of Post's least favorite responsibilities, casting, in his words, "a cloud of gloom" during his tenure.[6] He admitted to those at the Immigration Consultation in 1915, "I had an old grandmother who came from Revolutionary stock and she drilled into me . . . the essential ideals of human freedom and human liberty and equality irrespective of race and irrespective of nationality, and it took right, and I want to tell you that the immigration law rather worked crosswise with me . . . and I am not coming over a full convert to the immigration law."[7]

Post's views stood in sharp contrast to the Bureau of Immigration's traditional restrictionist stance, which jealously guarded the agency's authority over aliens and alleged citizens and defended its summary procedures. It is perhaps tempting to see Post's denunciations as the idiosyncrasies of a "crotchety reformer."[8] Yet other cabinet officials in Washington responsible for supervising the Bureau of Immigration after 1905 shared Post's liberal sympathies and revealed that the complaints of foreign-born groups were having some effect on the agency. Two men holding the office of secretary of commerce and labor—Oscar Straus (1906–9) and Charles Nagel (1909–13)—proved to be much more responsive to immigrants than previous officials. Straus, who emigrated from Germany as a young child, had been appointed in 1906 by Theodore Roosevelt during the furor over the Chinese boycott and segregation of Japanese students in San Francisco schools. Roosevelt also sought with the appointment to woo the support of the growing number of foreign-born voters. As evidenced in his article urging a less stringent enforcement of Chinese exclusion laws, Straus proved to be a counterweight to the restrictionist approach of the Bureau of Immigration. While in office, Straus opposed nativists' attempts to impose greater restraints upon immigrants, taking a particularly strong stand against the proposed literacy test. Straus gained the reputation for using his discretion to admit immigrants whom the commissioner general had rejected, thereby earning the enmity of the Immigration Restriction League and organized labor.[9] Straus later served on the advisory board for the Hebrew Sheltering and Immigrant Aid Society and continued to speak out against nativist legislation.[10] His successor, Charles Nagel, a corporate attorney and the son of German immigrants, also committed himself to a more "humane" approach to the administration of the immigration laws and adopted a somewhat more conciliatory approach to immigrants' demands for procedural rights.

Such officials wanted to portray a more positive image of the Bureau of Immigration and its work, moving away from the stereotypes of immigration officials as "cold-hearted" and biased and toward an image of humane, objective, and sympathetic officials.[11] Frederick C. Howe, appointed commissioner of immigration at Ellis Island in 1914, inaugurated reforms to humanize the immigration station. Playgrounds, weekly concerts, recreational programs, and walls adorned with historical pictures and American flags not only alleviated the tedium of detention but, in Howe's opinion, exposed immigrants to the American way of life.[12]

The efforts of such officials were not always appreciated by other leaders within the Bureau of Immigration. Until 1913, men filling the position of commissioner general continued to come from prominent labor organizations and to press for more rather than less restrictive policies.[13] Commissioner General Keefe, for example, chafed at the rulings of the Department of Commerce and Labor and took stands opposed to those of his superiors. Keefe ardently supported the literacy test as a condition for admission, which both Straus and Nagel actively opposed.[14] Local commissioners proved unenthusiastic about the liberal leanings of the Department of Commerce and Labor as well. Commissioner Williams at Ellis Island complained, "Straus claimed that he was 'humanizing' the law, but in fact he was disregarding it, with the result that the asylums and the charitable institutions of the state were being filled to capacity." What Straus really stood for, accused Williams, was "a lax application of the law."[15]

Yet officials within the Bureau of Immigration at times grudgingly bowed to the pressure of immigrant supporters and their superiors at the Department of Commerce and Labor. Commissioner of Immigration Henry M. White of Seattle recognized that the immigration service "is not popular."[16] Even Williams felt compelled to recommend the landing under bond of five Jewish children from Austria-Hungary who, "while not suffering from any disease, do not present a strong appearance," and whose impoverished parents in the United States lived in "squalid" conditions. Although Williams firmly believed that it would be in the "best interest of the country not to allow them to land," he also thought that "if we send them back our action is sure to be misunderstood and our motives misrepresented."[17]

Immigration officials also felt constrained in their actions by the threat of litigation. The bureau generally fared well in the federal courts but, perhaps for that reason, it took any judicial decision against it seriously. Dr. P. L. Prentis of the Chicago immigration office admitted to his colleagues at the immigration consultation, "I dislike, as you all do, of course, to be censured in any way by the courts. It gets us into a bad attitude and goes out to the public and gives encouragement to the attorneys which we dislike."[18] Commissioner J. H. Barbour of Oregon agreed, saying that in conducting investigations, "I try to bear in mind always, that some day the court will review this record which I am preparing at this particular time and I wonder what he [*sic*] will think about it, I wonder whether he will think that I have been fair or . . . unfair with the alien. In such cases," Barbour concluded, "I would rather go to the extreme of being fair to the alien."[19] Similarly, A. Warner Parker bolstered the regulations he drafted for the bureau with extensive legal citations to court decisions and congressional debates and reports, not only for the inspectors' benefit but with the hope that the regulations would "stand the test . . . of judicial consideration."[20]

The combined forces of sympathetic cabinet officials, the threat of legal challenges, and public criticism of the Bureau of Immigration led to some procedural reforms and curbs on the agency's discretion. The bureau, for example, changed several of its regulations governing the enforcement of Chinese exclusion laws after the public furor created by the Chinese boycott in 1905–6 and the appointment of Straus.[21] It explicitly guaranteed the right of Chinese to present witnesses and allowed counsel to make copies of the testimony to prepare for an appeal. The latter was an important change because attorneys previously were forced to make their appeals with little knowledge of the evidence used to deny their clients' entry. They continued to operate somewhat in the dark, however, because the bureau's internal memoranda, which included the inspector's evaluation of the evidence and recommendation, was still kept from them.[22] The bureau also extended the time to take appeals and allowed exempt Chinese to be released on $2,000 bond, rather than requiring detention, until their cases had been determined.[23]

In a further concession to Chinese and Chinese Americans, the commissioner general of immigration ordered in 1907 that Chinese applying for admission could have their attorneys and interpreters present at the hearing, though their representatives could not participate in the proceeding. The commissioner general rescinded that order in 1908, however, concluding that few Chinese had availed themselves of the privilege so that "no good purpose is served by allowing the said privilege."[24] After Secretary of Commerce and Labor Charles Nagel visited San Francisco in 1910, he reinstituted the rule allowing Chinese to have their attorneys and interpreters present at admission hearings. Nagel observed, "The situation on the western coast is a delicate one and we are desirous of doing too much rather than too little." Not only was the rule fair and just and "in keeping with the spirit of our own institutions," but it would also, in Nagel's opinion, "serve to maintain confidence in the integrity of our proceedings."[25] Commissioner General Daniel Keefe was clearly unenthusiastic about Nagel's decision, arguing that Chinese complaints "are really directed toward obtaining, if possible, the adoption of a procedure which would turn the examination of applicants into a judicial trial." To protect against that possibility, the rule again forbade the participation of the attorneys, allowing only their presence at the hearings. Keefe also stressed that the right to an attorney had to be confined to Chinese admission cases as "we could not afford to make any such concession in [non-Chinese] immigration cases."[26]

Non-Chinese aliens also appeared to gain some favorable procedural changes. In its 1911 rules the bureau cautioned its inspectors of the "necessity of giving the alien a fair hearing" before the board of special inquiry though, as in the courts, the precise definition of a "fair hearing" remained unelaborated. The right of aliens to an attorney in deportation proceedings appeared to be one element of a fair hearing. The bureau in 1911 explicitly provided that at some point during the examination the inspector should advise aliens arrested for deportation of their right to be represented by an attorney.[27] At the Immigration Consultation in 1915, A. Warner Parker reminded the commissioners that the aliens under investigation for deportation have "certain property rights, or other rights, family ties and things of that kind, we have to be more careful, we have to go into more detail, we have to allow the lawyers more liberty than we have in the cases of those applying for admission." The right to counsel, the bureau clarified in 1917, should be afforded "preferably at the beginning of the hearing" though the primary concern governing the timing was whether the "hearing has proceeded sufficiently in the development of the facts to protect the Government's interests."[28]

Also by 1917, attorneys representing aliens appeared to have the potential to play a more active role in the hearings. When Congress provided immigration inspectors with the power to subpoena witnesses and documents, the bureau extended the privilege to aliens under certain conditions and also conceded to aliens' attorneys the right to cross-examine witnesses and provided that the bureau would subpoena the government's witnesses whom counsel had not had an opportunity to cross-examine.[29] Such rules appeared to respond to criticism that the right to representation in hearings was meaningless if attorneys did not possess the basic tools to defend their clients' interests adequately.[30]

The bureau proved more resistant to demands that aliens have the right to representation in admission hearings before the board of special inquiry. Even Post, who harshly condemned the lack of procedural rights in deportation and alleged citizens' cases, thought the subjection of aliens applying for admission to summary administrative processes completely justifiable. "Inasmuch as immigrants never yet landed have no personal rights under our laws," Post clarified, "their exclusion does not raise questions of personal rights. The questions are of national policy alone."[31] Despite such resistance, immigrants did gain a small concession when Congress provided in 1917 that aliens could have a friend or relative present at the hearing before the board of special inquiry. The bureau, no doubt fearing the privilege could be used to turn the summary hearing into a trial, specifically prohibited attorneys and representatives of immigrant aid societies from appearing as a "friend or relative."[32]

The bureau also responded to challenges to the independence and neutrality of the boards of special inquiry. Critics like Max Kohler charged that inspectors on the boards, "instead of enforcing the law . . . seek now—almost to a man—to reach the results which their superior requires. . . . Inspectors know merely that they are expected to exclude with great frequency." As proof, Kohler pointed to the high reversal rate of board exclusions upon appeal, claiming that the secretary of labor sustained more than two-thirds of appeals taken by the Hebrew Sheltering and Immigrant Aid Society.[33] The U.S. Immigration Commission, reporting to Congress in 1911, bolstered such criticisms in its recommendation that "in justice to the immigrant, and to the country as well, the character of these boards should be improved." The commission found that "at all the important ports the boards of special inquiry are composed of immigrant inspectors, who are generally without judicial or legal training. This, together with the fact that they are selected by the commissioners of immigration at the ports where they serve, tends to impair the judicial character of the board and to influence its members in a greater or lesser degree to reflect in their decisions the attitude of the commissioner in determining the cases." The commission recommended that the hearings be public and that men "whose ability and training fit them for the judicial functions performed" be recruited.[34] Senator William Dillingham in his immigration bill submitted in 1911 proposed to make board members more independent by transferring the power to appoint members from the local commissioners of immigration to the secretary of commerce and labor.[35]

The bureau resisted public hearings and the transfer of appointment power to the Department of Commerce and Labor, but it agreed that the caliber of the inspectors had to be improved. As early as 1907, the commissioner general of immigration had stated that "members of these boards should be men qualified by temperament and training for the weighing of evidence and the application of law to the varying circumstances constantly being brought out in the examinations they conduct; they should be men of judicial and discriminating mind." Such men could be obtained, he continued, only if the bureau paid salaries equal to those earned by judges.[36]

The bureau's push for boards with a greater judicial character did not evolve only as a response to external criticism; it also reflected internal objectives to rationalize decision making within the agency and to make procedures more uniform. Though the bureau deflected legal challenges to its summary procedures by stressing the administrative nature of its work, it often noted that its tasks were not much different from those of a court.[37] The immigration officers heard testimony, found facts, weighed evidence, and applied law to particular cases. Some officials, seeing their inspectors drowning in a sea of documents and facts, argued that judicial methods of sifting evidence and narrowing the questions involved would help the immigration officers to make their decisions in a rational way. Collector John Wise in 1895 had complained to the secretary of the treasury that the Chinese inspectors "do not know the legal value of the evidence presented, not being versed in the law, they are not able to cross-question the witnesses with success. In this way very much time is lost and a vast amount of useless and immaterial evidence gathered which only tends to obscure the main facts in the case and to encumber the record."[38] Responding to similar problems, Commissioner of Immigration White of Seattle argued at the 1915 consultation that immigration hearings should use the "same procedure as the court," with both the government and the immigrants having full opportunity to present their evidence. Parker agreed; the judicial methods had been developed "hundreds and hundreds of years ago . . . because the courts recognized the necessity of getting the matter to an issue and it seems to me that we do not get the matter to an issue unless we follow that method."[39]

Such concerns prompted the bureau to establish a law division in its central office to oversee the legal work of the agency and guide inspectors in their investigations.[40] A. Warner Parker appears to have been the first designated "chief law officer" for the bureau and, in that capacity, also served as a special assistant to the attorney general.[41] It fell to Parker to draft departmental regulations, to propose revisions of the immigration laws, and to monitor litigation and its effects on the bureau's practices. The fact that Parker gave the opening remarks at the 1915 Immigration Consultation, setting out the dual objectives of administrative uniformity and fairness to aliens, suggests the more central role that lawyers were coming to play in the Bureau of Immigration.

At the local level as well, attorneys became more of a presence. Collector Wise at San Francisco had suggested hiring attorneys as inspectors in 1895; in 1909, Hart H. North, the commissioner of immigration at that port and a lawyer as well, urged a similar course, saying, "If we had a good law clerk whose whole time could be devoted to reviewing the records and pointing out to inspectors wherein they were deficient, I have no doubt that good results would ensue."[42] The commissioner general sent Fred Watts, the assistant chief of the bureau's law division, to San Francisco to evaluate whether such a clerk would be helpful. Watts strongly urged that "an officer of legal mind and training" be hired who could closely supervise the inspectors and drill them in proper methods of interrogation. With the guidance of a legally trained official, the inspectors would know what evidence was material or immaterial and the bureau in Washington would have less occasion to criticize their work.[43] Gradually, the number of lawyers increased, as did the importance of the agency's law division. By 1913, only four years after the first law clerk was appointed, the immigration service at San Francisco had a law section with five employees.[44]

The bureau's incorporation of lawyers increased the tendency toward a more legalistic approach. The lawyers brought with them a professional perspective that highlighted the importance of legal forms and procedures. Not surprisingly, officials with legal training tended to be the primary advocates at the Immigration Consultation for more uniformity, more courtlike hearings, and greater procedural protections for aliens.[45] Standardized forms, presumably prepared by the law division, prompted inspectors to consider and report on the relevant aspects of the case, asking such questions as, "What was the demeanor of witnesses during exam? Any discrepancies on material points? Do you believe alleged relationship exists? If not, is your adverse opinion based upon the discrepancies in testimony?"[46] If inspectors submitted incomplete reports or omitted certain procedures, the law officer could send the case back for further investigation.[47] To keep its field officers abreast of changes in the law or regulations and recent court decisions, the bureau began to publish a monthly newsletter, the *U.S. Immigration Service Bulletin*, in 1918.[48] Eventually, inspectors who had no formal legal training found themselves approaching their work more as lawyers would. In the process of enforcing the complex immigration laws, said Parker, "whether we have a legal training or not, we very soon pick up such of the little details of legal procedure as we need to put [our special knowledge] into proper form."[49]

The bureau's move toward a more legalistic approach and its granting of certain procedural protections would appear, at first glance, to indicate that immigrants and their supporters were succeeding in attaining a system of executive justice. They had sought to transform inspectors into judges and administrative hearings into trials with the attendant rights and practices. They hoped to replace administrative discretion with law, uniformity, and a regard for precedents, in other words, to subject the bureau to the "rule of law." Immigrant groups advocated such principles for strategic reasons; they thought that the greater emphasis on procedural justice would lead to fewer exclusions and deportations. Yet legalism did not automatically lead to more favorable outcomes for immigrants. For the most part, the bureau's turn to procedural reform and its elevation of the role of lawyers reflected its own desire to strengthen its gatekeeping role.

Secretary of Commerce and Labor Charles Nagel warned a gathering of the Union of American Hebrew Congregations of the dangers of insisting upon less administrative discretion and greater uniformity and reliance on precedents. In line with many legal progressives of his day, Nagel believed that substantive justice could be obtained only through the wise exercise of discretion by experts rather than through reliance on legal forms. If, as Max Kohler (the other speaker at the meeting) suggested, the bureau issued written reports of all of its decisions, Nagel argued that "the general consequences will be worse, and the law more severely construed . . . because [it would] make it necessary for me not to admit anybody unless I am clearly willing to admit everybody upon the same basis." In Nagel's opinion, "one of the great dangers to our country now is that we are loaded down" with law that prevented justice being done in individual cases. He admitted he often acted "contrary to strict law," but "if I break the law it is in behalf of the alien and not against him. If I strain it to meet the case, it is to help out a case of hardship, to prevent the separation of members of a family, to do what I think must have been intended to be done, treating it as an administrative law." Nagel cited as an example his refusal to sign a warrant for the deportation of a man who had been convicted of a crime many years before he came to the United States because Nagel did not believe that he was guilty, despite his conviction. Although the law, as written, required the deportation of all aliens who had been convicted of a felony before entry, Nagel was satisfied that he was carrying out the spirit if not the letter of the law. Without administrative discretion, such intervention on behalf of deserving aliens would be impossible, Nagel cautioned.[50]

But as Nagel conceded, discretion could also be a threat to aliens' interests. Much depended on the proclivities of the officials exercising discretion, and, for the most part, the bureau used both its discretion and its legalizing tendency to make enforcement of the laws more restrictive and the agency more powerful. Nativism, both from within and without the Bureau of Immigration, continued to have a powerful influence on the agency's practices. For example, after the bureau made several changes favorable to the Chinese in 1911, it informed President Taft, "We have gone as far as we possibly can to yield to the demands of the commercial interests of the coast. . . . The danger is . . . that our present course may invite popular condemnation on the part of labor unions and perhaps even the legislature."[51] At the same time that Chinese were agitating for procedural reforms, the anti-Asian campaign in California—aimed especially at Japanese and Asian Indians—grew increasingly hostile. The Bureau of Immigration at San Francisco was already under severe attack by California nativists for admitting Indians, and any sign of laxity regarding Chinese was interpreted as government corruption.[52]

The central Bureau of Immigration received protests from nativists regarding non-Chinese immigrants as well. Petitions calling for more restrictive legislation and more rigid enforcement of the existing immigration laws poured into the bureau at Washington, D.C.[53] Commenting on a speech by Secretary Nagel about "humanizing" the immigration laws, one man from Missouri wrote that such a proposal confirmed "a strong suspicion that prevails among members of my class, which is that of unskilled labor, that the immigration authorities have entirely too much 'heart' in the matter."[54] Another man, who signed his letter "One of your real Americans," put his case bluntly: "I am very interested in the immigration movement. It is ridiculous! There are altogether too many foreigners moving into our country. . . . I am a poor man and live among these dirty devils and I do not like it! They are eating up my share of the profits which really belong to me and my American neighbors. Our country is the Best Country in the World and you men of rank and authority can keep it so if you make strict laws to keep out paupers, bad men, and disease."[55] Secretary Nagel, caught between the conflicting demands of immigrants and nativists, responded to the complaints of Prescott Hall of the Immigration Restriction League: "I cannot expect to please everybody. In fact I am surprised when I please anybody."[56]

But in general, the bureau's policy catered more to nativists than to immigrants. At the 1915 Immigration Consultation held at San Francisco a division existed between commissioners who held liberal views toward immigrants and those who were restrictionist. If we can rely on the stenographer's notes indicating the applause given by the audience of commissioners to different speakers, the nativist speech given by Commissioner Henry J. Skeffington of Boston was much more popular than others emphasizing fairness to immigrants. Skeffington roused the commissioners, saying, "I want to see the meshes of the sieve drawn closer and tighter. . . . We have a right to invite into our house virile men, strong men. . . . We have a right to protect ourselves, and say: 'Stop this stream until we have assimilated what has come in here.' . . . That is the position I would like to see this Conference take."[57]

In its content and tone, Skeffington's speech reflected the dominant approach of Bureau of Immigration leaders to immigration policies and their enforcement. The bureau had always been in the vanguard of the movement for restrictive immigration laws. In every annual report, the commissioner general advocated expanding the excludable and deportable classes as well as lengthening the time limits for deportation. Concessions to aliens, such as the right to an attorney in deportation proceedings and the right to have a friend or relative present at admission hearings, were more than outweighed by the adoption of procedures working to their disadvantage. The commissioner general in 1917 praised the new immigration law, which he saw as providing a "much more intensive examination of aliens than ever [before]."[58] The law lengthened the time limit for deportation from three to five years and eliminated time limits for alien prostitutes and those advocating radical beliefs. The law also provided for the inspection by two, rather than one, inspectors of aliens applying for admission, a procedure advocated by Commissioner Williams in 1913 as a way to protect the government against "improper admissions." By 1917, the basic provisions for admission and deportation remained the same and aliens' critiques had penetrated only superficially.

Similarly, though Chinese made some inroads in liberalizing the agency's procedures, their lobbying and economic pressure generally failed to effect important changes. They had gained the right to have attorneys present at admission investigations, but because attorneys could not participate in the hearings, there was little hope that they could bring about significant changes in the outcomes of their cases, except, perhaps, on appeal. According to Commissioner General Keefe, attorneys for Chinese seldom used their privilege to be present at admission hearings because, they complained, "to be present without taking part in the proceedings was an empty form"; as a result, the bureau by 1914 had again rescinded the privilege to an attorney.[59] The bureau refused to remain bound by the weight of the evidence, insisting that it needed discretion to act upon its evaluation of the credibility of Chinese testimony. Both Chinese nationals and Chinese Americans remained subject to raids by immigration officials.[60] During the lull of immigration at the beginning of World War I in 1914, A. Warner Parker, the bureau's law officer, who would speak so passionately of the need to be fair at the Immigration Consultation one year later, suggested, "Why not avail ourselves of the lull in this work to get a better grip on and rid the country of Asiatic aliens—Chinese, Japanese, etc. . . . Of course, the adoption of such a policy would have to be kept quiet, and the matter handled discretely [*sic*] and not in such a way as to give the impression we were engaging in '*raids*.' "[61]

The bureau also continued to recommend procedures to make the exclusion laws even more stringent.[62] Parker made a concerted effort during his tenure to consolidate the administration of the Chinese and general immigration laws. For the most part, the move consisted of trying to combine the most restrictive elements of both laws. His proposed bill in 1909 sought to retain the full force of the Chinese exclusion laws while eliminating some of the protections Chinese enjoyed, particularly their right to a judicial hearing before deportation, and calling for a new registration of Chinese similar to that required by the Geary Act of 1892.[63] By 1919 Parker had authored a bill to admit aliens on a provisional basis and to expand the system of registration to non-Chinese as a "way of keeping tab on our alien population." Under his program, aliens would be subject to continual surveillance and possible deportation until they became naturalized citizens.[64] The bureau sought to expand its investigations into the alien's homeland as well, increasingly relying on preembarkation inspections to restrict immigration.[65]

The restrictive mind-set revealed in the bureau's legislative proposals influenced its objectives in adopting procedural reforms and limited the significance of the rights it did extend to aliens. The bureau's concessions tended to be ones that led to little real benefit for aliens but promoted the image of a fair, humane administration. When the bureau's office at San Francisco once again in 1919 became the source of vociferous complaints from Chinese groups, the commissioner of immigration there suggested reinstituting the right to an attorney in admission hearings because "the Service would be subjected to less criticism" from Chinese. White reassured the central office that "in practice, the privilege was never availed of by counsel" in the past because of the limits on counsel's participation, "but at the same time it afforded no grounds for attack."[66]

Commissioner Williams similarly sought to handle attacks on his discretion with public demonstrations of his fairness which ultimately left his discretion intact. When Williams returned to Ellis Island in 1909 after a four-year absence, he provoked a bitter controversy when he established the guideline that immigrants should have at least $25 to prove they were not excludable as aliens "likely to become a public charge." Williams argued that it was not a "hard and fast rule" for admission, but his critics charged him with imposing a money test not required by statute and unlawfully excluding hundreds of immigrants.[67] Lawyers for various Jewish organizations sought to challenge Williams's rule in federal court, but before the cases reached resolution, Williams had agreed to rehear the cases in a special, public administrative proceeding to which Secretary of Commerce and Labor Charles Nagel and representatives of various immigrant aid societies were invited to attend. Upon rehearing, Williams admitted seventeen of eighteen aliens previously excluded for lack of funds. With his public handling of the case, Williams succeeded in foreclosing judicial review of his rule and quieting public furor, but it does not appear that he substantially altered his ongoing policy. Williams removed the public notice of the $25 rule, but he did not modify his internal instructions to inspectors until two years later. Even then, Williams's staff continued to use $25 as "a convenient yardstick" in determining the admission of aliens.[68]

Aliens did gain some procedural rights that were more than window dressing, but those rights or procedures often ultimately served to strengthen the bureau's power. For example, after much lobbying, the bureau in the Immigration Act of 1917 gained the power to subpoena witnesses and documents; it subsequently allowed aliens the power to subpoena and cross-examine witnesses, a right aliens had tried, unsuccessfully, to obtain through litigation in the federal courts. In extending the privilege to aliens, the bureau appeared to be expanding the boundaries of due process, and Parker, in justifying the legislative proposal for the subpoena power, argued that it "would operate distinctly in the interest of justice" for both the alien and the government.[69] Yet the bureau undoubtedly expected the power of subpoena to work primarily to its own benefit, improving the ability of inspectors to obtain the necessary evidence to exclude or deport aliens.[70]

Parker made that primary objective clear when he discussed the possibility of adding to the bureau's rules a provision that evidence obtained from subpoenaed witnesses would not be used in criminal or penal proceedings against them.[71] Such a provision, Parker conceded, might forestall witnesses' refusal to testify on the grounds of the Fifth Amendment protection against self-incrimination. But Parker doubted whether the Fifth Amendment even applied to deportation proceedings, referring again to their civil nature, and he stressed the benefits to be obtained from not granting the exemption because the government "gains a chance . . . of obtaining voluntary confessions from witnesses" which could lead to further prosecutions or deportations. Parker felt the bureau could eliminate the provision and the rule "would doubtless operate successfully despite the constitutional provision against convicting any person out of his own mouth."[72] The final rules adopted did not offer witnesses immunity from civil or criminal proceedings, and the bureau placed further conditions on the alien's right to subpoena witnesses; the alien had to establish in writing "what he expects to prove by such witness or the books, papers and documents and to show affirmatively that the proposed evidence is relevant and material and that he has made diligent efforts without success to produce the same." Once a witness was subpoenaed, the alien could examine the witness only on the issues stated in the written application for the subpoena.[73] These conditions clearly limited the significance of the right for aliens, leaving its exercise to the discretion of immigration inspectors.

In fact, most of the protections given to aliens rested on the shaky ground of administrative discretion and thus were not very secure. The effective enforcement of the immigration laws required, in the bureau's opinion, an administrative system that vested ample discretion in the hands of local immigration inspectors. Commissioner Barbour urged at the Immigration Consultation that effective enforcement could not be accomplished simply through "uniformity . . . rule or regulation." Discretion remained a key component because "you have to depend upon the [immigration inspector's] individual common sense in such things."[74] Similarly, Commissioner White of Seattle warned that too much emphasis on "fairness" might make inspectors overly cautious and turn the immigration service into a "drone system." Let the chief officers worry about fairness, he suggested, while the inspectors concentrate on active, enthusiastic enforcement of the law.[75]

Because of such attitudes, the local commissioners and immigration inspectors retained significant latitude in determining the extent of aliens' rights, as can be seen in the implementation of the bureau's rule granting aliens the right to an attorney in deportation proceedings. Parker, the main proponent of forging greater uniformity in agency practices, admitted that the rule governing the right to attorneys "is drawn in very broad and general terms" to allow for diverse circumstances.[76] Commissioners at the Immigration Consultation in 1915 disagreed over when the attorney should be called in and how much the counsel should be allowed to participate in the hearing. Because of the difficulty in holding attorneys "within reasonable bounds" and the desire to establish the government's case, some districts did not inform the alien of the right to an attorney until the end of the hearing. Sometimes inspectors gained the cooperation of aliens by promising the opportunity to consult with an attorney later. By that point, however, an attorney could do little except review the recorded evidence and submit additional evidence; seldom could he repair damaging testimony unwittingly given by aliens.[77] For that reason, other commissioners argued "that an attorney has a perfect right to be in the case at its inception . . . that all the rights of the alien may be protected."[78] But even more liberal commissioners who wanted to protect aliens' rights believed that the need for administrative efficiency should circumscribe the extent of the attorney's participation in the hearing. Louis F. Post observed during the consultation that "lawyers will string out examinations uselessly." Thus the "inspector should use discretion and strength in restraining the cross-examination and the examination of witnesses within reasonable bounds; that there is where the line lies, to allow the man his full rights but to protect the Government from immaterial and long-drawn-out examinations."[79]

Of course, noted another official, F. W. Berkshire, inspectors could avoid the controversy about the timing and extent of attorneys' participation altogether by ensuring that the case against the alien was secure from the start. Berkshire advocated a full preliminary investigation before an inspector applied for a warrant for arrest. Like several other practices of the Bureau of Immigration, the preliminary investigation had the advantage of appearing to be more fair and protective of aliens while increasing the bureau's success in securing their deportation. Bureau officials in Washington, D.C., were enthusiastic supporters of the preliminary investigation because they received numerous complaints about arrests made without sufficient evidence for deportation. The secretary of labor, who held the authority for issuing the warrants for arrest, supposedly examined the evidence before issuing the warrant, but often he had little but the assurances of immigration officials before him. This was especially true in applications made by telegraph when speed in apprehending an alien was said to be essential. Telegraphic warrants gave local inspectors significant leeway to proceed without immediate administrative supervision and, according to Parker, were looked upon by the courts "with no degree of favor."[80] Abuse of discretion in such circumstances could, and did, occur, resulting in aliens being arrested and detained for several days upon suspicion or flimsy evidence. An extensive preliminary investigation would allow superior officials to review the evidence in the case more thoroughly and protect aliens against needless arrests.

The problem for aliens, however, was that preliminary investigations constricted the meaning and scope of the deportation hearings. For the bureau, the beauty of preliminary investigations was that the government could have its case prepared and decided before the actual hearing occurred. All of the material gathered in the investigation—which might include the unsworn statements of witnesses, anonymous tips, and incriminating remarks made by the aliens—could be submitted as evidence to support deportation.[81] According to Berkshire, the average deportation hearing in such cases should "not consume more than a few minutes"; simply "hand the alien the record, notify him of his right to be released on bond and of his right to have an attorney."[82] At that point, "it does not matter much when the attorney appears in the case," presumably because the government had already established its case, and "we eliminate the question of unfairness about the appearance of the attorney."[83]

By the eve of World War I, then, the bureau had adopted the rhetoric of "fairness to aliens" and under the leadership of certain sympathetic officials had even taken steps to provide some safeguards, particularly in deportation proceedings. But the bureau's move toward legalism remained confined by administrative exigencies and nativist policies. In the bureau's view, concerns about legal form should not be allowed to obscure the policy goals embodied in the Chinese exclusion and general immigration laws.

Legal procedures might prove useful or politically prudent, but the ends were still more important than the means. Administrative discretion could not be tamed too much. "The practical situation," the bureau argued, "absolutely demands" an administrative procedure of "summary character."[84] The bureau's tenuous commitment to proceduralism and "fairness to aliens" would become all too clear as the nation succumbed to widespread nativism in the aftermath of the world war.

THE RED RAIDS

On the night of January 2, 1920, Harry G. Steiner showed up for a committee meeting at a building known to Department of Justice officials as the Communist party headquarters in Boston, Massachusetts. Soon after his arrival, three men in civilian clothes burst in with guns and, without identifying themselves or disclosing a warrant, searched the people in the building, confiscated all their belongings, and took them to a city jail where Steiner was detained until the next afternoon. Two days later, a Department of Justice official came to Steiner's house and, again without a warrant, searched through his belongings and took Steiner and his papers to a federal office. After releasing him, Department of Justice officials approached Steiner the next day while he was at work and again took him into custody. Finally, Steiner substantiated his claim that he was an American citizen, born in Manchester, New Hampshire, and escaped the government's dragnet. Steiner proved more fortunate than thousands of others arrested that night throughout the nation. Of an estimated 600 to 1,000 persons arrested in the Boston vicinity and southern New Hampshire, 440 (almost all aliens) were imprisoned for weeks in the dilapidated and unsanitary facilities at Deer Island while they awaited deportation hearings, without the opportunity to consult attorneys.[85] Prisoners in other districts experienced similar problems and also reported beatings and threats made by government officials during interrogations.[86] Few of those detained were able to post the unusually high bail set by the bureau. By the end of the antiradical raids, the Bureau of Immigration had deported 760 aliens of the "anarchist and kindred classes."[87]

Such details of the so-called Red Raids have become well-known through the accounts of participants and the work of historians. There is a tendency in those accounts to see the raids as an aberration, the product of a particularly volatile era when the nation's fears became raised to a fevered pitch. Certainly the Red Raids were unique in their scope and intensity; but the administrative practices and assumptions that were exposed to the public, practices that emphasized results over rights, had a firm foundation in the

Bureau of Immigration's past policies, as historian William Preston has also pointed out.[88] With the rise of the Red Scare, the bureau dropped any pretense of concern about due process, using its considerable power and discretion to devise means to deport radical aliens.

Even before the Red Scare of 1919, Commissioner General of Immigration Anthony Caminetti had targeted radicals—especially members of the Industrial Workers of the World—as one of the bureau's special concerns.[89] Swept along by the demands for "Absolute and Unqualified Loyalty" during World War I, the bureau did its part to purge the United States of radical aliens who opposed the war and who were thus, by the agency's definition, pro-German and un-American.[90] The bureau continually advocated more restrictive legislation to enable it to exclude and deport aliens for their radical beliefs and associations as well as for their explicit advocacy and actions. By 1918, the bureau had succeeded in obtaining legislation which provided for the deportation, without time limit, of any alien who belonged to organizations that advocated certain radical doctrines (such as the forceful overthrow of government, the unlawful destruction of property, anarchy, or the assassination of public officials).

As the bureau's jurisdiction over perceived radical aliens expanded, so, too, did the willingness of immigration officials to use their discretion to limit the procedural rights of aliens and facilitate deportation proceedings. The first victims were aliens arrested for suspected association with the IWW in Seattle, Washington. The city had become a hotbed of conflict as relations between labor and employers worsened in 1917, culminating in a bitter strike in the lumber industry; employers, patriotic groups, and other Seattle residents laid the blame on the agitation of the IWW and beseeched the federal government to take action to repress the organization. The local Bureau of Immigration, led by Commissioner Henry White, responded readily to the call for help.

The subsequent actions by the bureau's Seattle office revealed the degree to which aliens' rights depended upon the good faith of local officials. Although Commissioner White had been one of the more vocal advocates at the Immigration Consultation of incorporating "as much of the judicial attitude" as possible in deportation hearings, he now struck a quite different stance.[91] White's staff began by ignoring rulings of Department of Labor officials that membership in the IWW did not, per se, violate the immigration laws and proceeded to arrest scores of Wobblies in the area, relying on telegraphic warrants of arrest, which made it difficult for the department to detect the deviance from its policy. According to William Preston's detailed account of the raids, immigration inspectors used loose standards in determining who to arrest, targeting not only those thought to be prominent leaders and members of the IWW but those "who looked like I.W.W.'s."[92] Once arrested, aliens waited from two to four months for their deportation hearings; as had been the practice in Seattle before the raids, immigration officials did not inform aliens of a right to an attorney until the end of the hearing. The inspectors conducting the hearing appeared determined to prove their cases against the aliens, relying on surmise or the appearance and attitude of the alien when firm evidence was lacking. Despite the secretary of labor's reminders that mere membership in the IWW or belief in its principles could not be grounds for deportation, the Seattle bureau continued to recommend deportation based on aliens' beliefs rather than their individual acts. In the end, federal court decisions and, even more important, the restraining hand of the secretary of labor drastically reduced the effects of the raids against the IWW. Of more than 150 aliens arrested, only 27 were eventually deported.[93]

Though the final deportations numbered far fewer than the bureau had expected, its enthusiasm for expelling alien radicals had not been dampened. Thus when J. Edgar Hoover from the Department of Justice approached Caminetti about the possibility of joint, massive raids on radicals, Caminetti proved a willing and energetic partner. Certain obstacles stood in their path, however, one being the lack of any legal authority for cooperative endeavors between the two agencies. For that reason, the Department of Labor was hesitant to accede to Attorney General Palmer's request for joint action. The department's caution was indicative of its general reluctance to embrace the antiradical campaign, a reluctance that would pose difficulties for Caminetti and Hoover. William B. Wilson, appointed secretary of labor in 1913, did not necessarily share the active sympathy for immigrants evident in his predecessors, Oscar Straus and Charles Nagel, but, as a former organizer and official of the United Mine Workers, Wilson did identify strongly with workers. It was in part his understanding of difficult working conditions and of the appeal certain groups such as the IWW could have for workers caught in intolerable jobs that led to his refusal to endorse the wholesale deportation of IWW members.[94] His assistant secretary, Louis F. Post, maintained a fundamental distrust of administrative power and a dislike of restrictive immigration policies.

Department of Labor officials thus proved less willing to bend the rules to facilitate the deportation of radicals. Secretary Wilson, in fact, took steps in the midst of the IWW hearings to afford aliens greater procedural protections. The summary methods of the Bureau of Immigration had become a source of controversy during the IWW raids, especially once George Vandeveer became the lawyer for the aliens. He publicly denounced the lack of due process afforded those arrested, particularly their inability to consult with counsel, and published a pamphlet advising aliens to refuse to answer questions if arrested in order to avoid self-incrimination. Secretary Wilson, in response, revised the bureau's rules regarding the right to an attorney in March 1919. Whereas the 1917 rules provided that it was preferable, when possible, to advise the alien of the right to counsel at the beginning of the hearing, Wilson's new rule left nothing to the discretion of the inspector, explicitly mandating that aliens be allowed counsel from the start.[95] The Bureau of Immigration and the Department of Justice perceived the new rule as a severe blow to their ability to obtain the necessary evidence for deportation. They had expected in the upcoming raids to rely heavily on the self-incriminating remarks of unrepresented aliens to secure their cases.

The Department of Labor thus posed a central obstacle to the plans of Caminetti and Hoover. Somehow, they had to persuade its high officials to endorse their proposed raids and, further, to relax their insistence upon procedural regularities, particularly the right to counsel. Through a combination of deceit and exaggeration on the part of Caminetti and Hoover and bureaucratic neglect or laxity on the part of Secretary Wilson, the Bureau of Immigration and the Department of Justice achieved their objectives. The onset of the Red Scare in 1919, sparked by violent riots on May Day and by revelations of bombing attempts on several prominent Americans (including Attorney General Palmer) in May and June, undoubtedly worked in Caminetti and Hoover's favor.[96] Bloody race riots and an outburst of labor strikes following on the heels of the May Day riots and June bombings pushed the nation on edge and created widespread fear of impending revolution in the United States. Under intense pressure to take action against alien radicals, the Department of Labor agreed in the fall of 1919 to work with the Department of Justice to embark upon a massive roundup and deportation of suspected radicals.

Secretary Wilson and Attorney General Palmer left the details of the raids to Caminetti, Hoover, A. Warner Parker, and John W. Abercrombie, the solicitor general of the Department of Labor. The basic plan divided the tasks between the two departments. Hoover's division within the Department of Justice did the investigatory work and gave the names of suspected aliens to the Bureau of Immigration. After the secretary of labor signed warrants for the aliens' arrest, Department of Justice officials apprehended them in mass roundups and turned them over to the Bureau of Immigration for deportation hearings. When the first joint raid of the Union of Russian Workers was carried out in November 1919, it became clear that the Department of Justice was as little concerned as the Bureau of Immigration with legal niceties and procedures. Arrests far exceeded the number of warrants issued; in New York, for example, officials armed with only 27 warrants arrested about 650 people. Allegations of beatings by arresting officers, long detentions without hearings, and seizure and destruction of personal property were common but apparently ignored by supervising officials in the initial roundups.[97]

Wilson's rule providing the right to an attorney at deportation hearings gave aliens one of their few protections against officials' zeal. The commissioner general complained in his 1919 annual report of the suspected radicals' readiness to claim "most vociferously . . . the right to be protected in every manner and to every degree."[98] As his remarks suggest, aliens, when advised of the right to counsel, tended to seize it and generally refused to answer questions that might lead to their deportation. As a consequence, the bureau deported far fewer aliens than expected at the end of the first raid. Thus in approaching the Department of Labor for approval of another, more extensive raid aimed at the newly formed Communist party and Communist Labor party, Caminetti and Hoover urged the reinstatement of the 1917 rule on the right to counsel, arguing that well-organized radicals posed an imminent danger to the nation's security. Secretary Wilson and Post reluctantly agreed to the new raid though Wilson continued to insist that individual wrongdoing, in addition to party membership, must be evident before warrants would be issued. The department's solicitor who signed the actual warrants, John Abercrombie, however, failed to scrutinize the evidence closely, relying instead on the commissioner general's recommendations in individual cases. It was also Abercrombie who, in Wilson's absence, authorized the change in the bureau's rule three days before the massive raids again to grant the immigration inspector the discretion to determine when to allow an alien the right to counsel. Once again, as had repeatedly happened in the past, central authorities deferred to the discretion of officers in the field, sacrificing the few procedural protections enjoyed by aliens in the process.

Those departmental concessions enabled Caminetti and Hoover to set into place the summary administrative apparatus necessary to carry off their widespread dragnet. Historians have aptly captured the excesses of the officials' actions in the raids carried out in January 1920. Hoover had obtained approximately three thousand warrants from the Department of Labor, but his enthusiastic force arrested an estimated ten thousand people, both aliens and citizens. In William Preston's words, the raids were characterized by "indiscriminate arrests of the innocent with the guilty, unlawful searches and seizures by federal detectives, intimidating preliminary interrogations of aliens held incommunicado, high-handed levying of excessive bail, and denial of counsel."[99] But once again, the success of the bureau—

measured in the number of deportations—must have been disappointing. Thousands of arrests netted deportations numbering only in the hundreds.

More deportations would probably have been forthcoming were it not for the shocked response of vocal, well-placed critics and federal judges and the restraining hand of the Department of Labor. Attorneys for those arrested turned to the federal courts to challenge the legality of the raids. They found powerful allies among the legal elite, including such luminaries as Felix Frankfurter, Roscoe Pound, Ernst Freund, and Zechariah Chafee. By May 1920, they formed with others the National Popular Government League and published a devastating denunciation of the Department of Justice's actions using exhibits from the department's own files as evidence of malfeasance. Frankfurter and Chafee also served as counsel in one of the most dramatic federal court cases arising out of the raids in Boston, *Colyer* v. *Skeffington.*

Judges usually spent very little time on immigration cases, often making their determinations on habeas corpus petitions in chambers. But in the *Colyer* case, District Court Judge George W. Anderson subjected the officials' actions in the raids to detailed scrutiny in a hearing lasting fifteen days, resulting in a trial record of almost sixteen hundred pages. As the testimony proceeded to reveal the number of arrests and detentions without warrants, the lack of access to counsel, the poor conditions at detention centers, and the active role played by the Department of Justice in the deportation proceedings beyond its statutory authorization, Anderson cried, "A more lawless proceeding it is hard for anybody to conceive. Talk about Americanization! What we need is to Americanize people that are carrying out such proceedings as this. We shall forget everything we ever learned about American Constitutional liberty if we are to undertake to justify such a proceeding as this."[100] Anderson's written opinion was only slightly more restrained; he concluded that the "terroristic methods" of the arrests, detentions, and hearings and the "lawless disregard of the rights and feelings of these aliens as human beings" made the proceedings as a whole unfair and a violation of due process. He referred the cases back to the Department of Labor for new hearings.[101]

District Court Judge George Bourquin in Montana used similar language in his holding that the raiding officials had violated the Fourth Amendment protection against unlawful searches and seizures. While conceding the summary character of deportation proceedings and the limited jurisdiction of the federal courts in immigration matters, Bourquin ruled that resident aliens were entitled to the protection of the Fourth Amendment, a significant victory given previous judicial reluctance to extend constitutional protections to aliens in deportation proceedings. The extent of the government's abuses appeared to prompt Bourquin's protective stance toward aliens. The officials, in his words, "perpetuated an orgy of terror, violence, and crime against citizens and aliens. . . . They are the spirit of intolerance incarnate, and the most alarming manifestation in America today."[102]

Even before Anderson and Bourquin voiced their condemnation of the raids, officials within the Department of Labor were taking steps to curb the Bureau of Immigration. By January 26, 1920, Secretary Wilson had reinstated his previous rule allowing aliens counsel from the beginning of the deportation hearings and had reaffirmed their right to reasonable bail if their hearings were delayed. He then reviewed all of the cases with great care before signing a warrant for deportation; Louis Post subjected the cases to even closer scrutiny when he became acting secretary after Wilson became ill. Caminetti and Hoover had planned their arrests on the theory that anyone who belonged to the Communist party or the Communist Labor party could be deported because both groups advocated the forceful overthrow of the government. Wilson distinguished between the two groups, ruling that mere membership in the Communist Labor party was not a deportable offense. Post, in his review of the cases, went further to adopt a more nuanced definition of membership, refusing to order the deportation of those who did not fully understand or know the principles of the organization or whose names had been transferred to the organization's membership lists without their knowledge.[103] Post also dismissed cases involving certain procedural irregularities, such as evidence obtained through unlawful searches and seizures or through incriminating remarks made before the alien had been advised of the right to counsel. Together, Wilson and Post canceled 2,202 warrants for deportation.[104]

The National Popular Government League praised Post for his "courageous reestablishment of American Constitutional Law," but not everyone was as pleased with his and Wilson's actions. Attorney General Palmer cast aspersions upon Post's "Americanism" and prompted a movement to investigate Post's loyalty, eventually leading to impeachment proceedings before the House of Representatives. As Post's treatment suggests, the raids had broad support among a public inflamed by antiradical, nativist sentiment. Congress, in passing the Immigration Act of 1920, indirectly declared its support of the Bureau of Immigration in its struggle with Post and Wilson. The law adopted the Bureau of Immigration's broad definition of guilt by association over the more narrow interpretations of membership and advocacy embraced by the Department of Labor. The act provided for the deportation of aliens who simply possessed radical literature, who showed support for radical groups through financial contributions, or who "advised" as well as advocated radical doctrines.[105]

Similarly, though the impassioned opinions of such judges as Bourquin and Anderson provided a needed tonic against the excesses of administrative officials and prevented the deportation of some aliens, the bureau generally found little opposition to its methods and interpretations in the federal courts during and after the Red Raids. Following the pattern set in earlier litigation, federal judges and Supreme Court justices continued to allow the Bureau of Immigration and the Department of Labor broad discretion in enforcing the law. For the most part, they readily accepted the theory of guilt by association, upholding the convictions of aliens for mere membership and for possessing leaflets or selling books of a radical nature on the grounds that as long as there was "some evidence" for the bureau's deportation order, the courts would not intervene.[106] Nor did most federal judges object to the lack of procedural protections.[107] Federal judges did continue to insist, however, that aliens were entitled to all the rights explicitly granted them in statutes and agency regulations and that the bureau's failure to afford such rights constituted a denial of due process.[108]

The Supreme Court continued to defer to the Bureau of Immigration's jurisdiction over aliens, yet its opinions in *Kwock Jan Fat* and *Ng Fung Ho*, decided soon after the Red Raids, suggests that administrative abuses during the raids prompted the Court to be more circumspect in subjecting *citizens* to the broad discretion of immigration authorities. Part of the horror expressed in Anderson's and Bourquin's decisions lay in the revelation that officials had treated citizens, as well as aliens, with a summary disregard for their procedural rights. Anderson, for example, cited at length the testimony of American citizen Harry Steiner to highlight the violations of due process. The Supreme Court made no explicit links between the Red Raids and the cases involving alleged Chinese-American citizens, yet its invigorated defense of the rights of citizens, made only six months after the well-publicized raids and only weeks after the National Popular Government League published its attack on them, suggests that the controversy over the raids provided the backdrop for its opinions. In *Kwock Jan Fat*, Justice John H. Clarke stressed the great power vested in administrative authorities and cautioned that "it is a power to be administered, not arbitrarily and secretly, but fairly and openly, under the restraints of the tradition and principles of free government applicable where the fundamental rights of men are involved." Clarke concluded, "It is better that many Chinese immigrants should be improperly admitted than that one natural born citizen of the United States should be permanently excluded from his country." Two years later, the Court held in *Ng Fung Ho* that alleged citizens were entitled to a judicial hearing, with its greater security of impartiality and procedural protections, before being deported, a position long advocated by critics of the Bureau of Immigration.[109]

These decisions undoubtedly marked a significant victory for those critics, yet they may have not been so advantageous for aliens who had gained indirectly from the bureau's previous power over alleged citizens. It is not surprising that the Supreme Court laid down the "fair hearing" requirement in a case involving an alleged citizen soon after its controversial decision in *Ju Toy* giving the bureau jurisdiction over alleged citizens. Though never treated with the same concern as alleged citizens, aliens also drew upon the fair hearing requirement, sometimes successfully, to carve out some procedural protections in immigration proceedings. In other words, they were able to "ride on the coattails" of the doctrines established in cases involving citizens. But the *Kwock Jan Fat* and *Ng Fung Ho* opinions served to reinforce the distinctions made in landmark cases such as *Fong Yue Ting* between the procedural rights due citizens and those granted to aliens. Once alleged citizens facing deportation had been removed from administrative authority, there might be less pressure to impose procedural restraints upon the Bureau of Immigration and, ironically, potentially less protection for aliens who remained within the agency's power.

When federal judges did find a violation of due process, they tended to refer the case back to the Department of Labor for reconsideration rather than discharge the alien. Even Anderson, who in his long opinion voiced little confidence in the administrative process used to deport aliens, allowed the department an opportunity to afford the petitioners in *Colyer* v. *Skeffington* a fair rehearing within a reasonable time. The referral to administrative authorities for remedial action had become more common before the Red Raids, but Anderson's deference to the department, in addition to being the established practice in his circuit, probably reflected his confidence that reforms taking place under the guidance of Wilson and Post would successfully curb administrative excesses.[110]

Such confidence may have been well placed in the short term for the Department of Labor took a variety of measures to require greater accountability from immigration officials and to leave less to the discretion of inspectors. Not only did it reaffirm and expand the rights of aliens in hearings, providing the right to an attorney and reasonable bail and protection against unlawful arrests and searches, but the department also instituted organizational reforms designed to bolster its supervision of the bureau. Post had recommended the establishment of an advisory committee within the Department of Labor to assist the secretary in reviewing deportation cases. By 1922, the committee had become the Secretary and

Commissioner-General's Board of Review, or more commonly, the board of review. Created by the discretionary authority of the secretary of labor, the board evaluated appeals from aliens denied admission, reviewed the entire records in deportation cases, and made recommendations to the secretary. The board occasionally returned the cases to inspectors for further investigation and also conducted oral hearings (in a room labeled "Courtroom") if requested by attorneys or congressional members. Its role remained purely advisory though its recommendations carried great weight in the final disposition of cases, especially as the number of deportation cases continued to climb in the 1920s.[111]

Critics, on the whole, tended to hail the creation of the board, seeing it as an "embryonic administrative court" that would provide the vehicle to incorporate a "judicial attitude" and judicial procedures in immigration proceedings.[112] Yet their approval of the board lay primarily on the role it *could* come to play, rather than upon its actual operations in the aftermath of the Red Raids. Similarly, most of the reforms instituted under Secretary Wilson's leadership remained aspirations rather than realities, as a flurry of studies completed in the early 1930s revealed.[113] Jane Perry Clark at Barnard College, William C. Van Vleck, with the support of the Commonwealth Fund, and Reuben Oppenheimer, under the auspices of the National Commission on Law Observance and Enforcement, all carried out independent studies of the Bureau of Immigration. Relying on in-depth reviews of administrative records and personal observation, the studies found many of the same practices used in the era leading up to the Red Raids still in place.

The right to counsel, for example, still remained elusive. In 1924, the bureau had dropped the requirement that aliens be advised of the right to counsel at the beginning of the hearing, providing simply that "at the hearing under the warrant of arrest the alien . . . shall be advised that he may be represented by counsel."[114] Although the wording allowed inspectors more discretion over the timing of the attorney's appearance, in practice, inspectors continued to inform the aliens of their right to counsel at the beginning of the hearing.[115] Few aliens (one-fifth in Van Vleck's estimation and one-sixth according to Oppenheimer) took advantage of that right, primarily, it appears, because they could not afford an attorney.[116] The lack of an attorney could materially influence the outcome of the case. Oppenheimer reported that deportation occurred in 70 percent of the cases in which attorneys appeared on behalf of the alien, but if no attorneys were involved, the deportation rate increased to 85 percent.[117] Even when attorneys were present, the inspectors' hostility toward them, made manifest in the limits placed on the right to subpoena and efforts to limit their participation, reduced the effectiveness of the right to counsel.

In part to avoid the influence of attorneys, inspectors continued to rely heavily on the controversial preliminary examinations to secure their case before the actual hearing.[118] Similarly, Wilson's attempt to protect aliens from arrests made on insufficient evidence and from lengthy detentions without bail faltered. Wilson had emphasized that telegraphic warrants should be issued only when "absolutely necessary"; a decade later, Van Vleck reported that telegraphic warrants, issued only upon the assurances of local immigration officials that evidence existed, were relied on in 36 percent of the cases in his sample.[119] Bail, though generally set well below the rates of the Red Raid era, remained out of reach for the vast majority of aliens. They remained in detention at immigration stations or, more commonly, at local jails for weeks or even months.[120] By 1926, Congress debated legislation that aimed to strengthen the deportation laws by expanding the power of the commissioner general of immigration and, concomitantly, reducing the supervisory function of the secretary of labor, by extending or eliminating time limits for deportation and by raising the minimum bail amount.[121]

The difficulty in securing a system of executive justice drove some observers to push for judicial hearings in deportation cases as well as those involving the claims of alleged citizens. Even before the reforms had been tested, Louis Post declared in 1921 that administrative processes were "too arbitrary to be suited to American ideals of fair-play when humane considerations are involved. . . . There is really no very good reason," Post continued, "why an alien who has acquired resident rights in the United States should not have his day in the courts of his vicinity before any administrative office of the central government is permitted . . . to deny him of those rights." Zechariah Chafee agreed that aliens deserved "the best legal machinery we can devise" before "we throw them out neck and heels."[122] William Van Vleck came to a similar conclusion after his in-depth review of the deportation process a decade later.

If aliens were not to have a judicial hearing, critics fell back on the standard secondary offensive, calling yet again for a more thorough system of executive justice. Clark in 1931 advocated more "adequately trained and qualified personnel" with a "judicial turn of mind," the adoption of procedures used in "ordinary courts of justice," and "more adequate representation of the alien by counsel." She and Van Vleck also urged broadening the authority and responsibilities of the board of review to make it analogous in structure and function to the Interstate Commerce Commission, the Federal Trade Commission, and the Board of Tax Appeals. The transformation of the board of review into a "kind of administrative court" would increase the procedural safeguards in the agency and more adequately protect the interests of aliens, according to Clark and Van Vleck.[123]

The recommendations of such scholars were strikingly similar to those made by immigrants and their advocates twenty years earlier. The persistent calls for greater executive justice reveal, on the one hand, the continuing existence of a core of critics who rejected several of the central doctrines—such as the nonpunitive nature of deportation, the extraconstitutional status of aliens, the distinctive character of immigration law, and judicial deference to immigration authorities—established in the formative period of immigration law. Yet, on the other hand, the reforms suggested by scholars in the 1930s show how impervious the Bureau of Immigration had been to earlier attacks on its discretion. Despite litigation and political pressure brought by immigrants and their allies and the vigorous attacks by legal elites during the Red Raids, the bureau emerged in 1924 virtually unscathed and fundamentally unchanged.

Certainly the federal courts' hesitancy to intervene in immigration matters contributed to the failure of the executive justice campaign. Left by the courts to regulate itself, the Bureau of Immigration, not surprisingly, maintained its gatekeeping function as its primary focal point; questions of fairness and aliens' rights were secondary concerns, if at all, and always to be addressed within the context of administrative efficiency and effectiveness. Administrative review by higher officials in the Department of Labor might act as a temporary and important restraint on the bureau, as is revealed by the actions of Post and Wilson, but ultimately failed to sustain lasting procedural reforms in immigration. Supervisory officials, occupied with numerous other duties, did not have the resources to monitor the agency on an ongoing basis. They also generally agreed with the bureau that local discretion was essential in enforcing the immigration laws, a concession that undercut departmental desires for uniformity and procedural regularity. Finally, and probably most important, the campaign for curbs on the bureau failed because the agency's restrictionist mind-set found broad support among the growing number of nativist Americans. In an era when the United States enacted its most restrictive immigration laws and aliens were increasingly identified as "dangerous menaces," questions about the procedural rights of aliens remained the concern of a limited, though vocal, number of people.

EPILOGUE

Immigration Law in American Legal Culture

> Administrative law . . . is an alien immigrant which not only comes to us without authentic letters of credence, but which brings with it suggestions of a questionable past if not of actual moral turpitude.
> —John Dickinson, 1928

The year 1924 marked the culmination of many of the events and movements set into motion in 1891. Nativists reached the pinnacle of their success with the passage of the act of 1924, which perfected the exclusion of Asians and severely curtailed the immigration of southern and eastern Europeans. The Bureau of Immigration had developed from a relatively small, nebulous body in 1891 into a powerful centralized agency by 1924. It had expanded and consolidated control over all phases of immigration, reaching into the immigrants' native lands for preembarkation investigations as well as into the aliens' lives after they settled in the United States. New federal judges staffed the San Francisco courts by 1924. William W. Morrow ended his long career on the federal bench in California in 1923, retiring as judge for the Ninth Circuit Court of Appeals. Maurice Dooling died the following year.

Most important, certain fundamental principles governing immigration regulation had been established between 1891 and 1924. The struggles over the enforcement of the Chinese exclusion and general immigration laws led policy makers to reshape government structures and to create new procedures. Courts and judicial methods were rejected in favor of an agency with broad discretion, operating according to summary administrative proceedings. Immigration law had developed its distinctive characteristics which would increasingly alienate it from other branches of public law.

The shift from judicial to administrative process, in itself, was not unique to immigration, nor was the concern aroused by that shift. "Summary justice becomes the fashion," proclaimed Roscoe Pound in 1913.[1] While even the harshest critics of administrative power conceded that it was an "inevitable and necessary" fact of modern life, they remained anxious about its implications for American governance.[2] Many Americans, John Dickinson suggested in 1928, associated administrative agencies with the dreaded bureaucracies of continental Europe, perceived to be governments of arbitrary officials and "repugnant to some of our most time-honored legal principles."[3] Woodrow Wilson, writing forty years earlier, attempted to persuade doubters that administration could be safely employed in the United States if shorn of its foreign ways and thoroughly "Americanize[d]." "It must learn our constitutions by heart; must get the bureaucratic fever out of its veins; must inhale much free American air," said Wilson.[4]

The closing of America's gates in 1924 temporarily eased anxieties about assimilating alien immigrants, but concerns about Americanizing administrative law only grew, especially as New Deal agencies proliferated.[5] The basic dilemma for both critics and supporters of the new administrative state was how to secure the benefits of administrative processes while respecting Anglo-American ideals of the rule of law. Discretion, "our principal source of creativeness in government and in law," was an essential tool for administrative agencies.[6] Yet, as Felix Frankfurter recognized in 1927, the expansion of administrative discretion "opened the door to its potential abuse, arbitrariness."[7] Republican ideology had placed great faith in the structure of American government, particularly the separation of powers among the executive, legislature, and judiciary, as the primary means to curb the possibility of official abuse of power.[8] The introduction of the so-called fourth branch of government, which exercised all these powers simultaneously, threatened to upset the careful system of checks and balances and create conditions ripe for the rise of despotic government.[9] "If we are to continue a government of limited powers," warned American Bar Association president Elihu Root in 1916, "these agencies of regulation must themselves be regulated."[10]

Increasingly, proceduralism became the preferred means to tame administrative discretion.[11] Due process challenges to administrative power, as we have seen in the immigration cases, certainly flourished in the Progressive Era; but by the 1930s, New Deal programs that vastly expanded government regulation provoked ever more vigorous attacks on administrative procedures. The Administrative Procedures Act, passed in 1946, sought to preserve administrative efficiency and, at the same time, address concerns about the lawlessness of administration. The act established the basic procedural principles and practices to govern administrative adjudication and administrative rulemaking, requiring higher standards of due process for adjudicatory tribunals. Since the act's passage, judicial norms of due process have increasingly become the baseline for determining administrative due process in both adjudication and rulemaking; in Martin Shapiro's assessment, "more and more agency behavior" had been made to become "court-like" by the 1970s.[12]

Until recently, immigration law has escaped much of this judicializing trend in administrative law. At a superficial level, perhaps, the Immigration and Naturalization Service took on a more adjudicatory appearance. In 1952, for example, Congress turned board of special inquiry officers into "immigration judges" and required some separation of functions, forbidding them from hearing cases in which they had already been involved as an investigator or prosecutor. But resistance to significant procedural reform has remained more characteristic of immigration law. The Administrative Procedures Act has only limited application to immigration, for example, Congress having expressly exempted immigration hearings from some of its provisions.[13] Modern-day critics complain of the same practices challenged by immigration lawyers in 1910 and scholars in the 1930s: the largely unchecked discretion of officials to apply the laws, the vulnerability of aliens to raids and official intimidation, the widespread use of preliminary investigations, the lack of procedural protections for aliens, and the enforcement-minded approach of immigration officials.[14] Even the in-depth questioning developed to detect fraud in Chinese cases has survived in a different context, used now to test the validity of marriages between aliens and American citizens, and has prompted one British victim of the interrogation to denounce the "un-American Immigration and Naturalization Service."[15]

Why have attempts to "Americanize" administrative law left immigration law relatively untouched and alien to what Schuck terms "those fundamental norms of constitutional right, administrative procedure, and judicial role that animate the rest of our legal system"?[16] The answer lies partly in the particular historical circumstances, described in this book, that shaped early immigration law. The doctrines providing the foundation for immigration law arose out of struggles on the West Coast among Chinese immigrants, government officials, and federal judges over the enforcement of the Chinese exclusion laws. Though on the margins of society, Chinese immigrants in their resistance to exclusion laid claim to principles and practices—habeas corpus, due process, evidentiary rules, judicial review— that were at the heart of Anglo-American jurisprudence. Officials were forced with the choice of extending those core principles to Chinese, with the practical effect of undermining exclusionist aims and the symbolic effect of recognizing Chinese as functional, if not formal, members of the society with legitimate claims to its cherished legal heritage. Rejecting that option, government officials instead persuaded Congress and the Supreme Court that the nation's gates could be effectively guarded only if they were allowed full authority and discretion over immigration policy without interference from the federal courts. Ironically, in their efforts to secure the door against Chinese immigration, officials undermined the very principles they accused the Chinese of subverting. The immigration law resulting from this struggle stood at odds with one of the most esteemed Anglo-American legal principles—the rule of law.

Within the space of a few years, the Supreme Court elaborated in *Chae Chan Ping, Nishimura Ekiu,* and *Fong Yue Ting* the basic doctrines that would serve as a bulwark against later attempts to submit the Immigration and Naturalization Service to judicial procedures. The Court began with the premise that Congress had the inherent sovereign power to police its borders, which included the power to exclude and deport aliens for any policy reasons it chose. As an incident of the plenary power to exclude and deport, the Court continued, Congress also had the power to devise whatever procedures it desired to implement its policies. Aliens, who entered and remained in the United States only at the sufferance of Congress, were not protected by explicit constitutional procedural guarantees. They enjoyed only those privileges the government expressly allowed them. The only procedural restraint the Court imposed was that aliens should have a fair opportunity to be heard in immigration proceedings. But fairness would be defined within the parameters of the other premises of immigration law, which placed a high premium on government objectives and saw aliens' rights as virtually nonexistent.

The basic doctrines established in the immigration cases set immigration law on a quite different trajectory from that of other branches of administrative law. While all administrative agencies shared certain characteristics—freedom from the technical rules of judicial procedure, flexibility, an emphasis on policy objectives, faith in experts—striking differences had developed among agencies by 1924.[17] At the same time that the Supreme Court was busily developing the doctrines freeing immigration officials from constitutional norms of due process, Interstate Commerce Commission chair Thomas Cooley complained that courts were forcing his agency to treat common carriers "precisely as . . . if charged with criminal conduct and arraigned upon an indictment."[18] The Supreme Court eventually acknowledged the authority of the ICC and other agencies in regulating the economy, but it continued to require higher procedural standards. In 1920, for example, when the federal courts were generally sanctioning the bureau's summary methods in the Red Raids, the Supreme Court struck down a Federal Trade Commission (FTC) order on the grounds that the agency's original complaint failed to meet the technical requirements of adequate notice.[19] This decision stands in stark contrast to the federal judiciary's willingness to uphold deportation orders made on warrants which it conceded were vague and technically inadequate.

The usual explanation for the judiciary's different treatment of immigration cases lies in the distinction between rights and privileges. Courts more closely regulated such agencies as the ICC and the FTC, it is said, because they governed businesses that had common law rights, previously under the jurisdiction of judges. Conversely, they allowed other agencies that dispensed government largesse or benefits (title to public land, the privilege to enter the country, postal services) much greater discretion. Aliens, it was thought, had no greater entitlement to be in the country than did a citizen to the use of the postal services. Because the government created the privilege, it could also regulate it.

The distinction is useful but not sufficient in understanding why aliens, particularly those facing deportation, became seen as clothed merely with suspendible privileges rather than rights. Changing perceptions of membership and its entitlements also explain the distinctive characteristics of immigration law. More expansive and variegated notions of membership existed in the nineteenth century before immigration restriction took hold. The Burlingame Treaty of 1868 between the United States and China affirmed the "inherent and inalienable right of man to change his home and allegiance." That natural right, argued Senator Watson C. Squire of the Select Committee on Immigration and Naturalization in 1890, could not be denied without also negating the basic principles on which the country was founded.[20] Once in the country, resident aliens were considered by many to be more analogous to citizens than immigrants and entitled to full constitutional rights and protections.[21]

The nation's move to close its borders against the perceived dangers of unlimited immigration prompted challenges to its earlier liberal definition of membership. Rejecting both natural rights assumptions about the right to migrate and the "stakes" theory of membership applied to resident aliens, judges drew sharper distinctions between aliens and citizens.[22] Rights were to be determined more strictly according to an individual's formal legal status. Aliens, regardless of their material and emotional investments in the country, were not formal members and could not lay claim to the panoply of constitutional rights enjoyed by citizens. By 1924, distinctions made in immigration law between the procedural rights of alleged citizens versus those owed aliens reveal the importance of formal membership in triggering recognition of due process claims.[23]

More recently, commentators have noted changes in administrative law and in legal thought more generally, which have the potential to assimilate immigration law into mainstream American legal culture. One development is the challenge to the traditional rights/privilege distinction in administrative law, most strikingly illustrated by the Supreme Court's opinion in *Goldberg* v. *Kelly*. In requiring trial-type hearings in the Aid to Families with Dependent Children program, the Court suggested that government benefits should be treated as entitlements deserving protection similar to that given to traditional property rights. At the same time, Paul Verkuil argues, courts have allowed agencies responsible for regulating economic interests, previously treated as rights, greater procedural flexibility. The result, Verkuil suggests, is the emergence of a unitary standard of administrative due process, applicable to all agencies regardless of the programs they administer.[24] Presumably, this development would result in higher standards of due process in immigration proceedings.

Peter Schuck sees greater possibilities in the transformative capacity of a new "communitarian legal order," which he believes is redefining concepts of membership and governmental obligations to citizens and aliens alike. Twentieth-century liberalism has increasingly emphasized the duty of government actively to protect the interests and rights of individuals, particularly those belonging to groups experiencing systematic discrimination. The result has been the so-called revolution in due process and equal protection as well as dramatic shifts in private law. The repeal of the Chinese Exclusion Act in 1943 and the national origins quota system in 1965 in favor of a less discriminatory policy also reflects the influence of the new liberalism.[25]

Accompanying this development has been a broadening definition of membership and the rights pertaining thereto, which once again emphasizes the individual as a member of an international community with certain inherent, universal rights. Such developments, Schuck suggests, promise to alter immigration law in a fundamental way. The central premise of immigration law—that government owes nothing to aliens except the privileges it explicitly grants them—is being supplanted, Schuck argues, by a "communitarian" norm "that the government owes duties to all individuals who manage to reach America's shores, even to strangers whom it has never undertaken, and has no wish, to protect."[26] In Schuck's opinion, the communitarian norm has begun to influence lower federal court opinions, stirring judges out of their traditional deference to immigration officials.

Some judges have subjected immigration procedures and official discretion to greater scrutiny and higher standards, beginning a trend which Schuck believes could lead to the dismantling of "classical" immigration law.

Whether such predictions are borne out will depend both on the relative strength of "communitarian" legal norms in the legal system and the general climate of opinion regarding immigration. The same forces that have sought to stem the so-called due process revolution will likely oppose an expanded notion of government's obligations to aliens, especially as a resurging nativist movement in the United States stresses once again the detriments of immigration.[27] Americans increasingly voice concerns about the economic and social impact of "new" immigrants, both legal and illegal, who now come primarily from Southeast Asia, the Caribbean, Latin America, and the Philippines. Some worry, too, about the ability of the newcomers to assimilate.[28] A chapter in a recent book on immigration is entitled "How Many Can America Absorb?" The authors put forth as their basic arguments:

A basic definition of *sovereignty* is control over a nation's own borders.

The United States is no longer an empty continent that can absorb endless streams of population.

The melting pot, like any pot, is finite.[29]

Such views not only echo the nativist arguments of the Progressive Era but reaffirm the basic premise of national sovereignty established in early immigration law. Thus far, pro-immigrant groups, who are more powerful and active than their Progressive Era counterparts, have managed to prevent significant restrictions on immigration.[30] But as politicians increasingly seize upon immigration regulation as a central problem and Americans continue to hear of floods of refugees poised to enter and the smuggling of illegal immigrants, it becomes increasingly unlikely that "communitarian" legal norms will take hold in immigration law.

Procedural reform, if it comes, may aim to restructure the Immigration and Naturalization Service and improve its enforcement efforts rather than to expand aliens' rights. The tension between administrative efficiency and due process, always present in administrative law, has become especially acute in immigration regulation. Beginning in the 1960s, commentators observe, a "breakdown in immigration enforcement" occurred which has only become more acute as new policies expand the agency's duties and the number of legal and illegal immigrants and asylum seekers increases.[31] The *New York Times* suggests that the Immigration and Naturalization Service may be "the most troubled major agency in the Federal Government" as it confronts a staggering workload, handled by an insufficient, underpaid, and demoralized staff.[32]

Given this administrative context, the push for more procedural protections and less administrative discretion will encounter difficulties. Even commentators sympathetic to alien rights recognize the difficulties the Immigration and Naturalization Service would confront if required to follow more formal procedures.[33] The service relies primarily on informal methods and voluntary compliance by aliens to accomplish the great majority of its enforcement efforts. If aliens demanded the procedural rights already secured to them, argues Edwin Harwood, "immigration enforcement would collapse."[34]

For the moment, the competing demands of restrictionists and immigration proponents and of administrative efficiency and respect for individual rights have thrown immigration reform into limbo. Treated as a pariah and virtually unsupervised by Congress, the immigration agency continues much as it has in the past but less efficiently.[35] Similarly, immigration law remains a resident alien, only partially integrated into American legal culture.

APPENDIX

Methodology

From 1891 to 1911, both the district and circuit courts were federal trial courts. The circuit court was abolished in 1911, and the district court became the sole federal trial court. Petitioners could file for writs of habeas corpus in either court, but they almost always filed their petitions in the district court.

I obtained data on both courts from two sources. From the courts' docket books, I recorded the disposition (as well as other basic information) for all the immigration and deportation cases filed during the period. From these cases, I drew a random sample (using a random number chart), choosing 10 percent or five cases, whichever was larger, from each year for an in-depth review of the case files. The files often contained the transcripts of the court hearings, which were the primary sources used, and the notes and transcripts from the agency's investigation. I adopted the same method in analyzing the deportation cases handled by the U.S. commissioner, who kept his own docket and case files.

NOTES

ABBREVIATIONS

Admiralty Casefiles

Admiralty Casefiles, 1891–1924, U.S. District Court for the Northern District of California, Records of the District Courts of the United States, RG 21, National Archives, San Francisco Branch.

Chinese Exclusion Cases

Chinese Exclusion Cases, Records of the Immigration and Naturalization Service, RG 85, National Archives, San Francisco Branch.

CG-AR

Annual Report of the Commissioner-General of Immigration

Collec. Corres.

Correspondence from the Collector to Other Federal Agencies and the General Public, Bureau of Customs, Port of San Francisco, RG 36, National Archives, San Francisco Branch, San Bruno, California.

Commissioner Casefiles

U.S. Commissioner Casefiles, U.S. District Court for the Northern District of California, Records of the District Courts of the United States, RG 21, National Archives, San Francisco Branch.

Cong. Rec.

Congressional Record

Criminal Casefiles

Criminal Casefiles, 1891–1924, U.S. District Court for the Northern District of California, Records of the District Courts of the United States, RG 21, National Archives, San Francisco Branch.

C. Seg. Files

Chinese Segregated Files, Records of the Immigration and Naturalization Service, RG 85, National Archives.

DJ

Department of Justice

DJ Let. Recd.

Letters Received, Records of the Department of Justice, RG 60, National Archives.

INS Subj. Corres.

Subject Correspondence, Central Office, Records of the Immigration and Naturalization Service, RG 85, National Archives.

RG

Record Group

ST-AR

Annual Report of the Secretary of the Treasury

255

1. Fritz, *Federal Justice in California*; see also Janisch, "The Chinese, the Courts, and the Constitution," 476–519, 654–762, 931–1045.

2. Patricia Evans's dissertation, "'Likely to Become a Public Charge,'" is an exception, as she studies the enforcement of a particular section of the immigration laws—the provision for the exclusion of aliens "likely to become a public charge." For a study of modern immigration administration, see Morris, *Immigration*.

3. Schuck, "Transformation of Immigration Law," 1; see also Note, "Developments in the Law—Immigration Policy and the Rights of Aliens," 1312–13.

4. Preston, *Aliens and Dissenters*, 19.

5. Schuck, "Transformation of Immigration Law," 14.

6. Ibid., 1.

7. See McClain, *In Search of Equality*; Mooney, "Matthew Deady and the Federal Judicial Response to Racism in the Early West"; Wunder, "Chinese and the Courts." For a general overview of American law relating to Asian Americans, see Kim, *Legal History of Asian Americans*.

8. Chinese immigrants and Chinese Americans provide a striking example of marginalized groups who appealed to the Constitution to develop an alternative view of the right to defend themselves against discriminatory acts. Their demonstration of what Hendrik Hartog has called "constitutional rights consciousness" is particularly interesting given exclusionists' stereotypes of Chinese as the slavish, obedient subjects of a despotic government (Hartog, "Constitution of Aspiration").

9. Paul, *The Conservative Crisis and the Rule of Law*; Twiss, *Lawyers and the Constitution*; Boudin, *Government by Judiciary*; Swindler, *Court and Constitution in the Twentieth Century*.

10. Recent studies have begun to modify the realists' interpretation of that era, revealing that the Supreme Court and state courts were not always bulwarks against Progressive reforms and that principle, as well as politics, guided the judges' decisions. See Semonche, *Charting the Future*; McCurdy, "Justice Field and the Jurisprudence of Government-Business Relations"; Urofsky, "State Courts and Protective Legislation during the Progressive Era."

11. On the potential influence of institutional roles and perspectives, see Shapiro, *Law and Politics in the Supreme Court*, 35–37. The judges' actions suggest the inadequacy of interpretations of legal formalism which stress that formalism, as a style of reasoning, simply favored the interests of a privileged, capitalist class. For another view of legal formalism, see William Nelson, *Roots of American Bureaucracy*, which argues that formalistic styles of reasoning grew out of the search by antislavery groups for a higher-law jurisprudence (133–55).

12. Stephen Skowronek has analyzed a similar shift in power from courts to agencies, using the Interstate Commerce Commission as an example; see *Building a New American State*, 121–62, 248–84. Another study of the rise of administrative discretion during the Progressive period is Nonet, *Administrative Justice*.

13. The concept of "radiating effects" is elaborated by Galanter, "Radiating Effects of Courts."

14. Gordon, "Legal Thought and Legal Practice in the Age of American Enterprise," 94–96.

15. The flowering of the substantive due process doctrine has absorbed historians' attention, and very little scholarly work has been done on the development of procedural due process during the Progressive Era. Brief analyses of the issue can be found in Verkuil, "The Emerging Concept of Administrative Procedure," 262–64; C. Miller, "The Forest of Due Process of Law"; Howard, *Road from Runnymede*.

CHAPTER ONE

1. In 1890, 14.8 percent of the United States population was foreign-born, and 33 percent of the population was born of foreign parents. The proportion of foreigners was much greater in western states like California. In that state, 30.3 percent were foreigners and 56.7 percent were born of foreign parents (U.S. Immigration Commission, *Reports of the Immigration Commission: Statistical Review of Immigration, 1820–1910*, Table 7, pp. 470–71).

2. Richmond Mayo Smith, *Emigration and Immigration*, 293.

3. U.S. Congress, House, Select Committee on Immigration and Naturalization, *Report*, 2:ii.

4. Practically any book discussing immigration restriction uses the growing excludable classes as the main legal evidence of restrictive policies. See, for example, Curran, *Xenophobia and Immigration*, 109–28, and Kraut, *Huddled Masses*.

5. 26 Stat. 1084.

6. Legomsky, *Immigration and the Judiciary*; Schuck, "Transformation of Immigration Law."

7. Proper, *Colonial Immigration Laws*; Curran, *Xenophobia and Immigration*, 11–20; Kettner, *Development of American Citizenship*, 108–10.

8. Calavita, *U.S. Immigration Law and the Control of Labor*, 39–41; M. Jones, *American Immigration*, 177–211.

9. Higham, *Strangers in the Land*, 20–21.

10. *Essays and Poems of Emerson with an Introduction by Stuart P. Sherman* (New York, 1921), xxxiv, quoted in Gossett, *Race*, 288.

11. Higham, *Strangers in the Land*, 19–21.

12. Oliver Wendell Holmes, *The Autocrat of the Breakfast Table* (Boston, 1858), 21, quoted ibid., 288.

13. Handlin, *Boston's Immigrants*, 200–206.

14. Higham, *Strangers in the Land*, 4–9, 23–24; Brown, *Immigration*, 92–102.

15. 3 Stat. 488; Hutchinson, *Legislative History*, 21–22.

16. One might suspect that the act, in limiting the number of passengers per ship and in keeping statistics on aliens, may have been an anti-immigrant measure. Unfortunately, there are no published debates on the act and thus no evidence of congressional intent. There are good reasons, however, for believing the law was genuinely designed to protect immigrants. Stories existed at the time describing the wretched conditions on board ships. Furthermore, according to histories of nativ-

ism, this was not a period of widespread xenophobia, which, presumably, would have had to exist for the statute to be anti-immigrant in nature.

17. Blodgett, "Colorado Territorial Board of Immigration"; Blegen, "Competition of the Northwestern States for Immigrants." For a list of state legislation regarding immigration, see U.S. Immigration Commission, *Reports of the U.S. Immigration Commission: Immigration Legislation*.

18. Hutchinson, *Legislative History*, 400; Brown, *Immigration*, 79–80, 87–92, 95–96.

19. *The City of New York* v. *Miln*, 11 Peters 102 (1837). The New York statute required masters to list the "name, place of birth and last legal settlement, age, and occupation of every person brought as a passenger."

20. *Passenger Cases*, 48 U.S. 282 (1849). Eight justices wrote individual opinions, but the majority agreed on the essential points as stated in the text.

21. Ibid., 409.

22. *Henderson* v. *Wickham, and Commissioners of Immigration* v. *The North German Lloyd*, 92 U.S. 259 (1876).

23. *Chy Lung* v. *Freeman*, 92 U.S. 275, 281 (1876).

24. Ibid., 278–80. See also Chan, "Exclusion of Chinese Women," 97–109. By the time the Court had invalidated the California law, Congress had already passed the Page Law which, among other things, excluded women prostitutes and thus accomplished part of California's goals.

25. Act of March 3, 1875, 18 Stat. 477.

26. The act also forbade the entry of convicts.

27. Higham, *Strangers in the Land*, 44.

28. The Supreme Court found this head tax to be constitutional in *Edye* v. *Robertson*, 112 U.S. 580 (1885).

29. Immigration Act of August 3, 1882, 22 Stat. 214. See Hutchinson, *Legislative History*, 77–80, for history of the act.

30. This was the wording of Article V of the Burlingame Treaty of 1868. See Parry, *Consolidated Treaty Series*, vol. 137.

31. Act of May 6, 1882, 22 Stat. 58.

32. For discussion of reasons for Chinese emigration, see Tsai, *China and the Overseas Chinese*; Chan, *This Bittersweet Soil*, 7–26, 37–39.

33. Takaki, *Strangers from a Different Shore*, 79–99. For Chinese in agriculture, see Chan, *This Bittersweet Soil*. For Chinese in fishing, see McEvoy, *Fisherman's Problem*, 75–79.

34. U.S. Bureau of the Census, *Statistical Historical Abstracts*, series A91-104, 14.

35. S. Miller, *Unwelcome Immigrant*, 36. One scholar argues that such stereotypes had been established long before American traders visited Asia. See Okihiro, *Margins and Mainstreams*, 3–30.

36. S. Miller, *Unwelcome Immigrant*, 83–94.

37. Saxton, *Indispensable Enemy*, 17–18.

38. R. Paul, "Origin of the Chinese Issue in California."

39. The Foreign Miners Tax of 1850, aimed at Latin American and Australian as well as Chinese miners, stipulated that miners who were not citizens must pay $20 a month for a license to work the mines. Similar laws passed in 1852, 1854,

1855, and 1856 placed the license fee variously at $3 to $6 a month. See Sandmeyer, *Anti-Chinese Movement*, 41–43; McClain, "Chinese Struggle," 539–48.

40. The court expanded the category of "Indian" in an amazing way: it argued that when Columbus landed in America, he thought he had reached an island in the Chinese Sea and named the inhabitants "Indians." Henceforth, an "Indian" and an "Asiatic" were seen as synonymous. Thus, in the statute, Chinese fell under the category of "Indian" and their testimony was forbidden. The judge also made the argument that by excluding the testimony of blacks and Indians, the statute actually intended to forbid all testimony by nonwhites.

41. *People* v. *Hall*, 4 Cal. 399, 405 (1854).

42. Takaki, *Iron Cages*, 229–36.

43. Gardner, "Image of the Chinese," 92–123.

44. McClain, "Chinese Struggle," 546–47; Gardner, "Image of the Chinese," 124–47; Seager, "Some Denominational Reactions to Chinese Immigration," 49–66.

45. For the effects of the Civil War on ideas about racial equality and the fate of those ideas during Reconstruction, see Foner, *Reconstruction*.

46. The resulting Burlingame Treaty was especially supported by commercial and religious sectors in the Northeast as well as in California. The major opponents were labor groups on the West Coast. See Sandmeyer, *Anti-Chinese Movement*, 79.

47. *New York Times*, Feb. 25, 1871, p. 2, quoted in Tsai, *China and the Overseas Chinese*, 25.

48. Ibid., 8–11.

49. "Treaty of Trade, Consuls and Emigration between China and the United States," July 28, 1868, in Parry, *Consolidated Treaty Series*, vol. 137. For an interesting account of the Chinese perspective on the Burlingame Treaty, see Tsai, *China and the Overseas Chinese*, 24–29.

50. Saxton, *Indispensable Enemy*, 104.

51. Takaki, *Iron Cages*, 229–40.

52. Ibid., 232, 216.

53. Saxton, *Indispensable Enemy*, 100–101.

54. Takaki, *Iron Cages*, 232–35; S. Miller, *Unwelcome Immigrant*, 175–84.

55. Whether a coolie trade actually existed in the United States has been hotly debated, but most recent scholars argue that it did not. Chinese either paid their own passage or bought their tickets on credit. Under the "credit-ticket" system, a Chinese immigrant agreed to pay for his ticket with a portion of his wages after he arrived in the United States. See Tsai, *Chinese Experience*, 3–10; Chan, *Bittersweet Soil*, 21–26; Sandmeyer, *Anti-Chinese Movement*, 25–29. Gary Okihiro argues, however, that in practice the credit-ticket system "was a scant advance over the earlier forms of coolie and contract labor" (*Margins and Mainstreams*, 47).

56. See S. Miller, *Unwelcome Immigrant*, 150–54, for analysis of how stories of the coolie trade in Latin America influenced American views of Chinese labor.

57. *San Francisco Chronicle*, Mar. 6, 1879, quoted in Sandmeyer, *Anti-Chinese Movement*, 26.

58. Barth, *Bitter Strength*, 42–45, 131–37, 210–11, 212–13; Takaki, *Iron Cages*, 216–17.

59. Takaki, *Iron Cages*, 216–24.

60. Stanton, *Leopard's Spots*.

61. For a discussion of the influence of Spencer on American ideas of race, see Hofstadter, *Social Darwinism*.

62. Gossett, *Race*, 73–82.

63. Ibid., 84–122; Hofstadter, *Social Darwinism*, 172–77; Saveth, "Race and Nationalism."

64. Saveth, "Race and Nationalism," 434–41.

65. S. Miller, *Unwelcome Immigrant*, 170.

66. Ibid., 160; Kraut, *Silent Travelers*, 58.

67. S. Miller, *Unwelcome Immigrant*, 163; see 160–66 for general discussion of Chinese and disease. See also Kraut, *Silent Travelers*.

68. Saxton, *Indispensable Enemy*, 113–37; Mink, *Old Labor and New Immigrants*, 71–112.

69. For a summary of this argument, see Saxton, *Indispensable Enemy*, 261–65.

70. Swisher, *Motivation and Political Technique in the California Constitution*, 10–15, 32–39, 42–44, 86–92; Saxton, *Indispensable Enemy*, 127–32.

71. Janisch, "The Chinese, the Courts, and the Constitution," 382–92.

72. See, for example, *In re Tiburcio Parrott*, 6 Sawyer 349 (1880), overturning the law forbidding corporations to employ Chinese; *In re Ah Chong*, 6 Sawyer 451 (1880), invalidating legislation that prohibited Chinese from fishing in public waters, denied state business licenses to Chinese, and authorized local towns to take all necessary measures to remove Chinese from their borders. For discussion of cases, see Janisch, "The Chinese, the Courts, and the Constitution," 370–93; McEvoy, *Fisherman's Problem*, 112–14; Przybyszewski, "Judge Lorenzo Sawyer and the Chinese." For the influence of these decisions on British Columbia judges dealing with similar anti-Chinese legislation in Canada, see McLaren, "Early British Columbia Judges."

73. For discussion of the legislative debate, see Janisch, "The Chinese, the Courts, and the Constitution," 184–97.

74. *In re Ah Yup*, 5 Sawyer 155 (1878).

75. Janisch, "The Chinese, the Courts, and the Constitution," 201–7.

76. The law appears to have had little effect on Chinese laborers but did result in reduced immigration of Chinese women. See Chan, "Exclusion of Chinese Women," 105–9; Peffer, "Forbidden Families."

77. Sandmeyer, *Anti-Chinese Movement*, 82–88.

78. Janisch, "The Chinese, the Courts, and the Constitution," 424–35. For a more in-depth analysis of the various presidents' views on Chinese exclusion, see Hune, "Politics of Chinese Exclusion."

79. The nationalization of the Chinese issue had been under way for at least a decade (S. Miller, *Unwelcome Immigrant*, 194).

80. Sandmeyer, *Anti-Chinese Movement*, 111. See also Saxton, *Indispensable Enemy*, 259–61. Stuart Creighton Miller has criticized Sandmeyer's thesis, particularly because of Sandmeyer's emphasis on California as the progenitor of the Chinese exclusion campaign and his tendency to dismiss eastern anti-Chinese rhetoric as guided by political expedience rather than genuine "sinophobia." Miller argues

instead that negative cultural and racial stereotypes of Chinese dominated the national imagination and led to the passage of the Chinese Exclusion Act (*Unwelcome Immigrant*, 3–15). Miller's argument is persuasive but does not necessarily eliminate the political balance of power analysis. Both political expediency and racial bias played roles in the national exclusion campaign.

81. Hutchinson, *Legislative History*, 625.

82. See Janisch, "The Chinese, the Courts, and the Constitution," 441–49, for the history of the Chinese issue in the 1880 campaign.

83. Treaty between the United States and China concerning Immigration, November 17, 1880, Art. I, 22 U.S. 826.

84. Ibid., Art. II.

85. *Cong. Rec.*, 47th Cong., 1st sess., 1484, 1485. See also 1483, 1637, 1644–45 for similar arguments.

86. Ibid., 1483–84.

87. Ibid., 1484; Senator James H. Slater (Ore.), 1635–36; Senator George F. Edmunds (Vt.), 1674.

88. Ibid., Senator Miller, 1483, 1486; Senator Slater, 1636.

89. All but one of the petitions sent to Congress in opposition to the bill came from New York and Massachusetts (Sandmeyer, *Anti-Chinese Movement*, 93).

90. *Cong. Rec.*, 47th Cong., 1st sess., Senator Hoar, 1521–22.

91. Ibid., 1643.

92. Ibid., 1516, 1518–19.

93. Ibid., Senator Brown, 1643.

94. Ibid., Senator Slater, 1634–35.

95. Ibid., Senator La Fayette Grover, 1546.

96. Ibid., Senator James T. Farley (Cal.), 1586.

97. Ibid., 2973. The House of Representatives voted 201 in favor, 37 against, and 51 absent. All of the western and southern representatives voted in favor of the bill. Of the eastern representatives, 53 voted in favor and 24 against, while 59 midwestern representatives supported the bill and 23 opposed (S. Miller, *Unwelcome Immigrant*, 189). The Senate voted 32 in favor, 15 against, and 29 absent. The Senate vote reflected a similar regional pattern, with the fifteen opposition votes coming exclusively from the Northeast and Midwest.

98. Act of May 6, 1882, 22 Stat. 58, Section 3.

99. The certificate of identification contained the laborer's "name, age, occupation, last place of residence, personal description, and facts of identification." The collector recorded the same information in registry books and kept them in his office (ibid., Section 4).

100. Ibid., Section 6.

101. Ibid., Section 14.

102. Until 1911, there were two federal trial courts—the district and circuit courts. Chinese could file their petitions in either court. The circuit court also heard appeals from the lower federal courts. When hearing appeals, the circuit court consisted of the regularly appointed circuit judge and the justice of the Supreme Court responsible for that circuit. The Circuit Court of Appeals was created in 1891, but the lower circuit court was not abolished until 1911.

103. For in-depth analyses of the San Francisco federal courts' treatment of the Chinese cases between 1882 and 1891, see Janisch, "The Chinese, the Courts, and the Constitution," 482–504, 655–69; Fritz, *Federal Justice*, 223–49. For slightly different versions of Fritz's discussion of the Chinese, see his articles, "A Nineteenth Century 'Habeas Corpus Mill' " and "Due Process, Treaty Rights, and Chinese Exclusion, 1882–1891."

104. *In re Chin Ah On*, 18 F. 506 (1883).

105. *In re Low Yam Chow*, 13 F. 605 (1882).

106. *In re Tung Yeong*, 19 F. 184, 187–88 (N.D. Cal. 1884).

107. Janisch, "The Chinese, the Courts, and the Constitution," 495–96.

108. 23 Stat. 115.

109. Fritz, *Federal Justice*, 236–37.

110. *In re Chew Heong*, 21 F. 791 (C.C. Cal. 1884); *Chew Heong* v. *United States*, 112 U.S. 536 (1884). Even though he was in the minority, Justice Field's opinion prevailed in the circuit court because he was the presiding justice (Fritz, *Federal Justice*, 237).

111. *In re Look Tin Sing*, 21 F. 905, 910–11 (1884).

112. *In re Tung Yeong*, 19 F. 184 (1884).

113. *In re Ah Moy*, 21 F. 785 (1884).

114. Janisch, "The Chinese, the Courts, and the Constitution," 678–79.

115. *Cong. Rec.*, 50th Cong., 1st sess., Senator Stewart, 7304; "Collector of the Port," *Alta California*, Sept. 23, 1885, quoted in Janisch, "The Chinese, the Courts, and the Constitution," 671.

116. Janisch, "The Chinese, the Courts, and the Constitution," 695. Representative Joseph McKenna from California reported a petition from his home state to impeach Judge Sawyer of the circuit court and Judge Sabin of the federal district court in Nevada for their handling of the Chinese cases (*Cong. Rec.*, 50th Cong., 1st sess., 7322).

117. Leigh Chalmers to Attorney General, Dec. 5, 1887, pp. 22–23, File 980-84, DJ Let. Recd. While newspapers targeted the courts as the prime culprits for the landing of Chinese, they also blamed the lax enforcement of administrators and called Secretary of the Treasury McCulloch "The Champion Nullifier" (Sandmeyer, *Anti-Chinese Movement*, 97).

118. Saxton, *Indispensable Enemy*, 201–13; Wunder, "Anti-Chinese Violence in the American West," 214–15.

119. See, for example, letters from U.S. Attorney White of Seattle to the Attorney General, Apr. 26, 1887; U.S. Attorney Campbell of Rock Springs, Wyoming, to Attorney General, Oct. 8, 1885, and other correspondence in File 980-84, DJ Let. Recd.

120. Hoffman to Felton, Jan. 16, 1888, reprinted in *Cong. Rec.*, 50th Cong., 1st sess., 6569.

121. Tsai, *China and the Overseas Chinese*, 81–89.

122. Act of September 13, 1888, 25 Stat. 476; Tsai, *China and the Overseas Chinese*, 89–93; Sandmeyer, *Anti-Chinese Movement*, 99–101.

123. Scholars have attributed the congressional haste to pass the Scott Act to political concerns. It was an election year, and the Democrats were anxious to

secure support for the incumbent, President Cleveland. The author of the bill was William L. Scott, chairman of the National Democratic Campaign Committee. See Tsai, *China and the Overseas Chinese*, 90–91; Sandmeyer, *Anti-Chinese Movement*, 101; Janisch, "The Chinese, the Courts, and the Constitution," 699–751.

124. Act of October 1, 1888 (25 Stat. 504). See Janisch, "The Chinese, the Courts, and the Constitution," 699–751, for legislative history.

125. The petitioner also made an argument based on a contract analogy. He asserted that the return certificate constituted a contract between the United States and the petitioner, which gave him certain vested rights. These rights, he argued, were protected by the constitutional provisions forbidding laws that impair the obligation of contracts. The circuit court rejected the contract analogy, saying instead that any benefits deriving from the certificates were merely privileges that could be revoked at will (*In re Chae Chan Ping*, 36 F. 431, 433–34 [C.C. Cal. 1888]). This was an important elaboration of the rights/privilege distinction which would reappear in future immigration decisions.

126. Ibid., 434–36.

127. U.S. Const., art. I, sec. 8, cl. 3.

128. *Chae Chan Ping* v. *United States*, 130 U.S. 581, 603–10 (1889).

129. This is the argument elaborated by Stephen H. Legomsky in *Immigration and the Judiciary*, 177–211. For another critique of the *Chae Chan Ping* decision, see Konvitz, *The Alien and the Asiatic in American Law*, 1–22.

130. Coolidge, *Chinese Immigration*, 280.

131. Chang Yin-huan to Secretary of State Blaine, July 8, 1889, quoted in Tsai, *China and the Overseas Chinese*, 94.

132. *ST-AR* (1892), lx.

133. Ibid., lxi–lxii; Higham, *Strangers in the Land*, 36–52; Mink, *Old Labor and New Immigrants*, 45–68.

134. Employers were permitted to bring in contract laborers under a law passed in 1864. For history of the contract labor issue, see Erickson, *American Industry and the European Immigrant*.

135. 23 Stat. 322 (1885).

136. Higham, *Strangers in the Land*, 54.

137. Richmond Mayo Smith, "Control of Immigration. I," 76.

138. Ibid., 75. Ironically, nativists had voiced the same complaints about Irish immigrants who preceded the Chinese by a generation (Sandmeyer, *Anti-Chinese Movement*, 38–39).

139. Richmond Mayo Smith, "Control of Immigration. II," 220–25.

140. U.S. Congress, House, Select Committee on Immigration and Naturalization, *Report*, 51st Cong., 2d sess., ii.

141. 26 Stat. 1084.

142. *Cong. Rec.*, 51st Cong., 2d sess. (1891).

143. This fact was pointed out to me by Archivist James L. Harwood, Projects Branch, Legislative Archives Division, National Archives, letter of Oct. 7, 1987. For customs law, see Title 34, Chapter 6, Section 2931, Revised Statutes, 43d Cong., 1st sess. (1873–74). For interpretation of the finality clause regarding the General Land Office, see *Johnson* v. *Towsley*, 13 Wall. 72 (1871).

144. See, for example, the testimony of Edmund Stephenson, New York commissioner of emigration, in which he criticizes a federal court decision admitting immigrants but advocates changes in the substantive law rather than curbs on courts (U.S. Congress, House, Select Committee on Immigration and Naturalization, *Report*, 149).

145. A search through the WESTLAW database for all federal court cases concerning immigrants before 1891 drew only sixteen cases.

146. *ST-AR* (1892), lix.

147. Act of September 13, 1888, 25 Stat. 476, section 12.

148. *Cong. Rec.*, 50th Cong., 1st sess., 6568–69.

149. *United States* v. *Loo Way*, 68 F. 475, 477 (S.D. Cal. 1895).

150. *U.S.* v. *Gee Lee*, 50 F. 271, 273 (9th Cir. 1892); *Li Sing* v. *United States*, 180 U.S. 486, 488–90 (1901).

151. U.S. Congress, Select Committee on Immigration and Naturalization, *Chinese Immigration*, 51st Cong., 2d sess., 272–73.

152. See Chapter 3.

153. The immigration inspector also suspected from Ekiu's "general appearance" and language that she was a prostitute (Secretary of Immigration Owens to Robert McPherson, Mar. 9, 1892, Letters Sent, Superintendent of Immigration, Secretary of the Treasury, RG 56, National Archives).

154. *Nishimura Ekiu* v. *United States*, 142 U.S. 651, 660 (1892) (emphasis added).

155. Schuck, "Transformation of Immigration Law," 14.

156. Freund, *Administrative Powers*, 288; Goodnow, *Principles of the Administrative Law*, 340–43. Courts might intervene in questions of fact if the administrative decision was "absolutely unsupported by evidence" (Goodnow, "Writ of Certiorari," 529).

157. *Philadelphia and Trenton Railroad Co.* v. *James Stimpson*, 14 Pet. 448, 458 (1840). Courts also applied the principle guiding appellate review of jury verdicts: the jury findings of facts were considered to be final whereas questions of law were amenable to appellate review. Last but not least among the reasons for judicial restraint was the practical desire to avoid overburdening the judicial system with routine or controversial policy decisions.

158. Freund, *Administrative Powers*, 289; Dickinson, *Administrative Justice*, 41–42, 307.

159. *Johnson* v. *Towsley*, 80 U.S. 72, 83 (1871).

160. Even in questions of law, however, the Supreme Court had exercised a limited review in land cases. If more than one interpretation of the law was possible, the Court often found the Land Office's construction to be conclusive (Dickinson, *Administrative Justice*, 284).

161. The Court, in explaining its holding on due process in *Ekiu*, cited *Murray's Lessee* v. *Hoboken Land Co.*, 18 How. 272, and *Hilton* v. *Merritt*, 110 U.S. 97, both tax cases. See also Dickinson, *Administrative Justice*, 268–74, and Goodnow, *Principles of the Administrative Law*, 334–38.

162. Dickinson, *Administrative Justice*, 39.

163. Ibid., 55; for an example of difficulties in distinguishing fact and law, see ibid., 274–76.

164. Ibid., 71.

165. Ibid., 56–71. The more active judicial review of the ICC also stemmed from provisions in the Interstate Commerce Act of 1887. The ICC had to petition the federal circuit court to enforce its orders against common carriers, thus allowing courts an opportunity to review its decisions (Freund, *Administrative Powers*, 280–81). The extent of judicial review also hinged on the type of remedy sought (ibid., 227–69; Freund, "Writ of Certiorari"; and Dickinson, *Administrative Justice*, 62–67).

INTRODUCTION TO PART I

1. Fritz, *Federal Justice*, Table I, Appendix. For antagonism toward the court during this period, see Janisch, "The Chinese, the Courts, and the Constitution," 671–80, 683–84.

2. Leigh Chalmers to Attorney General, Dec. 5, 1887, pp. 21–22, File 980-84, DJ, Let. Recd.

3. U.S. Congress, Select Committee on Immigration and Naturalization, *Chinese Immigration*, see statements of Clement Bennett, 332–33, and Stephen Houghton, 344.

4. *Chae Chan Ping v. United States*, 130 U.S. 581 (1889).

5. *Cong. Rec.*, 52d Cong., 1st sess., 3559.

6. U.S. Congress, Select Committee on Immigration and Naturalization, *Chinese Immigration*, 323. Houghton served as referee for the federal courts under Judge Hoffman, hearing admiralty and the Chinese habeas corpus cases until 1892.

7. See Appendix for methodology.

CHAPTER TWO

1. Lai, Lim, and Yung, *Island*, 42.

2. *CG-AR* (1901); *CG-AR* (1909), 127.

3. Act of May 6, 1882, 22 Stat. 58.

4. Act of July 6, 1884, 23 Stat. 115, section 6.

5. Act of May 5, 1892, 27 Stat. 25, section 6.

6. In 1897, for example, the collector at San Francisco supervised 250 employees ("List of Employees at San Francisco Customs Office," vol. 3, Collec. Corres.).

7. See, for example, account of civil service violations by Collector John Wise of San Francisco, "Against Collector Wise," *San Francisco Call*, Jan. 10, 1895. For the continuing influence of the collector, see Collector Frederick Stratton to Senator M. Welch, Feb. 1, 1902; Stratton to Hon. E. H. Heacock, Feb. 1, 1902; Stratton to Senator Thomas Bard, Feb. 11, 1902, in Correspondence and Papers of Frederick Stratton, Outgoing Letters, vol. 1.

8. See, for example, critique of Democratic administration of the exclusion laws in "Republicans and Exclusion—Enforcing the Law to the Very Letter," *San Francisco Chronicle*, Oct. 31, 1900.

9. "Exit Collector Wise," *San Francisco Call*, June 2, 1897.

10. Democratic senator Stephen M. White of California warned the attorney general of the United States in 1893 that the "situation in California regarding the

Chinese is critical" and could lead to "the destruction of the democratic party in that State" (White to Attorney General, Sept. 4, 1893, File 980-84, DJ Let. Recd.).

11. For an example of coverage of routine cases, see "Forty Chinese Come Ashore," *San Francisco Call*, Oct. 2, 1897; for corruption exposés, see "Watching the Bureau Chief," *San Francisco Call*, Sept. 4, 1898; "Wise Comes to Williams Rescue," *San Francisco Call*, Sept. 1, 1896; "Chinese Coolies Flocking to America Despite Laws Framed to Exclude Them," *San Francisco Call*, Sept. 26, 1902.

12. It was because of the "glare of publicity" that Collector Hager took his uncompromisingly restrictive stance in the 1880s, discussed in Chapter 1. See Janisch, "The Chinese, the Courts, and the Constitution," 480.

13. See, for example, Stratton to the Commissioner General of Immigration, June 8 and Oct. 26, 1901, Collec. Corres., box 2, vol. 6; Collector Jackson to Commissioner General of Immigration, June 29, 1900, ibid., box 2, vol. 5.

14. Collector Frederick Stratton, for example, was an attorney who showed a great concern for procedural regularity in investigations and for an accurate interpretation of the rules. In contrast, Collector John Wise expressed frustration with rules he felt got in the way of stringent enforcement. He grudgingly followed the rules because of the department's orders, but he tried in some cases to negate their effect, as is discussed below.

15. Sawyer, Diaries, Nov. 7, 1917, vol. 2.

16. *CG-AR* (1904), 137; Stratton to Commissioner General of Immigration, Jan. 22, 1903; Wise to all Collectors of Customs, Dec. 24, 1896, Collec. Corres.

17. Nee and Nee, *Long Time Californ'*, 64–65; Ma, "Chinatown Organizations," 14.

18. U.S. Congress, Select Committee on Immigration and Naturalization, *Chinese Immigration*, testimony of Consul Bee, 398.

19. Tsai, *China and the Overseas Chinese*, 35; see also 31–38; Lyman, "Conflict," 473–99, esp. 482; Nee and Nee, *Long Time Californ'*, 64–65; Ma, "Chinatown Organizations," 149–51.

20. Nee and Nee, *Long Time Californ'*, 65–66; Barth, *Bitter Strength*, 79–102. On the organization of the Chinese-American community in contesting discriminatory policies, see generally McClain, *In Search of Equality*.

21. Ma, "Chinatown Organizations," 148–49, 153–54; Nee and Nee, *Long Time Californ'*, 67–69; Lyman, "Conflict," 484–90.

22. Lyman, "Conflict," 489–90. Other Chinese organizations existed as well. See Ma, "Chinatown Organizations," 151–52.

23. Ma, "Chinatown Organizations," 154–56; Lyman, "Conflict," 486–88, 490–94.

24. Lyman, "Conflict," 497.

25. Ma, "Chinatown Organizations," 147.

26. Ibid., 163–65.

27. See Chapter 1.

28. Tsai, *China and the Overseas Chinese*, 68–70, 75–80; see also discussion of treaty of 1894 below.

29. Wakeman, *Fall of Imperial China*, 19–35.

30. *Cong. Rec.*, 53d Cong., 1st sess., Oct. 12, 1893, 2457.

31. U.S. Congress, House, *Facts Concerning the Enforcement of the Chinese-Exclusion Laws*, 6.

32. For an extensive analysis of the application of exclusion laws to Chinese women, see Chan, "Exclusion of Chinese Women."

33. *In re Ah Moy*, 21 F. 785 (C.C. Cal. 1884); *In re Ah Quan*, 21 F. 182 (C.C. Cal. 1884).

34. *Ex parte Chin King*, 35 F. 354 (C.C. Ore. 1888); *In re Yung Hing See*, 36 F. 437; *Tsoi Sim* v. *United States*, 116 F. 920 (9th Cir. 1902).

35. *In re Wo Tai Li*, 48 F. 668 (N.D. Cal. 1888); *In re Li Foon*, 80 F. 881 (C.C.S.D.N.Y. 1897); *In re Chung Toy Ho and Wong Choy Sin*, 42 F. 398 (C.C. Ore. 1890); *United States* v. *Mrs. Gue Lim*, 83 F. 136 (N.D. Wash. 1897).

36. *United States* v. *Mrs. Gue Lim*, 176 U.S. 459 (1900).

37. Secret Service agent Oscar Greenhalge to Walter S. Chance, Supervising Agent, Mar. 16, 1899, File 52730/84, INS Subj. Corres. See also File 13928/1, C. Seg. Files.

38. U.S. Congress, Senate, *Exclusion of Chinese Laborers*, 57th Cong., 1st sess., Dec. 10, 1901, Sen. Doc. 162, 22.

39. *Cong. Rec.*, 52d Cong., 1st sess., Senator Charles N. Felton, 3561.

40. Ibid., Senator Wilbur F. Sanders, 3566.

41. S. Steiner, *Fusang*, 178.

42. Chan, *This Bittersweet Soil*, 16–20, 29.

43. Tsai, *Chinese Experience in America*, 98–99; S. Steiner, *Fusang*, 168–71.

44. See, for example, the account by Wong Yow of his entry into the United States as a "paper son" in Leung, "When a Haircut Was a Luxury," 212–13.

45. The Act of September 11, 1957, provided that Chinese who had entered as "paper sons" could not be deported if they had a parent, spouse, or child who was a U.S. citizen or a permanent resident alien (71 Stat. 639). In response to this act, eight thousand Chinese had confessed by 1969 that they were paper sons (Chinn, Lai, and Choy, eds., *History of the Chinese in California*, 28).

46. For examples of stories about officials selling documents to Chinese, see "Door Opened to Illegal Admission of Chinese," *San Francisco Call*, May 5, 1898. A major investigation of the San Francisco immigration force in 1917 revealed many instances of official corruption and Chinese fraud. See the "Densmore Investigation" file, Immigration District 13, San Francisco, Box 7, Records of the Immigration and Naturalization Service, RG 85, National Archives.

47. For the effect of these restrictions on Chinese families, see Peffer, "Forbidden Families."

48. For official correspondence concerning Chinese prostitution, see File 1855/01, DJ Let. Recd.; File 12811, C. Seg. Files.

49. Hirata, "Free, Indentured, Enslaved," 8–10.

50. U.S. Attorney Marshall Woodworth reported to the attorney general that Chinese "slave girls" were worth from $1,000 to $3,000 (June 24, 1901, File 1855/01, DJ Let. Recd.). "Big Pete," a Chinese man involved in the tongs after 1905, recalled that organizations might pay as much as $5,000 (Nee and Nee, *Long Time Californ'*, 92).

51. Oscar Greenhalge to Walter Chance, "Report on San Francisco," [1899], File 52730/84, INS Subj. Corres.

52. For example, the Asiatic Exclusion League in 1910 charged the commissioner of immigration at San Francisco, Hart H. North, with fraud in Chinese cases, but its real reason for attacking North was that he refused to exclude East Indians from California. The political pressure became so great that North was forced to resign. See Chapter 7.

53. See, for example, Ingersoll and Geary, "Should the Chinese Be Excluded?"; Sandmeyer, *Anti-Chinese Movement*, 103.

54. *Cong. Rec.*, 52d Cong., 1st sess., 3568.

55. Ibid., 3558.

56. Act of May 5, 1892, 27 Stat. 25. In a move to prevent the chance for fraud in court cases, the law also suspended the right to bail in habeas corpus proceedings. The attorney general had recommended that the law provide for the punishment of Chinese who were found to be unlawfully in the United States more than once (Attorney General to Senator Dolph, Jan. 7, 1892, DJ, Letters Sent to Executive Officers and Members of Congress, File 199-92/62, Microfilm Roll 28, National Archives).

57. "Tie No Tag on Us," *San Francisco Call*, Sept. 14, 1892.

58. "It May Lead to War," *San Francisco Call*, Sept. 20, 1892.

59. Letter of Sept. 19, 1892, reprinted in *Cong. Rec.*, 53d Cong., 1st sess., Oct. 12, 1893, 2443.

60. Letter of Sept. 15, 1892, reprinted in ibid.

61. Ibid.; "Chinese Will Resist," *San Francisco Call*, Sept. 10, 1892; "It May Lead to War," ibid., Sept. 20, 1892; "Asking a Governor's Aid," ibid., Sept. 30, 1892.

62. U.S. Attorney Charles Garter to the Attorney General, Mar. 31, 1893, 2, 4, File 980-84, DJ Let. Recd.

63. "Bars Are Down," *San Francisco Call*, Apr. 9, 1893.

64. "A Pagan Problem," *San Francisco Call*, Mar. 28, 1893.

65. "To Herd Heathen," *San Francisco Call*, Mar. 27, 1893.

66. On Ashton's connection to the Southern Pacific, see Sandmeyer, *Anti-Chinese Movement*, p. 105, n. 30. Evarts's father had been secretary of state during the negotiation of the treaty of 1880. For another account of the litigation over the Geary Act, see McClain, *In Search of Equality*, 203–13.

67. Paulsen, "Gresham-Yang Treaty," 281.

68. *Cong. Rec.*, 53d Cong., 1st sess., 2421.

69. Brief for Appellants, Joseph H. Choate and Maxwell Evarts, *Fong Yue Ting* v. *United States*, 58.

70. Ibid., 36.

71. Ibid., 19.

72. Ibid., 54.

73. Opinion by J. Hubley Ashton and James Carter, ibid., 10.

74. The attorneys reasoned that the failure to register was an "infamous crime" because the punishment, "transportation for life has always been, and must always be, an infamous punishment" (ibid., 75–77).

75. Ibid., 69–83.

76. Ibid., 71–72. Congress did, in fact, believe that the U.S. judges could not distinguish between genuine and false Chinese testimony. Judge Hoffman had admitted as much, and the inability of the courts to ferret out fraudulent Chinese cases provided much of the rationale behind congressional steps to remove jurisdiction over Chinese cases from the federal courts. See Chapters 3 and 4.

77. Brief for Appellants, J. Hubley Ashton, ibid., 37.

78. Opinion, J. Hubley Ashton, ibid., 15.

79. Brief for Appellants, J. Hubley Ashton, ibid., 40.

80. Brief for the Respondents, ibid., 12.

81. Ibid., 11.

82. Ibid., 5.

83. Ibid., 49. On the international law argument, see 22–33; on congressional control over foreign affairs, see 36–37; on the federal police power, see 44–50.

84. Ibid., 58, 40.

85. Ibid., 42, 39–43.

86. Ibid., 16, 44.

87. Ibid., 59.

88. *Nishimura Ekiu* v. *U.S*, 142 U.S. 651, 660 (1891).

89. Justice Harlan did not participate in the decision.

90. *Fong Yue Ting* v. *United States*, 149 U.S. 698, 713 (1893).

91. Ibid., 707.

92. Ibid., 723, 724.

93. Ibid., 730.

94. Ibid., 744.

95. Ibid., 746.

96. Ibid., 754.

97. Ibid., 738.

98. *Monongahela Navigation Company* v. *United States*, 148 U.S. 312, 336, quoted ibid., 738.

99. Ibid., 743.

100. Ibid., 759.

101. Ibid., 763.

102. Ibid., 741.

103. Ibid., 743; see also 750, 760–61.

104. Although the Supreme Court did not recognize aliens' claims to specific rights under the Bill of Rights, it would later hold that aliens *were* entitled to a "fair hearing" by administrative officials. See Part II.

105. "Now the Chinese Must Go," *San Francisco Call*, May 16, 1893.

106. "The Geary Act in California," *Nation* 56 (May 18, 1893): 365.

107. The briefs before the Supreme Court had addressed the effect of the Geary Act on the treaties—the Chinese arguing that it violated treaty rights and the United States arguing it did not—but the issue was not central. As J. Hubley Ashton advised the Chinese Six Companies in November 1892, the decision of the Supreme Court in *Chae Chan Ping* made it "immaterial whether or not the [act] . . . is in contravention of the express stipulations" of the Burlingame Treaty or the treaty of 1880 (Opinion by J. Hubley Ashton, *Fong Yue Ting*, 5).

108. Note, "The American Bar Association and the Chinese Exclusion Case," 289–90; Young, "Chinese Question Again," 596. See also Clayton, "A New View of the Deportation Cases in the Supreme Court," 299.

109. Ingersoll and Geary, "Should the Chinese Be Excluded?," 56; see also editorial, *Nation* 56 (May 18, 1893): 358.

110. Ingersoll and Geary, "Should the Chinese Be Excluded?," 57.

111. *Cong. Rec.*, 53d Cong., 1st sess., 2422.

112. Secretary of State Gresham assured the Chinese minister that Congress would amend the act in the next session to "moderate some of the measure's harsh provisions" (Paulsen, "Gresham-Yang Treaty," 285).

113. Letters of May 24, 1893, reprinted in *Cong. Rec.*, 53d Cong., 1st sess., 2444.

114. *San Francisco Call*, Sept. 16, 1893.

115. "Censured Grover," *San Francisco Call*, Sept. 15, 1893.

116. "Law Set Aside—Nullification with a Vengeance," *San Francisco Call*, Sept. 12, 1893.

117. Stephen M. White to Attorney General Olney, Sept. 4, 1893, File 980-84, DJ Let. Recd.

118. U.S. Attorney George Denis to the Attorney General, Sept. 5, 1893, ibid.

119. Ibid.

120. Ibid.; U.S. Attorney Charles Garter to the Attorney General, June 4, 1893, ibid.

121. Attorney General to U.S. Attorney Denis, Sept. 12, 1893, ibid.

122. *Cong. Rec.*, 52d Cong., 1st sess., 2915, 3480.

123. Act of November 3, 1893, 28 Stat. 7, section 2.

124. 28 Stat. 1210. See Paulsen, "Gresham-Yang Treaty," for details on the negotiations. This provision had been included in the unratified treaty of 1888 and the act of September 13, 1888. See Chapter 1.

125. "Republicans and Chinese Exclusion," *San Francisco Chronicle*, Oct. 31, 1900.

126. Ma, "Chinatown Organizations," 155–56; Lyman, "Conflict," 492. Though its authority had been diminished, the Chinese Six Companies continued to be considered by white Americans as the primary spokesman for the Chinese.

127. U.S. Congress, *Exclusion of Chinese Laborers*, 8.

128. "How Uncle Sam Watches the Immigrant and Catches the Smuggler," *San Francisco Call*, Jan. 28, 1900. Angel Island was used solely as a quarantine station from 1892 until 1910, when it also became the immigration headquarters (Evans and Heron, "Isla de Los Angeles," 37).

129. For a compelling story of the immigration experience from the Chinese perspective, see Kingston, *China Men*.

130. Oscar Greenhalge to Walter S. Chance, [1899], File 52730/84, INS Subj. Corres.; U.S. Congress, Select Committee on Immigration and Naturalization, *Chinese Immigration*, 300.

131. For a description of inspection procedures, see U.S. Congress, Select Committee on Immigration and Naturalization, *Chinese Immigration*, 279–82, 297–300, 324–28.

132. Lai, Lim, and Yung, *Island*, 116.

133. Ibid., 117.

134. Ibid.

135. Ibid., 114.

136. U.S. Congress, Senate, *Exclusion of Chinese Laborers*, 8.

137. As described in Chapter 1, the Chinese Exclusion Act of 1882 provided that Chinese exempt from exclusion had to present certificates from their government attesting to their exempt status.

138. U.S. Congress, House, *Facts Concerning the Enforcement of the Chinese-Exclusion Laws*, 45.

139. Collector Wise to U.S. Marshal Baldwin, May 13, 1896, Collec. Corres.

140. Collector Frederick Stratton to Commissioner General of Immigration, Dec. 20, 1900, ibid.

141. Collector Wise to Special Agent Moore, Dec. 8, 1896, ibid.

142. U.S. Congress, Select Committee on Immigration and Naturalization, *Chinese Immigration*, 296.

143. Collector Stratton to Commissioner General of Immigration, Dec. 20, 1900, and Jan. 4, 1901, Collec. Corres.; see also experience of Collector Jackson discussed below.

144. Greenhalge to Chance, "Report on San Francisco," File 52730/84, INS Subj. Corres.

145. "Composition on the Advantages and Disadvantages of America, from a Chinese Standpoint," File 13928/1, C. Seg. Files; see also remarks in "A Poem" confiscated from Wong Ngum Yin at Portland, Oregon, Inspector Barbour to Commissioner General, Oct. 29, 1906, ibid., and John Jeong's oral history in Nee and Nee, *Long Time Californ'*, 73.

146. Greenhalge to Chance, "Report on San Francisco."

147. Chinese Chamber of Commerce et al. to Secretary of Commerce and Labor, Jan. 27, 1909, File 52363/14, INS Subj. Corres.

148. Secretary of Treasury Metcalf to Assistant Secretary of Treasury Lawrence Murray, Oct. 1, 1904, File 12811, C. Seg. Files.

149. This was through the amendment of section 6 in the act of July 5, 1884, 23 Stat. 115.

150. 28 Stat. 7, section 2.

151. U.S. Treasury Department, *Laws, Treaty, and Regulations Relating to the Exclusion of Chinese* (1902), paragraph 28.

152. Ibid., paragraph 58.

153. Special Deputy Collector to R. P. Schwerin, Vice President and General Manager of Pacific Mail Steamship Co., Jan. 5, 1897, vol. 3, Collec. Corres.

154. U.S. Treasury Department, *Laws, Treaty, and Regulations Relating to the Enforcement of the Exclusion of Chinese* (1902), regulation 40.

155. "Treaty between the United States and China Concerning Immigration," Nov. 17, 1880, art. I, 22 Stat. 826.

156. Kohler, "Coolies versus the Privileged Classes."

157. 22 Op. Att'y Gen. 132 (1898).

158. Ibid.

159. Timothy Phelps served as collector of San Francisco from 1888 to 1892.

John Wise succeeded in the post from 1892 to 1898. John P. Jackson took over for a two-year appointment between 1898 and 1900. Frederick Stratton was the last collector to supervise Chinese immigration, serving between 1900 and 1912.

160. Special Deputy Collector to Henry Hogan, Feb. 4, 1896, Collec. Corres.; U.S. Treasury Department, *Laws, Treaty, and Regulations Relating to the Enforcement of the Exclusion of Chinese* (1902), regulation 88.

161. Collector Wise to Parke Godwin, Jan. 2, 1896; Collector Wise to U.S. Consul, Hong Kong, Apr. 7, 1896, Collec. Corres.

162. Assistant Secretary of the Treasury to Collector of Customs at San Francisco, Apr. 25, 1899, File 53108/9-B, INS Subj. Corres.

163. Special Agents Linck and Smith to the Secretary of the Treasury, Feb. 6, 1899, File 53108/9-A, ibid.

164. Collector Jackson to the Secretary of the Treasury, Mar. 30, 1899, File 53108/9-B, ibid.

165. Assistant Secretary of the Treasury to Collector Jackson, Apr. 25, 1899, ibid.

166. Linck and Smith to the Secretary of the Treasury, Feb. 6, 1899, 21, ibid.

167. For San Francisco figures for 1898, see B. E. Meredith, Inspector in charge of Chinese Bureau, to Special Agents John Linck and C. J. Smith, Jan. 12, 1899, File 53108/9-A, ibid. For 1901 San Francisco figures, see *CG-AR* (1901), 49. The majority of Chinese entered the United States at San Francisco throughout the period, though they increasingly came over the border from Mexico and Canada. In 1891, 97 percent of Chinese entered the United States through San Francisco, dropping to 78 percent in 1898 and 64 percent in 1901. See *ST-AR* (1891), lx; *ST-AR* (1898), 844–45; Meredith to Linck, *CG-AR* (1901), 49.

168. For example, 70 percent of the Chinese refused admission at San Francisco in 1898 were those claiming to be born in the United States, who relied solely on testimony to support their cases (B. E. Meredith to Special Agents John Linck and C. J. Smith, Jan. 12, 1899, File 53108/9-A, INS Subj. Corres.).

CHAPTER THREE

1. *Cong. Rec.*, 53d Cong., 1st sess., Representative Bartlett, 2454.

2. See McClain, "Chinese Struggle"; Janisch, "The Chinese, the Courts, and the Constitution," 296–314, 374–98, 581–653; Fritz, *Federal Justice*, 210–28; Mooney, "Matthew Deady and the Federal Judicial Response to Racism in the Early West"; Sandmeyer, "California Anti-Chinese Legislation"; Wunder, "Chinese and the Courts."

3. See, for example, the letter of Secret Service agent Oscar Greenhalge to Walter Chance, Supervisor of Special Agents, Mar. 11, 1899, File 52730/84, INS Subj. Corres.

4. Chalmers to Attorney General, Dec. 5, 1887, File 980-84, DJ Let. Recd.; Janisch, "The Chinese, the Courts, and the Constitution," 678.

5. See "Densmore Investigation" file, Immigration District 13, San Francisco, Box 7, Records of the Immigration and Naturalization Service, RG 85, National Archives, for the role of brokers and their relationship to attorneys.

6. For an example of a business card, see ibid.

7. Inspectors Henry Kennah, Ainsworth, and Rickards all became active attorneys for the Chinese.

8. *Cong. Rec.*, 50th Cong., 1st sess., Appendix, 451.

9. Fritz, *Federal Justice*, 229–49.

10. *Cong. Rec.*, 49th Cong., 1st sess., 6222.

11. See, for example, McKenna's speech in *Cong. Rec.*, 50th Cong., 1st sess., 7746–59. McKenna also strongly opposed bills to compensate Chinese victims of the series of riots in the 1880s. See *Cong. Rec.*, 49th Cong., 1st sess., 4427–28; *Cong. Rec.*, 49th Cong., 2d sess., 1510; *Cong. Rec.*, 50th Cong., 1st sess., 9150, 9339, 9342.

12. *Cong. Rec.*, 51st Cong., 1st sess., 522.

13. *Black's Law Dictionary*, s.v. "habeas corpus."

14. U.S. Const., art. I, sec. 9.

15. See discussion of the Habeas Corpus Act of 1867 in Duker, *Constitutional History of Habeas Corpus*, 189–94.

16. U.S. Congress, Select Committee on Immigration and Naturalization, *Chinese Immigration*, 111.

17. *In re Jung Ah Lung*, 25 F. 141, 142–43. The United States Supreme Court affirmed the district court's decision in *United States v. Jung Ah Lung*, 124 U.S. 621 (1888).

18. U.S. Congress, Select Committee on Immigration and Naturalization, *Chinese Immigration*, 345. Houghton was referring to 13 Rev. Stat. sec. 755 (1878).

19. Ibid., 364.

20. Examiner David Fisher to Attorney General, Mar. 16, 1886, File 980-84, DJ Let. Recd.

21. Carey to Attorney General, Sept. 7, 1888, ibid.

22. U.S. Congress, Select Committee on Immigration and Naturalization, *Chinese Immigration*, 344.

23. The United States commissioners were given power to hear habeas corpus cases brought by Chinese immigrants in 1888. Stephen Chase Houghton was appointed commissioner in the circuit court, Ward McAllister, Jr., commissioner in the district court. E. H. Heacock, appointed commissioner in 1892, heard such cases for both courts until 1910. Act of September 13, 1888, 25 Stat. 476.

24. *San Francisco Call*, Dec. 25, 1882; "U.S. Commissioner Retires from Bench," *San Francisco Examiner*, Mar. 18, 1910; "Noted Jurist Is Dead at Ripe Age," *San Francisco Chronicle*, Apr. 30, 1914.

25. The observations that follow were obtained from the transcripts of the hearings before Commissioner Heacock, found in the district court case files. See Appendix for details on methodology.

26. See Chapter 2.

27. *In re Wong Yen*, No. 11359, *Admiralty Casefiles* (1897).

28. Hoffman to Felton, Jan. 16, 1888, reprinted in *Cong. Rec.*, 50th Cong., 1st sess., 6569; see also Special Agents Linck and Smith to the Secretary of Treasury, Feb. 6, 1899, File 53108/9-A, INS Subj. Corres.

29. U.S. Congress, Select Committee on Immigration and Naturalization, *Chinese Immigration*, 344.

30. *In re Jew Wong Loy*, 91 F. 240 (N.D. Cal. 1898).

31. *Quock Ting v. United States*, 140 U.S. 417, 420 (1890).

32. Ibid., 418–22. Chinese often faced a "Catch-22" situation when courts and administrative officials evaluated the credibility of their testimony. Officials suspected Chinese of lying if their stories were either too pat and detailed or too vague.

33. *In re Woey Ho*, No. 12099, *Admiralty Casefiles* (1901).

34. *Woey Ho v. United States*, 109 F. 888, 890–91 (9th Cir. 1901).

35. See, for example, *In re Wong Sing*, No. 11361, *Admiralty Casefiles* (1897).

36. See, for example, differences in interpretations of the McCreary Amendment in Chapter 4.

37. The rarity of such a reversal was highlighted in an article in the *San Francisco Call*, Feb. 3, 1898, which noted (inaccurately), "This is the first time that Judge Heacock's report in a Chinese case has been disaffirmed."

38. See, for example, U.S. Congress, House, *Facts Concerning the Enforcement of the Chinese-Exclusion Laws*, 1905–6, pp. 101–2, and Ralph, "Chinese Leak," 525.

39. Collector Wise to U.S. Marshal Barry Baldwin, Mar. 13, 1896, Collec. Corres.

40. See Chapter 2 for a discussion of such fraud.

41. Collector J. C. Saunders to Secretary of the Treasury, Jan. 3, 1894, File 980-84, DJ Let. Recd.; see also Special Agent Charles W. Johnston to Collector J. C. Saunders, Dec. 31, 1893, ibid.

42. Wise to Secretary of Treasury, Oct. 7, 1893, ibid.

43. Regarding the difficulty of Chinese finding white witnesses who knew them well enough to provide the required testimony, see letters of Collector Frederick S. Stratton to the Commissioner General of Immigration, Feb. 6, 1901, and Sept. 18, 1902, Collec. Corres.

44. John H. Wise to Hon. Richard Olney, Attorney General, Dec. 14, 1893, in "Weller, C.," Appointment Files, 1893–97, Records of the Department of Justice, RG 60, National Archives; see also letter from attorney general to U.S. Attorney Garter, Oct. 20, 1893, informing Garter of complaints by the San Francisco collector about lax enforcement by Garter's office, File 980/84, Letters Sent, DJ.

45. Wise was a Democrat and the U.S. attorney a Republican, and thus party friction may have added to the dispute. See U.S. Attorney Charles Garter to Attorney General, Oct. 25, 1893, File 980/84, DJ Let. Recd. For a similar defense, see John Carey to Attorney General, Sept. 7, 1888, ibid.

46. U.S. Congress, Select Committee on Immigration and Naturalization, *Chinese Immigration*, 324.

47. Garter to Attorney General, Oct. 25, 1893, File 980/84, DJ Let. Recd.

48. Wise to the Secretary of Treasury, Aug. 27, 1895, Custom House Nominations, California, San Francisco, March 1894–June 1896, Records of the Treasury, RG 56, National Archives.

49. Special Deputy Collector to Commissioner Heacock, Jan. 3, 1896, Collec. Corres. Perhaps the collector was trying to enlighten the commissioner as well. In one part of the letter, the collector seems to be expressing his own opinion while purporting to ask for advice. In respect to the "reliability of documentary testimony of white people," the collector asked "whether or not you have not found that white

people sign such documents as a business accommodation to their Chinese customers."

50. Jackson to Secretary of Treasury, Mar. 30, 1899, File 53108/9-B, INS Subj. Corres. See Chapter 2 for further discussion of tension between the approach of Jackson and the secretary of the treasury.

51. Special Agents John W. Linck and Converse J. Smith to Secretary of the Treasury, Feb. 6, 1899, File 53108/9-A, INS Subj. Corres.

52. Jackson to Secretary of Treasury, Mar. 30, 1899, File 53108/9-B, ibid.

53. Assistant Secretary of Treasury to Collector Jackson, Apr. 25, 1899, ibid.

54. See Chapter 2 for a detailed description of the conflict between Californians and administrative officials.

55. *Cong. Rec.*, 51st Cong., 1st sess., 2309–13.

56. "The Geary Law," *San Francisco Call*, Oct. 18, 1893. See also "Send Them Away," *San Francisco Call*, Sept. 21, 1893.

57. U.S. Attorney Denis to Attorney General, Sept. 5, 1893; U.S. Attorney Garter to Attorney General, Sept. 13, 1893, File 980/84, DJ Let. Recd.

58. 25 Stat. 476, section 13 (emphasis added).

59. The act of September 13, 1888, was to take effect upon the ratification of a treaty between China and the United States. China never ratified the treaty, thus rendering the validity of the law uncertain. The courts had held that the portions of the law which did not rely on the treaty were still binding. The secretary of the treasury believed that section 13 *did* depend on the treaty's ratification and thus argued that the section never took effect and that the court's actions were wrong (Secretary of Treasury Carlisle to Acting Attorney General Lawrence Maxwell, Sept. 27, 1893, File 980-84, DJ Let. Recd.).

60. J. Hubley Ashton to the Attorney General, Sept. 7, 1893, ibid.

61. Garter to Attorney General, Sept. 13, 1893, ibid.

62. Denis to Attorney General, Aug. 1, 1893, ibid.

63. Judge Ross to President Cleveland, Sept. 26, 1893; Garter to Attorney General, Sept. 13, 1893, ibid.

64. Denis to Attorney General, Sept. 5, 1893, ibid.

65. "The Geary Law," *San Francisco Call*, Oct. 18, 1893.

66. No Chinese had actually been deported. They all appealed their cases to the U.S. Supreme Court, thereby postponing their deportation.

67. 28 Stat. 7, section 6.

68. The court generally allowed defendants to be released on a $500 or $1,000 bond pending their hearing. See, for example, *U.S. v. Lew Yuen*, No. 1431, *Commissioner Casefiles* (1903); *U.S. v. Dea Seak Ngee*, No. 1472, *Commissioner Casefiles* (1904). The commissioner always notified the defendant of his or her right to an attorney, and defendants generally took advantage of the right for representation. See, for example, *U.S. v. Chun Jee*, No. 910, *Commissioner Casefiles* (1901).

69. Act of November 3, 1893, 28 Stat. 7; Act of September 13, 1888, 25 Stat. 476, section 13.

70. 27 Stat. 25, section 6.

71. See, for example, *United States v. Wong Loy Jeong*, No. 3272, *Criminal Casefiles* (1896); *United States v. Ah Sout*, No. 3439, *Criminal Casefiles* (1897).

72. *United States* v. *Ah Hen [or Hew]*, No. 3348, *Criminal Casefiles* (1896); *United States* v. *Wong Ark*, No. 3446, *Criminal Casefiles* (1897).

73. "The First Case," *San Francisco Call*, Dec. 19, 1893.

74. U.S. Congress, Select Committee on Immigration and Naturalization, *Chinese Immigration*, 415–16; Light, "From Vice District to Tourist Attraction."

75. "The Geary Law," *San Francisco Call*, Oct. 18, 1893; Lyman, "Conflict," 473; Light, "From Vice District to Tourist Attraction," 377–94.

76. Wise to Benjamin Harrison, Inspector in Charge of the Chinese Bureau, Jan. 29, 1896, Collec. Corres.

77. For cases involving Chinese seamen, see *United States* v. *Chung Foo*, No. 3218, *Criminal Casefiles* (1895); *United States* v. *Go Yin*, No. 3219, *Criminal Casefiles* (1895); *United States* v. *Yip Ah Chow*, No. 3406, *Criminal Casefiles* (1897). Regarding Chinese working in Alaska, see *United States* v. *Gee Kee*, No. 3165, *Criminal Casefiles* (1895). For excuse of inclement weather, see *United States* v. *Yee Tang*, No. 1113, *Commissioner Casefiles* (1902).

78. *United States* v. *Chun Kow Gum*, No. 926, *Commissioner Casefiles* (1901); *United States* v. *Lee Soy Sum*, No. 931, *Commissioner Casefiles* (1901); *United States* v. *Sun Young*, No. 1082, *Commissioner Casefiles* (1902); *United States* v. *Lin Yem Shang*, No. 1318, *Commissioner Casefiles* (1903).

79. *United States* v. *Chune Shea Wun*, No. 1450, *Commissioner Casefiles* (1903).

80. The court generally relied solely on Chinese testimony in citizenship cases; see, for example, *United States* v. *Toy Ong*, No. 1435, *Commissioner Casefiles* (1903).

81. *United States* v. *Low Lin Jow*, No. 1043, *Commissioner Casefiles* (1902); *United States* v. *Ah Gee*, No. 1622, *Commissioner Casefiles* (1905). Such tactics were even more common in northern states bordering Canada. See *CG-AR* (1901), 51–52.

82. For the tension between law and politics, see Hay, "Property"; Shapiro, *Courts*; and Thompson, *Whigs and Hunters*.

83. *Woey Ho* v. *United States*, 891.

84. "The Habeas Corpus Mill," *San Francisco Call*, May 13, 1894.

85. See, for example, "Chinese Immigration," *San Francisco Call*, Jan. 18, 1898; *CG-AR* (1904), 137.

86. "Shall the Chinese Coolie Be Admitted Again to Compete with Free Labor?," *San Francisco Call*, Oct. 27, 1897.

87. *CG-AR* (1903), 98; U.S. Attorney Garter to Attorney General, Oct. 25, 1893, File 980/84, DJ Let. Recd.

88. That the courts were being "imposed upon" was a favorite phrase of many commentators. See, for example, John Carey to Attorney General, Oct. 27, 1888, File 980/84, DJ Let. Recd.; H. Scott, Deputy Collector, to Attorney General, Dec. 3, 1887, ibid.

89. *Cong. Rec.*, 52d Cong., 1st sess., 3480.

90. Attorney General to Judge Ray, Nov. 23, 1903, File 9473/03, DJ Let. Recd.

CHAPTER FOUR

1. *Cong. Rec.*, 52d Cong., 1st sess., 3567.

2. Ibid., 2915.

3. For more information on the acts of 1884 and 1888, see Chapter 1.

4. Brief for Appellants, p. 61, *Fong Yue Ting* v. *United States*, 149 U.S. 698 (1893).

5. 28 Stat. 7, section 2.

6. J. Hubley Ashton to Secretary of the Treasury Carlisle, May 1, 1894, File 5306/94, DJ Let. Recd.

7. *In re Quan Gin*, No. 10948, *Admiralty Casefiles* (1894).

8. *In re Quan Gin*, 61 F. 395, 396 (1894).

9. *In re Loo Yue Soon*, No. 10978, *Admiralty Casefiles* (1894).

10. Chinese Merchants Exchange to Yang Yu, Chinese Minister, Washington, D.C., May 14, 1894, File 980-84, DJ Let. Recd.; see also Acting Secretary of State Uhl to Attorney General, May 12, 1894, ibid.

11. *Lee Kan* v. *United States*, 62 F. 914, 918 (1894).

12. "The Habeas Corpus Mill," *San Francisco Call*, May 13, 1894.

13. 28 Stat. 390.

14. Brief for Appellants, 9–12, *Lem Moon Sing* v. *United States*, 158 U.S. 538. Evarts distinguished *Nishimura Ekiu* by pointing to the different language used in the act of 1891. In that act, immigration inspectors were given the final determination of the right of *all* aliens to enter, whereas the act of 1894 limited the collector's jurisdiction to only those aliens excluded by laws or treaties.

15. Brief for the United States, 11, *Lem Moon Sing*.

16. Ibid., 542–43, 546–47 (1894).

17. Ibid., 547, 549.

18. Thirty-five petitions were filed in 1896 and forty-two in 1897. See Table 3 in Chapter 3.

19. "Effect on the Chinese," *San Francisco Call*, May 29, 1895.

20. "Use the Boycott," *San Francisco Call*, Oct. 27, 1894.

21. *In re Look Tin Sing*, 21 F. 905, 910–11 (1884).

22. *In re Tom Yum*, 64 F. 485 (1894).

23. Collector Wise to Secretary of Treasury, Nov. 17, 1894, File 5306/94, DJ Let. Recd.

24. Collins, "Are Persons Born within the United States Ipso Facto Citizens Thereof?," 834. See also Webster, "Acquisition of Citizenship"; Woodworth, "Citizenship of the United States under the Fourteenth Amendment."

25. *United States* v. *Wong Kim Ark*, 169 U.S. 649, 694 (1898).

26. Collector Jackson to Secretary of the Treasury, Aug. 16, 1898, Special Agent Moore to Secretary of the Treasury, Aug. 30, 1898, Customs House Nominations, San Francisco, October 1897–November 1898, Records of the Department of Treasury, RG 56, National Archives; see also *ST-AR* (1898), 846.

27. Jackson to Secretary of the Treasury, Aug. 16, 1898, ibid.

28. "Judge de Haven Has Made a New Rule," *San Francisco Chronicle*, Sept. 8, 1904.

29. *ST-AR* (1896), 798.

30. "Says Chinese Is Wronged," *San Francisco Chronicle*, Sept. 24, 1904.

31. *CG-AR* (1904), 137.

32. 31 Stat. 588, 611.

33. 32 Stat. 825. The same law transferred the Bureau of Immigration from the

secretary of the treasury to the newly created Department of Commerce and Labor.

34. The circuit court ordered a remand in 101 cases, a dismissal in 4. The outcome was unknown in 44 cases. In the district court, 108 petitions for habeas corpus were filed by immigrants between 1897 and 1910. Of these cases, the court intervened in the immigration decision in only 6 instances; it ordered the petitioner remanded to the custody of the commissioner of immigration in 72 cases. The outcome was unknown in 28 cases, and the court ordered dismissal in 2 cases. The high number of unknown outcomes is owing to the poor condition of the records (U.S., District Court for the Southern District of New York, *Equity Docket, 1897–1915*, RG 21, National Archives, New York Branch, Bayonne, N.J.; U.S., Circuit Court for the Southern District of New York, *Habeas Corpus Docket, 1891–1906*, ibid.).

35. Pitkin, *Keepers of the Gate*, 27, 35.

36. McKee, *Chinese Exclusion*, 28–36, 67–77; McKee, "The Chinese Must Go!"

37. For a transcript, see *Proceedings of the Chinese Exclusion Convention*. For a copy of the memorial sent to the president and Congress, see American Federation of Labor, *Some Reasons for Exclusion*, 25–30.

38. American Federation of Labor, *Some Reasons for Exclusion*; see also Phelan, "Why the Chinese Should Be Excluded," and Beale, "Why the Chinese Should Be Excluded."

39. Letter from Chinese minister Wu Ting-Fang to Secretary of State, Dec. 10, 1901, in U.S. Congress, Senate, *Exclusion of Chinese Laborers*, 18–19; McKee, *Chinese Exclusion*, 35.

40. "Hordes of Coolies Camped in Hawaii Waiting to Come," *San Francisco Call*, Oct. 24, 1897; see also editorial, *San Francisco Call*, Oct. 5, 1897.

41. Joint Resolution of July 7, 1898, 30 Stat. 750.

42. Act of April 30, 1900, section 101, 31 Stat. 141, 161.

43. Major-General Elwell S. Otis ordered in 1899 that Chinese exclusion be applied in the Philippines, but the issue had yet to be finally determined by Congress (McKee, *Chinese Exclusion*, 35).

44. *Cong. Rec.*, 57th Cong., 1st sess., Senator Miller, 3654–65.

45. See criticism of section by Senator Jacob H. Gallinger, ibid., 3874.

46. Ibid., 4033. See also testimony of James R. Dunn, chief of Chinese Bureau at San Francisco, in U.S. Congress, Senate, Committee on Immigration, *Chinese Exclusion*, pt. 2, p. 321.

47. *Cong. Rec.*, 57th Cong., 1st sess., Senator Gallinger, 3874.

48. Ibid., Senator Gallinger, 3726, 3874–82.

49. Wu Ting-Fang to Secretary of State, Mar. 22, 1902, ibid., 3875.

50. *Cong. Rec.*, 57th Cong., 1st sess., 3875. See also U.S. Congress, Senate, *Exclusion of Chinese Laborers*, 17.

51. McKee, *Chinese Exclusion*, 15–18.

52. Hutcheson, "Why the Chinese Should Be Admitted," 63.

53. McKee, *Chinese Exclusion*, 16–20, 60–61; *Cong. Rec.*, 57th Cong., 1st sess., 3771, 3877.

54. See, for example, Ho Yow (Chinese consul-general at San Francisco), "Chi-

nese Exclusion"; Wu Ting-Fang, "Mutual Helpfulness between China and the United States."

55. Tsai, *China and the Overseas Chinese*, 100.

56. Quoted in McKee, *Chinese Exclusion*, 46.

57. See, for example, his speech to students at the University of Michigan, reprinted in *Truth versus Fiction*, 55–67.

58. Ibid., 20. On Wu Ting-Fang's influence in generating American support, see also Coolidge, *Chinese Immigration*, 241–43.

59. Ibid; see also J. Miller, "The Chinese and the Exclusion Act."

60. *Cong. Rec.*, 57th Cong., 1st sess., 3942.

61. Ibid., 3945.

62. Act of April 29, 1902, 32 Stat. 176, section 1.

63. The law excepted Hawaii from this provision because other laws already applied exclusion in that territory (ibid., section 4).

64. This section of the law responded to complaints that the Bureau of Immigration submitted Chinese coming to fairs and expositions to unreasonably rigorous and lengthy examinations and denied many entry. The bureau continued to make rigorous examinations after the law was passed because it believed many Chinese were entering illegally on the pretext of going to the fair (McKee, *Chinese Exclusion*, 72–74). For the bureau's defense, see U.S. Congress, House, *Facts Concerning the Enforcement of the Chinese-Exclusion Laws*, 36–43.

65. Secretary of the Treasury to Attorney General, June 17, 1903, File 9473/03, DJ Let. Recd.

66. *In re Lee Tan*, No. 12053, *Admiralty Casefiles* (1900).

67. Order of Aug. 21, 1903, in File 9473/03, DJ Let. Recd. Judge Morrow of the circuit court issued a similar rule (U.S. Attorney Woodworth to Attorney General, Aug. 24, 1903, ibid.).

68. Charles Mehan to Attorney General, through the Collector of Customs, June 30, 1903, File 14978, C. Seg. Files.

69. Amsterdam, "Criminal Prosecutions," 884–92. See also Duker, *Constitutional History of Habeas Corpus*, 181–224.

70. Lott to Attorney General, Sept. 23, 1903, File 11547/00, DJ Let. Recd.

71. See, for example, Attorney General to George B. Curtis, Oct. 8, 1903, DJ Let. Recd.

72. Attorney General to U.S. Attorney Woodworth, Dec. 22, 1903, File 19482/03, DJ Let. Recd.

73. *ST-AR* (1897), liii; *ST-AR* (1898), lvi; *CG-AR* (1901), 51–52; *CG-AR* (1904), 137–41.

74. *In re Moy Quong Shing et al.*, 125 F. 641 (1903).

75. U.S. Attorney Curtiss to Attorney General, Oct. 16, 1903, File 11547/00, DJ Let. Recd.

76. *In re Sing Tuck*, 126 F. 386 (1903).

77. *Sing Tuck v. United States*, 128 F. 592 (1904).

78. *Gee Fook Sing*, 49 F. 146 (9th Cir. 1892); *In re Chin Bak Bong*.

79. Petition for Writ of Certiorari to the Circuit Court of Appeals for the Second Circuit, and Brief Thereon, p. 8, *United States v. Sing Tuck*, 194 U.S. 161 (1904).

80. Ibid., 20.

81. *U.S.* v. *Sing Tuck*, 163.

82. Brief for Relators, 4, ibid.

83. *In re Tom Yum*, 64 F. 485, 490 (N.D. Cal. 1894).

84. Brief for Relator, 5–9, *U.S.* v. *Sing Tuck*.

85. Though the commissioner general promulgated these rules in 1903, the collectors had already followed such procedures for several years. For criticism of the Bureau of Immigration's procedures, see accounts of various authors, particularly attorney Max Kohler, in the pamphlet *Truth versus Fiction*. See also *CG-AR* (1904), 136–37, and *CG-AR* (1905), 78–81, for accounts of growing opposition and criticism of the Bureau of Immigration's enforcement of the Chinese exclusion laws.

86. U.S. Attorney George Curtiss to Attorney General, Nov. 16, 1903, File 11547/00, DJ Let. Recd. His letter was evidently forwarded to the secretary of commerce and labor, who replied that the present rules afforded sufficient opportunity for alleged citizens fully to present their cases (Secretary of Commerce and Labor to Attorney General, Dec. 4, 1903, File 9473/03, DJ Let. Recd.).

87. U.S. Department of Commerce and Labor, *Treaty, Laws, and Regulations Governing the Admission of Chinese* (1903).

88. Brief for Relators, 10–16, *United States* v. *Sing Tuck*.

89. Judicial opinion, ibid., 167–68.

90. Ibid., 168–69, 170.

91. Ibid., 171, 173, 178.

92. Curtiss to Attorney General, Apr. 29, 1904, File 11547/00, DJ Let. Recd.

93. U.S. Attorney Woodworth to Attorney General, May 3, 1904, acknowledging order of attorney general, DJ Let. Recd.

94. McKee, *Chinese Exclusion*, 77–86. The Chinese government did offer to negotiate a new treaty, but China and the United States were unable to agree upon the terms. China demanded that exclusion be repealed in the territories and that exempt Chinese entering and living in the United States be afforded better protection. The Department of Commerce and Labor opposed such demands, wanting instead a treaty that allowed more restrictive regulations and the registration of nonlaborers (ibid., 92–102).

95. Ibid., 86–87.

96. *Cong. Rec.*, 58th Cong., 2d sess., 5031–38, 5413–16.

97. McKee, *Chinese Exclusion*, 90–91.

98. There was little debate on the section so the reason for its failure is unclear. Senator Platt of Connecticut claimed that the bill was unconstitutional (*Cong. Rec.*, 58th Cong., 2d sess., 5417). It was one of several sections that opponents of the bill advocated removing for being overly harsh.

99. *United States* v. *Sing Tuck*, 168.

100. Transcript of hearing before Heacock, p. 21, in *In re Ju Toy, Admiralty Casefiles*, No. 13397 (1905).

101. Motion to Advance, p. 5, *United States* v. *Ju Toy*, 198 U.S. 253 (1905).

102. Brief for the United States, 27, ibid.

103. Ibid., 21.

104. Supplemental Brief for Appellee, 5, ibid.

105. Notes from Felix Frankfurter's Seminar in Administrative Law, Harvard Law School, 1932, Frankfurter Papers, Box 188, Folder 2.

106. *United States* v. *Ju Toy*, 263.

107. Ibid., 262.

108. Ibid., 263.

109. Ibid.; *Murray's Lessee* v. *Hoboken Land & Improvement Co.*, 18 How. 272 (1855).

110. *United States* v. *Ju Toy*, 269.

111. Ibid., 268, 273; Brewer here drew upon *Hagar* v. *Reclamation District*, 111 U.S. 701, 708.

112. *United States* v. *Ju Toy*, 268, 273, 279–80.

113. Dickinson, *Administrative Justice*, 293.

114. Freund, *Administrative Powers*, 292; Drake, "The Chinaman before the Supreme Court," 266.

115. Freund, *Administrative Powers*, 292.

116. Drake, "The Chinaman before the Supreme Court," 266–67.

117. *CG-AR* (1910), 133.

118. Ibid.

119. U.S. Congress, House, *Facts Concerning the Enforcement of the Chinese-Exclusion Laws*, 8.

120. Immigration Act of 1917, 39 Stat. 874, section 19.

121. Act of March 3, 1901, 31 Stat. 1093; for correspondence regarding problem with deportations, see File 11547/00, DJ Let. Recd.

122. For a good summary of the issues involved in the debate, see A. Warner Parker, "Memorandum in re Proposition to Arrest and Deport, under the Provisions of the Immigration Act, Chinese Aliens Who Enter Surreptitiously," July 7, 1908, File 52541/27, INS Subj. Corres.

123. *Wong You* v. *United States*, 223 U.S. 67 (1912); *U.S.* v. *Woo Jan*, 245 U.S. 552.

124. *CG-AR* (1913), 25.

INTRODUCTION TO PART II

1. Bowman, "American Administrative Tribunals," 616.

CHAPTER FIVE

1. On growth of nativism, see, generally, Higham, *Strangers in the Land*; Kraut, *Huddled Masses*, 148–78. The term "aliens in our midst" was used frequently by nativists and agency officials. See, for example, *CG-AR* (1919), 291.

2. The state of the economy did not always spark nativist policies, however. The immigration acts of 1882 and 1891, for example, were not passed in depression years.

3. Higham, *Strangers in the Land*, 66–96. Employers often encouraged the divisions and hostilities between American workers and immigrants as a way to make unionization more difficult (ibid., 114–15). See also Mink, *Old Labor and New Immigrants*; Asher, "Union Nativism and the Immigrant Response."

4. Higham, *Strangers in the Land*, 301.

5. Wiebe, *Search for Order*, 12, 42.

6. On Italians and organized crime, see Nelli, *Business of Crime*; for the association of prostitution with immigration, see Rosen, *Lost Sisterhood*, 44, 62, 123; on the exaggerated fear of foreign radicals, see Preston, *Aliens and Dissenters*, 21–34.

7. Irish Catholics had been a target of nativists since the 1840s. See Leonard and Parmet, *American Nativism*. For anti-Semitism in America, see Higham, *Send These to Me*, 95–174.

8. See, for example, Grant, *Passing of the Great Race*.

9. Higham, *Strangers in the Land*, 147; Gossett, *Race*, 287–309; Altschuler, *Race, Ethnicity and Class*.

10. *CG-AR* (1907), 5.

11. *CG-AR* (1909), 111–12.

12. Kevles, *In the Name of Eugenics*.

13. *CG-AR* (1910), 5.

14. Limerick, *Legacy of Conquest*, 260; see also Pomeroy, *Pacific Slope*, 262–89, and R. White, "Race Relations in the American West."

15. Limerick, *Legacy of Conquest*, 269.

16. Rowell, "Chinese and Japanese Immigrants," 230.

17. "Shut the Gate to the Hindoo Invasion," *San Francisco Examiner*, June 6, 1910.

18. Matthews, "White Community and 'Yellow Peril.'"

19. Rowell, "Chinese and Japanese Immigrants," 224.

20. Daniels, *Asian America*, 100–154; Daniels, *Politics of Prejudice*, 1–9; Takaki, *Strangers from a Different Shore*, 132–229.

21. Jensen, *Passage from India*, 1–23; Misrow, *East Indian Immigration*.

22. Jensen, *Passage from India*, 24–36.

23. *CG-AR* (1924), Table XIV, 113–14.

24. North recalled his early apprehension about Japanese immigration in an article, "Chinese and Japanese Immigration to the Pacific Coast."

25. Irish, "Reasons for Encouraging Japanese Immigration," 296, 295. Irish certainly had his own reasons for championing Japanese immigration. Not only was he a landowner and farmer, but he was also the president of the Delta Association of California, an organization of farmers who relied on Japanese as farmworkers and tenants. See U.S. Congress, House, Committee on Immigration and Naturalization, *Japanese Immigration*. See also Gowen, "Problem of Oriental Immigration," 335.

26. Coryn, "Japanese Problem," 263–64.

27. On Japanese in agriculture, see Daniels, *Asian America*, 107–9, 133–37.

28. Phelan, "The Japanese Evil in California," 323–24.

29. Macfarlane, "Japan in California."

30. Daniels, *Politics of Prejudice*, 69–77.

31. "Advance Guard of Hindu Horde Has Arrived," *San Francisco Examiner*, Aug. 7, 1910.

32. "The Watchdog States," *San Francisco Post*, May 24, 1910; "Queer Argument for the Hindu," *San Francisco Call*, Aug. 1, 1910.

33. Burnett, "Misunderstanding of Eastern and Western States Regarding Ori-

ental Immigration," 258. Though most Indian immigrants were Sikhs, not Hindus, Americans invariably referred to them as Hindus. The argument that the immigrants were "caste-bound" revealed Americans' ignorance about the Indians, as Sikhs rejected the caste system (Jensen, *Passage from India*, 8, 24).

34. "Shut the Gates to the Hindu Invasion," *San Francisco Examiner*, June 16, 1910; see also "The Watchdog States," *San Francisco Post*, May 24, 1910.

35. On anti-Japanese agitation, see Daniels, *Politics of Prejudice*, 31–64, 79–91; on the campaign against Asian Indians, see Jensen, *Passage from India*, 42–56, 101–20.

36. For details on the events leading to the Gentlemen's Agreement, see Daniels, *Politics of Prejudice*, 31–45.

37. This event is described in greater depth in Chapter 7.

38. *CG-AR* (1913), 21–22; Daniels, *Politics of Prejudice*, 44–45; California, State Board of Control, *California and the Oriental*; for works on Japanese immigrant women, see Ichioka, "*Amerika Nadeshiko*"; Glenn, *Issei, Nissei, War Bride*.

39. The San Francisco commissioner of immigration reported to the commissioner general of immigration in 1920 that there was "universal sentiment" in California for the exclusion of Japanese (*CG-AR* [1920], 364).

40. "Stop the Hindoo Immigration," *Oakland Tribune*, Oct. 15, 1910.

41. Macarthur, "Opposition to Oriental Immigration," 246, 242.

42. U.S. Congress, Select Committee on Immigration and Naturalization, *Chinese Immigration*, 439.

43. In 1920, California was the fourth most popular destination of immigrants (*CG-AR* [1920], 43). For the history of Italian immigration in California, see Cinel, *From Italy to San Francisco*. On Portuguese immigration, see Williams, *And Still They Come*.

44. Higham, *Strangers in the Land*, 168.

45. *Santa Barbara Star*, Jan. 22, 1910.

46. Higham, *Strangers in the Land*, 172.

47. *Fresno Republican*, Apr. 28, 1900, quoted in Daniels, *Asian America*, 117.

48. Higham, *Strangers in the Land*, 165–66; Saxton, *Indispensable Enemy*, 273–78.

49. Cardoso, *Mexican Emigration*, 22.

50. Ibid., 20, 27–34, 120–32. See also Acuña, *Occupied America*, 123–35.

51. Higham, *Send These to Me*, 25, 32, 40, 48–49, 52.

52. The pro-immigrant newspapers in the Hearst press detailed the trials and tribulations of new immigrants (Higham, *Strangers in the Land*, 127).

53. Link and McCormick, *Progressivism*, 72–79, 99–104. For different interpretations of settlement workers, see A. Davis, *Spearheads of Reform*, and Lissak, *Pluralism and Progressives*.

54. See Chapter 1 for state and federal immigration legislation before 1891.

55. For enforcement of that provision, see P. Evans, " 'Likely to Become a Public Charge.' "

56. Hutchinson, *Legislative History*, 414–19.

57. *CG-AR* (1914), 7; Kraut, *Silent Travelers*.

58. Act of March 3, 1875, 18 Stat. 477. An exception was made for aliens convicted of political crimes.

59. Immigration Act of 1891, 26 Stat. 1084.

60. *CG-AR* (1909), 116.

61. Immigration Act of 1907, 34 Stat. 898.

62. Immigration Act of 1903, 32 Stat. 1203, section 2.

63. Preston, *Aliens and Dissenters*, 11–34.

64. The deportation time limit was extended to two years in the act of 1903, 32 Stat. 1203; to three years in the act of 1907, 34 Stat. 898; to five years in the act of 1917, 39 Stat. 874.

65. *CG-AR* (1909), 6.

66. Bouve, *Treatise*, 440.

67. On assimilation, see Higham, *Send These to Me*, 175–97; M. Gordon, *Assimilation in America*.

68. E. Evans, "Naturalizing and Nationalizing Alien," 162.

69. *CG-AR* (1914), 4. Approximately half were rejected on the grounds that they were likely to become public charges.

70. *CG-AR* (1924), 12.

71. Dubofsky, *We Shall Be All*, 376–422; Peterson and Fite, *Opponents of War*; Higham, *Strangers in the Land*, 194–222.

72. Higham, *Strangers in the Land*, 202–3.

73. Immigration Act of 1917, 39 Stat. 874; Jensen, *Passage from India*, 139–62.

74. Immigration Act of 1917, section 3.

75. Murray, *Red Scare*; Preston, *Aliens and Dissenters*; Coben, *A. Mitchell Palmer*.

76. Higham, *Strangers in the Land*, 222–27; Kennedy, *Over Here*, 258–84, 287–95.

77. On the role of Palmer, see Coben, *A. Mitchell Palmer*, 196–245.

78. Murray, *Red Scare*, 211, 210–22.

79. For Post's account of the raids, see *Deportations Delirium*. See Chapter 8 for a more in-depth discussion of the raids.

80. Murray, *Red Scare*, 239–62.

81. Higham, *Strangers in the Land*, 267.

82. *CG-AR* (1919), 62–63.

83. *CG-AR* (1921), 16.

84. Quota Act of 1921, 42 Stat. 5, section 2.

85. *CG-AR* (1923), 10.

86. Immigration Act of 1924, 43 Stat. 153; Higham, *Strangers in the Land*, 308–24.

87. Filipinos were the only Asians unaffected by the act of 1924. As noncitizen U.S. nationals (by virtue of their colonial status), Filipinos were exempt from the law. Their immigration to the United States became restricted in 1934. See Hing, *Making and Remaking Asian America*, 30–36.

88. *Ozawa v. United States*, 260 U.S. 178 (1922).

89. Parker, "The Ineligible to Citizenship Provisions," 24–25; Daniels, *Politics of Prejudice*, 92–105. The law exempted government officials, returning domiciled residents, teachers, and students. For a study of the effects of the law on Japanese immigration, see McKenzie, *Oriental Exclusion*.

90. Of course, the particular details of administrative proceedings differed in the Chinese cases because of the unique provisions of the exclusion laws. But the general character of the Bureau of Immigration's proceedings in Chinese and non-Chinese immigration cases was the same.

91. For analyses of these cases, see Chapters 1 and 2.

92. *CG-AR* (1915), 43.

93. Van Vleck, *Administrative Control*, 241.

94. Ibid., 224.

95. *Fong Yue Ting v. United States*, 149 U.S. 698, 711 (1893).

96. Van Vleck, *Administrative Control*, 83–148. For an in-depth description of deportation procedures, see Clark, *Deportation of Aliens*, 323–482.

97. Quoted in Pitkin, *Keepers of the Gate*, 23–24.

98. Preston, *Aliens and Dissenters*, 221.

99. Ibid., 18–20. For a similar argument, see Claghorn, *Immigrant's Day in Court*, 466.

100. Preston, *Aliens and Dissenters*, 18, 19.

101. For a collection of Kohler's writings on immigration law, see Kohler, *Immigration and Aliens*.

102. *Cong. Rec.*, 66th Cong., 2d sess., Appendix, quoted in Preston, *Aliens and Dissenters*, 227.

103. Preston, *Aliens and Dissenters*, 229–37.

CHAPTER SIX

1. *CG-AR* (1905), 78–81.

2. Higham, *Strangers in the Land*, 123.

3. Ibid., 111.

4. This narrative is reconstructed from the Transcript of Record in *United States ex. rel. Turner v. Williams*, 194 U.S. 279 (1904).

5. Act of March 3, 1893, sec. 5, 27 Stat. 569.

6. William Williams, "The Relations between Boards of Special Inquiry and Their Superiors," June 1913, Box 6, folder 1, Williams Papers.

7. Exhibit A, "Extracts from Speech Delivered by John Turner," in Transcript of Record, 10, *Turner v. Williams*.

8. "Minutes of a Board of Special Inquiry Convened at U.S. Immigrant Station, Ellis Island, October 24, 1903, at Noon," 6–7, 10–11, ibid.

9. Ibid., 8.

10. "Mass Meeting against Law Holding Turner," *New York Times*, Dec. 4, 1903, 1:1.

11. "Fight Turner Deportation," *New York Times*, Jan. 15, 1904, 3:3. For Samuel Gompers's support of Turner, see Gompers to George W. Perkins, Aug. 23, [1896], in Kaufman, Albert, and Palladino, *Gompers Papers*, 4:216–17; Affidavit of Samuel Gompers in support of motion to admit to bail, *Turner v. Williams*.

12. Masters, *Across Spoon River*, 275. Masters is better known for his literary work such as *Spoon River*.

13. Brief and Argument of Appellant, 96, *Turner v. Williams*.

14. Act of March 3, 1903, section 2.

15. See statements of Louis F. Post and Bolton Hall in Motion of Appellant to be Admitted to Bail, 6, 4, *Turner v. Williams*.

16. "Bail for John Turner," *New York Times*, Mar. 4, 1904, 14:3.

17. On rejection of due process arguments, see *Turner* v. *Williams*, 289–91; on interpretation of "anarchist," see 292–94.

18. Ogg, "New Plan for Immigrant Inspection," 33–36; William Williams, "Annual Report," Sept. 15, 1904, pp. 3–4, box 5, folder 2, Williams Papers.

19. Sargent, "Need for Closer Inspection." Before becoming commissioner general of immigration, Sargent served as grand master of the Brotherhood of Locomotive Firemen (*Dictionary of American Biography*, 47:358). Williams, "Annual Report," 1903, 14, box 5, Folder 1, Williams Papers.

20. *CG-AR* (1906), 100, 104; William Williams, "Annual Report," Oct. 10, 1911, 7, box 5, folder 19, Williams Papers.

21. La Guardia, *Making of an Insurgent*, 63–64.

22. Williams to Frank Sargent, Dec. 3, 1904, box 1, folder 12, Williams Papers.

23. In 1905, for example, the Ellis Island immigration station admitted 788,219 immigrants while San Francisco admitted 6,377 (*CG-AR* [1905], 4).

24. Special Immigration Inspector to Acting Commissioner General of Immigration, Oct. 15, 1909, File 52270/21, INS Subj. Corres.

25. John Sawyer, Diary, Feb. 15, 1917.

26. The procedures at Ellis Island are documented in Sayles, "Keepers of the Gate"; "Rules for the United States Immigrant Station at Ellis Island" (issued October 1910; revised January 1913), in box 6, folder 2, Williams Papers.

27. Sayles, "Keepers of the Gate," 919–20; E. H. Mullan, "Mental Examination of Immigrants, Administration and Line Inspection at Ellis Island," *U.S. Public Health Reports*, report 398, May 18, 1917, in G. Abbott, *Immigration*, 244–51. Though Sayles's and Mullan's descriptions of the medical inspection were written ten years apart, the procedures appear to be substantially the same.

28. Act of March 3, 1903, 32 Stat. 1203, section 2.

29. Williams, "Annual Report," Sept. 15, 1904, box 5, folder 2, Williams Papers.

30. This rule was rescinded by Williams's successor, Robert Watchorn, in 1905 but was reinstituted when Williams again became commissioner at Ellis Island in 1909 (Pitkin, *Keepers of the Gate*, 56–57).

31. La Guardia, *Making of an Insurgent*, 66.

32. Rules for the Registry Division, box 6, folder 2, Williams Papers.

33. Sayles, "Keepers of the Gate," 917.

34. 32 Stat. 1203, sec. 24.

35. See letter from Williams to E. I. Hajos, manager of the Home of the Hungarian Relief Society, Dec. 21, 1904, in which Williams refers "to a late case before the Board of Special Inquiry, in which your representative appeared on behalf of two aliens" (box 1, folder 12, Williams Papers).

36. "Testimony of Mr. Edward B. Holman," in U.S. Industrial Commission, *Reports of the Industrial Commission on Immigration*, 134. See also Williams to Sargent, Dec. 3, 1904, box 1, folder 12, Williams Papers.

37. Rules for Special Inquiry Division, box 6, folder 2, Williams Papers.

38. Williams, "The Relations between Boards of Special Inquiry and Their Superiors," June 1913, box 6, folder 1, ibid.

39. In that case, the board's decision was final (32 Stat. 1203, sec. 10).

40. Ibid., sec. 25.

41. U.S. Department of Commerce and Labor, *Immigration Laws and Regulations*, Aug. 26, 1903, rule 9.

42. The Immigration Act of 1903 did not explicitly allow aliens the right to an attorney on appeal. But rule 9 of the immigration regulations established by the Department of Commerce and Labor suggests that attorneys were allowed to appeal cases as early as 1903; the rule allows additional time "to the friends or counsel of an appealing alien to prevent a miscarriage of justice" (U.S. Department of Commerce and Labor, *Immigration Laws and Regulations*, Aug. 26, 1903).

43. U.S. Department of Commerce and Labor, *Treaty, Laws, and Regulations Governing the Admission of Chinese* (1903), rule 7.

44. Ibid., rule 21.

45. Ibid., rule 7.

46. Miner, "American Barbarism and Chinese Hospitality"; Fu Chi Hao, "My Reception in America"; McKee, *Chinese Exclusion*, 69–71.

47. See, for example, File 9781/188, Chinese Exclusion Cases, which shows the immigration service's tracking of a family from the entry of the grandfather as a native-born in 1900, to his children, and to his grandchildren in 1959 in an attempt to prove the fraudulent status of the whole family.

48. U.S. Department of Commerce and Labor, *Treaty, Laws, and Regulations Governing the Admission of Chinese* (1903), rule 28.

49. *CG-AR* (1906), 566.

50. Wong Gan, File 10036/6002, Chinese Exclusion Cases.

51. Dunn to Chinese Inspector in Charge, Feb. 3, 1905, case of Wong Gan.

52. North to Chinese Inspector in Charge, Feb. 6, 1905, ibid.

53. Dunn to Charles Mehan, Chinese Inspector in Charge, Feb. 17, 1905, ibid.

54. The certificate also listed the sex as "male," but because the occupation given was "housekeeper," Dunn was willing to concede that a mistake had been made as to the sex.

55. North to Chinese Inspector in Charge, Feb. 18, 1905; Assistant Secretary Murray to Commissioner of Immigration, Mar. 8, 1905, case of Wong Gan.

56. U.S. Department of Commerce and Labor, *Treaty, Laws, and Regulations Governing the Admission of Chinese* (1903), rule 23.

57. U.S. Congress, House, *Facts Concerning the Enforcement of the Chinese-Exclusion Laws*, 128–29.

58. Foster, "Chinese Boycott," 122–23.

59. U.S. Congress, House, *Facts Concerning the Enforcement of Chinese-Exclusion*, 128–29. There has been some confusion in historical accounts both as to the date of the raid and the number of Chinese arrested. John Foster gave the date as October 11, 1902, but it is clear from other sources, especially the official documents, that the correct date is 1903. Foster also implied in his article that only five Chinese were actually deported. The secretary of commerce and labor in his report to Congress stated that forty-five were deported, and I have chosen to accept the official's account.

60. Foster, "Chinese Boycott," 123.

61. Adamic, *Laughing in the Jungle*, 43–45.

62. Mei, Yip, and Leong, "*Bitter Society*," 50–51.

63. Pitkin, *Keepers of the Gate*, 48.

64. "Recommendations to U.S. Immigration Commission," in Kohler, *Immigration and Aliens*, 2.

65. Kohler, "Jewish Immigrants," 166–67, 169.

66. Chew, *Treatment of the Exempt Classes*, 8.

67. Mei, Yip, and Leong, "*Bitter Society*," 44–45.

68. For a typical list of grievances, see "Memorial to His Excellency the President of the United States of America," 1911, File 52961/24-E, INS Subj. Corres.

69. Chew, *Treatment of the Exempt Classes*.

70. 24 *Op. Atty. Genl.* 706 (June 24, 1903); U.S. Department of Commerce and Labor, *Treaty, Laws, and Regulations Governing the Admission of Chinese* (1903), rule 28. For Chinese protest, see unsigned complaint, Jan. 8, 1910, File 52961/24-B, INS Subj. Corres.

71. A. W. Parker, "Addendum to Memorandum in re administrative advisability and legal possibility of arresting *under the provisions of the immigration law* Chinese who cross the land boundaries in a surreptitious manner," July 21, 1910, File 52541/27-A, INS Subj. Corres. For more discussion of the plan, see Chapter 4.

72. Chinese Consolidated Benevolent Association to the President, Feb. 9, 1909, File 52423/40, INS Subj. Corres.

73. "Recommendations to U.S. Immigration Commission," in Kohler, *Immigration and Aliens*, 3.

74. Unsigned complaint, Jan. 8, 1910, File 52961/24-B, INS Subj. Corres.

75. Chinese Chamber of Commerce of San Francisco to Secretary of Labor, Mar. 22, 1927, quoted in McKenzie, *Oriental Exclusion*, 43.

76. The U.S. Immigration Commission in 1911 referred to a reversal rate of nearly 50 percent as proof of the insufficiency of the boards ("Brief Statement," from *Reports of the U.S. Immigration Commission*, vol. 1, in G. Abbott, *Immigration*, 207). Max Kohler argued that reversals in Jewish cases were even higher, saying that in November 1910, two-thirds of the appeals brought by the Hebrew Sheltering and Immigrant Aid Society were sustained ("Jewish Immigrants," 169).

77. Kohler, "Jewish Immigrants," 169.

78. *Volksblatt* (Cincinnati), n.d., translation of article in box 6, folder 9, Williams Papers.

79. Williams, "Annual Report," June 30, 1913, box 5, folder 4, Williams Papers.

80. Lombardi, *Labor's Voice*, 125–29.

81. Higham, *Strangers in the Land*, 123–30, 186–88.

82. See, for example, Daniels, "The Japanese," 41–45; Rischin, *Promised City*, 95–111; Glazer, "The Jews"; Sachar, *History of the Jews in America*, 116–39, 150–58.

83. For criticism of the societies' activist role, see Williams to E. I. Hajos, Manager, Home of the Hungarian Relief Society, Dec. 21, 1904, box 1, folder 12, Williams Papers.

84. Jenks and Lauck, *Immigration Problem*, 250.

85. "Testimony of Mr. Simon Wolf," Mar. 9, 1901, in U.S. Industrial Commission, *Reports on the Industrial Commission on Immigration*, 245–52.

86. "Louis Marshall—70th Birthday Tribute," in Kohler, *Immigration and Aliens*, 430–37; *Dictionary of American Biography*, 12:326; *National Cyclopedia of American Biog-*

raphy, 26:115; Handlin, "American Jewish Committee"; Auerbach, *Rabbis and Lawyers*, 94–99, 109–22.

87. Kohler, *Immigration and Aliens*, vii–ix.

88. Handlin, "American Jewish Committee," 6.

89. "Address of Hon. Charles Nagel," in Kohler, *Immigration and Aliens*, 193–94.

90. "Simon Wolf—In Memoriam," ibid., 425.

91. See, for example, the letter from the assistant U.S. attorney for the Southern District to Max Kohler, Nov. 4, 1911, in box 2, folder 15, Williams Papers, which acknowledges (and rejects) Kohler's charges of illegal conduct by immigration authorities at Ellis Island. Members of Jewish organizations were not always critical of the Bureau of Immigration and Naturalization. In 1912, one of the leaders of B'nai B'rith defended Commissioner Williams, for example, against criticisms made by Kohler and others (Pitkin, *Keepers of the Gate*, 63).

92. On Kohler's background, see Kohler, *Immigration and Aliens*, vii–viii. For his views on Chinese exclusion, see Kohler, "The Administration of Our Chinese Immigration Laws," ibid., 251–74, and "Un-American Character of Race Legislation."

93. Wittke, *German-Language Press*, 197–210.

94. See, for example, "Ask Immigration Reforms," *New York Times*, Jan. 5, 1911. Commissioner Williams kept a file of articles from foreign-language newspapers criticizing him. See box 6, folders 7–10, Williams Papers. See also Cizmic, "Experiences of South Slav Immigrants on Ellis Island."

95. Pitkin, *Keepers of the Gate*, 48–55; Higham, *Strangers in the Land*, 188.

96. Steiner, *From Alien to Citizen*, 322–23.

97. Steiner, *On the Trail of the Immigrant*, 72.

98. Ibid., 65–66.

99. Ibid., 69–70.

100. Steiner addresses his book explicitly to the "lady of the first cabin" (ibid., 9).

101. Ibid., 77.

102. Safford, *Immigration Problems*, 260–61.

103. Pitkin, *Keepers of the Gate*, 36.

104. Sayles, "Keepers of the Gate," 913.

105. *United States v. Sing Tuck*, 194 U.S. 161, 171, 177–79 (1904); *United States v. Ju Toy*, 198 U.S. 253, 268 (1905).

106. Currier, "Government by Executive Rulings," 107; Bowman, "American Administrative Tribunals," 616. See also Dickinson, "Administrative Law." On Brewer, see Fiss, "David J. Brewer."

107. Higham, *Strangers in the Land*, 126.

108. Safford, *Immigration Problems*, 88.

109. K'ang Yu-wei to Theodore Roosevelt, Jan. 30, 1906, reprinted in Tsai, *China and the Overseas Chinese*, 149.

110. Wong Kai Kah, "A Menace to America's Oriental Trade," 421.

111. The Chinese draft of the treaty also asserted a right of Chinese to free transit across the United States and provided exempt Chinese with certificates while in the United States to protect them from harassment (McKee, *Chinese Exclusion*, 96).

112. For the importance of nationalism in sparking the boycott, see Iriye, *Across*

the Pacific, 94; Tsai, "Reaction to Exclusion," 95–110; Fu Chi Hao, "My Reception in America," 770–73.

113. The boycott was to begin in July, allowing the United States time to ameliorate its exclusion policy (McKee, "Chinese Boycott of 1905–1906 Reconsidered," 178).

114. Ibid., 173–74. See also U.S. Congress, House, *Facts Concerning Enforcement of the Chinese-Exclusion Laws*, 151–54.

115. For example, Chinese in America who favored revolution in China tended to push for the repeal of the exclusion laws and free admission of all Chinese into the United States (Ma, "Chinatown Organizations," 158).

116. Boycotters also demanded that Chinese be granted the same privilege of transit across the United States when traveling to another destination as extended to non-Chinese (K'ang to Roosevelt, in Tsai, *China and the Overseas Chinese*, 150; "China and America," 952).

117. "The Chinese Boycott," *New York Times*, May 16, 1905. For a critique of the Bureau of Immigration by the former secretary of state, see Foster, "Chinese Boycott."

118. Roosevelt to George Bruce Cortelyou, Jan. 25, 1904, in Morison, ed., *Letters of Theodore Roosevelt*, 3:709–10; Roosevelt to Leslie Mortier Shaw, Mar. 27, 1902, ibid., 249.

119. Roosevelt to Secretary of Commerce and Labor Victor Howard Metcalf, June 16, 1905, ibid., 9:1235. For Metcalf's instructions to the Bureau of Immigration, see Department of Commerce and Labor, "Enforcement of the Chinese Exclusion Laws—General Instructions," June 24, 1905, Department Circular 81.

120. A bill to that effect never made it out of committee in the House of Representatives (McKee, *Chinese Exclusion*, 172–82). On Roosevelt's proposal, see ibid., 141.

121. Roosevelt to Acting Secretary of State Herbert Henry Davis Peirce, June 24, 1905, in Morison, ed., *Letters of Theodore Roosevelt*, 4:1251–52. For the development of Roosevelt's thinking on Chinese exclusion, see McKee, *Chinese Exclusion*, 126–45, 185–98.

122. For a report on the boycott by bureau inspector Harold Boyce, see File 53059/8, INS Subj. Corres.

123. *CG-AR* (1905), 81.

124. *CG-AR* (1906), 76, 84–85; U.S. Congress, House, *Facts Concerning the Enforcement of Chinese-Exclusion Laws*, 55.

125. U.S. Congress, House, *Facts Concerning the Enforcement of Chinese-Exclusion Laws*, 27–30.

126. Straus, "Spirit and Letter of Exclusion," 484–85.

127. U.S. Department of Commerce and Labor, *Treaty, Laws, and Regulations Governing the Admission of Chinese* (1907), rule 31a.

128. Acting Commissioner General of Immigration F. H. Larned to Commissioner of Immigration, San Francisco, Sept. 9, 1908, File 55079/203, INS Subj. Corres.

129. McKee, *Chinese Exclusion*, 209; Tsai, *China and the Overseas Chinese*, 115–21.

130. U.S. Congress, House, *Facts Concerning the Enforcement of Chinese-Exclusion Laws*, 29–30.

131. For an example of a handbill posted in Chinatown by the Six Companies protesting immigration procedures, see Commissioner North to Commissioner General of Immigration, Feb. 4, 1910, 52961/24, INS Subj. Corres.

132. See, for example, the battle over the act of 1902 in Chapter 4.

133. Straus, "Spirit and Letter of Exclusion," 484–85.

134. On agitation for new boycotts, see John Endicott Gardner to Commissioner North, Mar. 19, 1907, 14983/1, INS Subj. Corres.; Commissioner North to Commissioner General of Immigration, Nov. 12, 1907, 14983/4c, ibid.

135. The Chamber of Commerce of San Francisco to the Secretary of Commerce and Labor, July 13, 1910, File 52961/24-B, INS Subj. Corres.; see also Robert Dollar, The Robert Dollar Company, to L. C. Steward, Acting Commissioner of Immigration at San Francisco, Jan. 24, 1911, ibid.; Chamber of Commerce of San Francisco to the President of the United States, May 20, 1911, File 52961/24-C, ibid.; San Francisco Chamber of Commerce to the Secretary of Commerce and Labor, Dec. 20, 1912, File 52961/24-E, ibid.

136. Hoexter, *From Canton to California*, 216, 244–46.

137. Coolidge, *Chinese Immigration*, 312–13.

138. The publishers, upon complaints of her portrayal of immigration officials, temporarily withdrew the book from circulation. See "America and Oriental Labour," *China Mail* (Hong Kong), Feb. 16, 1910, clipping in File 52600/48, INS Subj. Corres.; "Memorandum in re book 'Chinese Immigration' by Mrs. Mary Roberts Coolidge, Berkeley, California," ibid.; editorial, *Nation* 89 (Dec. 23, 1909): 626.

139. Librarian of Congress to Acting Commissioner General of Immigration, Oct. 27, 1909, File 52600/48, INS Subj. Corres.

140. "Our Treatment of the Chinese," *Nation* 89 (Dec. 9, 1909): 574; "Fouling Their Nests," *Hong Kong Telegraph*, Feb. 15, 1910, clipping in File 52600/48, INS Subj. Corres.; "America and Oriental Labour," *China Mail*, Feb. 16, 1910, ibid.

141. Sui Sin Far was the pseudonym of Edith Eaton (1867–1914), the daughter of an English man and a Chinese woman who came to Canada and the United States with her family as a young child. For an autobiographical sketch, see Sui Sin Far, "Leaves from the Mental Portfolio of an Eurasian."

142. Sui Sin Far, "In the Land of the Free," 505.

143. Ibid., 508.

144. See Tables 8 and 9 in Chapter 7.

145. *CG-AR* (1905), 86.

146. Supplemental Brief for Appellee, *United States v. Ju Toy*, 198 U.S. 253 (1905).

147. See Chapter 3.

148. *Nishimura Ekiu v. United States*, 142 U.S. 651, 659–60 (1892).

149. *Fong Yue Ting v. United States*, 149 U.S. 698, 730 (1893).

150. Act of May 5, 1892, 27 Stat. 25.

151. *Wong Wing v. United States*, 163 U.S. 228 (1896), 237.

152. *Turner v. Williams*, 292.

153. *United States v. Ju Toy*, 198 U.S. 253 (1905).

154. Brief of Appellant, 5, *Japanese Immigrant Case* (Yamataya v. Fisher), 189 U.S. 86 (1903).

155. Ibid., 16. On the challenge to the act's constitutionality, see 10–16.

156. Brief for the United States, 3, ibid.

157. Ibid., 11–12.

158. Ibid., 10, 12.

159. *Japanese Immigrant Case*, 100–101.

160. The Court had elaborated a similar "fundamental principles" definition of due process in *Hurtado* v. *California*, 110 U.S. 516, 535–37 (1884), a challenge to a state criminal procedure, and would do so again in *Twining* v. *New Jersey* in 1908, 211 U.S. 73, 106.

161. *Japanese Immigrant Case*, 102.

162. Assistant Attorney General to Woodworth, Nov. 29, 1904, File 19482/03, DJ Let. Recd.

163. *United States* v. *Ju Toy*, 260–61.

164. W. W. Morrow to John W. Griggs, U.S. Attorney General, Aug. 10, 1898, and Seymour Thompson to Attorney General, Dec. 10, 1900, in "Woodworth, M. B.," Appointment Files of Judges, U.S. Attorneys, and Marshals, 1897–1901, Records of the Department of Justice, RG 60, National Archives.

165. The evidence of Stidger's work as a Chinese inspector rests on a warrant of arrest for deportation in *United States* v. *Ah See*, No. 3240, *Commissioner Casefiles*, in 1896, in which Stidger appears as the complaining officer. After being admitted to the bar in 1898, Stidger represented the Chinese Six Companies for the "term ending in 1909" and was the attorney for the Chinese Chamber of Commerce, the Chinese Merchants Association, and the Chinese Republic Association (Bates, ed., *History of the Bench and Bar of California*, 519). He also allegedly acted as a legal adviser to Sun Yat-sen and, in that capacity, drafted the Republic of China's Declaration of Independence. See Stidger's obituary in *San Francisco Chronicle*, Sept. 5, 1959.

166. See, for example, *In re Gin Yoke*, Case no. 13516, *Admiralty Casefiles* (1906); *In re Chew Duck*, Case no. 14069, ibid.; *In re Lee Wah*, Case no. 13514, ibid.

167. The facts surrounding Chin Yow's case are somewhat confusing because his name appears to have been spelled in a variety of ways in court and administrative records and the specific information regarding the date of his arrival in the United States and his occupation conflict in the records. The court record lists him as "Chin Yow," but records in the Bureau of Immigration refer to a "Chan You." The bureau, in its investigation, listed his date of arrival as August 2, 1905, and his occupation as a vegetable peddler, while the habeas corpus petition stated that he arrived in the United States on July 2, 1905, and worked for the Sawyer Tanning Company before leaving for a visit to China (Commissioner General Sargent, Memorandum on appeal of Chan You, Aug. 24, 1905, in File 19482/03, DJ Let. Recd.).

168. Brief of the Appellant, 6, *Chin Yow* v. *United States*, 208 U.S. 8 (1908).

169. A very similar argument would be accepted by the Court in *Powell* v. *Alabama* in 1932 to establish a right to an attorney in criminal proceedings (Howard, *Road from Runnymede*, 359).

170. Brief of the Appellant, 14–17, *Chin Yow* v. *United States*.

171. U.S. Attorney, San Francisco, to Attorney General, June 11, 1906, File 19482/03, DJ Let. Recd.

172. Brief for the United States, 6–7, *Chin Yow* v. *United States*.

173. *Chin Yow* v. *United States*, 11–12.

174. Ibid., 11–13.

175. "Pacific Mail Dock," *Hong Kong Telegraph*, Oct. 2, 1909, clipping in File 52270/2, box 92, INS Subj. Corres.

176. Powell, "Judicial Review," 363–65.

177. Ibid., 363–64.

178. U.S. Congress, *Operation of Present Immigration Law*, 3.

179. Pitkin, *Keepers of the Gate*, 52–53.

CHAPTER SEVEN

1. Nelson, *Fourteenth Amendment*, 199; Corwin, "Doctrine of Due Process" and "The Supreme Court and the Fourteenth Amendment"; Graham, *Everyman's Constitution*, 242–65.

2. A. Paul, *Conservative Crisis*, 42–43, and more generally, 39–60. See also Kales, "New Methods in Due-Process Cases"; Ross, *Muted Fury*.

3. Rothman, *Conscience and Convenience*, 43–81.

4. For the deployment of due process arguments by groups with quite different objectives, see Sterett, " 'Entitled to Have a Hearing.' "

5. *CG-AR* (1909), 124.

6. *Chin Yow* v. *United States*, 12 (emphasis added).

7. See, for example, *Hurtado* v. *California*, 110 U.S. 516 (1884); *Twining* v. *New Jersey*, 211 U.S. 78 (1908).

8. *Japanese Immigrant Case*, 100–101. For example, the right to notice and a hearing had been considered the most basic of rights protected by due process. Yet Justice Stephen J. Field noted in *Hagar* v. *Reclamation District*, 111 U.S. 708 (1884), that the right did not apply in all proceedings, such as in the collection of taxes levied by the legislature, because the tax collector exercised no discretion over the amount of taxes to be paid.

9. Bowman, "American Administrative Tribunals," 620.

10. *Sing Tuck* v. *United States*, 194 U.S. 161, 170 (1904).

11. Goodnow, *Principles of the Administrative Law*, 371.

12. Skowronek, *Building a New American State*, 121–62, 248–84; Dickinson, *Administrative Justice*, 56, 67. Dickinson points out, however, that especially after 1906, the Supreme Court increasingly treated ICC decisions of fact as final and adopted a more restrained judicial review. See 159–67.

13. R. Pound, "Executive Justice," 72–73.

14. *United States ex rel. Buccino et al.* v. *Williams*, 190 F. 897, 900 (C.C.S.D.N.Y. 1911).

15. *In re Can Pon*, 161 F. 618, 625 (W.D. Wash. 1908).

16. *In re Ung King Ieng*, No. 15496, *Admiralty Casefiles* (1914).

17. *United States ex rel. Bosny* v. *Williams*, 185 F. 598, 599 (S.D.N.Y. 1911).

18. Brief in Opposition to Motion to Dismiss or Affirm and in Support of Appeal, 9, 22, 29, *Low Wah Suey* v. *Backus*, 225 U.S. 460 (1912); see also petitions in *In re Leong Sai Moy*, No. 15116 (1911); *In re Helen Marequa*, No. 15267 (1912); and *In re Kimi Terada*, No. 15086, *Admiralty Casefiles* (1912).

19. *In re Leong Sai Moy*, Memorandum Opinion, Judge Dietrich; *Ex parte Kwan So*, 211 F. 772, 773 (N.D. Cal. 1913).

20. *Low Wah Suey* v. *Backus*, 468–72.

21. See, for example, Judge Learned Hand's opinion in *United States ex rel. Hom Yuen Jum* v. *Dunton*, 291 F. 905 (S.D.N.Y. 1923). See also *Chew Hoy Quong* v. *White*, 249 F. 869 (9th Cir. 1918); *Ex parte Keisuki Sata, Sike Sata, and their infant child*, No. 15592, *Admiralty Casefiles*, 215 F. 173, 176 (N.D. Cal. 1914).

22. The 1914 regulations specifically denied attorneys access to "memoranda of comment or letters of transmittal" unless they contained additional evidence (U.S. Department of Commerce and Labor, *Treaty, Laws, and Regulations Governing the Admission of Chinese* [1914], rule 5b).

23. *Ex parte Keisuki Sata, Sike Sata, and their infant child*, No. 15592, *Admiralty Casefiles*, 215 F. 173, 176 (N.D. Cal. 1914).

24. *Chin Yow*, 11.

25. *In re Low Yin Chow*, No. 17818, *Admiralty Casefiles*. The court's opinion is discussed in Memorandum on Behalf of the Petitioner, *In re Tom Shee*, No. 18354, ibid.; *U.S. ex rel. Weinstein et al.* v. *Uhl*, 266 F. 929 (S.D.N.Y. 1920); *U.S. ex rel. Chin Fook Wah* v. *Dunton*, 288 F. 959 (S.D.N.Y. 1923).

26. *United States* v. *Wong You*, 223 U.S. 67, 69 (1912), rev'g 181 F. 313 (2d 1910). *United States* v. *Woo Jan*, 245 U.S. 556 (1918). Congress in 1917 appeared to respond to the *Woo Jan* decision by submitting Chinese to administrative proceedings in all cases, a development the bureau applauded (*CG-AR* [1917], xxi). The *Woo Jan* opinion rested on analysis of the 1907 immigration law, but in 1922, the Supreme Court held that the 1917 law had eliminated judicial hearings for Chinese (though not for alleged citizens) arrested for deportation (*Ng Fung Ho* v. *White*, 259 U.S. 276, 274–81 [1922]).

27. On May 31, 1907, the bureau allowed Chinese the right to have an attorney and interpreter present during the admission hearing, though they could not participate in the hearing. The right was rescinded in 1908 but reinstated in 1910. See Acting Commissioner General of Immigration F. H. Larned to Commissioner of Immigration, San Francisco, Sept. 9, 1908, File 55079/203, INS Subj. Corres.; U.S. Department of Commerce and Labor, *Treaty, Laws, and Regulations Governing the Admission of Chinese* (1910), rule 4(b).

28. Commissioner General of Immigration to Commissioner of Immigration at San Francisco, n.d., quoted in Reply Brief of Government, *In re Keisuki Sata*, No. 15592, *Admiralty Casefiles* (1914).

29. Ibid.; Department of Commerce and Labor to Attorney General, Sept. 8, 1910, #153288, DJ Numerical File. The U.S. attorney at San Francisco disagreed with the Bureau of Immigration, arguing that a "fair hearing" required that aliens' attorneys have the opportunity to cross-examine the government's witnesses.

30. Commissioner General of Immigration to Commissioner of Immigration at San Francisco, n.d., quoted in Reply Brief of Government, *In Re Keisuki Sata*.

31. Brief on Behalf of Petitioner, *In re Li Yau Ngan*, No. 15411, *Admiralty Casefiles* (1913).

32. Petition for Habeas Corpus, *In re Pedro Garcia*, No. 15338, *Admiralty Casefiles* (1913).

33. *Buccino; United States ex rel. Falco* v. *Williams*, 191 F. 1001 (C.C.S.D.N.Y. 1911).

34. The Ninth Circuit had held as early as 1909 that due process does not require that an applicant and his attorney be present during the taking of a witness's testimony (*In re Can Pon*, 168 F. 479 [9th Cir. 1909]).

35. *In re Pedro Garcia*, No. 15338, *Admiralty Casefiles* (1913), 205 F. 53, 56–57 (N.D. Cal. 1913). Dietrich was a district court judge in Boise, Idaho, who was sitting temporarily on the bench in San Francisco.

36. Ibid., 57–58. A hearing on ex parte affidavits was acceptable to the courts even if the people who made the statements were dead and could not clarify or explain problems arising from their testimony. See *Ex parte Chan Wy Sheung*, No. 16672, *Admiralty Casefiles*, 262 F. 221 (N.D. Cal. 1919), *rev'd*, *White* v. *Chan Wy Sheung*, 270 F. 764 (9th Cir. 1921).

37. *U.S. ex rel. Bosny* v. *Williams*, 600–603. Having held the hearing unfair, Judge Holt proceeded to decide the merits of the case and subsequently discharged the Bosnys. For a similar decision in the Ninth Circuit, see *Roux* v. *Commissioner of Immigration at the Port of San Francisco*, No. 15213, *Admiralty Casefiles*, *rev'd*, 203 F. 413, 414 (9th Cir. 1913).

38. Dettweiler, "Maurice T. Dooling," 67; Franaszek, "Judge Dooling's Contribution to the Law," 70–74.

39. *In re Ung King Ieng*, No. 15496, *Admiralty Casefiles* (1914).

40. *In re Wong Quen Luck*, No. 15895, *Admiralty Casefiles* (1915).

41. *Ex parte Lew Lin Shew*, No. 15693, *Admiralty Casefiles*, 217 F. 317, 318 (N.D. Cal. 1914).

42. The number of petitions filed by Chinese more than doubled after Dooling's first year in office, from sixteen in 1913 to thirty-four in 1914, and, more important, they met with greater success. Between 1908 and 1913, Chinese had filed a total of eighty-eight petitions but had obtained favorable rulings in only five cases; in 1914, the court discharged the petitioner in eleven cases, a third of the cases filed that year. A similar pattern of increased filings and more favorable rulings occurred in non-Chinese immigrant cases. Non-Chinese immigrants filed a total of forty-nine habeas corpus petitions between 1908 and 1913 and were discharged from immigration officials' custody in eight of those cases. In 1914, non-Chinese immigrant cases totaled eighteen, eight of which resulted in rulings favorable to the immigrants. See Tables 8 and 9.

43. A. Warner Parker to Commissioner General Caminetti, n.d., note attached to Feb. 1919 monthly statistical report from San Francisco, File 54515/27, INS Subj. Corres. Parker was complaining because there were twenty immigration cases pending before the district court. For further discussion of Dooling's decisions, see *CG-AR* (1914), 322; U.S. Attorney Preston to Attorney General, Jan. 31, 1916, File 179713, DJ Let. Recd.

44. See, for example, *Choy Gum* v. *Backus*, 223 F. 487 (9th Cir. 1915); *In re Yee Chee Shim*, No. 16136, *Admiralty Casefiles* (1917); and *In re Chan Dong Quan*, No. 18004, *Admiralty Casefiles* (1923).

45. *Ex parte Kwan So*, 211 F. 772 (N.D. Cal. 1913); *In re Louie Hong*, No. 18507, Admiralty Docket (1924) (dismissed challenge to board that included a stenographer as a member and whose composition changed several times throughout the investigation); *United States ex rel. Goldbaum v. Curran*, 298 F. 118 (S.D.N.Y. 1924) (appeal board of medical officers not unfair because two of medical officers made the original decision to exclude).

46. *Pearson v. Williams*, 136 F. 734 (2d Cir. 1905), aff'd, 202 U.S. 281 (1906); *Ex parte Stancampiano*, 161 F. 164 (C.C.S.D.N.Y. 1908); *Haw Moy v. North*, 183 F. 89 (9th Cir. 1910); *White v. Chan Wy Sheung*, 270 F. 764 (9th Cir. 1921), rev'g 262 F. 221 (N.D. Cal. 1919).

47. *Lewis v. Frick*, 233 U.S. 291 (1914); *Williams v. United States ex rel. Bougadis*, 186 F. 479 (2d Cir. 1911).

48. *Buccino v. Williams*, 900.

49. *In re Lee Sing Wo*, No. 15160, *Admiralty Casefiles* (1911).

50. *United States ex rel. Freeman v. Williams*, 175 F. 274 (S.D.N.Y. 1910); *United States ex rel. Rosen v. Williams*, 200 F. 538 (2d Cir. 1912) (irregularities in warrant for arrest do not invalidate the warrant for deportation if a fair hearing has been afforded the alien after arrest); *United States ex rel. Bauder v. Uhl*, 211 F. 628 (2d Cir. 1914).

51. Although judges refused to impose technical legal requirements on the bureau, they also did not allow the bureau to hold the immigrants to a higher procedural standard than the agency was itself willing to follow. See *Ex parte Chooey Dee Ying*, No. 15118, *Admiralty Casefiles*, 214 F. 873 (N.D. Cal. 1911); *United States ex rel. Yee Loy Gee v. Pierce*, 289 F. 233 (2d Cir. 1923).

52. Dickinson, *Administrative Justice*, 293.

53. *Interstate Commerce Commission v. Union Pacific Company*, 222 U.S. 541, 548 (1912).

54. *In re Sannoza Nakawatase*, No. 18524, *Admiralty Casefiles* (1924).

55. *Chin Yow v. United States*, 203.

56. *Ex parte Lee Soo*, 291 F. 271, 274 (N.D. Cal. 1923).

57. *United States ex rel. Bauder v. Uhl*, 211 F. 628 (2d Cir. 1914). For similar holdings in the Northern District of California, see *In re Mon Singh*, No. 16738, *Admiralty Casefiles* (1920); *In re Haru Tanoue*, No. 15291, ibid. (1912); *In re Dong Wing*, No. 15000, ibid. (1910); *In re Jeung Bock Hong and Jeung Bock Ning*, No. 15322, ibid., affm'd, 258 F. 23, 24 (9th Cir. 1919).

58. *United States ex rel. Canfora v. Williams*, 186 F. 354, 356–57 (S.D.N.Y. 1911). For a similar decision, see *In re Giovanna*, 93 F. 659 (S.D.N.Y. 1899).

59. The Supreme Court reiterated that the Bureau of Immigration had exclusive jurisdiction to weigh evidence though it appeared to imply that the agency's decisions had to be supported by some evidence. See *Tang Tun v. Edsell*, 223 U.S. 673 (1912); *Zakonite v. Wolf*, 226 U.S. 272 (1912) (evidence was adequate to support finding of facts for deportation); *Lewis v. Frick*, 233 U.S. 291 (1914) (holding that the secretary of commerce and labor had sufficient evidence to justify his order of deportation).

60. *Bauder v. Uhl*, 633.

61. *In re Jew Shee*, No. 18102, *Admiralty Casefiles* (1924).

62. *United States ex rel. Glavas v. Williams*, 190 F. 686, 687 (C.C.S.D.N.Y. 1911).

63. *United States ex rel. Gegiow* v. *Uhl*, 211 F. 236, 237 (S.D.N.Y. 1914).

64. *United States ex rel. Rosen* v. *Williams*, 200 F. 538, 541–42 (1912). The Ninth Circuit shared the Second Circuit's view in *Ex parte Chan Kam*, 230 F. 990 (9th Cir. 1916) *rev'd* on rehearing, *Chan Kam* v. *United States*, 232 F. 855 (9th Cir. 1916).

65. Immigration Act of February 20, 1907, 34 Stat. 898, section 2. The act of 1903 allowed for the exclusion of those *convicted* of crimes involving moral turpitude; the 1907 act also allowed for exclusion if an alien *admitted* to such a crime.

66. *In re Kornmehl*, 87 F. 314, 315 (C.C.S.D.N.Y. 1898).

67. On the debate on journalistic ethics provoked by the case, see "Slander and Journalism," *Outlook* 103 (Mar. 1, 1913): 465–66.

68. *United States ex rel. Mylius* v. *Uhl*, 203 F. 152, 153 (S.D.N.Y. 1913); *affm'd*, 210 F. 860 (2d Cir. 1914).

69. Lombardi, *Venezuela*, 201–5.

70. Ibid.; see also Corsi, *In the Shadow of Liberty*, 229–45.

71. Quoted in Corsi, *In the Shadow of Liberty*, 233.

72. Quoted ibid., 236.

73. Quoted in *United States ex rel. Castro* v. *Williams*, 203 F. 155, 157–58 (S.D.N.Y. 1913).

74. Ibid., 157.

75. "Castro and Mylius," *Outlook* 103 (Mar. 1, 1913): 464–65.

76. "The Castro Decision," *New York Tribune*, Feb. 1, 1913.

77. Higham, *Strangers in the Land*, 158–233.

78. Jensen, *Passage from India*, 101–2.

79. *CG-AR* (1919), 56–58.

80. The district court upheld the bureau's decision, finding that there was some evidence for its conclusions (*In re Shina Ryu*, No. 15805, *Admiralty Casefiles* [1915]).

81. See Chapter 5.

82. "Summary Report upon the Administration of Immigration Commissioner, H. H. North, by Clayton Herrington, Special Agent, Department of Justice," Mar. 25, 1911, pp. 29–30, File 53108/24-A, INS Subj. Corres.

83. See resolutions sent to the Commissioner General of Immigration, May 1910, File 52961/16, ibid.

84. Inspector Ainsworth to Commissioner General Daniel O'Keefe, May 18, 1910, ibid.

85. "Hindus Will Find Bars to Entrance," *San Francisco Call*, Aug. 18, 1910; President Taft to Secretary of Commerce and Labor Charles Nagel, Oct. 22, 1910, File 52961/16B, INS Subj. Corres.

86. "Be Not Deceived by the Hindu," *San Diego Tribune*, Oct. 25, 1910.

87. "Hookworm to Stop Hindu Invasion," *San Francisco Chronicle*, Sept. 29, 1910; "The Hookworm as an Aid to Exclusion," *San Jose Mercury*, Oct. 31, 1910.

88. *In re Rhagat Singh, et al.*, No. 15479, *Admiralty Casefiles* (1913); *In re Sundar Singh, et al.*, No. 15480, *Admiralty Casefiles* (1913).

89. Brief of Petitioner, 4, *In re Rhagat Singh*.

90. Brief of Government's Points and Authorities, 4–5, *In re Rhagat Singh*.

91. Memorandum Brief on Nature of Evidence Offered by Government, 2, *In re Rhagat Singh*.

92. *In re Bhagat Singh,* 209 F. 700, 702 (1913).

93. Exhibit B in Transcript of Record, *Gegiow* v. *Uhl,* 239 U.S. 3 (1915). See Exhibit A for minutes before the board of special inquiry and its decision to exclude. Gegiow's name is written as "Gegiew" in the immigration documents but as "Gegiow" in the court records. I have chosen to use the spelling in court records.

94. *United States ex rel. Gegiow et al.* v. *Uhl,* 211 F. 236–37 (S.D.N.Y. 1914).

95. *United States ex rel. Gegiow* v. *Uhl,* 215 F. 573, 574 (1914). Judge Ward dissented. See also *White* v. *Gregory, et al.,* 213 F. 768, 769 (2d Cir. 1914), for a very similar case and ruling arising on the West Coast.

96. The other immigrants did not appeal and were deported to Russia. Petition for Certiorari, *Gegiow* v. *Uhl,* 6–7. Although Kohler and Elkus were particularly interested in the effects of the bureau's policies on Jewish immigrants, it is doubtful that the immigrants in this case were Jewish because they were Osetins, a people who embraced the Christian or Islamic faith.

97. Kohler, "Jewish Immigrants," in *Immigration and Aliens,* 168.

98. Petition for Certiorari, Brief and Notice of Filing, in *Gegiow* v. *Uhl,* 2–3.

99. *CG-AR* (1915), 16.

100. *Interstate Commerce Commission* v. *Louisville and Nashville Railroad Company,* 227 U.S. 88, 91, 93 (1913).

101. Ibid., 91.

102. Ibid., 93.

103. *Whitfield* v. *Hanges,* 222 F. 745 (1915) (see esp. 754–55).

104. Brief for Petitioner, *Gegiow* v. *Uhl,* 15, 35, 16.

105. Brief for Respondent, ibid., 20.

106. Ibid.

107. Ibid., 29, 32.

108. Ibid., 19.

109. Ibid., 44. Davis argued that Congress, if it desired, could exclude immigrants with no hearing at all. He distinguished the *Japanese Immigrant Case,* conceding that in deportation cases aliens have a right to a hearing because of the greater stakes involved (ibid., 40–43).

110. *Gegiow* v. *Uhl,* 239 U.S. 3, 9–10 (1915).

111. *Healy* v. *Backus,* 243 U.S. 657 (1917). Exclusionists did have the last say, however, as they succeeded in barring all further Indian immigration in the Immigration Act of 1917. The bureau also persuaded Congress to amend the immigration law so as to make it more apparent that the "likely to become a public charge" clause had a broader meaning than that imputed by the Court (*CG-AR* [1917], xviii–xix). For stricter judicial scrutiny of likely to become a public charge cases in California, see *Ex parte Kichmiriantz,* No. 17559, *Admiralty Casefiles,* 283 F. 697 (N.D. Cal. 1922); see also *In re Nunziata Schiaroni,* No. 17756, ibid. (1923); *In re Matsutaro Nakao,* No. 15998, *Admiralty Casefiles* (1916); *In re Yee Quong,* No. 17761, *Admiralty Casefiles* (1923). For New York cases, see *United States ex rel. Mantler* v. *Commissioner of Immigration,* 3 F.2d. 234, 235 (2d Cir. 1924); *United States ex rel. Cavanaugh* v. *Howe,* 235 F. 990 (S.D.N.Y. 1916); *Howe* v. *United States ex rel. Savitsky,* 247 F. 292 (2d Cir. 1917);

United States ex rel. Brugnoli v. *Tod*, 300 F. 913 (S.D.N.Y. 1923); *United States ex rel. Engel* v. *Tod*, 294 F. 820 (2d Cir. 1923).

112. See, for example, *United States ex rel. Boxer* v. *Tod*, 294 F. 628 (2d Cir. 1923); *Chryssikos* v. *Commissioner of Immigration, Ellis Island, New York, N.Y.*, 3 F.2d 372 (2d Cir. 1924); *United States ex rel. Haft* v. *Tod*, 300 F. 918 (2d Cir. 1924).

113. Rogers Smith, "The 'American Creed.'"

114. Ibid.

115. U.S. Const. amend. XIV, section 1; Act of July 14, 1870.

116. *Wong Kim Ark* v. *United States*. For discussion of case, see Chapter 4. See alsoKettner, *Development of American Citizenship*, 317–18, 342–44, and Schuck and Smith, *Citizenship without Consent*.

117. *In re Ah Yup*, 5 Sawyer 155 (C.C. Cal. 1878).

118. *Ozawa* v. *United States*, 260 U.S. 178, 197 (1922); *United States* v. *Bhagat Singh Thind*, 261 U.S. 204 (1922).

119. *United States* v. *Ju Toy*, 198 U.S. 253, 263 (1905).

120. *Haw Moy* v. *North*, 183 F. 89, 91 (9th Cir. 1910); see also *Hoo Choy* v. *North*, 183 F. 92 (9th Cir. 1910).

121. *CG-AR* (1916), xvi.

122. *CG-AR* (1907), 108.

123. Ibid.

124. The law provided, however, that the "rights of citizenship shall not de-scendto children whose fathers never resided in the United States" (Rev. Stat. sec. 1993). That provision was modified in 1907 to require children of citizens to register at the age of eighteen their intention to become residents of the United States and to take an oath of allegiance when they reached the age of majority (34 Stat. L. 1228). The Bureau of Immigration lobbied for even more restrictive legislation. See, for example, *CG-AR* (1916), xvi–xvii.

125. Rule 9(d–g) provided that male children under age fourteen were presumed to be members of the father's household, as were sons between fifteen and eighteen, though the latter's claims were "subject to rebuttal" by inspectors. Sons between the ages of eighteen and twenty-one had to prove affirmatively that they were dependents of their fathers and those over twenty-one were not admitted at all unless they could prove their exemption from the Chinese exclusion laws, independent from their father's status. The rule did not apply to the Chinese daughters of Chinese-American citizens (rule 9 [c]). See U.S. Department of Commerce and Labor, *Treaty, Laws, and Regulations Governing the Admission of Chinese* (1915), rules approved Oct. 15, 1915.

126. *Ex parte Leong Wah Jam*, No. 15937, *Admiralty Casefiles*, 230 F. 540 (1916).

127. *Ex parte Lee Dung Moo*, No. 15947, *Admiralty Casefiles*, 230 F. 746, 747 (N.D.Cal. 1916); see also *Ex parte Tom Toy Tin*, No. 15942, ibid., 230 F. 747 (N.D. Cal. 1916); *Ex parte Ng Doo Wong*, No. 15887, ibid., 230 F. 751 (N.D. Cal. 1915). The Ninth Circuit supported Dooling's approach in *Quan Hing Sun* v. *White*, 254 F. 402 (9th Cir. 1918).

128. *Kwock Jan Fat* v. *White*, 253 U.S. 454, 464 (1920).

129. *Ng Fung Ho* v. *White*, 259 U.S. 276 (1922). The Court's decisions may have

been influenced by the Bureau of Immigration's excesses during the Red Raids of 1919–20. See Chapter 8 for an elaboration of that argument. For an application of the opinion to the foreign-born daughter of an American citizen, see *Lew Shee* v. *Nagle*, 7 F.2d 367 (9th Cir. 1925).

130. *Ng Fung Ho* v. *White*, 284.

131. Ibid., 282.

132. *Ex parte Chan Shee*, 2 F.2d 998 (N.D. Cal. 1924); *Chang Chan* v. *Nagle*, 268 U.S. 346 (1925). Its decision reversed an earlier judicial policy established in 1902 in *Tsoi Sim* v. *United States*, 116 F. 920 (9th Cir. 1902). Ironically, the Court held that Chinese merchants, protected by treaty and exempt from the Quota Act, could still bring their Chinese wives to the United States (*Cheung Sum Shee* v. *Nagle*, 268 U.S. 336 [1925]). As a result of persistent lobbying by the Chinese-American Citizens' Alliance, Congress amended the law in 1930 to admit Chinese women who had married American citizens before the 1924 act went into effect. See Chan, "Exclusion of Chinese Women," 125–27.

133. Hall, "Citizenship of Married Women," 722–23.

134. Act of September 22, 1922, 42 U.S. 1021.

135. American men who married women "ineligible for citizenship" still retained their citizenship, however (Hall, "Citizenship of Married Women," 727).

136. Through the efforts of the Japanese American Citizens League and the Chinese-American Citizens' Alliance, this law was amended in 1931 to allow women who had lost their citizenship by marrying men ineligible to become citizens the opportunity to regain their citizenship through naturalization (Chan, "Exclusion of Chinese Women," 128–29; Daniels, *Asian America*, 180–81).

137. *United States ex rel. D'Amato* v. *Williams*, 231.

138. *White* v. *Wong Quen Luck*, 243 F. 547 (9th Cir. 1915), 549.

139. See, for example, *In re Tong You and Tong Mi*, No. 16349, *Admiralty Casefiles* (1918). Dooling thought he continued to exercise some discretion over whether to hear the case on its merits and sometimes he did rather than remand it to the bureau. See *In re Tom Sue*, No. 16185, *Admiralty Casefiles* (1917).

140. *Tod* v. *Waldman*, 266 U.S. 113 (1924), 119, 120–21.

141. Gellhorn, *Administrative Law*, 919.

142. A few cases that expanded the definition of the "fair hearing" requirement developed in response to the Red Raids of 1919–20 and are discussed in the next chapter.

143. "Immigration Consultation at San Francisco," [transcript], Aug. 9–11, 1915, 5, File 53990/52, INS Subj. Corres.

144. See, for example, Dooling's decision in *In re Rhagat Singh*, discussed above.

145. *In re Peter and Sophie Beliaew*, No. 17956, *Admiralty Casefiles* (1923).

CHAPTER EIGHT

1. "Immigration Consultation at San Francisco," [transcript], Aug. 9–11, 1915, p. 4, File 53990/52, INS Subj. Corres.

2. Ibid., 22.

3. Post, "Administrative Decisions in Connection with Immigration," 256, 260–61.

4. *Dictionary of American Biography*, 15:118; Lombardi, *Labor's Voice*, 89–92.

5. See Chapter 6.

6. Louis F. Post, "Living a Life Over Again," unpublished manuscript, Library of Congress, quoted in Lombardi, *Labor's Voice*, 132.

7. "Immigration Consultation," 363.

8. The description is John Higham's, though Higham does not suggest Post was idiosyncratic (*Strangers in the Land*, 232).

9. Ibid., 127–28, 188; McKee, *Chinese Exclusion*, 206–9; Lombardi, *Labor's Voice*, 59–60. Straus defended himself against such charges, arguing that in his first year in office, deportations had increased over 47 percent (Pitkin, *Keepers of the Gate*, 98).

10. Straus's name appears on the letterhead of the organization in a letter of complaint from Samuel Littman to William B. Wilson, Secretary of Labor, Mar. 6, 1915, File 53775/222, INS Subj. Corres. For Straus's opposition to nativist legislation, see Kohler, *Registration of Aliens a Dangerous Project*, 32. For Straus's account of his experience as secretary, see Straus, *Under Four Administrations*, 207–47.

11. "Nagel Stands for More Humanity," newspaper clipping in letter from Robert M. Wilson, St. Louis, Missouri, to the Secretary of Commerce and Labor, Mar. 14, 1911, File 53072/2-A, INS Subj. Corres.; "Immigration Consultation," 79–92, 392.

12. Pitkin, *Keepers of the Gate*, 112–14.

13. Terence V. Powderly (1897–1902) had been the leader of the Knights of Labor; Frank P. Sargent (1902–8) was the grand master of the Brotherhood of Locomotive Firemen; Daniel Joseph Keefe (1908–13) had served as president of the longshoremen's union and had also been a vice-president of the American Federation of Labor (Lombardi, *Labor's Voice*, 125–28; Powderly, *Path I Trod*).

14. Lombardi, *Labor's Voice*, 127–28; Higham, *Strangers in the Land*, 128, 189–91.

15. Note, Williams scrapbook, vol. 2, [p. 7], Williams Papers. For tensions between Washington and local officials, see Safford, *Immigration Problems*, 205–6.

16. "Immigration Consultation," 13.

17. Williams to the Commissioner General of Immigration, Dec. 6, 1910, box 2, folder 8, Williams Papers.

18. "Immigration Consultation," 14.

19. Ibid., 313–14.

20. A. Warner Parker, Memorandum for the Commissioner General, Dec. 5, 1913, File 52903/59, INS Subj. Corres.

21. See Chapter 6 for discussion of the boycott and changes made in the regulations.

22. Commissioner General Daniel J. Keefe to Commissioners of Immigration, Apr. 5, 1912, File 55079/203, INS Subj. Corres. The right to inspect and make copies of the record was given in the Chinese Regulations of February 26, 1907. Rule 4b of the Chinese Regulations of 1914 specified that the record available to attorneys did not include "memoranda of comment" or "letters of transmittal" unless they included additional evidence.

23. The time for appeal was extended from two to five days in 1907 and to ten days by 1910. See Secretary of Commerce and Labor Charles Nagel to H. S. Smith, Board of Trade of San Francisco, May 26, 1911, File 52961/24-C, INS Subj. Corres.; U.S. Department of Commerce and Labor, *Treaty, Laws, and Regulations Governing the Admission of Chinese* (June 22, 1911); "Release on Bond of Chinese of Exempt Classes Pending Final Determination of Their Right to Enter the United States," Jan. 14, 1911, Department Circular No. 220, File 52961/24-C, INS Subj. Corres.

24. Acting Commissioner General of Immigration F. H. Larned to Commissioner of Immigration, San Francisco, Sept. 9, 1908, File 55079/203, INS Subj. Corres.

25. Nagel to Commissioner General of Immigration Keefe, Oct. 20, 1910, ibid.

26. Daniel Keefe to Charles Nagel, Oct. 27, 1910, File 52961/24-B, ibid. The bureau also took steps to protect itself against the charge that the agency's interpreters did not have an adequate grasp of the various Chinese dialects. The commissioner of immigration at San Francisco instructed the Chinese Division in 1911 to make a list of all its interpreters and the dialects they spoke. The dialect spoken by each applicant was noted in the record of the hearing, and at the end of each examination the applicant was asked if he or she had understood the interpreter (Luther Steward to Inspector in Charge, Chinese Division, May 29, 1911, File 52961/24-E, ibid.).

27. U.S. Department of Labor, *Immigration Laws and Rules, Rules of November 15, 1911*, rule 15, subdivision 2; rule 22, subdivision 4(b). The bureau retained the right to regulate who could practice before it and to set the maximum fees that attorneys could charge. See rule 31.

28. "Immigration Consultation," 5; U.S. Department of Labor, *Immigration Laws and Rules, Rules of 1917*, rule 22, subdivision 5(b).

29. Immigration Act of 1917, section 16; U.S. Department of Labor, *Immigration Laws and Rules, Rules of 1917*, rule 24, subdivision 1.

30. See Chapter 7 for further discussion of the conflict over the participation of attorneys.

31. Post, "Administrative Decisions," 258.

32. Immigration Act of 1917, section 17; U.S. Department of Labor, *Immigration Laws and Rules, Rules of 1917*, rule 15, subdivision 2.

33. Kohler, "Jewish Immigrants," 169. The society claimed an even higher rate of reversal of 75 percent in 1914. See letter from Samuel Littman to William Wilson, Secretary of Labor, Mar. 6, 1915, File 53775/222, INS Subj. Corres.

34. "Recommendations for Changes in the Federal Immigration Laws, 1911," in G. Abbott, ed., *Immigration*, 206–7.

35. See Appendix B in Jenks and Lauck, *Immigration Problem*, for text of proposed bill.

36. *CG-AR* (1907), 127–28. Low salaries continued to be a problem for the bureau and were used by critics of the agency to bolster the claims that the inspectors were not competent. For the general allegation that Congress continually failed to appropriate adequate funds to enforce the immigration laws, see Safford, *Immigration Problems*, 195–96.

37. See, for example, *CG-AR* (1915), 43–44.

38. Collector Wise to the Secretary of Treasury, Aug. 27, 1895, Custom House Nominations, California, San Francisco, Mar. 1894–June 1896, Records of the Treasury, RG 56, National Archives.

39. "Immigration Consultation," 13–14.

40. The bureau sought in 1915 to expand the staff of its law division, stressing its importance in dealing with complicated legal issues (*CG-AR* [1915], 43–44).

41. Parker served as law officer for the bureau from 1906 to 1919 and had a significant impact on bureau policies. He helped to draft the Immigration Law of 1917 (*Who Was Who in America*, vol. 1). After leaving the agency, Parker set up a private practice and, as had other former government attorneys, he represented immigrants.

42. Commissioner North to Commissioner General, May 3, 1909, File 52999/44, INS Subj. Corres.

43. Fred Watts to Acting Commissioner General of Immigration, Oct. 15, 1909, and Commissioner General Daniel J. Keefe to Secretary of Commerce and Labor, Jan. 7, 1910, File 52999/44, INS Subj. Corres. The commissioner of immigration at San Francisco from 1898 to 1910, Hart H. North, was also a lawyer, but, according to Watts, did not have the time to supervise the inspectors' examinations and records.

44. Lauritz Lorenzen, Inspector-in-Charge, Records and Accounts Division, to Commissioner of Immigration, Angel Island, June 16, 1913, File 52999/44-G, INS Subj. Corres. The staff at Ellis Island also included an attorney, a law clerk, and inspectors and stenographers serving under the law clerk (Rules for the Executive Division, Feb. 1912, box 6, folder 2, Williams Papers).

45. The two strongest proponents, Commissioner H. M. White of Seattle and A. Warner Parker, were both lawyers.

46. Abstract of Record and Report, quoted in Application to Reopen Case made to Commissioner White, Sept. 4, 1916, in *In re Mah Shee*, No. 16118, Admiralty Docket.

47. See, for example, Lee Gow Huey, #10420/6135, [1910], Chinese Exclusion Act Cases, INS/SF.

48. *CG-AR* (1918), 36–37.

49. "Immigration Consultation," 325–26.

50. Speech of Charles Nagel, in Kohler, *Immigration and Aliens*, 196–98. Post also called for greater discretion for the secretary of labor to ameliorate the harshness of the immigration laws ("Administrative Problems").

51. Draft of letter to the President, Feb. 1911, File 52961/24-B, INS Subj. Corres.

52. The Asiatic Exclusion League, angered by Commissioner North's refusal to exclude Indians, trumped up allegations of corruption in his enforcement of the Chinese laws. Their complaints prompted an investigation and eventually the forced resignation of North (Jensen, *Passage from India*, 117).

53. See, for example, resolutions of the Junior Order United American Mechanics and other labor groups in File 53072/2, INS Subj. Corres.

54. Robert M. Wilson to Secretary Nagel, Mar. 14, 1911, File 53072/2-A, ibid.

55. Silas E. Champe, Detroit, Michigan, to President Taft, Feb. 27, 1911, ibid.

56. Nagel to Hall, Mar. 18, 1911, ibid.

57. "Immigration Consultation," 166–67.

58. *CG-AR* (1917), xv.

59. Keefe to Nagel, Oct. 27, 1910, File 52961/24-B, INS Subj. Corres.; A. Warner Parker, Memorandum for the Commissioner General, Dec. 5, 1913, p. 3, File 52903/59, ibid. The 1914 edition of the Chinese Regulations omit the right to an attorney. See U.S. Department of Commerce and Labor, *Treaty, Laws, and Regulations Governing the Admission of Chinese* (January 24, 1914).

60. Native Sons of California Chinese to Julius Kahn, House of Representatives, Oct. 24, 1923, File 55383/30, INS Subj. Corres.

61. A. Warner Parker to the Commissioner General of Immigration, Aug. 7, 1914, File 53775/202-A, ibid.

62. "Memorandum for the Secretary," [1922], File 54261/147-A, ibid.

63. For copy of bill, see *CG-AR* (1910), 179–92; see also A. Warner Parker, Memorandum for the Commissioner General, Mar. 16, 1910, File 52730/8-A, INS Subj. Corres. His bill was never fully adopted, though the 1917 immigration law did submit Chinese to administrative deportation proceedings (Immigration Act of 1917, sections 19 and 38).

64. Parker, "Immigration Control," 79.

65. See P. Evans, " 'Likely to Become a Public Charge,' " 165–83.

66. White to Commissioner General, Sept. 12, 1919, File 54261/147, INS Subj. Corres.

67. See annual report of Williams in *CG-AR* (1909), 132–33. For criticism, see Kohler, "Jewish Immigrants," 169.

68. Pitkin, *Keepers of the Gate*, 57–59.

69. A. Warner Parker, Memorandum for the Commissioner General, Mar. 16, 1919, File 52730/8-A, INS Subj. Corres. Parker may have also feared that the federal courts would extend the right to aliens if the bureau did not. The earlier court cases denied aliens the right to subpoena and cross-examine witnesses because the statute did not allow inspectors the power to subpoena witnesses. But once Congress had extended such a power, it is likely that courts would have found that aliens had the right to take advantage of it. See Chapter 7.

70. Ibid.; Memorandum for Commissioner Williams, Nov. 15, 1909, File 52730, INS Subj. Corres.

71. Parker cited a similar provision in a statute relating to proceedings before the Interstate Commerce Commission (Act of February 11, 1893, 27 Stat. 443) as the model for the proposed Bureau of Immigration rule.

72. Ibid.

73. U.S. Department of Labor, *Immigration Laws and Rules, Rules of 1917*, rule 24, subdivision 1.

74. "Immigration Consultation," 311.

75. Ibid., 24–25.

76. Ibid., 4.

77. Ibid., 6–8. Commissioner White of the Seattle office stated that it was the practice in his district to inform the alien of the right to an attorney at the end of the hearing.

78. Commissioner H. H. Moler, ibid., 10.

79. Ibid., 11.

80. Ibid., 3.

81. See Van Vleck, *Administrative Control*, 90–95, 107–8, for examples of the type of evidence obtained in preliminary examinations.

82. "Immigration Consultation," 16.

83. Ibid.

84. *CG-AR* (1915), 16.

85. Steiner's account is drawn from *Colyer* v. *Skeffington*, 265 F. 17 (D. Mass. 1920), as are the estimates of the number of arrests. Local Bureau of Investigation officials estimated that 600 people had been arrested, but Judge Anderson thought, based on the evidence he heard in fifteen days of testimony, that the figure was closer to 800 to 1,200.

86. See exhibits 1–1c, 2–2f, 5a, 5b, and 9 in National Popular Government League, *Illegal Practices*.

87. *CG-AR* (1920), 200–201; *CG-AR* (1921), 14.

88. Preston, *Aliens and Dissenters*, 11.

89. The following account of the Red Raids is drawn from Preston, *Aliens and Dissenters*, 153–237; Coben, *A. Mitchell Palmer*, 196–245. Unfortunately, the Immigration and Naturalization Service withdrew the records upon which these histories relied (soon after their publication) and thus they were not available for this study.

90. Higham, *Strangers in the Land*, 200.

91. "Immigration Consultation," 13.

92. Preston, *Aliens and Dissenters*, 166.

93. Judge Frank H. Rudkin of the Eastern District of Washington held in September 1918 that mere membership in the IWW did not constitute a deportable offense and, as a result, many of the Wobblies arrested were released. Soon thereafter, Judge Jeremiah Netterer of the Western District of Washington came to the opposite conclusion, supporting the bureau's ruling that membership in the IWW constituted advocacy of unlawful doctrines. Judge Augustus Hand of the Southern District of New York distinguished between membership and advocacy, releasing IWW members who had not personally advocated unlawful doctrines but upholding the orders of deportation for several others based on their distribution, and by implication, their advocacy of IWW literature that proposed sabotage as a strategy in labor conflicts. See Preston, *Aliens and Dissenters*, 185–86, 189–90, 204–6.

94. Lombardi, *Labor's Voice*, 341.

95. U.S. Department of Labor, *Immigration Laws and Rules, Immigration Rules of May 1, 1917*, 3d ed., March 1919, rule 22, subdivision 5(b).

96. Stanley Coben has argued that A. Mitchell Palmer did not become firmly committed to the antiradical program until the bombing attack on his house in June 1919. Before that, Palmer took a more liberal stance toward radicals and resisted public pressure to adopt more repressive measures (*A. Mitchell Palmer*, 196–207).

97. Ibid., 220–21.

98. *CG-AR* (1919), 34.

99. Preston, *Aliens and Dissenters*, 221.

100. Exhibit 13 in *Illegal Practices*, 46.

101. *Colyer* v. *Skeffington*, 47, 45. For discussion of insufficiency of procedures, see 45–51.

102. *Ex parte Jackson*, 263 F. 110 (D. Mont. 1920); see also Bourquin's decision in *Ex parte Radivoeff*, 278 F. 227 (D. Mont. 1922).

103. Apparently, when the Communist party splintered off from the Socialist party, some members had.been shifted to the Communist party's membership lists without their knowledge (Coben, *A. Mitchell Palmer*, 223–24).

104. Higham, *Strangers in the Land*, 231.

105. Act of June 5, 1920, 41 Stat. 1008.

106. *Tisi* v. *Tod*, 264 U.S. 131 (1924) (holding there was some evidence for secretary of labor to infer that alien knew of the seditious character of leaflets in his possession, despite alien's claim that he could not read English); *U.S. ex rel. Georgian* v. *Uhl*, 271 F. 676 (2d Cir. 1921) (found there was some evidence that bookstore owner advocated, through his selling of publications of a radical nature, the unlawful doctrines contained therein; Circuit Judge Ward dissented, saying there was no proof of his personal advocacy of or belief in the doctrines); *Guiney* v. *Bonham*, 261 F. 582 (9th Cir. 1919); *United States ex rel. Rakics* v. *Uhl*, 266 F. 646 (2d Cir. May 12, 1920).

107. *Ex parte Caminita*, 291 F. 913 (S.D.N.Y. 1922) (limited reach of Fourth Amendment); see also *Weinstein* v. *Attorney General*, 271 F. 673 (2d Cir. 1921), *affm'g In re Weinstein*, 271 F. 5 (S.D.N.Y. 1920). *Guiney* v. *Bonham*; *United States ex rel. Diamond* v. *Uhl*, 266 F. 34 (2d Cir. 1920) (rejected challenge to affidavits).

108. See, for example, *United States ex rel. Weinstein* v. *Uhl*, 266 F. 929 (S.D.N.Y. 1920) (denial of bail when profferred according to regulations constitutes a violation of due process).

109. *Kwock Jan Fat* v. *White*, 253 U.S. 454, 464 (1920); *Ng Fung Ho* v. *White*, 259 U.S. 276, 285 (1922).

110. Anderson cited *Ex parte Petkos* as authority for his action.

111. Clark, *Deportation of Aliens*, 302–3, 377–81, 383–87; Van Vleck, *Administrative Control*, 78–81, 146–48.

112. Clark, *Deportation of Aliens*, 386–88; Van Vleck, *Administrative Control*, 218–19.

113. Preston, *Aliens and Dissenters*, 235–37.

114. U.S. Department of Labor, *Immigration Laws and Rules, Rules of 1924*, rule 19, subdivision D.

115. Clark, *Deportation of Aliens*, 365–66; Van Vleck, *Administrative Control*, 97–99.

116. Clark, *Deportation of Aliens*, 365–66; Van Vleck, *Administrative Control*, 231–34; U.S. National Commission on Law Observance and Enforcement, *Report on the Enforcement of the Deportation Laws*, 83–86.

117. U.S. National Commission on Law Observance and Enforcement, *Report on the Enforcement of the Deportation Laws*, 107.

118. Van Vleck, *Administrative Control*, 228–34; Clark, *Deportation of Aliens*, 366–67. Oppenheimer found that preliminary investigations were used in 85 percent of

the cases in his study (U.S. National Commission on Law Observance and Enforcement, *Report on the Enforcement of the Deportation Laws*, 60).

119. Van Vleck, *Administrative Control*, 91. Of 597 applications for warrants of arrest in deportation cases examined for his study, Van Vleck found 213 were telegraphic applications.

120. Van Vleck reported that the usual bond was $500, but only 14 percent of aliens in his study were able to pay the bond. An additional 6 percent were released on their own cognizance or to the custody of attorneys or family (ibid., 97).

121. The bill's provisions are discussed in Freund, "Deportation Legislation," 46–57. The bill passed the House with a wide majority but died in the Senate (Hutchinson, *Legislative History*, 199–200).

122. Chafee, *Free Speech in the United States*, 236.

123. Clark, *Deportation of Aliens*, 386–88, 487–90; Van Vleck, *Administrative Control*, 247.

EPILOGUE

1. R. Pound, "Executive Justice," 64–65.

2. Sutherland, "Private Rights and Government Control," 168.

3. Dickinson, "Administrative Law and the Fear of Bureaucracy," 513.

4. Wilson, "Study of Administration," 202.

5. Verkuil, "Emerging Concept of Administrative Procedure," 268–74.

6. K. Davis, *Discretionary Justice*, 3.

7. Frankfurter, "Task of Administrative Law," 4.

8. Bailyn, *Ideological Origins of the American Revolution*, 75–77, 284–85; Wood, *Creation of the American Republic*, 446–52, 547–52.

9. Sutherland, "Private Rights and Government Control," 169–70; C. Pound, "Judicial Power," 787–90.

10. Root, "Public Service by the Bar," 41 *A.B.A. Rep.* (1916): 355, 368–69, quoted in Verkuil, "Emerging Concept of Administrative Procedure," 266.

11. See Mashaw, *Due Process in the Administrative State*, for discussion of the various models of due process applied in administrative law.

12. Shapiro, *Who Guards the Guardians?*, 111. For a somewhat different assessment, see Verkuil, "Emerging Concept of Administrative Procedure." He argues that administrative law has developed new norms of due process, independent of judicial models, which balance fairness with concerns for efficiency and the satisfaction of parties.

13. Schuck, "Transformation of Immigration Law," 31–33.

14. See Note, "Developments in the Law—Immigration Policy and the Rights of Aliens," 1358–1400; Crewdson, *Tarnished Door*, 113–41; K. Davis, *Administrative Law*, 85–92.

15. "Doctors, Spaghetti and My American Wife," *New York Times*, June 7, 1993.

16. Schuck, "Transformation of Immigration Law," 1.

17. On similarities in administrative process, see Stephens, *Administrative Tribunals and the Rules of Evidence*; Albertsworth, "Judicial Review of Administrative

Action"; Brinton, "Some Powers and Problems of the Federal Administrative," 138; Martin, "The Lines of Demarcation between Legislative, Executive [*sic*], and Judicial Functions," 734.

18. U.S. Interstate Commerce Commission, *Annual Report* (1890), 12, quoted in Sterett, " 'Entitled to Have a Hearing,' " 55.

19. *Federal Trade Commission* v. *Gratz*, 253 U.S. 421 (1920). The Court further limited the agency's authority to determine what were "unfair business practices," substituting its own definition instead. This and similar rulings "completely devitalized" the commission, in the opinion of its advocates (G. Davis, "Transformation of the Federal Trade Commission," 441–42).

20. Parry, ed., *Consolidated Treaty Series*, article V; U.S. Congress, Select Committee on Immigration and Naturalization, *Chinese Immigration*, 439.

21. Federal courts initially held, for example, that resident aliens were not subject to the immigration laws. See *In re Martorelli*, 63 F. 437 (C.C.S.D.N.Y. 1894); *In re Maiola*, 67 F. 114 (C.C.S.D.N.Y. 1895). See also petitioners' brief in *Fong Yue Ting* v. *United States*, 149 U.S. 698 (1893).

22. *In re Moses*, 83 F. 995 (C.C.S.D.N.Y. 1897); *Lapina* v. *Williams*, 232 U.S. 78 (1914).

23. See Chapter 8 for judicial distinctions between the procedural rights due aliens and alleged citizens in immigration proceedings. See also Schuck, "Transformation of Immigration Law," 2–3.

24. Verkuil, "Emergence of a Concept of Administrative Procedure," 283–86; Reich, "The New Property"; Van Alstyne, "The Demise of the Right-Privilege Distinction in Constitutional Law."

25. Act of December 17, 1943, 57 Stat. 600; Act of October 3, 1965, 79 Stat. 911.

26. Schuck, "Transformation of Immigration Law," 4, 47–73. Schuck sees *Plyler* v. *Doe*, in which the Supreme Court invalidated a Texas law denying alien children access to public education, as a particularly significant shift toward a functional, rather than a formal, definition of membership.

27. "On These Shores, Immigrants Find a New Wave of Hostility," *New York Times*, June 13, 1993.

28. LeMay, *From Open Door to Dutch Door*, xiii–xiv, 120–21.

29. Lamm and Imhoff, *The Immigration Time Bomb*, x.

30. "Two in Congress Who Fought to Improve Immigration Policy," *New York Times*, Sept. 15, 1994, p. 18.

31. Harwood, "How Should We Enforce Immigration Law?," 73–74.

32. "At Immigration, Disarray and Defeat," *New York Times*, Sept. 11, 1994, p. 1.

33. Schuck, "Transformation of Immigration Law," 76–83.

34. Harwood, "How Should We Enforce Immigration Law?," 86.

35. See series of articles "Chaos at the Gates," *New York Times*, Sept. 11–15, 1994.

BIBLIOGRAPHY

UNPUBLISHED MATERIALS

Bancroft Library, University of California, Berkeley
    Papers of Hart H. North
    Papers of James D. Phelan
    Diaries of John Sawyer
    Correspondence and Papers of Frederick Stratton

Harvard Law Library, Cambridge, Mass.
    Felix Frankfurter Papers

National Archives, Washington, D.C.
    Records of the Department of Treasury. RG 56. Letters Sent, Superintendent
        of Immigration.
    Records of the Department of Treasury. RG 56. Customs House Nominations.
        San Francisco.
    Records of the Immigration and Naturalization Service. RG 85. Central Office.
        Subject Correspondence.
    Records of the Immigration and Naturalization Service. RG 85. District 13.
        San Francisco.
    Records of the Immigration and Naturalization Service. RG 85. Segregated
        Chinese Files.
    Records of the Department of Justice. RG 60. Appointment Files of Judges,
        U.S. Attorneys, and Marshals, 1853–1905.
    Records of the Department of Justice. RG 60. Appointment Files for Offices in
        Federal Judicial Districts, 1901–33.
    Records of the Department of Justice. RG 60. Letters Received, 1849–1903.
    Records of the Department of Justice. RG 60. Letters Sent, 1849–1918.

National Archives, New York Branch, Bayonne, New Jersey
    Records of the District Courts of the United States. RG 21. U.S. Circuit Court
        for the Southern District Court of New York. *Habeas Corpus Docket, 1891–*
        1906.
    Records of the District Courts of the United States. RG 21. U.S. District Court
        for the Southern District of New York. *Equity Docket, 1897–1915.*

National Archives, San Francisco Branch, San Bruno, California
    Records of the Bureau of Customs. RG 36. Port of San Francisco.
        Correspondence from the Collector to Other Federal Agencies and the
        General Public, 1895–1915.
    Records of the District Courts of the United States. RG 21. U.S. District Court
        for the Northern District of California. *Admiralty Casefiles, 1891–1924.*
    Records of the District Courts of the United States. RG 21. U.S. District Court

for the Northern District of California. *Admiralty Docket, 1891–1924.* [Located in Archives Room, U.S. District Court, San Francisco.]

Records of the District Courts of the United States. RG 21. U.S. District Court for the Northern District of California. *Commissioner's Docket.*

Records of the District Courts of the United States. RG 21. U.S. District Court for the Northern District of California. *Criminal Casefiles, 1891–1924.*

Records of the District Courts of the United States. RG 21. U.S. District Court for the Northern District of California. *Criminal Docket, 1891–1924.* [Located in Archives Room, U.S. District Court, San Francisco.]

Records of the District Courts of the United States. RG 21. U.S. Circuit Court for the Northern District of California. *Common Law and Equity Casefiles, 1891–1911.*

Records of the District Courts of the United States. RG 21. U.S. Circuit Court for the Northern District of California. *Common Law Docket, 1891–1911.* [Located in Archives Room, U.S. District Court, San Francisco.]

New York Public Library
William Williams Papers

PUBLISHED MATERIALS

Abbott, Edith. *Historical Aspects of the Immigration Problem.* 1924; repr. New York: Arno Press, 1969.

Abbott, Grace. *Immigration: Select Documents and Case Records.* 1924; repr. New York: Arno Press, 1969.

Acuña, Rodolfo. *Occupied America.* San Francisco: Canfield Press, 1972.

Adamic, Louis. *Laughing in the Jungle: The Autobiography of an Immigrant in America.* 1932; repr. New York: Arno Press, 1969.

Albertsworth, E. F. "Judicial Review of Administrative Action by the Federal Supreme Court." *Harvard Law Review* 35 (1921–22): 127–53.

Altschuler, Glenn C. *Race, Ethnicity, and Class in American Social Thought, 1865–1919.* Arlington Heights, Ill.: Harlan Davidson, 1982.

American Federation of Labor. *Some Reasons for Exclusion, Meat vs. Rice, American Manhood against Asiatic Coolieism, Which Shall Survive?* 57th Cong., 1st sess., S. Doc. 137. Washington, D.C.: GPO, 1902.

Amsterdam, Anthony G. "Criminal Prosecutions Affecting Federally Guaranteed Civil Rights: Federal Removal and Habeas Corpus Jurisdiction to Abort State Court Trial." *University of Pennsylvania Law Review* 113 (April 1965): 793–912.

Asher, Robert. "Union Nativism and the Immigrant Response." *Labor History* 23 (1982): 325–48.

Auerbach, Jerold S. *Rabbis and Lawyers: The Journey from Torah to Constitution.* Bloomington: Indiana University Press, 1990.

Bailyn, Bernard. *The Ideological Origins of the American Revolution.* Cambridge, Mass.: Belknap Press of Harvard University Press, 1967.

Barth, Gunther. *Bitter Strength: A History of Chinese in the United States, 1850–1870.* Cambridge, Mass.: Harvard University Press, 1964.

Bates, J. C., ed. *History of the Bench and Bar of California*. San Francisco: N.p., 1912.

Beale, Truxton. "Why the Chinese Should Be Excluded." *Forum* 33 (March 1902): 53–58.

Blegen, Theodore C. "The Competition of the Northwestern States for Immigrants." *Wisconsin Magazine of History* 3 (1919): 3–29.

Blodgett, Ralph E. "The Colorado Territorial Board of Immigration." *Colorado Magazine* 46 (Summer 1969): 245–56.

Boudin, Louis. *Government by Judiciary*. New York: W. Godwin, 1932.

Bouve, Clement. *A Treatise on the Laws Governing the Exclusion and Expulsion of Aliens.* Washington, D.C.: John Byrne & Co., 1912.

Bowman, Harold M. "American Administrative Tribunals." *Political Science Quarterly* 21 (1906): 609–25.

Brinton, Jasper Yeates. "Some Powers and Problems of the Federal Administrative." *University of Pennsylvania Law Review* 61 (1913): 135–62.

Brown, Lawrence Guy. *Immigration: Cultural Conflicts and Social Adjustments*. New York: Longmans, Green, 1933.

Burnett, Albert G. "Misunderstanding of Eastern and Western States Regarding Oriental Immigration." *Annals of the American Academy of Political and Social Science* 34 (July–December 1909): 257–61.

Calavita, Kitty. *U.S. Immigration Law and the Control of Labor, 1820–1924*. London: Academic Press, 1984.

California. State Board of Control. *California and the Oriental*. Sacramento, 1922.

Cardoso, Lawrence A. *Mexican Emigration to the United States, 1891–1931*. Tucson: University of Arizona Press, 1980.

Chafee, Zechariah, Jr. *Freedom of Speech*. New York: Harcourt, Brace, 1920.

Chan, Sucheng. "European and Asian Immigration into the United States in Comparative Perspective, 1820s to 1920s." In *Immigration Reconsidered: History, Sociology and Politics*, ed. Virginia Yans-McLaughlin, 37–75. New York: Oxford University Press, 1990.

———. "The Exclusion of Chinese Women, 1870–1943." In *Entry Denied: Exclusion and the Chinese Community in America, 1882–1943*, ed. Sucheng Chan, 94–146. Philadelphia: Temple University Press, 1991.

———. *This Bittersweet Soil: The Chinese in California Agriculture, 1860–1910*. Berkeley: University of California Press, 1986.

Chase, William C. *The American Law School and the Rise of Administrative Government.* Madison: University of Wisconsin Press, 1982.

Chew, Ng Poon. *The Treatment of the Exempt Classes of Chinese in the United States.* San Francisco: Published by the author, 1908.

"China and America." *Outlook* 81 (December 30, 1905): 952.

Chinn, Thomas W., H. Mark Lai, and Philip P. Choy, eds. *A History of the Chinese in California*. San Francisco: Chinese Historical Society, 1969.

Cinel, Dino. *From Italy to San Francisco: The Immigrant Experience*. Stanford: Stanford University Press, 1982.

Cizmic, Ivan. "The Experiences of South Slav Immigrants on Ellis Island and the Establishment of the Slavonic Immigrant Society in New York." In *In the Shadow of the Statue of Liberty: Immigrants, Workers, and Citizens in the American*

Republic, ed. Marianne Debouzy, 67–82. Urbana: University of Illinois Press, 1992.

Claghorn, Kate Holladay. *The Immigrant's Day in Court*. 1923; repr. New York: Arno Press, 1969.

Clark, Jane Perry. *Deportation of Aliens from the United States to Europe*. New York: Columbia University Press, 1931.

Clayton, J. C. "A New View of the Deportation Cases in the Supreme Court." *New Jersey Law Journal* 16 (1893): 292–99.

Coben, Stanley. *A. Mitchell Palmer: A Biography*. New York: Columbia University Press, 1963.

Collins, George D. "Are Persons Born within the United States Ipso Facto Citizens Thereof?" *American Law Review* 18 (1884): 831–38.

Commager, Henry Steele, ed. *Immigration and American History*. Minneapolis: University of Minnesota Press, 1961.

Coolidge, Mary Roberts. *Chinese Immigration*. New York: Henry Holt, 1909.

Corsi, Edward. *In the Shadow of Liberty*. 1935; repr. New York: Arno Press, 1969.

Corwin, Edward Samuel. "The Doctrine of Due Process before the Civil War." In *Corwin on the Constitution*, ed. Richard Loss, 2:149–79. Ithaca: Cornell University Press, 1981.

——. "The Supreme Court and the Fourteenth Amendment." In *Corwin on the Constitution*, ed. Richard Loss, 2:123–48. Ithaca: Cornell University Press, 1981.

Coryn, Sidney G. P. "The Japanese Problem in California." *Annals of the American Academy of Political and Social Science* 34 (July–December 1909): 262–68.

Crewdson, John. *The Tarnished Door: The New Immigrants and the Transformation of America*. New York: Times Books, 1983.

Curran, Thomas J. *Xenophobia and Immigration, 1820–1930*. Boston: Twayne, 1975.

Currier, Albert Dean. "Government by Executive Rulings." *North American Review* 186 (September 1907): 98–108.

Daniels, Roger. *Asian America: Chinese and Japanese in the United States since 1850*. Seattle: University of Washington Press, 1988.

——. *Coming to America*. New York: Harper Collins, 1990.

——. "The Japanese." In *Ethnic Leadership in America*, ed. John Higham, 36–63. Baltimore: Johns Hopkins University Press, 1978.

——. *The Politics of Prejudice: The Anti-Japanese Movement in California and the Struggle for Japanese Exclusion*. Berkeley: University of California Press, 1962.

Davis, Allen F. *Spearheads of Reform: The Social Settlements and the Progressive Movement, 1890–1914*. New York: Oxford University Press, 1967.

Davis, G. Cullom. "The Transformation of the Federal Trade Commission, 1914–1924." *Mississippi Valley Historical Review* 49 (December 1962): 437–55.

Davis, Kenneth Culp. *Administrative Law—Cases—Texts—Problems*. 2d ed. St. Paul: West, 1965.

——. *Discretionary Justice: A Preliminary Inquiry*. Baton Rouge: Louisiana State University Press, 1969.

Dettweiler, Alma Dooling. "Maurice T. Dooling, 1860–1924." In *A Judicial Odyssey: Federal Court in Santa Clara, San Benito, Santa Cruz, and Monterey Counties*, ed. Christian G. Fritz, Michael Griffith, and Janet Hunter, 63–70. San Jose: Advisory Committee, San Jose Federal Court, 1985.

Dickinson, John. *Administrative Justice and the Supremacy of Law in the United States.* Cambridge, Mass.: Harvard University Press, 1927.

———. "Administrative Law and the Fear of Bureaucracy—I." *American Bar Association Journal* 14 (1928): 513–16.

Drake, B. Frank. "The Chinaman before the Supreme Court." *Albany Law Journal* 67 (1905): 258–67.

Dubofsky, Melvyn. *We Shall Be All.* 2d ed. Urbana: University of Illinois Press, 1988.

Duker, William F. *A Constitutional History of Habeas Corpus.* Westport, Conn.: Greenwood Press, 1980.

Erickson, Charlotte. *American Industry and the European Immigrant, 1860–1885.* Cambridge, Mass.: Harvard University Press, 1957.

Evans, Elliot A. P., and David W. Heron. "Isla de Los Angeles: Unique State Park in San Francisco Bay." *California History* 66 (March 1987): 24–39.

Evans, Evan A., Judge. "Naturalizing and Nationalizing Alien." *Journal of the American Bar Association* 7 (November 1920): 161–62.

Evans, Patricia Russell. " 'Likely to Become a Public Charge': Immigration in the Backwaters of Administrative Law, 1882–1933." Ph.D. dissertation, George Washington University, 1987.

Fiss, Owen M. "David J. Brewer: The Judge as Missionary." In *The Fields and the Law*, 53–71. San Francisco: United States District Court for the Northern District of California Historical Society, 1986.

Foner, Eric. *Reconstruction: America's Unfinished Revolution, 1863–1877.* New York: Harper & Row, 1988.

Foster, John W. "The Chinese Boycott." *Atlantic Monthly* 97 (January 1906): 118–27.

Franaszek, Joseph. "Judge Dooling's Contribution to the Law in the Northern District of California." In *A Judicial Odyssey: Federal Court in Santa Clara, San Benito, Santa Cruz, and Monterey Counties*, ed. Christian G. Fritz, Michael Griffith, and Janet Hunter, 70–74. San Jose: Advisory Committee, San Jose Federal Court, 1985.

Frankfurter, Felix. "The Task of Administrative Law." *University of Pennsylvania Law Review* 75 (1927): 614–21.

Freund, Ernst. *Administrative Powers over Persons and Property: A Comparative Survey.* Chicago: University of Chicago Press, 1928.

———. "Deportation Legislation in the Sixty-Ninth Congress." *Social Service Review* 1 (March 1927): 46–57.

———. "The Law of Administration in America." *Political Science Quarterly* 9 (Fall 1894): 403–25.

Fritz, Christian G. "Due Process, Treaty Rights, and Chinese Exclusion, 1882–1891." In *Entry Denied: Exclusion and the Chinese Community in America, 1882–1943*, ed. Sucheng Chan, 25–56. Philadelphia: Temple University Press, 1991.

———. *Federal Justice in California: The Court of Ogden Hoffman, 1851–1891.* Lincoln: University of Nebraska Press, 1991.

———. "A Nineteenth Century 'Habeas Corpus Mill': The Chinese before the Federal Courts in California." *American Journal of Legal History* 32 (October 1988): 347–72.

Fu Chi Hao. "My Reception in America." *Outlook* 86 (August 10, 1907): 770–73.

Galanter, Marc. "The Radiating Effects of Courts." In *Empirical Theories about Courts*, ed. K. Boyum and L. Mather. New York: Longmans, 1983.

Gardner, John. "The Image of the Chinese in the United States, 1885–1915." Ph.D. dissertation, University of Pennsylvania, 1961.

Gellhorn, Walter. *Administrative Law: Cases and Materials*. Chicago: Foundation Press, 1940.

Glazer, Nathan. "The Jews." In *Ethnic Leadership in America*, ed. John Higham, 19–35. Baltimore: Johns Hopkins University Press, 1978.

Glenn, Evelyn Nakano. *Issei, Nissei, War Bride: Three Generations of Japanese American Women in Domestic Service*. Philadelphia: University of Pennsylvania Press, 1986.

Goodnow, Frank. *The Principles of the Administrative Law of the United States*. New York: G. P. Putnam's Sons, 1905.

———. "The Writ of Certiorari." *Political Science Quarterly* 6 (September 1891): 493–536.

Gordon, Milton M. *Assimilation in America: The Role of Race, Religion, and National Origins*. New York: Oxford University Press, 1964.

Gordon, Robert W. "Legal Thought and Legal Practice in the Age of American Enterprise, 1870–1920." In *Professions and Professional Ideologies in America*, ed. Gerald L. Geison, 70–110. Chapel Hill: University of North Carolina Press, 1983.

Gossett, Thomas F. *Race: The History of an Idea in America*. New York: Schocken Books, 1965.

Gowen, Herbert H. "The Problem of Oriental Immigration in the State of Washington." *Annals of the American Academy of Political and Social Science* 34 (July–December 1909): 329–37.

Graham, Howard Jay. *Everyman's Constitution*. Madison: State Historical Society of Wisconsin, 1968.

Grant, Madison. *The Passing of the Great Race*. New York: Scribner's Sons, 1916.

Hall, Cyril D. "Citizenship of Married Women." *American Journal of International Law* 18 (1924): 720–36.

Handlin, Oscar. "The American Jewish Committee: A Half-Century View." *Commentary* 23 (January 1957): 1–10.

———. *Boston's Immigrants: A Study in Acculturation*. New York: Atheneum, 1968.

Hansen, Marcus. *The Immigrant in American History*. Cambridge, Mass.: Harvard University Press, 1940.

Hartog, Hendrik. "The Constitution of Aspiration and the Rights That Belong to Us All." *Journal of American History* 74 (December 1987): 1013–34.

Harwood, Edwin. "How Should We Enforce Immigration Law?" In *Clamor at the Gates: The New American Immigration*, ed. Nathan Glazer, 73–91. San Francisco: Institute for Contemporary Studies, 1985.

Hay, Douglas. "Property, Authority, and the Criminal Law." In *Albion's Fatal Tree:*

Crime and Society in Eighteenth-Century England, 17–63. New York: Pantheon Books, 1975.

Higham, John. *Send These to Me: Immigrants in Urban America.* Rev. ed. Baltimore: Johns Hopkins University Press, 1984.

——. *Strangers in the Land: Patterns of American Nativism, 1860–1925.* 2d ed. New York: Atheneum, 1978.

Hing, Bill Ong. *Making and Remaking Asian America through Immigration Policy, 1850–1990.* Stanford: Stanford University Press, 1993.

Hirata, Lucie Cheng. "Free, Indentured, Enslaved: Chinese Prostitutes in Nineteenth-Century America." *Signs* 5 (Autumn 1979): 3–29.

Ho Yow. "Chinese Exclusion: A Benefit or a Harm?" *North American Review* 173 (September 1901): 314–30.

Hoexter, Corinne K. *From Canton to California: The Epic of Chinese Immigration.* New York: Four Winds Press, 1976.

Hofstadter, Richard. *Social Darwinism in American Thought.* Boston: Beacon Press, 1944.

Hofstadter, Richard, et al. *The American Republic.* Vol. 2. Englewood Cliffs, N.J.: Prentice-Hall, 1970.

Holder, Charles Frederick. "The Chinaman in American Politics." *North American Review* 166 (January 1898): 226–33.

Hough, Charles M. "Due Process of Law—To-Day." *Harvard Law Review* 32 (1918–19): 218–33.

Howard, A. E. Dick. *The Road from Runnymede: Magna Carta and Constitutionalism in America.* Charlottesville: University Press of Virginia, 1968.

Hune, Shirley. "Politics of Exclusion: Legislative-Executive Conflict, 1876–1882." *Amerasia Journal* 9 (1982): 5–27.

Hutcheson, Robert. "Why the Chinese Should Be Admitted." *Forum* 33 (March 1902): 59–67.

Hutchinson, E. P. *Legislative History of American Immigration Policy, 1798–1965.* Philadelphia: University of Pennsylvania Press, 1981.

Ichioka, Yuji. "*Amerika Nadeshiko*: Japanese Immigrant Women in the United States." *Pacific Historical Review* 49 (1980): 339–57.

——. "The Early Japanese Quest for Citizenship: The Background for the 1922 Ozawa Case." *Amerasia Journal* 4 (1977): 1–22.

Ingersoll, Col. R. G., and Thomas J. Geary. "Should the Chinese Be Excluded?" *North American Review* 157 (July 1893): 52–67.

Irish, John P. "Reasons for Encouraging Japanese Immigration." *Annals of the American Academy of Political and Social Science* 34 (July–December 1909): 294–99.

Iriye, Akira. *Across the Pacific: An Inner History of American–East Asian Relations.* New York: Harcourt, Brace & World, [1967].

Janisch, Hudson N. "The Chinese, the Courts, and the Constitution: A Study of the Legal Issues Raised by Chinese Immigration, 1850–1902." J.S.D. dissertation, University of Chicago Law School, 1971.

Jenks, Jeremiah W., and W. Jett Lauck. *The Immigration Problem.* New York: Funk & Wagnalls, 1912.

Jensen, Joan M. *Passage from India: Asian Indian Immigrants in North America.* New Haven: Yale University Press, 1988.

Jones, David. *The Surnames of the Chinese in America*. San Francisco: Chinese Name Spelling Company, 1904.

Jones, Maldwyn Allen. *American Immigration*. 2d ed. Chicago: University of Chicago Press, 1992.

Kales, Albert M. "New Methods in Due-Process Cases." *American Political and Social Science Review* 12 (1918): 241–50.

Kaufman, Stuart B., Peter J. Albert, and Grace Palladino, eds. *The Samuel Gompers Papers*. Urbana: University of Illinois Press, 1991.

Kennedy, David M. *Over Here: The First World War and American Society*. New York: Oxford University Press, 1980.

Kettner, James H. *The Development of American Citizenship, 1608–1870*. Chapel Hill: University of North Carolina Press, 1978.

Kevles, Daniel. *In the Name of Eugenics: Genetics and the Uses of Human Heredity*. New York: Knopf, 1985.

Kim, Hyung-chan. *A Legal History of Asian Americans, 1790–1990*. Westport, Conn.: Greenwood Press, 1994.

Kingston, Maxine Hong. *China Men*. New York: Knopf, 1980.

Kohler, Max J. "The Administration of Our Chinese Immigration Laws." *Journal of American Asiatic Association* 5 (July 1905): 176–79.

———. "Coolies versus the Privileged Classes." *Journal of the American Asiatic Association* 6 (March 1906): 49–52.

———. *Immigration and Aliens in the United States*. New York: Bloch, 1936.

———. "Jewish Immigrants." In *Immigration and Aliens in the United States*, ed. Max J. Kohler. New York: Bloch, 1936.

———. *Registration of Aliens a Dangerous Project*. N.p., 1926.

———. "Un-American Character of Race Legislation." *Annals of the American Academy of Political and Social Science* 34 (1909): 55–73.

Konvitz, Milton R. *The Alien and the Asiatic in American Law*. Ithaca: Cornell University Press, 1946.

———. *Civil Rights in Immigration*. Ithaca: Cornell University Press, 1953.

Kraut, Alan M. *The Huddled Masses: The Immigrant in American Society, 1880–1921*. Arlington Heights, Ill.: Harlan Davidson, 1982.

———. *Silent Travelers: Germs, Genes and the Immigrant Menace*. New York: Basic Books, 1994.

La Guardia, Fiorello H. *The Making of an Insurgent*. New York: J. B. Lippincott, 1948.

Lai, Him Mark, Genny Lim, and Judy Yung. *Island: Poetry and History of Chinese Immigration on Angel Island, 1910–1940*. San Francisco: HOC DOI, 1980.

Lamm, Richard D., Gov., and Gary Imhoff. *The Immigration Time Bomb: The Fragmentation of America*. New York: Truman Telling Book, 1985.

Legomsky, Stephen H. *Immigration and the Judiciary: Law and Politics in Britain and America*. Oxford: Clarendon Press, 1987.

Le May, Michael C. *From Open Door to Dutch Door: An Analysis of U.S. Immigration Policy since 1920*. New York: Praeger, 1987.

Leonard, Ira, and Robert Parmet. *American Nativism, 1830–1860*. New York: Van Nostrand Reinhold, 1971.

Leung, Peter C. Y. "When a Haircut Was a Luxury: A Chinese Farm Laborer in the Sacramento Delta." *California History* 64 (1985): 211–17.

Light, Ivan. "From Vice District to Tourist Attraction: The Moral Career of America Chinatowns, 1880–1940." *Pacific Historical Review* 43 (1974): 367–94.

Limerick, Patricia Nelson. *The Legacy of Conquest: The Unbroken Past of the American West.* New York: Norton, 1987.

Link, Arthur S., and Richard L. McCormick. *Progressivism.* Arlington Heights, Ill.: Harlan Davidson, 1983.

Lissak, Rivka Shpak. *Pluralism and Progressives: Hull House and the New Immigrants, 1890–1919.* Chicago: University of Chicago Press, 1989.

Lombardi, John. *Labor's Voice in the Cabinet: A History of the Department of Labor from Its Origin to 1921.* New York: Columbia University Press, 1942.

Lombardi, John V. *Venezuela: The Search for Order, the Dream of Progress.* New York: Oxford University Press, 1982.

Lyman, Stanford. "Conflict and the Web of Group Affiliation in San Francisco's Chinatown, 1850–1910." *Pacific Historical Review* 43 (November 1974): 473–99.

Ma, L. Eve Armentrout. "Chinatown Organizations and the Anti-Chinese Movement, 1882–1914." In *Entry Denied: Exclusion and the Chinese Community in America, 1882–1943,* ed. Sucheng Chan, 147–69. Philadelphia: Temple University Press, 1991.

Macarthur, Walter. "Opposition to Oriental Immigration." *Annals of the American Academy of Political and Social Science* 34 (July–December 1909): 239–46.

Macfarlane, Peter Clark. "Japan in California." *Colliers* 51 (June 7, 1913): 5–6.

McClain, Charles J., Jr. "The Chinese Struggle for Civil Rights in Nineteenth-Century America: The First Phase, 1850–1870." *California Law Review* 72 (1984): 529–68.

——. *In Search of Equality: The Chinese Struggle against Discrimination in Nineteenth-Century America.* Berkeley: University of California Press, 1994.

McCurdy, Charles W. "Justice Field and the Jurisprudence of Government-Business Relations: Some Parameters of Laissez-Faire Constitutionalism, 1863–1897." *Journal of American History* 61 (March 1975): 970–1005.

McEvoy, Arthur F. *The Fisherman's Problem: Ecology and Law in the California's Fisheries, 1850–1900.* Cambridge: Cambridge University Press, 1986.

McKee, Delber L. "The Chinese Boycott of 1905–1906 Reconsidered: The Role of Chinese Americans." *Pacific Historical Review* 55 (March 1986): 165–91.

——. *Chinese Exclusion versus the Open Door Policy, 1900–1906.* Detroit: Wayne State University Press, 1977.

——. "The Chinese Must Go! Commissioner General Powderly and Chinese Immigration, 1892–1902." *Pennsylvania History* 44 (1977): 37–51.

McKenzie, R. D. *Oriental Exclusion.* Chicago: University of Chicago Press, 1928.

McLaren, John. "The Early British Columbia Judges, the Rule of Law and the 'Chinese Question': The California and Oregon Connection." In *Law for the Elephant, Law for the Beaver: Essays in the Legal History of the North American West,* ed. John McLaren, Hamar Foster, and Chet Orloff, 237–73. Pasadena: Ninth Judicial Circuit Historical Society, 1992.

Martin, Edward D. "The Lines of Demarcation between Legislative, Exective [*sic*], and Judicial Functions, with Special Reference to the Acts of an Administrative Board or Commission." *American Law Review* 47 (1913): 715–39.

Mashaw, Jerry. *Due Process in the Administrative State*. New Haven: Yale University Press, 1985.

Masters, Edgar Lee. *Across Spoon River*. New York: Farrar & Rinehart, 1936.

Matthews, Fred H. "White Community and 'Yellow Peril.' " *Mississippi Valley Historical Review* 50 (1964): 612–33.

Mei, June, and Jean Pany Yip with Russell Leong. "*The Bitter Society: Ku Shehui*, A Translation, Chapters 37–46." *Amerasia Journal* 8 (1981): 33–67.

Miller, Charles. "The Forest of Due Process of Law: The American Constitutional Tradition." In *Due Process*, ed. J. Roland Pennock and John W. Chapman, 3–63. New York: New York University Press, 1977.

Miller, Joaquin. "The Chinese and the Exclusion Act." *North American Review* 173 (December 1901): 782–89.

Miller, Stuart Creighton. *The Unwelcome Immigrant: The American Image of the Chinese, 1785–1882*. Berkeley: University of California Press, 1969.

Miner, Luella. "American Barbarism and Chinese Hospitality." *Outlook* 72 (December 27, 1902): 984–88.

Mink, Gwendolyn. *Old Labor and New Immigrants in American Political Development: Union, Party, and State, 1875–1920*. Ithaca: Cornell University Press, 1986.

Misrow, Jogesh C. *East Indian Immigration to the Pacific Coast*. Stanford: N.p., 1915.

Modell, John. *The Economics and Politics of Racial Accommodation: The Japanese of Los Angeles, 1900–1942*. Urbana: University of Illinois Press, 1977.

Mooney, Ralph James. "Matthew Deady and the Federal Judicial Response to Racism in the Early West." *Oregon Law Review* 63 (1985): 561–644.

Morison, Elting, ed. *The Letters of Theodore Roosevelt*. Cambridge, Mass.: Harvard University Press, 1951.

Morris, Milton D. *Immigration—The Beleaguered Bureaucracy*. Washington, D.C.: Brookings Institution, 1985.

Mott, Rodney L. *Due Process of Law*. Indianapolis: Bobbs-Merrill, 1926.

Murray, Robert K. *Red Scare: A Study in National Hysteria, 1919–1920*. Minneapolis: University of Minnesota Press, 1955.

National Popular Government League. *To the American People Report upon the Illegal Practices of the United States Department of Justice*. 1920; repr. New York: Arno Press, 1969.

Nee, Victor B., and Brett de Bary Nee. *Long Time Californ': A Documentary Study of an American Chinatown*. New York: Pantheon Books, 1973.

Nelli, Humbert. *The Business of Crime: Italians and Syndicate Crime in the United States*. New York: Oxford University Press, 1976.

Nelson, William. *Fourteenth Amendment*. Cambridge, Mass.: Harvard University Press, 1988.

——. *The Roots of American Bureaucracy, 1830–1900*. Cambridge, Mass.: Harvard University Press, 1982.

Nonet, Philippe. *Administrative Justice: Advocacy and Change in a Government Agency*. New York: Russell Sage Foundation, 1969.

North, Hart H. "Chinese and Japanese Immigration to the Pacific Coast." *California Historical Quarterly* 28 (December 1949): 343–50.

Note. "The American Bar Association and the Chinese Exclusion Case." *American Law Review* 28 (1894): 289–93.

Note. "Developments in the Law—Immigration Policy and the Rights of Aliens." *Harvard Law Review* 96 (April 1983): 1286–1465.

Ogg, Frederic Austin. "A New Plan for Immigrant Inspection." *Outlook* 83 (May 5, 1906): 33–36.

Okihiro, Gary Y. *Margins and Mainstreams: Asians in American History and Culture.* Seattle: University of Washington Press, 1994.

Olin, Spencer. "European Immigrant and Oriental Alien." *Pacific Historical Review* 35 (August 1966): 303–15.

Parker, A. Warner. "Immigration Control." *Saturday Evening Post*, February 28, 1920.

———. "The Ineligible to Citizenship Provisions of the Immigration Act of 1924." *American Journal of International Law* 19 (1925): 23–47.

Parry, Clide, ed. *The Consolidated Treaty Series.* 233 vols. Dobbs Ferry, N.Y.: Oceana Publications, 1981.

Paul, Arnold M. *The Conservative Crisis and the Rule of Law: Attitudes of Bar and Bench, 1887–1895.* Ithaca: Cornell University Press, 1960.

Paul, Rodman W. "The Origin of the Chinese Issue in California." *Mississippi Valley Historical Review* 25 (1938): 181–96.

Paulsen, George E. "The Gresham-Yang Treaty." *Pacific Historical Review* 37 (August 1968): 281–97.

Peffer, George Anthony. "Forbidden Families: Emigration Experiences of Chinese Women under the Page Law, 1875–1882." *Journal of American Ethnic History* 6 (Fall 1986): 28–46.

Peterson, H. C., and Gilbert C. Fite. *Opponents of War, 1917–1918.* Madison: University of Wisconsin Press, 1957.

Phelan, James D. "The Japanese Evil in California." *North American Review* 210 (September 1919): 323–28.

———. "Why the Chinese Should Be Excluded." *North American Review* 178 (November 1901): 663–76.

Pitkin, Thomas. *Keepers of the Gate: A History of Ellis Island.* New York: New York University Press, 1975.

Pomeroy, Earl. *Pacific Slope.* New York: Knopf, 1968.

Post, Louis F. "Administrative Decisions in Connection with Immigration." *American Political Science Review* 10 (May 1916): 251–61.

———. *The Deportations Delirium of Nineteen-Twenty.* Chicago: Charles H. Kerr, 1923.

Pound, Cuthbert W. "The Judicial Power." *Harvard Law Review* 35 (May 1922): 787–96.

Pound, Roscoe. "Executive Justice." In *Selected Essays in Constitutional Law.* Book 4. Chicago: Foundation Press, 1938. Reprinted from *Columbia Law Review* 14 (1912): 12.

Powderly, Terence. *The Path I Trod.* New York: AMS Press, [1968].

Powell, Thomas Reed. "Judicial Review of Administrative Action in Immigration Proceedings." *Harvard Law Review* 22 (1909): 360–66.

Preston, William, Jr. *Aliens and Dissenters: Federal Suppression of Radicals, 1903–1933.* Cambridge, Mass.: Harvard University Press, 1963.

Proceedings of the Chinese Exclusion Convention, San Francisco, November 21, 22, 1901. San Francisco, 1901.

Proper, Emberson Edward. *Colonial Immigration Laws: A Study of the Regulation by the English Colonies in America.* New York: Columbia University Press, 1900.

Przybyszewski, Linda C. A. "Judge Lorenzo Sawyer and the Chinese: Civil Rights Decisions in the Ninth Circuit." *Western Legal History* 1 (Winter–Spring 1988): 23–56.

Ralph, Julian. "The Chinese Leak." *Harper's New Monthly Magazine* 82 (March 1891): 515–25.

Reich, Charles. "The New Property." *Yale Law Journal* 73 (1964): 733–87.

Reynolds, James Bronson. "Enforcement of the Chinese Exclusion Law." *Annals of the American Academy of Political and Social Science* 34 (July–December 1909): 363–74.

Rischin, Moses. *The Promised City: New York's Jews, 1870–1914.* Cambridge, Mass.: Harvard University Press, 1962.

Rosen, Ruth. *The Lost Sisterhood: Prostitution in America, 1900–1918.* Baltimore: Johns Hopkins University Press, 1982.

Ross, William G. *A Muted Fury: Populists, Progressives, and Labor Unions Confront the Courts, 1890–1937.* Princeton: Princeton University Press, 1994.

Rothman, David J. *Conscience and Convenience: The Asylum and Its Alternatives in Progressive America.* Boston: Little, Brown, 1980.

Rowell, Chester H. "Chinese and Japanese Immigrants—A Comparison." *Annals of the American Academy of Political and Social Science* 34 (July–December 1909): 223–30.

Sachar, Howard Morley. *A History of the Jews in America.* New York: Knopf, 1992.

Safford, Victor. *Immigration Problems: Personal Experiences of an Official.* New York: Dodd, Mead, 1925.

Sandmeyer, Elmer Clarence. *The Anti-Chinese Movement in California.* 1939; repr. Urbana: University of Illinois Press, 1973.

——. "California Anti-Chinese Legislation and the Federal Courts: A Study in Federal Relations." *Pacific Historical Review* 5 (September 1936): 191–211.

Sargent, Frank P. "The Need for Closer Inspection and Greater Restriction of Immigrants." *Century Magazine* 67 (January 1904): 470–73.

Saveth, Edward. "Race and Nationalism in American Historiography: The Late Nineteenth Century." *Political Science Quarterly* 54 (September 1939): 421–41.

Saxton, Alexander. *The Indispensable Enemy: Labor and the Anti-Chinese Movement in California.* Berkeley: University of California Press, 1971.

Sayles, Mary B. "The Keepers of the Gate." *Outlook* 87 (December 28, 1907): 913–23.

Scheiber, Harry N. *The Wilson Administration and Civil Liberties, 1917–1921.* Ithaca: Cornell University Press, 1960.

Schuck, Peter H. "The Transformation of Immigration Law." *Columbia Law Review* 84 (January 1984): 1–90.

Schuck, Peter H., and Rogers Smith. *Citizenship without Consent: Illegal Aliens in the American Polity*. New Haven: Yale University Press, 1985.

Seager, Robert. "Some Denominational Reactions to Chinese Immigration to California, 1856–1892." *Pacific Historical Review* 23 (1959): 49–66.

Semonche, John E. *Charting the Future: The Supreme Court Responds to a Changing Society, 1890–1920*. Westport, Conn.: Greenwood Press, 1978.

Shapiro, Martin. *Courts: A Comparative and Political Analysis*. Chicago: University of Chicago Press, 1981.

——. *Law and Politics in the Supreme Court: New Approaches to Political Jurisprudence*. New York: Free Press of Glencoe, 1964.

——. *Who Guards the Guardians?* Athens: University of Georgia Press, 1988.

Skowronek, Stephen. *Building a New American State: The Expansion of National Administrative Capacities, 1877–1920*. New York: Cambridge University Press, 1982.

Smith, John Morton. *Freedom's Fetters: The Alien and Sedition Laws and American Civil Liberties*. Ithaca: Cornell University Press, 1956.

Smith, Richmond Mayo. "Assimilation of Nationalities in the United States, I." *Political Science Quarterly* 9 (September 1894): 426–44.

——. "The Control of Immigration. I." *Political Science Quarterly* 3 (March 1888): 46–77.

——. "The Control of Immigration. II." *Political Science Quarterly* 3 (June 1888): 220–25.

——. *Emigration and Immigration: A Study in Social Science*. New York: Scribner's Sons, 1890.

Smith, Rogers M. "The 'American Creed' and American Identity: The Limits of Liberal Citizenship in the United States." *Western Political Quarterly* 41 (June 1988): 225–51.

Stanton, William Ragan. *The Leopard's Spots: Scientific Attitudes toward Race in America, 1815–1859*. Chicago: University of Chicago Press, 1960.

Steiner, Edward A. *From Alien to Citizen: The Story of My Life in America*. New York: Fleming H. Revell, 1914.

——. *On the Trail of the Immigrant*. New York: Fleming H. Revell, 1906.

Steiner, Stan. *Fusang: The Chinese Who Built America*. New York: Harper & Row, 1979.

Stephens, Harold M. *Administrative Tribunals and the Rules of Evidence: A Study in Jurisprudence and Administrative Law*. Cambridge: Cambridge University Press, 1933.

Sterett, Susan. " 'Entitled to Have a Hearing': Due Process in the 1890s." *Social and Legal Studies* 3 (1994): 47–70.

Stockwell, Alcott W. "The Immigrant's Bill of Rights." *American Journal of Sociology* 15 (July 1909): 21–31.

Straus, Oscar S. "The Spirit and Letter of Exclusion." *North American Review* 187 (April 1908): 481–85.

——. *Under Four Administrations*. Boston: Houghton Mifflin, 1922.

Sui Sin Far [Edith Eaton]. "In the Land of the Free." *Independent* 67 (September 2, 1909): 504–8.

——. "Leaves from the Mental Portfolio of an Eurasian." *Independent* 66 (January 21, 1909): 125–32.

Sutherland, George. "Private Rights and Government Control." *Central Law Journal* 85 (September 7, 1917): 168–75.

Swindler, William F. *Court and Constitution in the Twentieth Century*. 3 vols. Indianapolis: Bobbs-Merrill, 1969–74.

Swisher, Carl Brent. *Motivation and Political Technique in the California Constitution, 1878–79*. Claremont: Pomona College, 1930.

Takaki, Ronald T. *Iron Cages: Race and Culture in 19th Century America*. Seattle: University of Washington Press, 1979.

——. *Strangers from a Different Shore: A History of Asian Americans*. New York: Penguin Books, 1990.

Thompson, E. P. *Whigs and Hunters: The Origins of the Black Act*. New York: Pantheon Books, 1975.

Truth versus Fiction, Justice versus Prejudice, Meat for All, Not for a Few: A Plain and Unvarnished Statement Why Exclusion Laws against the Chinese Should Not Be Re-enacted. N.p., n.d. In John Fryer Collection, Doe Library, University of California, Berkeley.

Tsai, Shih-Shan Henry. *China and the Overseas Chinese in the United States, 1868–1911*. Fayetteville: University of Arkansas Press, 1983.

——. *The Chinese Experience in America*. Bloomington: Indiana University Press, 1986.

——. "Reaction to Exclusion: The Boycott of 1905 and Chinese National Awakening." *Historian* 39 (1976): 95–110.

Twiss, Benjamin R. *Lawyers and the Constitution: How Laissez-Faire Came to the Supreme Court*. Princeton: Princeton University Press, 1942.

U.S. Bureau of the Census. *Historical Statistics of the United States, Colonial Times to 1957*. Washington, D.C.: GPO, 1975.

U.S. Congress. *Operation of Present Immigration Law*. 63d Cong., 1st sess., 1913. S. Doc. 52.

U.S. Congress. House. *Facts Concerning the Enforcement of the Chinese-Exclusion Laws*. 59th Cong., 1st sess., May 25, 1906, H. Doc. 847.

——. Committee on Immigration and Naturalization. *Japanese Immigration*. 66th Cong., 2d sess., July 12, 13, and 14, 1920.

——. Select Committee on Immigration and Naturalization. *Report*. 51st Cong., 2d sess., 1890.

——. *Chinese Immigration*. 51st Cong., 2d sess., 1890.

U.S. Congress. Senate. *Exclusion of Chinese Laborers*. 57th Cong., 1st sess., Dec. 10, 1901, S. Doc. 162.

——. Committee on Immigration. *Chinese Exclusion*. 57th Cong., 1st sess., S. Rept. 776, 1902.

U.S. Department of Commerce and Labor. *Annual Report of the Commissioner-General of Immigration*, 1903–11.

——. *Immigration Laws and Regulations*, 1903–11.

——. *Treaty, Laws, and Regulations Governing the Admission of Chinese*, 1903–17.

U.S. Department of Labor. *Annual Report of the Commissioner General of Immigration*, 1911–24.

——. *Immigration Laws and Rules*. 1911–24.

——. *U.S. Immigration Service Bulletin*. Vol. 1 (1919).

U.S. Immigration Commission. *Reports of the U.S. Immigration Commission: Immigration Legislation*. 61st Cong., 3d sess., 1911. S. Doc. 758.

——. *Reports of the Immigration Commission: Statistical Review of Immigration, 1820–1910*. 61st Cong., 3d sess., 1911. S. Doc. 756.

U.S. Industrial Commission. *Reports of the Industrial Commission on Immigration: Including Testimony with Reviews and Digest*. 1901; repr. New York: Arno Press, 1970.

U.S. National Commission on Law Observance and Enforcement. *Report on the Enforcement of the Deportation Laws of the United States*, by Reuben Oppenheimer. Washington, D.C.: GPO, 1931.

U.S. Treasury Department. *Annual Report of the Commissioner General of Immigration*, 1894–1902.

——. *Annual Report of the Secretary of Treasury*, 1891–1901.

——. *Laws, Treaty, and Regulations Relating to the Exclusion of the Chinese*. 1902.

Urofsky, Melvin. "State Courts and Protective Legislation during the Progressive Era: A Reevaluation." *Journal of American History* 63 (June 1985): 63–91.

Van Alstyne, William. "The Demise of the Right-Privilege Distinction in Constitutional Law." *Harvard Law Review* 81 (1968): 1439–64.

Van Vleck, William C. *The Administrative Control of Aliens*. New York: Commonwealth Fund, 1923.

Verkuil, Paul. "The Emerging Concept of Administrative Procedure." *Columbia Law Review* 78 (March 1978): 258–329.

Wakeman, Frederic, Jr. *The Fall of Imperial China*. New York: Free Press, 1975.

Webster, Prentiss. "Acquisition of Citizenship." *American Law Review* 23 (1889): 759–74.

White, Richard. "Race Relations in the American West." *American Quarterly* 38 (1986): 396–416.

White, Leonard Dupee. *The Republican Era, 1869–1901: A Study in Administrative History*. New York: Macmillan, 1958.

Wiebe, Robert H. *The Search for Order, 1877–1920*. New York: Hill and Wang, 1967.

Williams, Jerry R. *And Yet They Come: Portuguese Immigration from the Azores to the United States*. New York: Center for Migration Studies, 1982.

Wilson, Woodrow. "The Study of Administration." *Political Science Quarterly* 2 (June 1887): 197–222.

Wittke, Carl. *The German-Language Press in America*. [Lexington]: University of Kentucky Press, 1957.

Wong, Kai Kah. "A Menace to America's Oriental Trade." *North American Review* 178 (January 1904): 414–24.

Wood, Gordon S. *The Creation of the American Republic, 1776–1787*. New York: Norton, 1969.

Woodworth, Marshall. "Citizenship of the United States under the Fourteenth Amendment." *American Law Review* 30 (1896): 535.

——. "Who Are Citizens of the United States?" *American Law Review* 32 (1898): 554–61.

Wu Ting-Fang. "Mutual Helpfulness between China and the United States." *North American Review* 171 (July 1900): 1–12.

Wunder, John R. "Anti-Chinese Violence in the American West, 1850–1910." In *Law for the Elephant, Law for the Beaver: Essays in the Legal History of the North American West*, ed. John McLaren, Hamar Foster, and Chet Orloff, 212–36. Pasadena: Ninth Judicial Circuit Historical Society, 1992.

——. "The Chinese and the Courts in the Pacific Northwest: Justice Denied?" *Pacific Historical Review* 52 (May 1893): 191–211.

Young, John Russell. "The Chinese Question Again." *North American Review* 154 (May 1892): 596–602.

INDEX

Abercrombie, John W., 236, 237

Act of Aug. 18, 1894: construed in *Sing Tuck*, 108–9; finality of inspectors' decisions, 97–98, 110, 112–14; requires exhaustion of remedies, 110

Adamic, Louis, 153

Administrative agencies: as distinct from courts, 180, 182, 183, 184, 186, 194; Progressives' faith in, 180

Administrative law: administrative finality in, 27, 29–30; as alien, 245–46; post–New Deal, 246–47, 250; questions of law vs. fact, 29–30, 195–96; rights-privilege distinction in, 31, 182, 249. *See also* Finality, administrative; Immigration law; Judicial review

Administrative Procedures Act, 246, 247

Administrative process: judicialization of, 247; and separation of powers, 29, 245; supplants judicial process, 246

Admissions procedures, 145–49; attorneys excluded under, 147, 222–23; board of special inquiry in, 147–48, 223; women and children under, 147

Aid to Families with Dependent Children, 250

Alien and Sedition Acts (1798), 3

Alien Contract Labor Law, 24

Alien Land Laws, 128

Aliens: possess privileges, not rights, 51, 53, 54, 170, 182–83, 194, 205–6, 215, 248; resident, status of, 48–49, 51, 53–54, 132, 249–50; rights of, compared to citizens', xviii, 48, 51–52, 114, 171, 207, 209, 215, 240–41, 249–50

American Asiatic Association, 105

American Bar Association, Committee on International Law, 55

American Federation of Labor, 102, 103, 105, 122

Americanization: of administrative process, 246; as Progressive strategy, 130; as test for admission, 151, 210

American Jewish Committee, 158

American Legion, 133

Anarchists: definition of, 141, 142–43; exclusion of, 131, 140

Anderson, George W., 238, 241

Angel Island, 59, 60, 167, 200; workload at, 144–45

Anti-Chinese Law and Labor League, 55

Anti-Chinese movement: arguments of, 10–11; in California, 5, 8, 9; federal judges' support of, 33–34, 72; labor's support of, 9, 12; in 1902 exclusion campaign, 102–3; opposition to, 8, 13. *See also* Chinese exclusion; Nativism

Anti-immigrant movement. *See* Nativism

Anti-radicalism: in immigration policy, 131–40; during Red Scare, 133–34, 233–38, 239

Arthur, Chester A., 15

Ashton, J. Hubley, 47, 49, 87

Asian Indians: exclusion of, 199, 200–201, 298 (n. 111); immigration of, 125–26; litigation by, 200–202, 206; naturalization denied to, 208

Asiatic Barred Zone, 133

Asiatic Exclusion League, 127, 199, 200

Assimilation: faith in, 3, 130; lack of faith in, 11, 15–16, 132, 251

Attorney, right to, 189, 222–23, 242–43; on administrative appeal, 148, 287 (n. 42); in Chinese exclusion proceedings, 62, 66, 83, 166, 189, 221–22; and deportation, 185, 189–90, 222, 231–32, 236–37, 242; litigation concerning, 185–86, 188–91; and right to be heard, 175–76, 185

Attorneys: in Bureau of Immigration, 224–25; in Chinese habeas corpus cases, xv, 70, 83; for Chinese Six Companies, 40, 47, 70, 112, 174; fees of, 70; importance to favorable outcomes, xv, 72, 83, 237, 242–43; in Jewish community, 137, 158–59, 202; oppose affidavits, 189–90. *See also* Attorney, right to; U.S. attorneys

Bail, 233, 237, 239, 243, 275 (n.68)
Barbour, J. H., 220–21, 231
Barnett, Ralph, 202
Berkshire, F. W., 231–32
Bill of Rights: limited application to aliens, 48–50, 52–53, 54, 136, 142, 143, 170–71, 230. *See also* Fifth Amendment; Fourth Amendment
Bitter Society, The, 153, 154, 163, 169
Board of Special Inquiry, 140–41, 149, 192–93, 247; in admissions, 147; discretion of, 148, 153–55; members' qualifications challenged, 156, 186, 204, 223; procedures of, criticized, 156, 223
Board of Tax Appeals, 244
Boston raid of 1903, 152
Bourquin, George, 238–39
Brewer, David: dissent in *Fong Yue Ting,* 53–54; dissent in *Ju Toy,* 113; dissent in *Sing Tuck,* 109–10; opposition to administrative power, 161–62
Brown, Joseph E., 16, 17
Bureaucracy: fear of, xvii–xviii, 161–62, 246
Bureau of Immigration: Chinese Americans suspected by, 115, 150–

51, 208–10, 299 (n. 125); and Chinese boycott, 164–66; criticism of, 139–40, 142–43, 152–56, 163–64, 185, 235–36, 238–39, 244, 247; defense against critics, 139, 144–45, 203; and enforcement of Chinese exclusion laws, 38, 100, 101–2, 114–15, 155, 187; freed from judicial practices, 186–87, 192–94, 196, 214, 245; and Interstate Commerce Commission, compared, 183, 204–5, 206; judicial deference to, xiv–xv, 28–29, 102, 114, 137, 139, 180, 184, 189, 196, 201, 202, 212–14, 215, 218, 240, 244; law division within, 224–25; procedural reform in, 217–33 passim; and Red Raids, 133–34, 137, 233–42; restrictionist perspective of, 143–44, 219, 220, 226–29, 232–33; supervision of, 149, 151–52, 156; unusual power of, xiv, 217–18; workload of, 144–45, 252. *See also* Chinese exclusion, enforcement of; Procedures, immigration
Burlingame Treaty, 9, 13, 14, 48; and right to migrate, 249

Cable Act of 1922, 212
California: anti-Asian campaign in, 5, 12, 127–29, 199–201, 226–27; and Geary Act, 55–56, 58; as key to national immigration law development, xvii, 247; role in Chinese exclusion, 13, 14, 260–61 (n. 80)
Caminetti, Anthony: and Red Raids, 134, 234, 235, 236, 237, 239
Canton certificate. *See* Section 6 certificates
Carey, John P., 76
Castle Garden, 25
Castro, Cipriano, 198
Certificates of identification, 17, 19, 20, 23
Chae Chan Ping v. United States, 22, 29; contract analogy in, 263 (n. 125);

opinion, 23; relied on, 28, 48, 50,
52, 53, 136, 248

Chafee, Zechariah, 238, 243

China: denounces treaty, 111, 163; emigration policy of, 9; negotiations on
exclusion, 21, 22, 57, 163

Chinese American organizations, 40–
41; conflict among, 41, 58, 89–90; in
resisting exclusion, 42, 57, 157. *See
also* Chinese Six Companies; Triad
societies

Chinese Americans: Bureau of Immigration's suspicions of, 115, 150–51,
208–10; citizenship of, 20, 98–99,
208; exempt from exclusion, 20;
foreign-born children of, 210, 299
(nn. 124, 125); inspection of, 59,
65–66, 151–53; jurisdiction over, in
exclusion proceedings, 98–100, 107–
10, 111–13; paper sons, 44, 61–62,
150; population of, 10; and Quota
Act of 1924, 212, 300 (n. 132); violence against, 21. *See also* Chinese
immigrants; Citizenship

Chinese boycott, 139, 153, 162, 163–
64; and Geary Act resistance,
compared, 166–67; mixed success
of, 165–67, 221; mobilizes anti-
exclusion opinion, 164, 167–69

Chinese Bureau, 38, 39, 59, 62, 70,
106

Chinese Consolidated Benevolent
Association. *See* Chinese Six Companies

Chinese exclusion: and Chinese government, 21, 22; Chinese resistance
to, xv, 18, 37, 43, 116, 137, 162–67,
247; citizens exempt from, 20; economic arguments for, 10, 12, 15, 103;
exempt Chinese under, 17, 20, 62,
64–65, 104, 154, 163, 164, 165, 166;
extended to Hawaii, 103; extended
to Philippines, 105–6; extended
without time limit, 111; labor's support of, 9, 12, 102, 103, 105; non-
Chinese opposition to, 8–9, 16, 17,

104–5, 167–69; as political issue,
39, 57–58, 85; racial arguments for,
10–11, 15–16, 17, 260–61 (n. 80);
repeal of, 250; women and families
under, 20, 43, 64, 65–66, 67–68. *See
also* Chinese exclusion, enforcement
of; Chinese exclusion legislation

Chinese exclusion, enforcement of:
and belief in Chinese fraud, xvi, 59,
62, 81–82, 150–51; and Chinese boycott, 163, 164–67; Chinese interpreters in, 62, 302 (n. 26); criticism
of, 59–62, 64, 100, 109, 110, 153,
154–55; and detention of Chinese,
63, 101, 152, 221; exempt classes'
treatment in, 62, 149–50, 154–55,
164, 165; finality of inspectors' decisions in, 97–98, 110, 112–14; fragmentation of, 40, 101–2, 104; inspection of Chinese, 59–63, 149–52;
judicial and administrative procedures, contrasted, 81–85, 101, 145;
officials' frustration with, 37, 104;
officials responsible for, 38–40,
101–2; and raids on Chinese, 152,
153, 228; restrictionist thrust of, 34,
59, 63–64, 75, 85; steamship companies, liability of, 63; and weighing of
evidence, 82, 155. *See also* Collector
of customs; Procedures, judicial;
U.S. district court (N.D. Calif.)

Chinese Exclusion Act of 1882: congressional debates on, 15–17; litigation concerning, 18–19; provisions
of, 17–18; vs. open-door policy, 7;
vote on, 261 (n. 97)

Chinese Exclusion Act of Sept. 13,
1888: administrative finality under,
27, 94; deportation under, 87; passage of, 22; validity of, 28, 87, 94,
275 (n. 59)

Chinese Exclusion Case. See *Chae Chan
Ping v. United States*

Chinese exclusion legislation: Act of
1882, 17–18; Act of 1884, 19–20;
Act of Sept. 13, 1888, 22; Scott Act

(1888), 22–23; Geary Act (1892), 45; McCreary Amendment (1893), 56; Act of Aug. 18, 1894, 97; Act of 1902, 102–5; Act of 1904, 111, 163. *See also* Act of Aug. 18, 1894; Chinese Exclusion Act of 1882; Chinese Exclusion Act of Sept. 13, 1888; Geary Act (1892); McCreary Amendment (1893)

Chinese foreign ministry: as immigrants' advocate, 41–42, 47, 58, 104, 105, 163. *See also* Wu Ting-Fang

Chinese immigrants: and African Americans, compared, 8, 10; and "coolie" trade, 10, 259 (n. 55); experience with bureaucracies, 42; and general immigration laws, 26, 31–32, 155; naturalization denied to, 13, 18; number admitted, 67. *See also* Chinese Americans

Chinese laborers: under exclusion laws, 17, 18, 21, 22, 64

Chinese litigation: challenging exclusion, xv, 18–19, 20, 34–35, 69–81 passim, 116; by Chinese Americans, 98–100; effects on immigration law, xv, xvii, 117–18, 248; against state laws, 13; strategy after *Ju Toy*, 170, 174–77, 179, 181–83; success of, 81

Chinese merchants: commercial allies of, 104–5, 167; defined, 57, 95; documentation required of, 17–18, 19–20; leadership role of, 41, 46, 162; under McCreary Amendment, 56–57, 95–96; right to bring families, 20, 300 (n. 132)

Chinese Merchants Exchange, 96

Chinese Six Companies: as community leader, 40–41, 46–47; competes with Triads, 89–90; criticizes *Ju Toy*, 155; litigation by, 13, 40, 47, 112

Chinese students, 64, 149–50, 166

Chin Yow v. United States, 175, 176–77, 183, 203, 205; fair hearing requirement in, 176–77, 179, 181, 187; juris-

diction if unfair hearing, 213; narrowed, 186–87; opinion, 175–77, 181; promise unrealized, 214; unresolved questions, 181–82

Choate, Joseph H., 47

Chune Shea Wun, 91

Chung Sai Yat Po, 167

Chy Lung v. Freeman, 5

Citizenship: and administrative due process, 174–76, 180, 207, 210–12, 214, 215, 240–41, 247–48; birthright, of Chinese recognized, 20, 98–99, 208; of Chinese, doubted, 115, 150–51, 208–10; competing definitions of, 99, 207–8; of foreign-born children, 210, 299 (n. 124); functional definition of, 48, 250; and jurisdiction in immigration proceedings, 98–101, 106, 108–10, 112–14, 171, 210–12, 240–41; of married women, 212; naturalization, denied to Asians, 13, 98, 208. *See also* Chinese Americans

Clark, Jane Perry, 242, 243, 244

Clarke, John H., 240

Cleveland, Grover, 55

Collector of customs: as administrator of Chinese exclusion, 18, 32, 34, 38–39, 58–59, 65–67, 75, 81–85, 102; discretion of, 65–66; political ties of, 38–39, 85; terms of service, 271–72 (n. 159); and U.S. attorneys, 84–85. *See also* Chinese exclusion, enforcement of

Collins, George D., 99

Colyer v. Skeffington, 238, 241

Commissioner general of immigration: and organized labor, 102, 156. *See also* Bureau of Immigration

Communist Labor party, 237, 239

Communist party, 237, 239

Congressional power: to deport aliens, 49, 50–51, 52, 53, 54, 248; over foreign commerce, 4, 23; over immigration procedures, 28–29, 136, 186–87, 248; inherent sovereign

power, 23; plenary, over immigration policy, 23, 28–29, 52–53
Cooley, Alford W., 176
Cooley, Thomas, 248
Coolidge, Mary Roberts: *Chinese Immigration*, 167–68
Corruption: of government officials, alleged, 45, 303 (n. 52)
Courts: as distinct from administrative agencies, 182, 183, 184, 186, 194. *See also* Judicial review; U.S. federal courts
Coxe, Alfred, 196

Darrow, Clarence, 142
Davis, John W. 205–6
Deer Island, 233
De Haven, John, 79–80, 92, 106, 108; anti-immigrant views of, 72, 215; on detention of Chinese, 101
Denis, George, 56
Deportation: of Chinese under Geary Act, 46, 49–50, 57, 86–88, 88–89; of Chinese under general immigration laws, 115, 155, 187, 294 (n. 26); defined as civil proceeding, 53, 136, 171, 230; legislation providing for, 26, 46, 115, 131–32, 230, 234, 239, 294 (n. 26); as nativist strategy, 131–32, 133; perceived as punishment, 49, 54; during Red Scare, 133–34, 233–38; time limits for, 131–32, 228, 234, 243. *See also* Deportation procedures
Deportation procedures, 136, 140–42, 145, 171, 172–73, 192–93; affidavits used in, 189–90; attorney, right to, 185, 189, 222; bail in, 233, 237, 239, 243; detention of aliens in, 233, 237, 243; judicial hearings in, for alleged citizens, 211; judicial hearings in, in Chinese cases, 46, 50, 52, 53, 115, 152, 187, 294 (n. 26); preliminary examination in, 231–32, 243; telegraphic warrants in, 232, 243; witnesses in, right to subpoena and

cross-examine, 189, 191, 222, 230, 304 (n. 69). *See also* Attorney, right to; Procedures, immigration
Dibble, Henry C., 112, 170
Dickinson, J. M., 98
Dickinson, John, 30, 31, 114, 194, 246
Dietrich, Frank, 190
Dillingham, William, 223
Discretion, administrative, 49, 148, 149; alleged abuse of, 152, 153–54, 174–75, 194–95, 203, 229; and efficient governance, 180, 183–84, 203, 205–6, 214, 230–31, 232–33, 244, 246; in evidentiary practices, 64–65, 82, 83, 195, 228; over immigration procedures, 185, 188–89, 214, 216, 230–32, 234–35; in interpreting law, 142–43, 146–47, 155, 196, 199–202, 206; and restriction of immigration, 58, 64–67, 196–97, 199–201, 202–3, 226–27, 229–33, 234; and rise of nativism, xvii, 136–38, 180, 199, 215; in rule-making, 64, 146–47, 154; for substantive justice, 226; vs. rule of law, xvii–xviii, 154, 201, 246. *See also* Procedures, immigration
Dolph, Joseph N., 27
Dooling, Maurice T., 194, 210, 213, 214, 215, 245; on Asian Indian exclusion, 201; disposition of immigration cases, 295 (n. 42); as proceduralist, 184, 191–92
Due process: under Fifth Amendment, 113; Progressives' view of, xviii, 179–80, 226; revolution, 251; substantive, 179–80. *See also* Due process, administrative
Due process, administrative: and administrative efficiency, xviii, 118, 145, 180, 182–84, 194, 205–6, 214, 230–31, 232–33, 244, 251–52; for aliens, xvii–xviii, 29, 30–31, 48–50, 51–54, 136, 170–71, 205; for alleged citizens, 110, 112, 113, 171, 174–77, 180, 207, 209, 210–12, 215, 249–50;

challenged as inadequate, xvii–xviii, 48–50, 54, 100, 101, 109, 136–37, 142, 143, 154, 156; fundamental principles approach, 172, 173, 181, 183, 184, 185; before Interstate Commerce Commission, 182, 183; judicial procedures, as the standard, xviii, 48–50, 118, 140, 156, 170, 186, 205, 243–44, 246–47; judicial standards, as inappropriate, 170–71, 182, 186, 199, 214; and nature of proceedings, 110, 113, 181–83, 186, 205; and policy objectives, 118, 138, 182, 198–99, 226, 232–33, 244; procedural rights sought, 155, 156, 163, 183, 184, 185; and right to be heard, xviii, 173, 183, 187, 203, 293 (n. 8); stakes theory as basis for, 175, 183, 186, 205; statutes and agency regulations, as standard for, 181, 183, 186–87, 214, 240; in tax proceedings, 30, 113, 293 (n. 8). *See also* Fair hearing requirement

Dunn, John R., 151

Eaton, Edith. *See* Sui Sin Far

Elkus, Abram, 202, 203–5, 206

Ellis Island, 140, 143, 144, 159, 220; inspection of immigrants at, 145–49, 153

Emerson, Ralph Waldo, 3

Ethnic organizations. *See* Immigrant aid societies

Eugenics movement, 124, 130

Evarts, Maxwell, 47, 97–98, 175–76, 183

Evidence: administrative discretion over, 64, 65–66, 83, 148, 154, 196; affidavits as, 189–91, 295 (n. 36); under Chinese exclusion legislation, 17–18, 19–20, 46, 57, 64, 88, 95; Chinese testimony as, 8, 59, 67–68, 77–81, 85, 91, 150, 259 (n. 40); in judicial hearings of Chinese cases, 18–19, 20, 77–79, 96–97, 100–101; white witnesses requirement, 65–66,

83, 95, 101. *See also* Evidence, evaluation of; Section 6 certificates

Evidence, evaluation of: differences in, 82–83, 195; in immigration proceedings, 66–67, 82, 147, 148; in judicial hearings, 69, 79–80, 91, 92, 100–101, 195; sufficiency of, in administrative proceedings, 194–95, 204, 207, 296 (n. 59). *See also* Evidence; Judicial review

Exhaustion of remedies, 106–7, 110

Ex parte Leong Wah Jam, 210

Ex parte Lew Lin Shew, 191

Ex parte Royall, 107

Fair hearing requirement, 136, 248; in *Chin Yow*, 176–77; citizens and, 210–11, 213–14; competing definitions of, 180, 181, 183; and evidentiary practices, 187, 194, 203, 204–5; litigation strategy concerning, 177, 180, 181, 185–86; manifest unfairness standard, 186; and procedural rights, 177, 179, 181, 183, 184, 186–87; procedure if not met, 212–14, 241. *See also* Due process, administrative

Federal Trade Commission, 244, 247–48, 308 (n. 19)

Federal Trade Commission v. Gratz, 248–49

Felton, Charles N., 21, 78

Field, Stephen J., 19, 20, 79; dissent in *Fong Yue Ting*, 53–54; opinion in *Chae Chan Ping*, 23, 28

Fifteen Passenger Bill, 14

Fifth Amendment, 113, 179–80, 230

Filipinos: under Quota Act of 1924, 284 (n. 87)

Finality, administrative: challenged, 176–77, 205; and citizens, 108–10, 112–14; legislative provisions for, 26–28, 97–98, 110. *See also* Judicial review

Fisher, David, 76

Fong Yue Ting v. United States, 47–48, 114, 171, 181, 241; immigration law, effect on, 54, 184–85, 248; relied upon, 113, 136, 143, 172; response to, 54–55, 58; in Supreme Court, 48–54, 269 (n. 107). *See also* Geary Act (1892)

Foreign-born population, 257 (n. 1)

Foreign-language press, 157, 159

Foster, John, 152

Fourteenth Amendment, 13, 179–80, 208

Fourth Amendment, 238–39

Frankfurter, Felix, 113, 238, 246

Fraud: suspected of Chinese, xvi, 101, 150–51

Free Speech League, 142

Freund, Ernst, 114, 238

Fu Chi Hao, 149–50

Fuller, Melville W.: dissent in *Fong Yue Ting*, 53–54

Garter, Charles, 56, 84

Geary, Thomas, 47

Geary Act (1892), 95, 102, 152, 229; Chinese resistance to, 46–48, 57, 166–67; deportation under, 46, 49–50, 57, 86–88; enforcement of, 38, 55, 57–58, 86–88; legal challenge of, 47–54; limits on judicial discretion, 46, 50, 94–95; McCreary Amendment to, 56; passage of, 45–46; section 4 invalidated, 171; upheld, 52–53. See also *Fong Yue Ting v. United States*

Gegiow, Ali, 202

General Land Office, 27, 29–30, 31

Gentlemen's Agreement, 128, 199

George, Henry, 10, 218

Goldberg v. Kelly, 250

Gompers, Samuel, 102, 105, 142

Goodnow, Frank J., 182

Gray, Horace: in *Fong Yue Ting*, 52–53; in *Nishimura Ekiu*, 29

Greenhalge, Oscar, 43, 59

Gresham-Yang Treaty (1894), 57, 163

Mrs. Gue Lim v. United States, 43

Habeas corpus, writ of: and Chinese exclusion litigation, 18, 21, 27, 34–35, 74–75; under Constitution, 75; and exhaustion of remedies, 106–7, 109–10; expansion of right to, 75, 107; judicial respect for, 35, 69, 72, 75, 92; petitions filed in California, 34, 98, 99, 169–70, 180, 191, 295 (n. 42); petitions filed in New York, 102, 278 (n. 34); right of Chinese to, 75; and rule of law, 75, 92. *See also* Procedures, judicial

Habeas Corpus Act of 1867, 107

Hagar v. Reclamation District, 293 (n. 8)

Hager, John, 34, 75

Hall, Prescott, 227

Hand, Augustus, 305 (n. 93)

Hand, Learned, 196, 213

Harlan, John Marshall, 98, 173–74

Hawaii: exclusion extended to, 103

Haw Moy v. North, 209

Hayes, Rutherford B., 14

Haymarket Affair, 25

Heacock, E. H., 77, 101, 106, 111; in Chinese deportation cases, 88, 91; evaluation of evidence by, 79–81, 91; habeas corpus hearings before, 77–81; on McCreary Amendment, 96–97. *See also* U.S. commissioners

Head tax, 4–6

Hebrew Sheltering and Immigrant Aid Society, 158, 219, 223

Henderson v. Wickham, and Commissioners of Immigration v. The North German Lloyd, 4–5

Hepburn Act of 1906, 204

Hoar, George Frisbie, 16, 17, 105

Hoffman, Ogden, 174; in Chinese habeas corpus cases, 19–21, 72, 76; on habeas corpus, right to, 75, 92

Holmes, Oliver Wendell, 3

Holmes, Oliver Wendell, Jr.: opinion in *Chin Yow*, 176–77, 181, 187, 195, 213; opinion in *Gegiow*, 206; opinion in *Ju Toy*, 113, 114, 174; opinion in *Sing Tuck*, 109–10, 111, 182

Holt, George Chandler, 190–91, 195, 215

Hoover, J. Edgar, 235, 236, 237, 239

Houghton, Stephen Chase, 34, 75, 76–77, 78

Howe, Frederick C., 220

Huiguan, 40–41, 58

Illegal immigration: of Chinese, 44–45, 61–62, 150; extent unknown, 45; as modern problem, 251; and triad societies, 41, 44–45

Immigrant aid societies, 137; in administrative proceedings, 147, 157, 223; as advocates for immigrants, 157–58, 177–78; Jewish, 157–59. *See also* Chinese American organizations

Immigrants, non-Chinese: allies of, 140, 157–62; criticize immigration procedures, xvii–xviii, 152–56, 185, 235–36; nativist reaction to, 121, 126–29; "new" immigrants, 24, 122–23, 251; number admitted, 67–68, 132; political power of, 130, 157, 162, 219, 251. *See also* Asian Indians; Immigrant aid societies; Japanese

Immigration: congressional investigation of, 25, 28

Immigration Act of 1875. *See* Page Law (1875)

Immigration Act of 1891, 131; administrative finality under, 1, 26–28, 155; Chinese, exempt from, 31, 32, 70; constitutionality upheld, 28, 29, 173; deportation under, 26; effect of Chinese litigation upon, 2, 27–28; and federal control over immigration, 26; and right to hearing, 173

Immigration Act of 1917, 133, 228; deportation under, 131; and power to subpoena witnesses, 230

Immigration and Naturalization Service. *See* Bureau of Immigration

Immigration Consultation, 217, 219, 224, 225, 227, 231

Immigration law: basic doctrines in, 54, 118, 248; and "communitarian legal order," 250–51; effect of Chinese litigation on, xv, xvii, 117–18, 248; and other administrative law, compared, xiv, 30, 113, 172–73, 182, 183, 203–4, 206–7, 248–49, 250; rights/privilege distinction in, 48–49, 51–53, 54, 136, 182–83, 205–6, 215, 248–50; as unique, xiv, 172, 245, 248, 252. *See also* Finality, administrative; Judicial review

Immigration legislation: Act of 1819, 3, 257 (n. 16); Page Law of 1875, 5; Act of 1882, 6, 7; Act of 1891, 26; Act of 1903, 131; Act of 1907, 131; Act of 1917, 133; Act of 1920, 239. *See also* Immigration Act of 1891; Immigration Act of 1917; Page Law (1875)

Immigration policy: Bureau of Immigration's shaping of, 134, 227–28, 228–29; and eugenics, 130; excludable classes, 130–31, 145; exclusion of Asians, 128, 133; federal administration of, xiii, 2, 25, 26; literacy test, 133; national origins provision, 135, 250; plenary congressional power over, 23, 28–29, 52–53; open-door policy, 2, 3; restrictionist, xiii, 5, 6, 17, 26, 121, 130–31, 132, 134–35; state administration of, 4, 25; World War I and, 132–33, 134–35. *See also* Chinese exclusion legislation; Immigration legislation

Immigration Restriction League, 124, 133, 218, 227

Imperialism: and exclusion, 103

Industrial Workers of the World, 133, 234–35

Inherent sovereign powers. *See* Congressional power

In re Ah Yup, 13

In re Can Pon, 295 (n. 34)

In re Chin An On, 19

In re Gee Fook Sing, 108
In re Jung Ah Lung, 75, 92
In re Kornmehl, 197
In re Look Tin Sing, 20
In re Loo Yue Soon, 96
In re Low Yam Chow, 19
In re Moy Quong Shing, 108
In re Pedro Garcia, 190
In re Quan Gin, 96
In re Rhagat Singh, 201, 206
In re Tom Yum, 99, 109
In re Tung Yeong, 19
In re Wong Quen Luck, 191
Interstate Commerce Commission, 243; compared to Bureau of Immigration, 204, 206; judicial scrutiny of, 31, 179, 182, 183, 194, 204, 248, 265 (n. 65)
Interstate Commerce Commission v. Louisville and Nashville Railroad Company, 204–5, 206
Interstate Commerce Commission v. Union Pacific Co., 194
Irish, John P., 126

Jablow, Morris, 202
Jackson, John P., 66–67, 85, 100, 171–72 (n. 159). *See also* Collector of customs
Japanese: allies of, 126; exclusion of, 128, 135; hostility toward, 126–28; immigration of, 125; naturalization denied to, 128, 208; women, 128, 199–200
Japanese Immigrant Case, 176, 181, 204, 205, 214; and fundamental principles of due process, 173, 177; opinion in, 172–73
Johnson, Albert, 138
Judicial review: of administrative agencies, compared, 182–83; of administrative evaluation of evidence, 194–212; attempts to restrict, 94–95, 97, 100–101, 106–7; in Chinese exclusion cases, 27–28, 31–32, 70; in immigration, limited, 26–27;

28–29, 31, 97–98, 116, 117, 139, 157, 169; involving alleged citizens, 101, 106, 108–10, 112–14, 171, 176–77, 210–12; after *Ju Toy*, 174–75, 176; of questions of fact, 29–31, 97–98, 195–97, 201–2, 207; of questions of jurisdiction, 109; of questions of law, 29–31, 197–98, 206–7, 214. *See also* Finality, administrative; Habeas corpus; U.S. federal courts
Jurisdiction: over alleged citizens in immigration cases, 100–101, 106, 108–10, 111–14, 171, 211; conflicting, in immigration, 100, 101, 114–15, 182; of courts, if hearing unfair, 177, 212–14; over deportation, 114–15, 187, 211–12; of immigration officials, 97–98, 99

K'ang Yu-wei, 163
Kearney, Dennis, 12, 87
Keefe, Daniel J., 124, 178, 180, 200, 301 (n. 13); opposes Chinese right to attorney, 221–22, 228; restrictionist views of, 220
King Ow-yang, 47
Knights of Labor, 102
Know-Nothing party, 3
Kohler, Max, 137, 155, 158, 159; criticizes administrative procedures, 154, 202–3, 223; in *Gegiow*, 203–5, 206
Kung Hsiang Hsi, 149–50
Kwangtung Province: Chinese emigration from, 40, 42, 125–26
Kwock Jan Fat v. White, 210–11, 240–41

Lacombe, Emile Henry, 184, 196, 197
La Guardia, Fiorello H., 144, 147
Lamar, Joseph Rucker, 204
Lea, Homer, 127
Lee Joe, 48
Lee Kan v. United States, 96
Lem Moon Sing v. United States, 97–98, 113, 277 (n. 14)
Lewis v. Frick, 296 (n. 59)
"Likely to become a public charge"

clause: Asian Indians excluded from, 200–201; and labor market conditions, 202; as primary grounds for exclusion, 130; restrictive interpretation of, 145–47, 196–97, 199–203; Supreme Court on, 206; women suspected of being, 147. *See also* Discretion, administrative

Linck, John, 66

Literacy test, 133, 219

Litigation: challenging immigration procedures, fails, 192–94, 214–15; by immigrants in New York, 102; to judicialize immigration proceedings, 179, 181–83, 204–5; by U.S., to foreclose judicial review, 55–56, 87–88. *See also* Chinese litigation

Lodge, Henry Cabot, 104

London, Jack, 129

Lott, John, 107

Low Wah Suey v. Backus, 185–86, 187

Macarthur, Walter, 128

McCreary, James B., 56

McCreary Amendment (1893), 88, 95; extends time for registration, 56; legal challenges to, 96–97; restrictions on merchants, 56–57, 64, 95–96

McKee, John J., 140

McKenna, Joseph, 72, 86–87

McKinley, William, 131, 140

McReynolds, J. M., 111, 112, 174

Mann Act, 131

Marshall, Louis, 158, 159

Masters, Edgar Lee, 142

Metcalf, Victor, 152; and Chinese boycott, 164–65

Mexican immigration, 129

Miller, John F., 15, 16

Miner, Luella, 149–50

Moore, H. A., 100

Moral turpitude, crime involving: restrictive interpretation of, 145, 196–98

Morrow, William, 33, 184, 209, 245; on administrative finality, 97, 99; anti-Chinese views of, xvi, 33–34, 72, 86–87, 215; in deportation cases, 86–88; on jurisdiction over alleged citizens, 99, 101, 109; opinions on McCreary Amendment, 96–97

Morton, Samuel George, 11

Murray's Lessee v. Hoboken Land and Improvement Co., 113

Nagel, Charles, 158, 227, 229; pro-immigrant sympathies of, 219–20, 226, 235; on right to attorney, 221–22

National Liberal Immigration League, 161

National origins provision, 135, 250

National Popular Government League, 238, 239, 240

Native-born Chinese. *See* Chinese Americans

Nativism, 3, 121; in American West, 124–29; against Asians, 125–28, 133, 199–201; and economic instability, 9–10, 24, 122; among middle class, 24, 122, 124; against "new" immigrants, 24, 123, 129; 1924 Quota Act as high point of, 135, 245; opposition to, 130, 157, 161; among organized labor, 12, 24, 122, 129, 156; racial, 10–11, 15–16, 17, 124–29; resurgence of, 251; and rise of administrative power, xvii, 121, 180, 199, 215, 244. *See also* Anti-Chinese movement

Naturalization: act of 1790, 207; act of 1906, 210; racial limits on, 13, 18, 128, 207, 208

Netterer, Jeremiah, 305 (n. 93)

New Deal, 246

New York, Southern District of: immigration litigation in, 102, 118, 278 (n. 34)

Ng Fung Ho v. White, 211–12, 240–41

Ng Poon Chew, 167

Nishimura Ekiu v. United States, 97, 102,

114, 136; effect on later cases, 48, 52, 113, 181, 184–85, 196, 205, 215, 248; opinion in, 28–31

North, Hart H., 126, 127, 151, 224; forced to resign, 128, 200

Olney, Richard, 48, 56
On the Trail of the Immigrant (Steiner), 159–60
Oppenheimer, Reuben, 242
Ozawa v. United States, 135, 208

Pacific Mail Steamship Company, 63
Pacific Mail Steamship dock, 63, 152, 153
Page Law (1875), 5, 14, 131
Palmer, A. Mitchell, 235, 236, 239, 305 (n. 96)
Panic of 1893, 56
Paper sons, 44, 61–62, 150. *See also* Illegal immigration
Paredes, Antonio, 198
Parker, A. Warner, 221, 224, 225, 231, 232, 236, 303 (n. 41); on fairness to aliens, 217, 222; restrictionist views of, 228–29
Partridge, John S., 215
Passenger Cases, 4
Peckham, Rufus W., 109, 113
People v. Hall, 8, 259 (n. 40)
Phelan, James D., 126–27
Phelps, Timothy, 33, 59, 84
Philippines: exclusion extended to, 105–6
Picture brides, 128
Post, Louis F., 222, 231; criticizes immigration procedures, 218–19, 235, 242–43; opposes Red Raids, 134, 239, 244; opposes Turner's deportation, 143, 218
Pound, Roscoe, 238, 246
Powderly, Terence, 102, 301 (n. 13)
Powell, Thomas Reed, 177, 180, 213
Prentis, P. L., 220
Proceduralism: to check discretion, 155, 246; to improve decision mak-

ing, 184, 218, 223–25. *See also* Due process, administrative
Procedures, immigration: and Chinese exclusion procedures, compared, 149, 166; criticism of, xvii–xviii, 152, 154, 155, 159–60, 185, 235–36, 247; distinct from judicial procedures, xviii, 180, 182, 184, 186, 194; in evaluation of evidence, 194–207 passim; as focus of litigation strategy, xvii–xviii, 118, 140, 170, 174–77, 179–216 passim; legalistic tendencies in, 217, 223–26, 243–44; reforms after Red Raids, 241–42, 242–43, 247; restrictionist thrust of, 136, 228, 229–33; summary nature of, 143, 147–48, 170–71, 182–83, 184, 206, 245; and tax procedures, compared, 113, 173, 182, 206. *See also* Admissions procedures; Chinese exclusion, enforcement of; Deportation procedures; Discretion, administrative; Due process, administrative
Procedures, judicial: in Chinese deportation, 88, 90–91; in Chinese habeas corpus cases, 34, 69–70, 72–81, 83, 92; as distinct from administrative, xviii, 81–85, 101, 145, 180, 182, 184, 186, 194. *See also* U.S. district court (N.D. Calif.); U.S. federal courts
Progressives, xviii, 179–80
Prostitutes: Chinese, 11, 44–45, 185–86; deportation of, 131; immigration restricted, 5, 14, 131; women suspected of being, 147, 200

Quinn, John, 46–47
Quock Ting v. United States, 79
Quota Act of 1921, 121, 134
Quota Act of 1924, 121, 135; and Chinese Americans, 212; exclusion of Asians under, 135, 245; Filipinos under, 284 (n. 87); as high point of nativism, 135, 245

Ray, George Washington, 108
Red Raids, 233–41; arrests and deportations during, 134, 233, 235, 237, 305 (n. 85); judicial decisions concerning, 238–39, 240–41; procedural irregularities during, 235–36, 237, 238–39; and protection of citizens' rights, 211, 240–41
Red Scare of 1919, 133, 137, 234, 236
Registration: of Chinese laborers, 46, 48, 56, 57, 229; extended to Hawaii, 103; extended to Philippines, 105–6. *See also* Geary Act (1892); McCreary Amendment (1893)
Resist Treaty Committee, 164
Riordan, Thomas, 47, 70, 90, 98
Rogers, Henry Wade, 195
Roosevelt, Theodore: and Chinese boycott, 163, 164–65, 166; courts immigrant vote, 162, 219; and Gentlemen's Agreement, 128; warns of "race suicide," 124
Root, Elihu, 246
Rosenberg, Ed, 93
Ross, Erskine, 87
Rowell, Chester H., 125, 129
Ruddell, S. J., 75
Rudkin, Frank H., 305 (n. 93)
Rule of law: and administrative process, xvii–xviii, 117–18, 154, 246; in Chinese habeas corpus cases, 69–70, 75, 92; undermined in immigration law, 248

Sabin, George M., 20, 21
Sanders, Wilbur F., 45
San Francisco: as port of entry, 272 (n. 167); segregation of Japanese in, 127–28. *See also* California; U.S. district court (N.D. Calif.)
San Francisco Chamber of Commerce, 167
San Francisco Labor Council, 86, 93
Sargent, Aaron Augustus, 14
Sargent, Frank P., 102, 124, 139, 140, 143, 144, 162, 301 (n. 13)

Sawyer, John, 39, 144–45
Sawyer, Lorenzo, 13, 20, 21, 22
Schiff, Jacob, 158
Scott Act (1888), 22–23
Section 6 certificates: as evidence in Chinese admissions, 17–18, 19–20, 62, 66, 149, 150, 155, 165
Shanghai Chamber of Commerce, 163–64
Skeffington, Henry J., 227
Smith, C. J., 66
Smith, Richmond Mayo, 25
Spencer, Herbert, 10, 128
Squire, Watson C., 75, 249
Steiner, Edward, 159–61
Stewart, William M., 34
Stidger, Oliver P., 174, 175, 292 (n. 165)
Stout, Arthur, 11
Straus, Oscar S.: appointed secretary of commerce and labor, 166, 221; pro-immigrant sympathies of, 166, 167, 219–20, 235
Sui Sin Far (Edith Eaton): "In the Land of the Free," 168–69
Sumner, Charles, 13

Taft, William Howard, 155, 200, 214, 226
Taney, Roger, 208
Tang Tun v. Edsell, 296 (n. 59)
Teller, Henry, 45
Tod v. Waldman, 213–14
Tongs. *See* Triad societies
Treaty of 1880, 14–15, 19, 22, 104; exempt Chinese under, 65
Triad societies, 40–41, 44–45, 89–90
Tsui Kwo Yin, 48
Turner, John, 140–42, 143, 145; supporters of, 142. See also *United States ex rel. Turner v. Williams*
Tuska, Waldemar, 78

Uhl, Byron, 202
Union of American Hebrew Congregations, 158, 226
Union of Russian Workers, 236–37

United States ex rel. Bosny v. Williams, 190–91

United States ex rel. Canfora v. Williams, 195

United States ex rel. Castro v. Williams, 198–99

United States ex rel. Gegiow v. Uhl, 199, 202–6

United States ex rel. Georgios Glavas v. Williams, 196

United States ex rel. Mylius v. Uhl, 197–98, 198–99

United States ex rel. Turner v. Williams, 142–43, 171

United States v. Ju Toy, 117, 121, 137, 139–40, 162, 169, 205, 241; alien/citizen distinction blurred by, 171; and Chinese boycott, 163; criticism of, 114, 115, 155, 162; establishes new doctrine, 114; and litigation strategy, 170, 174, 183; opinion in, 111–13

United States v. Sing Tuck, 108–10, 113, 182; questions unresolved in, 111, 112

United States v. Thind, 208

United States v. Wong Kim Ark, 99, 108, 208

United States v. Woo Jan, 115, 187

U.S. attorney general: opinion defining exempt Chinese, 65, 154–55, 163; opinion on firm name requirement, 95, 96; opinion subjecting Chinese to general immigration laws, 155

U.S. attorneys: as attorneys for immigrants, 70, 158, 174; in Chinese exclusion administration, 38, 76; in Geary Act struggle, 87–88; judicial perspective of, 83–84, 109. *See also,* Denis, George; Garter, Charles; Kohler, Max; Woodworth, Marshall

U.S. commissioners: in Chinese habeas corpus cases, 77, 293 (n. 23). *See also* Heacock, E. H.

U.S. consuls, 38, 165

U.S. Department of Commerce and Labor: oversees Bureau of Immigration, 149, 151–52, 156; reforms after boycott, 164, 165, 166. *See also* U.S. Department of Labor, U.S. Treasury Department

U.S. Department of Justice: and Geary Act, 55–56, 87–88; and Red Raids, 133–34, 137, 235–38, 238–39; strategy to limit judicial review, 106–9, 111–12. *See also* U.S. attorney general; U.S. attorneys

U.S. Department of Labor: board of review in, 242, 243; as curb on Bureau of Immigration, 218–20, 235–36, 241–42, 244; on membership in radical organizations, 234–35, 239. *See also* U.S. Department of Commerce and Labor; U.S. Treasury Department

U.S. district court (N.D. Calif.): anti-Chinese views of, xvi, 33, 69, 72, 86, 91–92; belief in Chinese fraud, 76–78, 79–80, 92; Chinese deportation, facilitated by, 86–89; Chinese exclusion policy, effect on, 19, 20, 28, 93, 94; on citizenship of Chinese, 98–99; criticism of, 19, 20, 33, 92–93, 97; defense of, 75, 84, 93; judicial practices of, followed in Chinese cases, xvi, 34–35, 69–70, 74–75, 80–81, 82–83, 90–91, 92; unique procedures in Chinese cases, 76–79, 87, 92. *See also* Chinese exclusion, enforcement of; U.S. federal courts

U.S. federal courts: in alleged citizen cases, 108, 113, 207, 209–12, 215; campaign to remove jurisdiction of, in Chinese exclusion, xvi–xvii, 93, 94–95, 97–102, 106–16, 182; on crimes involving moral turpitude, 197–98; deference to Bureau of Immigration, xiv–xv, 28–29, 102, 114, 137, 139, 180, 184, 189, 196, 201, 202, 212–14, 215, 218, 240, 244; as favorable forum for Chinese, xv, xvi,

13, 18–19, 20, 68, 79–81, 82–83, 91, 92; on likely to become a public charge, 197, 200, 201, 202, 206; limited judicial review, constrained by, 184–85, 188–89, 201, 215; in Progressive Era, xv–xvi; on Red Raids, 238–39, 240–41, 305 (n. 93); reject due process claims, xviii, 192–94, 180, 186; structure of, 261 (n. 102). *See also* Judicial review; Procedures, judicial; U.S. district court (N.D. Calif.)

U.S. Immigration Commission, 155, 223

U.S. Immigration Service Bulletin, 225

U.S. Supreme Court: limits judicial review in immigration, 31, 52–53, 111–13, 156–57, 169, 184–85. *See also* individual cases; Judicial review

U.S. Treasury Department: and Geary Act, 55; supervision of collectors, 39, 66–67, 85

Vandeveer, George, 235–36
Van Vleck, William, 242, 243, 244

Ward, Henry, 196, 198
Watts, Fred, 224–25
Weldon, Joseph, 140, 141
Wellborn, Olin, 27
Wheeler, Hoyt Henry, 108
White, Henry M., 220, 229, 231, 234, 235
White, Stephen M., 56
Whitfield v. Hanges, 204

Williams, William, 143, 144, 178, 220; interpretation of public charge, 146–47, 154, 229–30

Wilson, William B.: and Red Raids, 235, 236, 237, 239, 242, 243, 244

Wilson, Woodrow, 246

Wise, John, 39, 81, 83, 85, 84, 99, 224; restrictionist administration of, 62, 65. *See also* Chinese exclusion, enforcement of; Collector of customs

Woey Ho v. United States, 79–80, 92

Wolf, Simon, 158

Wong Gan, 151–52

Wong Quan, 47

Wong Wing v. United States, 171

Wong You v. United States, 115, 187

Woodworth, Marshall: as attorney for Chinese, 174, 175, 190; as U.S. attorney, 70, 111

Workingmen's party, 12

World War I: accelerates nativism, 132–33

Wu Ting-Fang: and American opposition to exclusion, 105; criticism of Chinese exclusion, 43, 58, 62, 104

Yamataya, Kaoru, 172, 173–74
Yamataya v. Fisher. See *Japanese Immigrant Case*
Yang Yu, 57
Young, John Russell, 55

Zakonite v. Wolf, 296 (n. 59)
Zarikoew, Sabas, 202